Counseling Children and Adolescents

To my precious sons, Joel and Cary, who teach me every day, in the most wonderful ways, that I have much to learn. Experiencing the world along with you and loving you just as you are has made me a better mom, counselor, and person. And to all of the other children in my life who have challenged me to imagine the world from their view. These experiences have truly shaped me as a person and as a counselor, and I am forever grateful.

—Sondra Smith-Adcock

To the memory of my maternal grandmother, Elizabeth Murphy Moseley, who taught me everything I know about the power of authentic presence and listening with the heart. She spent countless hours playing with, and listening to, me. You're still my guidepost.

—Catherine Tucker

Counseling Children and Adolescents

Connecting Theory, Development, and Diversity

Edited by

Sondra Smith-Adcock
University of Florida

Catherine Tucker
Indiana State University

SAGE

Los Angeles | London | New Delhi
Singapore | Washington DC | Melbourne

FOR INFORMATION

SAGE Publications, Inc.
2455 Teller Road
Thousand Oaks, California 91320
E-mail: order@sagepub.com

SAGE Publications Ltd.
1 Oliver's Yard
55 City Road
London, EC1Y 1SP
United Kingdom

SAGE Publications India Pvt. Ltd.
B 1/I 1 Mohan Cooperative Industrial Area
Mathura Road, New Delhi 110 044
India

SAGE Publications Asia-Pacific Pte. Ltd.
3 Church Street
#10–04 Samsung Hub
Singapore 049483

Development Editor: Abbie Rickard
Editorial Assistant: Carrie Montoya
Production Editor: Bennie Clark Allen
Copy Editor: Michelle Ponce
Typesetter: Hurix Systems Pvt. Ltd.
Proofreader: Rae-Ann Goodwin
Indexer: Terri Morrissey
Cover Designer: Anupama Krishnan
Marketing Manager: Shari Countryman

Printed in the United States of America

Library of Congress Cataloging-in-Publication Data

Names: Smith-Adcock, Sondra, editor, author. | Tucker, Catherine (Mary Catherine) editor, author.

Title: Counseling children and adolescents : connecting theory, development, and diversity / edited by Sondra Smith-Adcock, Catherine Tucker. Description: Los Angeles : SAGE, [2016] | Includes bibliographical references and index.

Identifiers: LCCN 2015040057 | ISBN 9781483347745 (pbk. : alk. paper)

Subjects: LCSH: Children–Counseling of. | Teenagers–Counseling of. | Neuropsychology. | Cognitive neuroscience.

Classification: LCC BF721 .C663 2016 | DDC 158.3083–dc23
LC record available at http://lccn.loc.gov/2015040057

This book is printed on acid-free paper.

16 17 18 19 20 10 9 8 7 6 5 4 3 2 1

Brief Contents

Detailed Contents

SECTION III

Acknowledgments

The authors gratefully acknowledge the contributions made by Naijian Zhang and Richard Parsons, series editors, to the development of this text. Thank you for the opportunity to write this text and for your guidance along the way. We also want to acknowledge the patience, professionalism, and creativity of the entire SAGE team, especially Kassie Graves, Carrie Montoya, and Bennie Clark Allen, as well as our copy editor Michelle Ponce, who worked most closely with us. Lastly, we are forever grateful to the amazing group of coauthors who helped us to achieve our goal of providing a comprehensive and rich resource for counselors who work with children and adolescents. The coauthors of the chapters in this text are our friends and colleagues, but moreover, they represent a diverse group of talented and caring practitioners and scholars who put young people at the heart of their work.

SAGE Publications gratefully acknowledges the following reviewers:

Charles Crews
Texas Tech University

Gaston Weisz
Adelphi University

Janet G. Froeschle
Texas Tech University

Jennifer Jordan
Winthrop University

Jonathan Lent
Marshall University

Karen Sue Linstrum
Northwestern Oklahoma State University

Kristina A. Peterson
Roosevelt University

Melissa Alvarado
University of Texas at Brownsville

Ronica Arnold Branson
Jackson State University

Susan Mendelson
Rutgers University

Ann M. McCaughan
University of Illinois - Springfield

LaTonya Wood
Pepperdine University

Mark F. Lepore
Clarion University

Saliwe M. Kawewe
Southern Illinois University, Carbondale

Stacy M. Van Horn
University of Central Florida

Section I

Chapter 1: Historical and Contextual Trends in Counseling Children and Adolescents: Guiding Frameworks

Chapter 2: Legal and Ethical Issues in Counseling Children and Adolescents

Chapter 3: Attachment, Trauma, and Repair From Infant to Adolescent Development: Counseling Implications From Neurobiology

Chapter 4: The Counseling Process: Establishing a Therapeutic Alliance

Historical and Contextual Trends in Counseling Children and Adolescents: Guiding Frameworks

CATHERINE TUCKER AND CEYMONE DYCE

Children are living beings—more living than grown-up people who have built shells of habit around themselves. Therefore it is absolutely necessary for their mental health and development that they should not have mere schools for their lessons, but a world whose guiding spirit is personal love.

—Rabindranath Tagore

If you don't know history, then you don't know anything. You are a leaf that doesn't know it is part of a tree.

—Michael Crichton

INTRODUCTION

Graduate students reading this text in the second decade of the 21st century are preparing for careers in a counseling field in the middle of a paradigm shift. In the past decade, the human brain has given up many of its secrets to scientists. The enormous surge in neurobiology findings has fundamentally shifted our understanding of our species and our profession. All areas of the counseling profession are impacted by this new knowledge, perhaps none more so than the area of child and adolescent counseling. Contributions by researchers and clinicians such as Bruce Perry, Stephen Porges, Bessel van der Kolk, Ed Tronick, Dan Siegel, and many others have drastically altered our understanding of brain development, the role of early attachments in the development of identity, the individual and environmental mechanisms that mitigate or aggravate early traumatic experiences, the process of change in the adolescent brain, and other crucial discoveries involving interpersonal relationships and the development of the brain and nervous system.

This new paradigm in the world of counseling signals the need for a change in how we think about and help people solve problems. For example, we now know that the brain can and does grow and change over the life span, not just during the first few years of life. We know that the brain changes structurally and functionally when confronted by stress and trauma and when the effect of traumatic experiences is resolved through counseling or empathetic relationships (van der Kolk, 2014). This text is written with the intention of weaving together the most recent findings from neurobiology with established developmental theories, theories of counseling, and social-historical context to provide the reader with a comprehensive foundation from which to build a solid practice in counseling young people in schools and clinical settings. The theories of counseling or development may be familiar to some readers, but the inclusion of that material against the backdrop of new scientific discoveries and a broad view of multicultural applications is, we believe, a unique contribution to the literature at this point in time.

In this introductory chapter, we introduce some of the ideas and philosophies underpinning this book and focus on some of the major social and historical problems young people have faced in the United States since its founding. We do acknowledge that myriad global issues affect children and families and are extremely important for counselors to understand. Though we will address issues of working with children of various backgrounds who live in the United States, we do not have enough space in one book to adequately cover all issues for counselors in all parts of the world. If you are a counseling student who lives in another country, or has recently come from another place, we hope you will do your own research to find out about these key issues and histories there. We also hope that our readers in the United States will take opportunities to learn more about systems of mental health care, education, labor practices, and child protection in other countries, especially when working with people who are immigrants to the United States. Throughout the text, we hope to provide meaningful resources related to multicultural counseling with youth and opportunities for personal reflection on your multicultural competencies.

The final section of this chapter concerns our ideas on what issues are emerging in the United States that may impact your career as a counselor working with young people. Again, this section could easily be a book on its own, and we hope some of the ideas we present will inspire you to continue learning about the topics after you finish reading this book. Our hope for you, as a counseling student, is that you find in this text the inspiration you need to relate confidently to young people as well as to gain the knowledge and the tools to help them succeed.

After reading this chapter, you will be able to

- explain why an understanding of social, cultural, and historical context is crucial for professional counselors;
- describe to colleagues how the key issues of child labor, education, and child protection have changed over the past 200 years in the United States;
- tell others why a strong understanding of developmental theory and neurobiology is crucial to effective work with young people in counseling; and
- point out current issues impacting counselors working with young people.

COUNSELING YOUTH: A DEVELOPMENTAL AND MULTICULTURAL PERSPECTIVE

Counseling children and adolescents is an important specialization area for counselors. The perspective we take in this text is that children and adolescents constitute a distinct, heterogeneous group deserving of separate study. The counseling needs of children and adolescents are unique relative to adults (Innerhofer, 2013). In our experience as clinical supervisors and counselor educators, many counseling students graduate without enough preparation in counseling this distinct population, even though most counselors work either directly or indirectly with young people during the course of their careers. A quick search of the national directory of Council for Accreditation of Counseling & Related Educational Programs (CACREP) accredited master's level programs in counseling shows that most (nine out of 10 randomly chosen clinical mental health counseling programs and six out of 10 randomly chosen school counseling programs) do not require specific coursework in counseling children and adolescents. All programs do require some coursework in human development and in counseling diverse populations, but it is not clear how many of these courses directly address theoretical and practical issues of working with young people (CACREP, retrieved August 27, 2014 from http://www.cacrep .org/directory).

Case Illustration 1.1 helps to illustrate why counseling children and adolescents is a unique specialty area. In this real-life example, note how the children manifest emotional difficulties in ways that differ greatly from adults.

Case Illustration 1.1

The purpose of this case illustration is to give the reader a real-life example of one way in which children manifest emotional difficulties in ways that differ greatly from adults. Being able to apply what you know about human development is critical in working with children and adolescents. Using what you know about developmental theories, explain the different reactions to grief expressed by each boy.

Donny, 14, and his brother, Randy, 5, have both recently experienced the death of their grandfather. Both boys were very close to their grandfather and are very sad and angry about his death. Consider the differences in how each boy, due to developmental stages, grieves for this loss.

Immediately after Grandpa's funeral, Donny becomes withdrawn. His parents rarely see him except at meal times, when he picks at his food. At other times, he stays in his bedroom, playing online video games or reading. He has not asked to go out with friends much lately and appears to be tired and irritable when he's interacting with the family. When his mom asks if he's ok, Donny often replies, "I'm fine, leave me alone. You can't possibly understand." Meanwhile, Randy has become much more anxious and clingy. His parents report that he is now "Always right under us," which is a change from his previous independent nature. Unlike his older brother, Randy is often emotionally more expressive than usual, with frequent bouts of tears and a recurrence of toddler-like tantrums over minor frustrations. His teacher reports that Randy often "daydreams" and gets into a lot of arguments with school friends.

Regardless of the setting they are in, counselors' use of specific counseling techniques and interventions, that are appropriate and established for use with widely different groups of children and adolescents, is important to learn about and practice. One of the foundational research studies that lead us to this conclusion is the landmark Adverse Childhood Experiences (ACEs) studies. The ACEs examined data from 17,000 adults from a wide variety of backgrounds across the United States. Participants were asked questions about their current health status and about various experiences in earlier life. To the great surprise of the researchers, a very strong correlation was discovered between negative early life experiences such as having a parent in prison, being beaten by a caregiver, or spending time in foster care and experiencing a wide range of negative mental and physical health outcomes as adults (Felitti et al., 1998). Several follow-up studies have been done with these data, all of them finding more links between a high number of ACEs and negative life outcomes. The ACEs research clearly shows that when children are subjected to trauma, there are very often serious negative outcomes for them as adults, making childhood trauma one of the largest public health threats in existence. Fortunately, the ACEs research also shows that prevention of or effective early intervention for trauma can reduce the risk of negative outcomes in adulthood (CDC, 2015). This evidence makes clear the need for counselors to be educated about intervening with families and children with high ACEs scores to prevent or mitigate the ongoing negative impact of those experiences on the well-being of the public.

In addition to understanding brain development and theories, counselors are expected to understand how to work across the lifespan and to be able to work with a wide variety of types of clients and client problems (ACA, 2014). In order to comply with ethical standards, counselors are expected to know and employ evidence-based practices. In a general sense, this implies that counselors should use strategies that have been thoroughly researched and tested for effectiveness (Marquis, Douthit, & Elliott, 2011). The shift away from using techniques created on the spot for individual clients, or using techniques the counselor likes, and toward the use of evidence-based practices requires that counselors continue reading professional journals, attending continuing education events, and continually updating their skills as new evidence emerges (Chorpita, Daleiden, & Collins, 2014). Although it is possible to integrate evidence-based approaches with emerging or creative practices, this should be done intentionally, with an eye toward building evidence that these practices are also effective (Chorpita et al., 2014).

Although children may differ greatly from each other, they also differ greatly from adults within their own cultural groups developmentally and in terms of relative power in society (Axline, 1969). Children and adolescents process information, express ideas, and behave differently from adults. Thinking of children and adolescents as a specific subset of a population assists clinicians in viewing their young clients different from themselves in critical ways, triggering the clinician to conceptualize the counseling relationship as occurring between members of different groups, even if the counselor and client share racial, ethnic, gender, and social class identities. It is our belief that considering children and adolescents in this way will help counselors, especially those new to the field, to keep these key differences in mind.

In Guided Exercise 1.1, you are asked to explore how human development impacts common daily chores and activities.

Guided Exercise 1.1

As children grow and develop, they are normally granted more freedom and power. Consider the following activities and at what age you remember first doing them. Do you think you were ready developmentally for the task? Would you allow a child of that age to do the activity? Why, or why not (using developmental theory to back up your answer)? Discuss your answers with classmates, noting cultural differences that may arise.

1. Use a gas-powered lawn mower without supervision

2. Stay at home alone for an hour

3. Walk alone to a friend's house in the same neighborhood

4. Use the stove unsupervised

5. Babysit a younger child

We also believe that in order to best understand how to work with any given population of people, counselors need to know at least the basic socio-historical context from which that population is emerging. Without studying the past, we are less able to understand the present.

SOCIO-HISTORICAL CONTEXT OF CHILDHOOD AND CHILDREN'S MENTAL HEALTH CARE IN THE UNITED STATES

Though parents throughout our history have cared for, loved, and done their best to raise their children according to the best wisdom of their times, the treatment of children within the context of the legal and social welfare systems has been inconsistent at best (Brenner, 1970). The primary legal responsibility for the care of minors has generally rested with the adults in their immediate families. However, society and its legal institutions have long played a role in protecting children considered to be dependent on the state, either because the family was too impoverished to care for them, parents died, or there was caregiver abuse or neglect (Myers, 2004).

The following four issues are central to the understanding of the social and historical context of childhood in United States. Education, child labor, child abuse and neglect, and children's mental health care are all critical components of a modern society that hopes to raise children who are capable, emotionally stable adults later in their lives.

Education

In the early years of the colonial United States, most education was driven by colonists' interest in ensuring that their children could read the Bible for themselves, an important goal for reformed Protestant believers (Cook & Klay, 2014). Many of the early colonists favored basic education, at least for boys, but were not always successful in providing it to all children due to lack of teachers, books, and space. The first colony to legally require every town to educate its children was Massachusetts, which passed a law in 1647 mandating that every town of more than 50 people have a functioning school (Brackemyre, 2015). This law was not always implemented and was not adopted in all colonies.

After the Revolutionary War, both George Washington and Thomas Jefferson lobbied Congress to pass laws requiring all children to be educated (Reisner & Butts, 1936). Both Washington and Jefferson, among other founders, believed strongly that a democracy's success rested on having a voting public, comprised of free White landowning men, who appeared to be able to read and reason well enough to make informed decisions at the polls (Cook & Klay, 2014). However, multiple attempts at passing a federal education law failed in the years following independence due to lawmakers' insistence on local control of education statutes. As a result, some states, such as Massachusetts, passed strong educational laws, while other states deferred to private educational enterprises (Reisner & Butts, 1936). Jefferson's Act to Establish Public Schools finally passed Congress in 1796 in a highly edited form (Brackemyre, 2015) but did not have a strong mandate to force states to comply. As a result, many states continued to consider education to be a private enterprise and did not establish public schools until well into the next century (Reisner & Butts, 1936). Churches, charities, and home-based schools educated the majority of United States students until the mid-1800s (Mintz, 2012).

By the 1840s, education was more accessible, at least for White families (Mintz, 2012). Parents who wanted their children to attend school had to enroll them and pay tuition. Families whose children were in school all day also lost the labor the children might have provided, often making schooling impractical for struggling families (Walters & James, 1992). Even families who could afford schools often had limited options for their daughters, as many schools did not accept girls (Graham, 1974). There were some excellent private schools for girls, but they were often expensive and difficult for many families to access (Graham, 1974). Children of slaves were specifically barred from schooling, as educating slaves was illegal in most southern states prior to the Civil War (Anderson, 1988). Only in 1918 were all states required to provide free compulsory elementary education for all nondisabled children, even though all states had public elementary schools by 1870 (Graham, 1974). Children with disabilities were not always afforded equitable opportunities in education until Congress passed the Individuals with Disabilities Education Act (IDEA) in 1975 (Walter & James, 1992). This means that until 1918, children in some states were not required by law to attend school, and that until 1974, not all children with disabilities were guaranteed a free and appropriate public education.

Schools varied greatly in quality of instruction and in the racial and gender makeup of the students they served (Herbst, 1996). Some public schools remained segregated by gender and/or race until the 1950s or even later (Graham, 1974). Secondary education evolved somewhat later in the United States. In 1940, only half of United States 18-year-olds had a high school diploma (Herbst, 1996). Today, 88% of United States citizens are high school graduates (U.S. Census Bureau, 2012). However, today achievement gaps still exist for students in inner cities, who come from low-income families, males, and students of color as compared to their wealthier and White peers (U.S. Department of Education, 2013).

Current Issues

Schooling is an important part of young peoples' lives. In the following section, we explore in greater detail a selection of a few of the important current policy issues in education. Please consider that policy issues can change quite a bit very quickly, so it is important to follow multiple news sources to stay current.

The Education Gap

According to the National Education Association, "The term 'achievement gap' is often defined as the differences between the test scores of minority and/or low-income students and the test scores of their White and Asian peers. But achievement gaps in test scores affect many different groups. Some groups may trail at particular points, for example, boys in the early years and girls in high school math and science. Differences between the scores of students with different backgrounds (ethnic, racial, gender, disability, and income) are evident on large-scale standardized tests. Test score gaps often lead to longer-term gaps, including high school and college completion and the kinds of jobs students secure as adults" (NEA, n.d.).

Counselors, in both school and clinical settings, can be important agents of change in the national effort to reduce these gaps. However, school counselors are in an advantaged position to do so. School counselors can use student data to inform how to best use their time for interventions to help close these gaps. For example, a high school counselor can sort the student database to find honor roll students who are on free or reduced lunch and offer those students additional guidance on applying for college and completing financial aid applications. An elementary school counselor might look at state achievement test data to find out how well or poorly students in first-year teachers' classrooms are scoring and offer additional support to the teachers the following year, as needed. School counselors should be on all school leadership teams that make decisions about grouping children, assigning teachers, and allocating assets because counselors often know critical "behind-the-scenes" information about individual or group student and teacher strengths and weakness, and they are trained to use data to inform decision making. The American School Counselor Association offers many articles on its website to assist counselors in developing strategies to reduce gaps between groups (ASCA, 2014).

Education for Children Whose Families Have Immigrated.

Immigration policy has been a contentious issue in the United States over the past several years. Many states, including most of the states that border Mexico, have attempted to limit the flow of immigrants into the United States by means of building walls, adding more border patrol agents, and refusing basic medical and educational services to undocumented adults and children (Hipsman & Meissner, 2013).

In 1996, the federal government passed a law barring undocumented immigrants from receiving in-state college tuition (Chen, 2011). Some states have amended their laws to widen immigrants' access to higher education, mostly by making it possible for them to register as in-state students if they meet certain requirements, such as having lived in the state for a certain number of years (Chen, 2011; Hooker, Fix, & McHugh, 2014). Other states, like Georgia, have allocated resources to support educational achievement of children who have immigrated, regardless of their legal status, in the K-12 public schools. The argument for this approach is that the children of illegal immigrants are not to blame for their parents' choices, and if allowed to do so, can become tax-paying adults (Hooker et al., 2014). Counselors should be aware of the laws in the states where they practice regarding health and educational resources for undocumented immigrants.

Special Education Issues—Race and Class

Closely related to the social justice issues and the achievement gap previously outlined, disproportionality of children who are receiving special education services by gender, race, and family income is a topic of much debate. The United States Department of Education and the Office of Civil Rights conducted a national investigation of school district practices related to discipline and special education placement by race, gender, and family income from 2011 to 2012 and from 2013 to 2014. The agencies had previously conducted limited studies of a sample of schools, but in 2011, they were given the power to require all schools in the United States to provide data (Office of Civil Rights, 2015). The study found startling discrepancies in the severity of punishment and the likelihood of special education placement for African-American, Hispanic, and multiracial males from poor families in many districts (Office of Civil Rights, 2015). Differential, and harsher, treatment of minority males begins in preschool and is consistently employed throughout the educational process. In Guided Exercise 1.2, you will take a closer look at the achievement gap in your own state, county, or city by referencing the Office of Civil Rights website: http://www2.ed.gov/about/offices/list/ocr/data.html?src=rt.

Guided Exercise 1.2

Use the Office of Civil Rights' website to look up data on your local school district. Are all children achieving equally where you live? If not, what role might you play in reducing the discrepancy? http://www2.ed.gov/about/offices/list/ocr/data.html?src=rt.

Charters and Vouchers

The political question surrounding whether or not the United States should have a strong centralized educational system, the central debate facing Thomas Jefferson's reform efforts, has resurfaced in recent years. Beginning with the No Child Left Behind (NCLB) Act of 2001, public schools have been made more accountable for student learning outcomes. The high stakes testing program from NCLB, along with new rules about teachers' roles and training, have led some states and districts to embrace charter schools and/or provide government funded vouchers for poor families to help them send their children to private schools in areas where public schools are struggling to perform up to standards (Richardson, 1994). Opponents of charters schools and voucher programs believe that giving public funds to these schools causes already struggling public schools to suffer more, while those in favor of the programs believe that public funds should be made available to create alternatives to public schooling. In Guided Exercise 1.3, you will learn more about how these issues play out in your local area.

Guided Exercise 1.3

What is the law in your state regarding charter schools and school vouchers? In your town or city, what percentage of school aged children attend a traditional public school, a charter school, a private school, or are home schooled? What are the graduation rates and college-going rates for each type of school in your state (these data are often available on the state's education website)? Are there differences in the racial or social class/income distribution of students in each type of school? What seems to be the strengths or weaknesses of each type of school in your local area? Does your state have laws prohibiting illegal immigrant children from attending school or receiving college loans? What is the race and gender breakdown of your area's special education program? Write a letter to your local school board applauding their efforts and outlining any concerns you have. Mail the letter, or share it with your class as a project.

Child Labor Practices

No federal legislation regulated child labor in the United States until 1938, when Congress passed the Fair Labor Standards Act (FLSA) (Rauscher, Runyan, Schulman, & Bowling, 2008). The FLSA created limits on the numbers of hours per week minors could work and the types of work they could do. The FLSA has been amended many times since 1938 and now restricts minors to less than 40 hours of work per week during the school year and bans the employment of children under age 14, except in family businesses or on family farms, where child labor remains unregulated (Kruse & Mahony, 2000). Until 1938, many children worked 12 or more hours a day, 6 or 7 days a week, often in dangerous conditions for little pay.

Currently, federal and state laws are in place to protect minors from hazardous work, long hours, and abusive employment practices. Illegal work among minors has been dramatically reduced in the past century but does still occur. Kruse & Mahony's (2000) research suggests that approximately 310,000 minors are in violation of labor laws either due to working excessive hours, in hazardous jobs, or under age each year in the United States. Children who have parents with less than a high school education appear to be much more likely than children whose parents graduated from college to report working too many hours or in hazardous occupations (Rauscher et al., 2008). The same study found significantly more African-American youth were working beyond allowed hours than were their White peers, meaning that although progress has been made in regulating child labor, it is certainly not a problem of the past, nor is it a problem that impacts all ethnic and social strata equally. More research needs to be done in order to verify the cause and effect between these demographic variables, over work, and negative academic and criminal justice outcomes, but it does seem that a conclusion may be drawn that counselors need to be extra vigilant in monitoring the work practices of at-risk youth in their care. One of the more interesting and interactive photographic archives will help you see the deeper issues of child labor in Guided Exercise 1.4.

Guided Exercise 1.4

Proponents of child labor regulation received a boost in evidence for their cause through the photographic work of Lewis Hine in the early 1900s. Mr. Hine traversed the country for several years in the early 20th century documenting harsh working conditions for children. His photographs of children at work are now available for online viewing via the National Archives (http://www.archives.gov/education/lessons/hine-photos). After exploring the photographs in the archives, reflect on the following questions in class:

1. How might working in a factory overnight or on third shift impact children's capacity to learn at school?

2. What types of work might children do in your local area? If the area is largely agricultural, what role might children play in migrant farm labor there?

3. Did any of your parents, grandparents, or other family members work long hours as children? How do they feel their work impacted their lives as adults? Do you, or would you, allow your own children to work? Under what circumstances would this be acceptable?

Child Abuse and Neglect

The rate of child abuse and neglect has always been difficult to estimate and was especially so prior to 1962 in the United States (Levine & Levine, 1992). During the Colonial period, local systems of justice sporadically adjudicated cases regarding the mistreatment of children, but child abuse was generally considered to be a family matter and was dealt with inside the family or local community (this was also true for spousal abuse). Prior to the 20th century, most cases of abuse and neglect were never investigated by police or adjudicated in court, since no laws were violated. One exception was *Pletcher v. People*, 1869 (cited in Myers, 2004).

In 1869, an Illinois father was prosecuted for confining his blind son in a cold cellar in the middle of winter. The father's attorney argued that parents have the right to raise their children as they see fit, but the Illinois Supreme Court disagreed, writing that parental "authority must be exercised within the bounds of reason and humanity. If the parent commits wanton and needless cruelty upon his child, either by imprisonment of this character or by inhuman beating, the law will punish him." Even though most cases of child abuse were never prosecuted, signal cases such as *Pletcher* built important legal foundations for future trials. This case laid the groundwork for the legal punishment of abusive and neglectful care taking of minors in the United States for years to come. Though many mores and laws have changed, to a large extent, this strong sense of parental domain still exists in the U.S. culture.

The *Pletcher* case and other well-publicized child abuse cases during the latter years of the 19th century eventually led to laws against child abuse and neglect. In 1912, the Federal Children's Bureau was created to monitor and enhance child welfare on a national level, and by 1918 all but three states had juvenile courts, which were able to handle cases of abuse and neglect (Myers, 2004). During the late 19th and early 20th century, the responsibility for the identification and care of abused and neglected children fell largely to private charitable organizations, such as the New York Society for the Prevention of Cruelty to Children (NYSPCC; Levine & Levine, 1992). Interestingly, the NYSPCC grew out of an earlier society that protected animals from abuse (Myers, 2004). Although these organizations did enormous amounts of work on the behalf of maltreated children, they were not authorized to punish perpetrators of abuse or neglect.

It was not until the publication in 1962 of the article "The Battered-Child Syndrome" (Kempe, Silverman, Steele, Droegemueller, & Silver, 1962) in the prestigious *Journal of the American Medical Association* and its subsequent widespread media coverage that average people in the United States recognized the extent and seriousness of the problems of child abuse and neglect. Public outrage following the release of "The Battered Child Syndrome" lead to legislation that both created government-run child protection agencies and pushed states to craft laws making child abuse and neglect criminal offenses (Myers, 2004). By 1967, all 50 states had laws that required medical doctors to report suspected abuse and neglect to child protective services (Myers, 2004).

Today, mandatory reporters include teachers, doctors, nurses, day care workers, mental health care providers, and other professionals who work with children (Child Welfare Information Gateway, 2014). The creation of child protection agencies and laws to punish perpetrators of abuse and neglect has likely saved the lives of thousands, if not millions, of children over the past half century. At this point in our history and with the mores of our current society, this seems unthinkable. Moreover, there are still serious flaws within the foster and adoptive care services, but certainly United States children are far safer and more protected today than at any prior point in history. In Case Illustration 1.2, we examine a possible case of child neglect through the eyes of a clinical mental health counselor working at a community agency.

Case Illustration 1.2

Veronica is a licensed professional counselor at the local family services agency. One of her young clients, Mason, who is 6, often comes to his sessions looking tired. He always has dark circles under his eyes and sometimes rests his head on the table as they play or talk. Lately, he has been wearing shorts and t-shirts with shoes that appear to be too big, none of which will keep him from being chilly in the autumn weather of the Midwest. Veronica knows that Mason's mother is a young single woman who works two jobs to support herself and Mason. Veronica also knows that Mason's mom has a history of alcohol abuse and unhealthy romantic relationships. Veronica is concerned about Mason's well-being. What steps should she take next? Consult with your peers and professors to create an ethically appropriate answer.

Children's Mental Health Care

Although children in the United States are better educated and more protected than before, children's mental health services remain underfunded, understaffed, and underused (SAMHSA, 2012). Prior to the 20th century, children's mental health care was not addressed on a federal level in the United States (Jenkins, 2011). Children were not considered capable of having mental health needs until at least the early 20th century (Salmon, 2006). Mental health care for children in the United States was brought to national attention in 1982 with the publication of Dr. Jane Knitzer's report "Unclaimed Children: The Failure of Public Responsibility to Children and Adolescents in Need of Mental Health Services." This report highlighted the enormous unmet mental health needs of children in the nation (Community Action Network, 2010).

Even though the 1974 Federal Community Mental Health Centers Act earmarked $20 million in federal spending for expansion of services for young people, Knitzer found that by the early 1980s, over two thirds of children with mental health needs were not receiving appropriate services (Children's Mental Health Network, n.d). One response to Knitzer's exposé of the crisis was the creation in 1984 of the Child and Adolescent Service System Program (CASSP) by the National Institute of Mental Health (Community Action Network, 2010). CASSP was given the task of both integrating children's services into existing mental health care frameworks and creating new services where none currently existed (Community Action Network, 2010). In spite of these efforts, unmet mental health needs remain in 2016, especially among low-income and minority children.

In the 2012 report "Behavioral Health in the U.S.," the federal Substance Abuse and Mental Health Administration estimates that 64% of children and adolescents who report symptoms of serious mental health problems receive treatment each year. This rate is lowest for adolescents who report problems with substance abuse, with only 12% reporting that they received treatment for the problem in the past year, while adolescents who report having attention deficit hyperactivity disorder (ADHD) report that about 60% have received treatment in the past year (SAMHSA, 2012). Although this is clearly a vast improvement over the treatment use patterns cited by Jane Knitzer in 1982, of the children and adolescents who reported receiving mental health services for any problem in the past year, most report six or fewer visits with any health professional, and the majority reported only receiving prescriptions for medication with no concurrent counseling (SAMHSA, 2012). Having access to mental health care also differs across groups. For example, children from minority cultures, including sexual minorities, children in juvenile justice settings, and children in foster care generally experience more problems related to anxiety, depression, and trauma than children in other population segments (SAMHSA, 2012). However, these children are also perhaps the most underserved of all population segments in the United States in terms of counseling programs (SAMHSA, 2012).

CURRENT PERSPECTIVES ON CHILDREN'S MENTAL HEALTH CARE

The early part of the 21st century has seen a continuation of many long-time problems in children's mental health, including depression, anxiety, academic problems, developmental delays, substance abuse, and residual issues related to trauma. Although the mental health professions have made some progress in identifying and treating these disorders, the majority of children suffering from them are still not adequately treated (SAMHSA, 2012). Additionally, dramatic increases in the diagnoses of autism, bipolar disorder, and obesity (which is not in itself a mental health problem but which is certainly a public health concern and has been linked to increased incidents of depression, anxiety, and poor academic outcomes) bring new challenges to counselors working with young people in the second decade of the 21st century. Growing diversity in the United States population overall also adds new layers of nuance to the training needs of mental health professionals, a goal prominently stated in the 2002 New Freedom Commission on Mental Health report (U.S. Department of Health & Human Services, 2003).

Advances in what we know about the structure and functions of the developing brain have also led to dramatic increases in our knowledge of the mechanisms of mental health problems (Perry, 2005; Schore, 2012), but problems with access to services cause long delays between the onset of problems and the initiation of treatment (SAMHSA, 2012). One of the greatest challenges, therefore, to the mental health of children and adolescents in the United States in the 21st century may be related to efficient and equitable delivery of services as well as knowing how to intervene. In Guided Exercise 1.5, you are directed to locate resources you may need in your career as a counselor.

Guided Exercise 1.5

Make a community resource guide for your local area. List all relevant human services agencies you might refer clients or students to, including counseling services for people without health insurance, domestic violence shelters, alcohol and drug addiction facilities, hospitals, child abuse and neglect hotlines, and other important resources. When you complete the list, consider how easy or difficult it might be for a low-income family in your area to obtain services, especially if they do not have their own transportation. What barriers do you see?

FUTURE TRENDS

Counseling Youth and Other Counseling Specialties

One of the most active research areas in child and adolescent counseling focuses on tailoring intervention for young people. In keeping with trends in counseling, it is important to be aware of increasingly new and effective approaches to the counseling experience for this unique population. Children and adolescents are extremely active participants in determining what they learn and how they understand their environment. Play therapy has become a powerful approach used by counselors to bring about changes in child behavior. A large and growing research base suggests that play therapy is effective with children from a wide variety of cultural backgrounds and with a wide variety of problems (Ray, 2015). Play therapy establishes an interpersonal process where counselors use the therapeutic powers of play to help clients prevent or resolve psychosocial difficulties and achieve optimal growth and development (Association for Play Therapy, n.d.; Blanco, Ray, & Holliman, 2012; Bratton, Rhine, Ray, & Jones, 2005). The Association for Play Therapy recently added a statement of evidence based practice outlining the research conducted on the use of play in various forms. You can access the statement on the APT website at http://www.a4pt.org/?page=evidencebased. In the fall of 2015, a group of play therapy researchers applied to the National Registry of Evidence-Based Programs and Practices for inclusion on the registry.

The creative experience is a crucial component of any child's education, fundamental for healthy development (Glassman & Prasad, 2013). Perhaps it is not surprising, then, that counseling youth requires a substantially different approach. Another example of innovative development in the area of counseling specialties is the use of art therapy. Art therapy can be effective in improving child self-esteem, self-direction, and prosocial behaviors. Studies show that the use of expressive arts significantly impacts children's engagement and response level during the counseling relationship, ultimately producing more effective and successful sessions (Howie, Prasad, & Kristel, 2013), both vital for counselors to be aware of as the profession begins to face great changes in functionality within a new healthcare system.

Affordable Care Act

One of the largest impacts on the practice of counseling in the next decade is likely to be the changes to the U.S. health care system begun under the Affordable Care Act (ACA). The ACA includes provisions for reforming how medicine, especially for Medicare/Medicaid patients, is accessed. Under the new federal laws, mental health services are covered along with nine other essential provisions for all policies sold on the federal exchanges (Mechanic, 2012). Counselors may find themselves working in integrated health practices alongside family physicians and nurses as this model is encouraged by increased federal funding (Mechanic, 2012). School counselors may notice that more of their students are able to access health care and health insurance, allowing more of them to use the counselor's referral to outside care. Older adolescents will likely benefit from both the new rule outlawing insurance companies to deny coverage to people with preexisting conditions and the rule allowing children to remain on their parent's employer-based insurance plans up to age 26 (Mechanic, 2012). Although this set of laws is still very new, and some state governments are seeking ways not to participate in the ACA, it is likely that the ACA will fundamentally change how counselors and other mental health professionals handle the financial and documentation aspects of their jobs.

More Discoveries From Neuroscience

New and increasingly effective treatments for trauma and other problems are likely to emerge from ongoing research. Methods for educating students who come to school with traumatic life histories or other problems that may lead to behavioral issues at school have already started to emerge from recent findings, making brain research highly relevant for school counselors (Cozolino, 2013).

The U.S. federal government began a new, large-scale push to fund more research on the human brain in 2013. The ultimate goal of this project is to create a map of the human brain similar to that of the human genome (National Institutes of Health, 2014). Many scientists from diverse agencies such as the U.S. Food and Drug Administration, Defense Advanced Projects Research Agency, and National Science Foundation are working with the National Institutes of Health to grant funding to promising projects in neuroscience labs across the United States. The first rounds of funding were granted in 2014 (National Institutes of Health, 2014). Counselors and other mental health professionals will need to be sure to keep up with findings as they emerge from these reports, as the new information will likely have a profound impact on the diagnosis and treatment of mental health issues.

COUNSELING KEYSTONES

- The concepts of childhood and adolescence as special, separate, and protected is new relative to many ideas about the progression of the stages of human life.
- Young people in the United States have only recently been protected by the government from abusive labor practices, substandard caregivers, poor or nonexistent educational opportunities, and other threats to their health and well-being.
- We still have a long way to go to reach the ideals of safe and healthy childhood and adolescence for all children in the United States.
- Appreciating differences in development and social power can help counselors better relate to young people.
- Children and adolescents are not small adults. Counselors working with these populations need special skills, especially strong backgrounds in developmental theories.
- Counselors in all settings can be powerful advocates for change in the lives of young people.

ADDITIONAL RESOURCES

In Print

Tronick, E., & Beeghly, M. (2011). Meaning making and infant mental health. *American Psychologist*, 107–119.

Online

Association for Play Therapy: http://a4pt.org

Centers for Disease Control and Prevention: ACE study: http://www.cdc.gov/violenceprevention/acestudy/index.html

Center for School Mental Health: http://csmh.umaryland.edu

National Child Traumatic Stress Network: http://www.nctsn.org

History of childhood in the United States. Primary sources from George Mason University: http://chnm.gmu.edu/cyh/primary-sources/browse/?tags=North+United States

United States School Counselor Association: http://schoolcounselor.org

Additional Resources on Children of Minority Groups in the United States Through History

Bronski, D. (2011). *A queer history of the United States*. Boston, MA: Beacon.

Illick, J. (2011). *United States childhoods*. Philadelphia: University of Pennsylvania Press.

Hungrywolf, A. (2008). *Tribal childhood: Growing up in traditional Native United States*. Summertown, TN: Native Voices.

Jorae, W. (2009). *The children of Chinatown: Growing up Chinese American in San Francisco, 1850–1920*. Chapel Hill: UNC Press.

Markowitz, G., & Rosner, D. (2013). *Children, race, and power: Kenneth and Mamie Clark's Northside Center*. New York, NY: Routledge.

Morgan, H. (1995). *Historical perspectives on the education of black children*. New York, NY: Praeger.

Nazario, S. (2007). *Enrique's journey*. New York, NY: Random House.

REFERENCES

American Counseling Association (2014). *ACA code of ethics*. Alexandria, VA: Author.

American School Counselor Association (ASCA). (2014). ASCA resource center. Retrieved from http://www.schoolcounselor.org/login.aspx?ReturnUrl=%2fschool-counselors-members%2fasca-resource-center

Anderson, J. D. (1988). *The education of Blacks in the South, 1860–1935*. Chapel Hill: University of North Carolina Press.

Association for Play Therapy. (n.d.). Evidence-based practice statement: Play therapy. Retrieved from http://www.a4pt.org/?page=EvidenceBased

Axline, V. M. (1969). *Play therapy.* New York, NY: Ballantine.

Blanco, P., Ray, D., & Holliman, R. (2012). Long-term child centered play therapy and academic achievement of children: A follow-up study. *International Journal of Play Therapy*, 21, 1–13.

Brackemyre, T. (2015). Education to the masses. *U.S. History Scene*. Retrieved from http://ushistoryscene.com/article/rise-of-public-education

Brenner, R. H. (1970). *Children and youth in United States: A documentary history, volume 1.* Cambridge, MA: Harvard University Press.

Bratton, S., Rhine, T., Ray, D., & Jones, L. (2005). The efficacy of play therapy and filial therapy with children: Summary of the meta-analytic findings. *Professional Psychology: Research and Practice, 36*(4), 376–390.

Centers for Disease Control and Prevention (CDC). (2015). Child maltreatment: Risk and protective factors. Retrieved from http://www.cdc.gov/violence prevention/childmaltreatment/riskprotectivefactors.html

Chen, G. (2011). Should illegal immigrants qualify for in-state tuition? *Community College Review Online.* Retrieved from http://www.communitycollegereview .com/articles/335

Children's Mental Health Network. (n.d.). History of the movement: Early days of CASSP. Retrieved from http://www.cmhnetwork.org/history

Child Welfare Information Gateway. (2014). Mandatory reporters of child abuse and neglect. Washington, DC: U.S. Department of Health and Human Services, Children's Bureau. Retrieved from https://www.childwelfare.gov/topics/ systemwide/laws-policies/statutes/manda

Chorpita, B., Daleiden, E., & Collins, K. (2014). Managing and adapting practice: A system for applying evidence in clinical care with youth and families. *Clinical Social Work Journal, 42*(2), 134–142. doi:10.1007/s10615-013-0460-3

Community Action Network. (2010). The historical perspective on children's mental health policy. Retrieved from http://www.caction.org/health/Prescrip tionForWellness/Appendices/AppendixA.htm

Cook, S., & Klay, W. (2014). George Washington and enlightenment ideas on educating future citizens and public servants. *Journal of Public Affairs Education*, *20*(1), 45–55.

Cozolino, L., (2013). *The social neuroscience of education.* New York, NY: Norton.

Felitti, V. J., Anda R. F., Nordenberg, D., Williamson, D. F., Spitz, A. M., Edwards, V., Koss, M. P., & Marks, J. S. (1998). Relationship of childhood abuse and household dysfunction to many of the leading causes of death in adults: The Adverse Childhood Experiences (ACE) Study. *American Journal of Preventive Medicine*, 14, 245–258.

Glassman, E. L., & Prasad, S. (2013). Art therapy in schools: Its variety and benefits. In P. Howie, S. Prasad, & J. Kristel (Eds.), *Using art therapy with diverse populations: Crossing cultures and abilities* (pp. 126–133). London, UK: Jessica Kingsley.

Graham, P. A. (1974). *Community and class in United States education, 1865–1918.* New York, NY: Wiley.

Herbst, J. (1996). *The once and future school: Three hundred and fifty years of United States secondary education.* New York, NY: Routledge.

Hipsman, F., & Meissner, D. (2013, April). Immigration in the United States: New economic, social, political landscapes with legislative reform on the horizon. *Migrant Policy Institute.* Retrieved from http://www.migrationpolicy.org/article/immigration-united-states-new-economic-social-political-landscapes-legislative-reform

Hooker, S., Fix, M., & McHugh, M. (2014, March). Education reform in a changing Georgia: Promoting high school and college success for immigrant youth. *Migrant Policy Institute.* Retrieved from http://www.migrationpolicy.org/research/education-reform-changing-georgia-promoting-high-school-and-college-success-immigrant-youth

Howie, P., Prasad, S., & Kristel, J. (2013). *Using art therapy with diverse populations: Crossing cultures and abilities.* London, UK: Kingsley.

Innerhofer, B. (2013). The relationship between children's outcomes in counselling and psychotherapy and attachment styles. *Counselling Psychology Review, 28*(4), 60–76.

Jenkins, P. (2011). Mental health services for children and young people: A new era of "joined up thinking"? *Healthcare Counselling & Psychotherapy Journal, 11*(2), 25–27.

Kempe, C. H., Silverman, F. N., Steele, B. F., Droegemueller, W., & Silver, H. K. (1962). The battered-child syndrome. *Journal of the United States Medical Association, 181,* 17–24.

Kruse, D. L., & Mahony, D. (2000). Illegal child labor in the United States: Prevalence and characteristics. *Industrial and Labor Relations Review, 54*(1), 17–40.

Levine, M., & Levine, A. (1992). *Helping children: A social history.* New York, NY: Oxford University Press.

Marquis, A., Douthit, K. Z., & Elliot, A. J. (2011). Best practices: A critical yet inclusive vision for the counseling profession. *Journal of Counseling & Development, 89*(4), 397–405.

Mechanic, D. (2012). Seizing opportunities under the Affordable Care Act for transforming the mental and behavioral health system. *Health Affairs, 31,* no.2, 376–382. doe: 10.1377/hlthaff.2011.0623

Mintz, S. (2012). Education in the early republic. *Digital History*. Retrieved from http://www.digitalhistory.uh.edu/disp_textbook.cfm?smtID=3&psid=242

Myers, J. E. B. (2004). *A history of child protection in United States*. Bloomington, IN: LIBRIS Corporation.

National Education Association (NEA). (n.d.). Students affected by achievement gaps. Retrieved from http://www.nea.org/home/20380.htm

National Institutes of Health. (2014). The brain initiative. Retrieved from http://www.nih.gov/science/brain

Office of Civil Rights. (2015). Civil rights data collection. Retrieved from http://www2.ed.gov/about/offices/list/ocr/data.html?src=rt

Perry, B. D. (2005). Maltreatment and the developing child: How early childhood experience shapes child and culture. The inaugural Margaret McCain lecture (abstracted); McCain Lecture series, The Centre for Children and Families in the Justice System, London, ON.

Pletcher v. People, 52 Ill. 395 (1869).

Ray, D. (2015). Research in play therapy: Empirical support for practice. In D. Crenshaw, & A. Stewart (Eds.), *Play therapy: A comprehensive guide to theory and practice* (pp. 167–183). New York, NY: Guilford.

Rauscher, K., Runyan, C., Schulman, M., & Bowling, J. M. (2008). U.S. child labor violations in the retail and service industries: Findings from a national survey of working adolescents. *United States Journal of Public Health*, 98(9), 1693. doi:10.2105/AJPH.2007.122853

Reisner, E., & Butts, R. F. (1936). History of United States education during the colonial period. *Review of Educational Research*, 63, 57–363.

Richardson, J. (1994). Common, delinquent, and special: On the formalization of common schooling in the United States. *United States Educational Research Journal*, 31(4), 695–723.

Salmon, T. W. (2006). Mental hygiene. *United States Journal of Public Health*. 96(10), 1740–1742.

Schore, A. (2012). *The science of the art of psychotherapy*. New York, NY: Norton.

Substance Abuse and Mental Health Services Administration (SAMHSA). (2012). *Mental health, United States, 2010. HHS Publication No. (SMA) 12-4681*. Rockville, MD: Substance Abuse and Mental Health Services Administration.

van der Kolk, B. (2014). *The body keeps the score*. New York, NY: Norton.

Walters, P., & James, D. R. (1992). Schooling for some: Child labor and school enrollment of Black and White children in the early twentieth-century South. *American Sociological Review, 57*(5), 635–650.

U.S. Census Bureau (2012). Educational attainment in the United States: 2012—Detailed Tables. Retrieved from http://www.census.gov/hhes/socdemo/education/data/cps/2012/tables.html

U.S. Department of Education, National Center for Education Statistics. (2013). The condition of education 2013 (NCES 2013-037), Status dropout rates. Retrieved from http://nces.ed.gov/pubs2014/2014083.pdf

U.S. Department of Health & Human Services. (2003). New freedom commission on mental health: Achieving the promise: Transforming mental health care in United States. Final Report. DHHS pub no SMA-03-3832. Rockville, MD: Department of Health and Human Services. Retrieved from http://www2.nami.org/Template.cfm?Section=New_Freedom_Commission&Template=/ContentManagement/ContentDisplay.cfm&ContentID=28335

Chapter 2

Legal and Ethical Issues in Counseling Children and Adolescents

SONDRA SMITH-ADCOCK AND SANDRA LOGAN

All children have the right to protection. They have the right to survive, to be safe, to belong, to be heard, to receive adequate care and to grow up in a protective environment.

—United Nations Children's Fund [UNICEF], 2010, p. 149)

INTRODUCTION

Constitutional governments construct laws in order to grant basic freedoms and protections to their citizens. Children and adolescents occupy a particularly precarious position within the balance of freedom and protection. They are not yet old enough to hold complete power over their own choices, but at the same time, are sentient beings who we generally view as having basic rights. The struggle to strike the best possible balance between the competing needs for freedom and protection for young people has long roots, going back at least as far as the late 1800s, when child protection laws first began to appear in the United States (Myers, 2004). A decade into the 21st century, we are still striving to provide protection from abusive and neglectful caregivers while allowing children and adolescents some control over their own lives. The statistics cited in "Each Day in America for All Children" (Children's Defense Fund, 2014) suggest that the United States has not yet discovered an ideal way to protect children in a diverse democracy:

- 4 children are killed by abuse or neglect
- 187 children are arrested for violent crimes
- 408 children are arrested for drug crimes
- 838 public school students are corporally punished
- 1,837 children are confirmed as abused or neglected
- 4,028 children are arrested

As counselors, our professional ethics echo the need for protections that are specific for children and adolescents. Counselors working with youth rely on legal and ethical principles that are unique relative to their work with adults—and make clinical decisions that can be complicated by children's limited legal rights and an ethical imperative to help keep them safe. At the same time, children of all ages also are capable of making developmentally appropriate decisions and benefit from some autonomy and personal agency. Maintaining this balance tasks professional counselors with having an extensive and specialized knowledge and skills base related to legal and ethical decision making.

Critical variables in each and every decision counselors make are their own beliefs and cultural biases about how children should be treated. The reflective counselor practices with insight and intent (Parsons & Zhang, 2014). Before making decisions, we must examine our own relationships to the decisions we are making. Counselors also have varied personal ideas and attitudes related to the topics we address in this chapter, such as parents' rights in divorce, adolescent sexual behavior, and breaking confidentiality. A few key questions can help with reflective practice: (1) What is your relationship to the client? (2) What is your obligation to the client? (3) How does your own experience influence the decision you are making? (4) Should you reconsider it from another perspective such as the child's, the parents', or someone else's? (5) If you reconsider the issue from alternative perspectives, how might your decision be modified?

In the remainder of this chapter, we present a detailed overview of the legal and ethical issues related to counseling children and adolescents. We use illustrations and case examples to help counseling professionals in schools and clinical settings navigate the specialized legal and ethical standards and practices that are foundational for the child and adolescent counselor.

After reading this chapter you will be able to

- cite federal and state legal statutes that are related to counseling minors in school and clinical settings;
- cite relevant ethical standards for counseling children and adolescents, as published by counseling professional organizations (e.g., American Counseling Association [ACA, 2014], American School Counselor Association [ASCA, 2010]);
- recognize and apply ethical counseling practices such as informed consent;
- understand and apply ethical decision-making models that integrate knowledge of legal statues with ethical practices;
- reflect on your own personal ethics in counseling children and adolescents; and
- identify professional organizations related to counseling children and adolescents.

Imagine for a moment how commonly counselors encounter legal and ethical situations in schools or clinical settings. These situations happen every day, ranging from those that are relatively easy to address to those that are more ambiguous and subjective. Here are some examples:

- A school counselor welcomes a third-grade child to an elementary school. His mother states that he has attention deficit hyperactivity disorder (ADHD) and needs an accommodation for an upcoming exam. What laws are relevant, and how should the school counselor proceed?
- After a few sessions, an adolescent discloses recent risky sexual activity to her mental health counselor. Should the counselor break confidentiality and call her parents?
- A young mother is distraught because her son is having an increasing number of temper tantrums and asks for some parenting help. After a brief intake, the mother reports that she is separated legally from the child's father. Do both parents have to consent for the child to be counseled?
- A child who is 5 years old cries at school and tearfully tells his teacher, "My momma spanked me so hard last night." Should this be reported to a child welfare agency?

What legal and ethical principles are relevant in each scenario? In responding to each of these dilemmas, the answer is usually, it depends. The remainder of this chapter provides a trove of helpful information to help address these and other scenarios. In Guided Exercise 2.1, conduct informational interviews with counselors in a setting of your choice (schools, agencies, private practice, or medical settings) to better understand how they handle legal and ethical scenarios.

Guided Exercise 2.1

As you become a new professional in any field, it is helpful to gain insight from those who are currently practicing in the profession. Novice counselors can learn from the expertise of those who are more experienced. In the following exercise, interview a counseling professional (mental health or marriage and family counselor, school counselor, social worker, etc.) about their perspectives and experience regarding legal and ethical issues when working with children and adolescents. Reflect upon what you have learned from the expert in the field. Share with your classmates to compare and contrast the similarities and differences among those in the counseling profession.

Interview Questions:

1. Provide an overview of the education and training you have received related to counseling this particular population.

2. How familiar are you with the laws related to counseling minors in your state of practice? Are there any laws in particular that you personally have difficulty with?

3. How do you stay update on the ever-changing laws within your state?

4. Within your particular counseling specialty and setting, what are some of the most common legal and ethical situations that you face?

5. How do you deal with conflict that may arise between a minor and his or her parent/ guardian?

6. Tell me some of the challenges you have encountered when counseling minors who are living in separate households or their families have experienced or are experiencing the possibility of divorce?

7. Are there any particular resources that assist you when faced with legal and/or ethical dilemmas?

8. Have you ever been subpoenaed to court related to your counseling with minors? If so, tell me about that experience.

9. What advice or words of wisdom do you have for those new to the profession?

CHILDREN'S RIGHTS

Do children have rights? If so, what are they? Legally, it is clear that children have fewer rights than adults; children do not choose their own doctor, own their own home, or bring home their own pay check. However, children do have civil rights and many other legal rights that are designed to protect them (Legal Information Institute, n.d.). Children are protected by U.S. and state law and are generally considered to have civil rights. You will note that in Chapter 1 we provided a historical overview of children's rights in the United States. In the section that follows, we review some of the legal rights of children that have been passed. According to

"Children's Rights Overview" by the Legal Information Institute (LII) at Cornell University, the following federal statutes are related to children's rights (Legal Information Institute [LII], n.d.):

Table 2.1   Federal Statutes Related to Children's Rights

Civil Action for the Deprivation of Rights, 42 U.S.C. § 1983	Provides a basic human rights protection, including children, to people in a free society.
The Indian Child Welfare Act of 1978 (25 U.S.C., Ch. 21) and the Child Abuse Prevention and Treatment Act of 2010, 42 U.S.C. 5101 et seq; 42 U.S.C. 5116 et seq	U.S. federal laws provide protections related to fostering and adoption of minors that require basic rights of the child are met, with a respect for family bonds and ethnic and cultural background.
The Social Security Act (42 U.S.C., Ch. 7)	This act provides for children's welfare generally and more recently, states' responsibility to provide children's health insurance. The Social Security Act requires state governments to provide support for minors.
The Children's Bureau (42 U.S.C., Ch. 6)	This government division was developed to provide for the welfare of children by the U.S. Congress and its constituencies.

As advocates for children's rights, counselors need to be familiar with the 1989 *United Nations Convention on the Rights of the Child*, or UNCRC (UNICEF, n.d.) The UNCRC position is that children should have basic human rights, including input in regard to decisions that affect them (UNICEF, n.d.). Madeline Albright (the U.S. Ambassador to the United Nations at the time) signed the UNCRC in 1995, but the United States has not ratified the treaty. To do this, Congress must approve it, and the president must ratify it (UNICEF, 2005). The reasons the United States has not ratified the treaty are related to sociopolitical and ideological conflicts within the country about the role of government and the autonomy of citizens. Some factions within the population believe that this legally binding treaty would compromise U.S. sovereignty, the rights of states, and, ultimately, parents' rights to raise their children in the way they see fit (Cohen & DeBenedet, 2012). For a more detailed explanation about the UNCRC and its historical significance, consult the UNICEF website: http://www.unicef.org/crc/index_understanding.html. In Guided Exercise 2.2, we provide an activity related to Children's Legal Rights.

Guided Exercise 2.2

It is important to understand the history and the contributions that have led to the rights that children have in this modern day and age. Read the section on UNICEF's website, "Understanding the CRC." Additionally, read the section, "Rights under the Convention on Children's Rights," which presents guiding principles and three sets of rights: Survival and Developmental Rights, Protection Rights, and Participation Rights. Consult additional online resources concerning the rights of children in society as needed. Using what you have learned, create a 1 to 2 page newsletter or pamphlet that summarizes the rights given to children (and other vulnerable populations). Take the opportunity to use your creativity in presenting this important information. Consider not only including the historical dates and events but also highlighting the implications of such events.

THE CHILD AND ADOLESCENT COUNSELOR AND THE LAW: WORKING WITHIN THE LEGAL SYSTEM

Every U.S. state has different laws and agencies regulating children's welfare, including foster care, custody, and adoption. Reviewing all of these legal codes state-by-state is beyond the scope of this chapter. Laws related to what constitutes abuse of children, issues such as age of consent, statutory rape, and minors' access to reproductive health services also vary by state. The United States Department of Health and Human Services offers guidance on these statutes and how they apply to your location with their online resource, "Online Resources for State Child Welfare" "Law and Policy" (Child Welfare Information Gateway, 2013a). Counselors should conduct their own research into the laws and policies of the state in which they practice. Explore your state's laws in Guided Exercise 2.3.

Guided Exercise 2.3

While the intent of state laws is to protect and respect the rights of individuals, they are also designed to provide guidance. As such, it is important for counselors to be knowledgeable about laws specific to their state of practice. Go to the Child Welfare Information Gateway, housed by U.S. Department of Health & Human Services, at https://www.childwelfare.gov/topics/systemwide/laws-policies/state.

1. Select your state of practice.
2. Select a topic(s):
3. Click on the check boxes that relate to your counseling work within the three areas of child abuse and neglect, child welfare, and adoption.
4. Click the "go" button to begin your search for your state's statutes.
5. You will be provided with the specific citations and legal reference to those areas that you identified. Also, you should note that PDF files are available that correspond to these specific areas and that provide information so that you can better understand the issue across the states.

In the section that follows, we provide information on key legal issues in coun-seling children and adolescents, beginning with federal statutes. Throughout this chapter, we cite print and online resources that help the professional counselor in both school and clinical settings stay informed. In the section that follows, we provide an overview of some of the legal information most commonly referenced by professional counselors. Importantly, both federal and state laws continue to be updated; so while care has been taken to provide up-to-date information in this chapter, professional counselors need to stay abreast of changes in the law.

Federal Privacy Laws: HIPAA and FERPA

Federal statutes related to the protection of clients' privacy are important consid-erations in counseling children and adolescents. For example, the Health Insurance Portability and Accountability Act of 1997 (HIPAA) protects the privacy of any medical patient's health record including children (U.S. Department of Health and Human Services, n.d.). The Family Educational Rights and Privacy Act (FERPA, 20 U.S.C § 1232g; C.F.R § 34 CFR Part 99) provides for the confidentiality of students' educational records and pertains to all schools that receive federal funds. FERPA also provides for the privacy of all educational records including any documentation related to the Individuals With Disabilities Act (IDEA), which is discussed in a later section. For children and adolescents in substance abuse treat-ment, there are additional protections in the form of 42 CFR Part 2, which applies to the privacy of any records related to substance abuse education, treatment, or prevention programs that are related to or assisted by any department or agency of the U.S. government (Kunkel, 2012).

HIPAA governs the protection of medical records, while FERPA relates to edu-cational records. Counselors who work with children in clinical settings are more likely to encounter the rules outlined in HIPAA. Counselors in public schools, including colleges and universities, generally fall under FERPA regulations. However, this is not mutually exclusive, and counselors should have a working knowledge of both laws. For example, a school counselor who refers a student for mental health counseling might be asked for information regarding school perfor-mance. Similarly, a student's health records related to a mental health diagnosis have some relevance to the daily work of the school counselor to make accommo-dations for the student at school. In both cases, the records are private, and legal guardians should be contacted to provide a signed document releasing the relevant information to the collaborating counselor. Though privacy of records is of high importance, sharing information across settings is often vital to effective treatment outcomes and is in the best interest of the child.

Under each of these privacy provisions, records are considered private and con-fidential. However, a primary purpose of FERPA also is to provide legal guardians the right to view their children's records. In some cases, HIPAA allows for minors' individual rights to keep their health records confidential from parents or caregivers (e.g., if the minor can show that releasing records to caregivers would put them at risk), however, educational records are exempt from these HIPAA exclusions as FERPA provisions allow parents and caregivers access to their unemancipated minors' educational records (45 CFR § 160.103; Family Educational Rights and Privacy Act, 20 USC §§ 1232g; and 34 CFR, part 98) (U.S. Department of Health and Human Services & U.S. Department of Education, 2008). For more information, see "Joint Guidance on the Application of the Family Education Rights and Privacy Act (FERPA) and the Health Insurance Portability and Accountability Act of 1996 (HIPAA) To Students' Health Records" at http://www.hhs.gov/ocr/privacy/hipaa/understanding/coveredentities/hipaaferpajointguide.pdf.

Minors' Legal Consent

There are many legal and ethical guidelines that are specific to the status of minors in society. For example, the extent to which minors have legal rights to consent is a concept central to many legal and ethical issues in counseling children and adolescents. *Consent*, the ability to enter into binding contracts, is a right afforded to adults, at the age of majority. With few exceptions, minors cannot enter into binding legal contracts, which includes consenting to counseling services. The age of majority is defined in the United States at the state level. While it is generally understood that the age of majority is 18, state laws vary concerning at what age individuals may provide consent for health treatment. For example, in many states, adolescents can consent to certain types of treatment, including mental health care. The legal precedent is often whether or not the adolescent is of sufficient age to make mature decisions or if the disclosure to parents or caregivers would put the adolescent at risk for harm.

Consent and privacy laws also address a balance between minors' privacy and caregivers' rights to information concerning their unemancipated, or dependent, minor children. The concept of legal consent also relates to the age at which young people can make other adult-like decisions. For example, age of consent refers to the age at which a minor can consent to sexual activity or marriage without parental permission (U.S. Department of Health and Human Services, 2004). Without a legal authority to grant consent, adult caregivers must consent to treatment of their unemancipated minors, and, therefore, the young people do not have the same reasonable expectation of privacy, as do adults. This limits their rights to *confidentiality*. A related legal concept is *privileged communication,* which refers to a legal principle that protects information obtained in particular relationships (e.g., attorney-client, physician-client, spouse-spouse) from being entered into evidence in a legal proceeding. The privilege belongs to the client so counselors can provide information if the client requests or consents to have the information provided in a legal proceeding. In some states, the counseling relationship between a client and a licensed mental health provider is privileged, but most school counselors are state certified so they may not fit into this legal category (Hansen, 2009). Any time practicing counselors, regardless of the setting, have questions about whether the information obtained from their clients is privileged, they should contact legal counsel (Hansen, 2009).

Though minors cannot legally give their consent for treatment, their participation and involvement in decision making are critical to the success of counseling for all ages. Counselors focus on a developmental and strengths-based approach; counseling is not something we do *to* children, but *with* them. Therefore, measures can be taken to have minors provide their *assent*, which is a not a legally binding contract, but is a way for children and adolescents to communicate that they are fully committed to and in agreement with the services they are receiving. Counselors in any setting can secure an assent by explaining the following: an outline of the counseling approach in developmentally appropriate language, what they will be asked to do (e.g., how often you will meet), and what is required of them (e.g., what activities you will do together). Children, as young as 5 or 6 years old, can provide their signature, but assent can also be done verbally. For professional counselors who work with children, these two concepts, *consent* and *confidentiality,* provide a foundation for many of the legal and ethical questions we encounter in our work. More information related to consent and confidentiality is provided later on in this chapter.

Confidentiality is important to children and adolescents in counseling just as it is to adults. While it is important to protect the privacy of children and adolescents, there also are precedents that prioritize keeping caregivers informed. As professional counselors, the privacy of our clients is paramount, and federal privacy laws are an essential part of the legal knowledge required of counselors in any setting. Though these privacy laws may be more relevant for some counselors than others, all counselors need to be aware of their scope and importance to safeguarding client's records. For further guidance regarding a HIPAA or FERPA-related issue, search topics at the Office of Civil Rights website at http://www.hhs.gov/ocr/privacy/hipaa/faq/index.html.

Counseling Children With Disabilities: IDEA and Section 504

Two federal laws guide access to specialized educational services for children with disabilities. These laws are integral to the work of the school counselor but are also critical to the work of any counselor working with school-age youth.

IDEA

The IDEA mandates that children with disabilities receive an adequate and appropriate education and holds schools accountable for providing services that meet their developmental and educational needs and optimize their academic achieve-ment. Under IDEA (IDEA, 2004), children enrolled in K-12 public schools with 13 categories of identified disabilities are eligible for supportive educational and mental health services. Furthermore, any public school that receives federal funding is legislated to provide these services. The National Dissemination Center for Children with Disabilities (NICHCY) provides a brief explanation of each category:

Table 2.2 Categories of Childhood Disability

Autism	A developmental disability significantly affecting verbal and nonverbal communication and social interaction, onset is usually prior to age three, and educational performance is usually affected
Deafness	A hearing impairment that significantly impairs language ability and negatively affects educational performance
Deaf-Blindness	Combined hearing and visual impairments that cannot be accommodated in special education programs solely for children with deafness or children with blindness
Emotional Disturbance	A condition exhibiting one or more of the following characteristics over a long period of time that adversely affects a child's educational performance: (a) An inability to learn that cannot be explained by intellectual, sensory, or health factors (b) An inability to build or maintain satisfactory interpersonal relationships with peers and teachers (c) Inappropriate types of behavior or feelings under normal circumstances (d) A general pervasive mood of unhappiness or depression (e) A tendency to develop physical symptoms or fears associated with personal or school problems
Hearing Impairments	An impairment in hearing, that is not included in the definition of deafness but is significant to negatively affect educational performance
Intellectual Disability	A significantly subaverage general intellectual functioning that affects adaptive functioning and development
Multiple Disabilities	Combined impairments (such as intellectual disability-blindness, intellectual disability-orthopedic impairment) that cannot be accommodated in other specific categories of special education
Orthopedic Impairments	A severe orthopedic impairment that adversely affects a child's educational performance

Other Health Impairments	A limited strength, vitality, or alertness, including a heightened alertness to environmental stimuli, that results in limited alertness with respect to the educational environment, that
	(a) is due to related health problems such as asthma, attention deficit disorder or attention deficit hyperactivity disorder, diabetes, epilepsy, a heart condition, hemophilia, lead poisoning, leukemia, nephritis, rheumatic fever, sickle cell anemia, and Tourette syndrome; and
	(b) adversely affects a child's educational performance
Specific Learning Disabilities	A disorder of the basic psychological processes involved in language that negatively affects ability to listen, think, speak, read, write, spell, or do mathematics
Speech or Language Impairments	A speech or language impairment that adversely affects a child's educational performance
Traumatic Brain Injury	An acquired injury to the brain caused by an external physical force, resulting in physical disability or psychosocial problems, or both, that negatively affects educational performance
Visual Impairments	An impairment in vision that, even with correction, adversely affects a child's educational performance

Source: Adapted from National Dissemination Center for Children with Disabilities (NICHCY). (2012). *Categories of Disability Under IDEA.*

Counselors who work in schools implement direct services related to IDEA every day, primarily by providing counseling support to students with disabilities. School counselors are also usually intricately involved in the administration of these services, including Individualized Education Plans (IEPs). Importantly, IEPs often include counseling services. Sample IEP goals related to counseling might include *(1) Develop awareness of emotions, (2) Develop empathy for others, and (3) Communicate emotions effectively.* These are social and emotional goals that are often delivered within the context of a counseling relationship. Though counselors who work in clinical settings will usually not be directly involved in the administration of IEPs, they often find that having knowledge of these laws is an imperative because of the number of youth they see with one or more of these disabilities and their collaboration and consultation with school personnel.

Section 504

Section 504 of the Rehabilitation Act of 1973 mandates that public schools provide a free and appropriate education to students who have a physical or mental impairment that substantially limits one or more major life activities. An amendment to the American Disabilities Act of 2004 (enacted in 2009) continued a provision for 504 educational services and also expanded the definition of disability. An appropriate education for a student with a disability under the Section 504 regulations could consist of education in regular classrooms, education in regular classes with supplementary services, and/or special education and related service (Office for Civil Rights, 2015). Educational 504 plans are binding agreements between the school, student, and a student's legal guardian to have certain accommodations made for the student's schooling. Accommodations are related to providing access to educational services that help with a student's disability whether the disability is physical (e.g., ramps) or mental (e.g., extra time on tests or increased assistance with note taking).

Remember the school counselor who welcomed a third-grade child who had ADHD and had a 504 plan? As the test was approaching, the school counselor would have wanted to obtain a copy of the plan and coordinate with teachers and other staff to help make arrangements for the accommodations the child needed. This might have included having extra time, a quiet space, fewer items per page, or someone to read the test to him.

A comparison chart for IDEA and Section 504 can be found on the National Center for Learning Disability website (http://www.ncld.org/disability-advocacy/learn-ld-laws/adaaa-section-504/section-504-idea-comparison-chart). While these laws have been an important part of the legal landscape for counseling children and adolescents for decades, implementation of these laws can be uneven at best, and many issues may arise in which counselors will be called upon to advocate for youth with disabilities. Some troubling trends are noteworthy. Children from minority groups are disproportionately identified and classified as having disabilities (U.S. Department of Education, 2009). For example, Black children tend to be overidentified as having mental retardation and emotional disturbance (Donovan & Cross, 2002; USDE, 2009). Interestingly, the phenomenon also extends to the underidentification of giftedness among children from minority groups (USDE, 2009). Decades of research have examined this phenomenon, and the reasons why these disparities exist are varied and can be controversial (Klingner et al., 2005; Skiba et al., 2008). There does seem to be some consensus, however, that the problem is both historical and systemic, with systematic discrimination at its root (NASP, 2013). (Please also note the discussion of the achievement gap in Chapter 1.)

Counselor Advocacy for Children With Disabilities

Professional counselors can be a primary force in working within educational and mental health systems of care to advocate for children and adolescents who have disabilities. Trusty and Brown (2005) outlined an advocacy process for school counselors, although these steps would certainly be applicable to counselors working with children in any setting. Trusty and Brown recommend the following:

1. *The counselor develops advocacy dispositions.* Advocacy dispositions are the personal characteristics that motivate counselors to prioritize advocacy and are the foundation for advocacy skills. Autonomy, being guided by one's own decision making, is an important part of advocacy.

2. *Develop advocacy relationships and knowledge.* Find and learn about advocacy resources and build networks within and outside the school.

3. *Define the advocacy problem.* Gather information and define the problem within the context of systems.

4. *Develop action plans.* Create clear and specific plans using advocacy resources.

5. *Implement action plans.* Organize your action using advocacy skills such as problem solving, communication, and collaboration.

6. *Make an evaluation.* Assess whether the action mitigated the problem, as defined.

7. *Celebrate or regroup.* Encourage those involved to advocate for themselves (parents and children), and when problems are not changed, regroup. (Adapted from Trusty & Brown, 2005, p. 264.)

Tort Negligence or Malpractice

The word *tort* refers to an intentional or negligent civil wrongdoing. Though some torts committed by professional counselors are intentional wrongdoing and also meet the definition of criminal acts (e.g., stealing from clients or fraudulent insurance claims), most are unintentional and result in legal sanction but are not criminal acts (e.g., failing to report child abuse). For professional counselors, these are most often related to a specific kind of tort called *malpractice*. Malpractice is misconduct by a professional that violates a *standard of care* that is expected of that professional. According to Wheeler and Bertram (2012), *standard of care* is the expected level of attention that is consistent with the degree of learning, skill, and ethics typically possessed and carried out by professional counselors practicing under similar circumstances (p. 15). For counselors, as with other professionals, a failure to meet a standard of care involves *negligence*, or a situation in which a wrongful action by one person results in harm to someone else. Because professional counselors have a prescribed *duty* in relationship to the client, when that duty is not met appropriately, the counselor can be considered negligent (Wheeler & Bertram, 2012). Legally, a common threshold usually determines a reasonable standard of care—would another professional counselor in the same situation make the same or similar decision? In court cases, this usually means that professionals from the community would be called to establish this threshold. In ethical proceedings, this standard is similar and is usually determined by state licensing or certification boards.

There is a strong correlation between the legal definition and the professions' ethical definitions of standard practices (for professional counselors, ACA, ASCA, etc.). These professional standards often are statutory, meaning that these standards also are adopted as federal, state, or local laws, and violations of these express standards are considered malpractice and can be subject to both ethical and legal sanction. Within each state, there are both laws for professional counselors and legislated professional licensure boards, such as the National Board for Certified Counselors (NBCC) that oversee these standards and sanctions. Visit NBCC's website and navigate to the topic, Understanding Certification and Licensure (NBCC, 2014) for a comparison of national counselor certification and state counselor licensure (http://www.nbcc.org/Certification/CertificationorLicensure). For certification laws for school counselors, review the American School Counselor Association's webpage (http://www.schoolcounselor.org/school-counselors-members/careers-roles/state-certification-requirements), as well as to consult the Department of Education for the state in which you practice.

Parental Rights and Custody

The Uniform Parentage Act and the Uniform Child Custody Jurisdiction Act (Legal Information Institute, n.d.) are laws that are consistent across all states and the District of Columbia. Generally, these laws are intended to provide reciprocity across states so that states honor and enforce the parental rights and custody-related rulings of the other(s). Parental rights and custody laws are important for professional counselors primarily because there can be questions regarding who can provide *consent for treatment*, that is, who can make decisions in the interest of the child and who has rights to the child's educational and health records. When there are legal rulings such as custody or revocation of parental rights, the counselor is charged with finding this out up front.

What happens if a parent who is divorced seeks counseling for his or her minor child without the other parent's permission? In this case, the counselor should make sure he or she has a clear understanding of the custody agreement between the parents and to follow it. If both parents have custody of the minor child, both parents have rights to information about their child. Issues related to parental consent are commonly addressed across both school counseling and clinical settings.

Issues related to parenting rights and child custody can be highly emotionally charged. Counselors can become entangled in the perspectives of parents and/or children and unintentionally find themselves up against the boundaries of the legal.

For instance, a divorced mother brings her young child in to a clinical setting to seek help for her child, who is having tantrums. The counselor in this case should ask the mother for a copy of any legal documents that define the custody arrangements between the child's father and herself. This is important. If the father also has legal custody, it is important to have his consent and cooperation in working with the young child.

The complexities of family law are critical for counselors working with minors, but the volume of information that is available state by state is cumbersome and would be impossible to summarize well in this chapter. For more information on family law in the United States, explore a comprehensive electronic resource provided by the American Bar Association (ABA) in Guided Exercise 2.4.

Guided Exercise 2.4

As a helping professional, it is imperative that you familiarize yourself with the family laws pertinent to the state that your practice in. The *Family Law Quarterly*, published by the American Bar Association, provides a brief graphical representation that summarizes the laws by topic in each state, including alimony/spousal support, custody, child support guidelines, and grounds for divorce. To gain a better understanding of the laws that are in place in your state of practice and beyond, attempt to answer the following questions by accessing http://www.americanbar.org/groups/family_law/resources/family_law_in_the_50_states.html.

Review each of the charts, and identify what laws, provisions, and exceptions are applicable to your state of practice.

Questions:

1. According to Chart 1, *Alimony/Spousal Support Factors*, identify the only state that fails to include all four factors in its laws.

2. According to Chart 2, *Custody Criteria*, identify the state that currently has the largest number of legal codes that address family law and custody situations.

3. According to Chart 2, *Custody Criteria*, identify which states function under the presumption to be in favor of joint custody.

Mandated Reporting for Child Abuse and Neglect

All states and the District of Columbia have mandatory reporting laws that identify persons who are required to report suspected child maltreatment and abuse (Child Welfare Information Gateway, n.d.). Child maltreatment includes physical, emotional, and sexual abuse and neglect. Acts of omission, or a failure to take reasonable action to protect a child from harm, also constitute maltreatment

(Child Welfare Information Gateway, n.d.). Furthermore, all states identify professional counselors among those mandated to report. Other individuals who may be identified as mandated reporters include law enforcement officers, court-appointed special advocates, employees of youth campus and recreational centers, and commercial film or photograph processors.

When mandatory reporting occurs during the reporters' employment or volunteer service at an institution, such as a school or hospital, often there is what is called, "institutional reporting." In these cases, there often are internal policies and procedures about how reports are made. These procedures, however, do not release individuals of their responsibility to report, nor do they allow institutions to prohibit individuals from reporting (Child Welfare Information Gateway, 2013b). Though the details of these provisions vary from state to state, there are rules to which counselors and their supervisors should adhere. For a complete list of those mandated to report in your state, please refer to the Child Welfare Information Gateway links in the Additional Resources section at the end of this chapter.

Laws concerning when a report must be made also differs according to state. Generally, a report must be made when a mandated reporter, in an official capacity, has a reason to believe that a child has been neglected or abused and has knowledge of or has observed child maltreatment that has or might reasonably result in harm to the child. The responsibility is to report a suspicion of abuse or neglect are not usually eased by *privileged communication* (Child Welfare Information Gateway, 2013b). Both legally and ethically, the protection of children from harm takes precedence over privileged communication for mandatory reporters.

Let's return to the 5-year-old child who cries at school and tearfully tells his teacher, "My momma spanked me so hard last night." Because the child seems emotionally upset, the teacher quickly informs the school counselor and the principal. However, there is no evidence of bruises or other injuries. At what point would these mandatory reporters contact child welfare? The general legal definition for abuse is defined as the intent to inflict harm on a child (Child Welfare Information Gateway, n.d.). Spanking, while strongly discouraged by many child experts (e.g., Gershoff, 2008; MacKenzie, Nicklas, Waldfogel, & Brooks-Gunn, 2013), does not always constitute abuse. In this case, a report to child welfare would probably not be necessary. However, child abuse hotlines can be contacted with anonymity if there is any doubt about whether a situation like this rises to the threshold of physical abuse. Childhelp National Abuse Hotline (1-800-4-A-CHILD; https://www .childhelp.org/hotline) is available in the United States, U.S. territories, and Canada. Most states in the United States also have hotlines. For more information visit the National Council on Child Abuse and Family Violence at http://www .nccafv.org/index.htm.

Juvenile Justice

When minors commit crimes and delinquent acts, they come into contact with the legal system. However, children and adolescents may be treated differently by the legal system than adults because they are minors For example, juveniles do not have the right to a trial by jury unless they are transferred to the adult justice system and charged as adults (United States Department of Justice, n.d.). In addition, the term, *delinquency* refers to an act committed by a youth that would constitute a crime if committed by an adult. Traffic violations and petty offenses that are punished with small fines are generally not considered to be delinquent offenses, nor are status offenses like truancy or running away from home. Some states exclude certain serious offenses from the "delinquent act" definition so that youth who commit those acts will be tried in criminal court. In many states, murder is considered to be a criminal act rather than a delinquent act, even if the offender is a child (Griffin, Adams, & Firestine, 2011). This is a trend that has come under much scrutiny but is generally allowed in most states. Counselors should be aware that in some states, juveniles sentenced as adults are housed in adult prisons, sometimes with adult offenders. Additionally, there is a strong undercurrent of racial bias within the U.S. system of justice, including the juvenile system. African-American and Hispanic youth are arrested and incarcerated at far higher rates than their White counterparts. Nationally, 67% of incarcerated youth are racial minorities (Leadership Conference on Civil and Human Rights, 2014). Some states allow juveniles to be sentenced as adults, including the sentence of life without parole. There are currently around 2,570 youth serving life sentences in the United States, and 74% of them are African-American or Hispanic (Leadership Conference on Civil and Human Rights, 2014).

Another population that is overrepresented in the juvenile justice system is gay, lesbian, bisexual, and transgender (LGBT) youth. According to some estimates, LGBT youth comprise as much as 15% of the U.S. juvenile detention and incarcerated youth populations, even though they may only be 3% to 5% of the entire adolescent population in the United States (Hunt & Moodie-Mills, 2012). Once inside detention facilities, LGBT youth often face bullying, sexual harassment, and sexual assault at much higher rates than heterosexual youth (Hunt & Moodie-Mills, 2012).

As professional counselors, we come into contact with minors who are offenders in several ways. First, crimes and delinquency do occur on and around the school grounds (Florida Department of Juvenile Justice, n.d.), and school counselors may be required to interact on behalf of students or the institution within the legal system. Second, many professional counselors work within juvenile justice settings to provide case management or direct services to juvenile offenders. Counselors working within those settings interact with the legal system as a youth advocate and also within clinical settings as an agent of change for the individual children and adolescents and their families. Counselors have an ethical responsibility to advocate for best counseling practices within juvenile justice settings. Many institutions and organizations are committed to making the juvenile justice system rehabilitative and effective in mitigating juvenile crime as well as helping youth succeed. For more information, search the Coalition for Juvenile Justice, Juvenile Law Center, John D. and Catherine T. MacAuthor Foundation, the Annie E. Casey Foundation, or the Free Child Project.

Recent Legislation: State Laws to Mandate Bullying Prevention

Within the last decade, many states have passed antibullying legislation. According to StopBullying.gov, published by the U.S. Department of Health and Human Service, all states have bullying-related laws, with the exception of Montana, which has a policy. In *Analysis of State Bullying Laws and Policies* (Stuart-Cassel, Bell, & Springer, 2011), researchers found that 13 of the states specify that schools have jurisdiction over off-campus bullying behavior if it creates a hostile school environment. Given this small number and inconsistency throughout the states concerning off-campus policies, the handling of situations involving bullying and cyberbullying will greatly vary upon geographical location and work setting.

Counselors should be aware that some subsets of the youth population are at much higher risk for all forms of bullying and harassment than others.

Laws related to bullying are relatively recent, with most laws introduced within the last 10 to 15 years. In Guided Exercise 2.5, find out what, if any, policies your local community or state has related to bullying.

Guided Exercise 2.5

At Stopbullying.gov, you can research local and state policies. Go to http://www.stopbullying.gov/laws. Research the policies and laws that govern your local schools. To what extent are these policies effectively carried out in the settings in which counselors work? How do counselors use these laws and policies to advocate for children?

ETHICS OF COUNSELING CHILDREN AND ADOLESCENTS: BEST PRACTICES AND DECISION MAKING

In the section that follows, we address the counseling profession's ethical standards and models for ethical decision making. We take care in integrating the legal principles discussed above with what is considered as a *standard of care* outlined by the counseling profession's ethical standards related to the counseling of minors. Links to the most recent ethical standards adopted by counseling professional organizations (e.g., ACA, 2014; ASCA, 2010; AMHCA, 2010) are provided at the end of this chapter.

Counselor Competence

Counseling children and adolescents is an important specialty area. So first and foremost, counselors should be knowledgeable and competent in working with this distinct and vulnerable population in society. While there are no separate ethical standards related to the subspecialty we refer to as counseling children and adolescents (ASCA standards are for school counseling specifically, not counseling minors), the ACA (2014) Ethical Code C.2.a is clear about practicing within our competencies. The standard states,

C.2.a. Boundaries of Competence

Counselors practice only within the boundaries of their competence, based on their education, training, supervised experience, state and national professional credentials, and appropriate professional experience. Whereas multicultural counseling competency is required across all counseling specialties, counselors gain knowledge, personal awareness, sensitivity, dispositions, and skills pertinent to being a culturally competent counselor in working with a diverse client population. (p. 8)

Additionally, the ACA Code of Ethics C.2.b. cites the importance of developing skills in a new practice specialty area. For example, Lawrence and Kurpius (2000) recommend that counselors who work with children need specialized knowledge and specific diagnostic tools. Further, these authors are clear in their admonition that carelessly applying the same treatment and diagnostic tools used with adults to children is inappropriate and unethical.

As stated in Chapter 1, we strongly suggest that counseling children and adolescents is a specialty area that requires additional education, training, and dispositions.

This specialty area is an important one for counselors, whether in schools or clinical settings, because children are at a developmentally vulnerable stage (Remley & Herlihy, 2014). In sections that follow in this text, more elaboration of this specialization are forefront. Knowledge of developmental ages and stages, the use of developmentally appropriate interventions, childhood psychological disorders, and culturally centered and family-centered approaches are some of the specialized knowledge areas that counselors should obtain.

Informed Consent and Confidentiality

As we presented in the early sections of this chapter, because children and adolescents are generally minors and have limited legal rights as compared to adults, counselors navigate a different ethical and legal terrain. This makes the ethical standards related to counseling minors as well as ethical decision making of particular importance to practitioners. Though minors usually need their parents' consent to participate in treatment (except in schools, because counseling is usually considered part of the educational programming), it is an ethical imperative to give them as much confidentiality and agency in their own counseling as possible. This makes the ethical concepts related to *confidentiality* and *informed consent* of particular consideration. Last, while these legal directives and ethical codes are often consistent, in some instances, they might come into conflict with each other. Say, for example, a counselor is called as a witness in a hearing related to child custody but feels strongly that the need to protect the child's confidentiality takes precedence. In this case, the counselor is torn between a legal directive and an ethical imperative to protect the child.

While counselors are usually held to strict confidentiality concerning their clients, there are situations that require that oath to be broken, such as when issues of child abuse and neglect arise. Counselors also need to be aware of their work settings' particular procedures and protocols regarding breaking confidentiality and making reports. These procedures can also be beneficial in helping counselors to have adequate consultation and supervision during periods in which they must make reports.

ACA ethical codes address respect for confidentiality, which pertains to the privacy of any client, including minors. Standard B.1.c. states, "Counselors protect the confidential information of prospective and current clients. Counselors disclose information only with appropriate consent or with sound legal or ethical justification (2014, p. 7). For all clients, confidentiality is an ethical imperative. However, there are important limitations for the expectation of confidentiality. ACA standard B.1.d. maintains that counselors keep their clients informed throughout the counseling process about the conditions under which confidentiality might be broken.

In both clinical and school settings, care must be taken to help young people know that their counseling relationships are confidential. However, in schools, there may be an added pressure to release information to school personnel or parents. When the expectation of confidentiality is limited by these demands, children should be informed. You might say, for example, "in here what you say is private; however, in some cases, we will want to let your parents or your teachers know what we talk about because it will help you do better in school."

In Guided Exercise 2.6, practice role-playing a consent statement with a child or adolescent.

Guided Exercise 2.6

In small groups, have students take turns role-playing their confidentiality statement with a child or adolescent. For instance, student one will role-play as counselor with student two as the child or adolescent. Other group members serve as process observers and then provide feedback.

Counselors should also explain the limits of confidentiality (ACA, 2014, B.1.d.). These *limitations* involve the protection of the client from serious harm and have particular urgency when working with children and adolescents. ACA ethical code B.2.a. provides guidelines for breaking confidentiality under the condition that there is foreseeable harm for the client or when legal requirements demand that information be revealed. Wheeler and Bertram (2012) suggest that a variety of factors including "the age, maturity, and education level of the minor; the relationship with parents or guardians; whether disclosure can reasonably be expected to help the situation or could cause harm" should be considered in making decisions as to whether break confidentiality or not (p. 89). Additionally, it is important to consider one's place of employment and understand how the organization's perspectives on confidentiality and policy play into a counselor's decision-making process. As we presented earlier in this chapter, all states clearly mandate the need for counselors to report the abuse and neglect of their minor clients.

Standard A.2. of the ACA Code of Ethics (2014) outlines the importance of informed consent in the counseling relationship. A.2.a. states,

Clients have the freedom to choose whether to enter into or remain in a counseling relationship and need adequate information about the counseling process and the counselor. Counselors have an obligation to review in writing and verbally with clients the rights and responsibilities of both counselors and clients. Informed consent is an ongoing part of the counseling process, and counselors appropriately document discussions of informed consent throughout the counseling relationship. (p. 4)

Though minors do not have a legal right to contract for counseling services, informing them of the counseling process and obtaining their consent are nonetheless important. According to standard A.2.b., this information includes what to expect in counseling: the purposes, goals, techniques, procedures, limitations, potential risks, and benefits of services; the counselor's qualifications, credentials, relevant experience, and approach to counseling (p. 4). Importantly, ethics also make clear the importance of developmental and cultural sensitivity in the informed consent process, making sure that these informed procedures are understood by and appropriate for the client (ACA, 2014, A.2.c.). Lawrence and Kurpius (2000) recommend that children should be informed of the counseling process in language that they can understand and should be included in making decisions in developmentally appropriate ways.

Working With Parents and Other Adults

Although our legal system has come a long way and courts have often recognized that youth are individuals with their own rights, by and large, the law still favors biological parents' rights to make decisions on behalf of their children (Legal Information Institute [LII], n.d.). Therefore, there has been a general consensus among counselors to err on the side of releasing information to parents (Hendrix, 1991), while making sure that clients understand this when explaining informed consent. More recently, privacy laws have provided mixed advice to the practicing counselor, with most of the statutes favoring the release of information to parents.

Because minors usually do not have the capacity to provide their legal consent, ethical issues related to how best to protect their confidentiality quickly emerge. In the ACA Code of Ethics (2014), standards B.5 (a, b, & c) address a client's capacity to give informed consent. In fact, standard B.5.a. is specific to the importance of protecting confidentiality when clients demonstrate an inability to give voluntary informed consent, as directed by law and ethical standards. Standard B.5.b. relates directly to the legal rights of parents and caregivers (custodial arrangements) and the importance of a collaborative relationship between counselors and families or caregivers. As part of this relationship, it is important that counselors communicate to guardians the confidential nature of the counseling relationship. Finally, standard B.5.c. provides guidance to counselors regarding the release of confidential information to third parties. In these circumstances, counselors seek the permission of a caregiver or other appropriate third party and take steps to make sure that the client understands the need for disclosure and protects his or her confidentiality as much as possible. When releasing information, the minor's age and developmental level is of concern in making decisions to break or not break confidentiality. Because of their increasing autonomy and authority to make decisions for themselves, as children's age increases, counselors might less often believe that they should break confidentiality. Legally, they may be considered competent and able to *consent*. Remember that some privacy laws give older children a right to consent to treatment, and not in all cases, do they need their parents' consent to do so.

So if after a few weeks of counseling, an adolescent discloses risky sexual activity to her mental health counselor, should her counselor inform her parents? Should he or she break confidentiality? Our ethical guidelines as counselors maintain that we break confidentiality when there is a serious and foreseeable harm (ACA Code of Ethics, 2014, B.2.a., p. 7). A study by Moyer and Sullivan (2008) showed that school counselors made decisions to break confidentiality based on a number of factors, most prominent of which was the level of seriousness of the risky behavior and how likely it was that the risky behavior occurred. Other factors included the potential consequences of breaking confidentiality, protecting the adolescent, the likelihood that the risky behavior would stop without telling the parents, and the duration of the risk-taking behavior. In this case, there are many questions to be answered to help guide the counselor in making the decision whether or not to break confidentiality, including the age of the child reporting the behavior.

In counseling with minors, it is important to be mindful of the difference between *disclosing* and *informing*. It is often possible to inform caregivers, educators, or other health professionals without breaking your client's confidentiality and disclosing information. For instance, if a caregiver were to approach a school counselor, school social worker, or school psychologist, asking about the specifics of a recent counseling session with their fourth grade student, it would be appropriate to inform him or her that in the counseling session you spoke with the student about his or her aggressive behavior. While this provides some information as to the topic or content of the session, it maintains the confidentiality of the student's specific contributions in the session.

Importantly, this approach is not likely to damage the therapeutic alliance that the counselor has established with the client, especially if the counselor communicates with the adolescent prior to the disclosure to the parent. Above all and regardless of the setting in which you work, remember that the goal is to offer a trusting environment that allows children and adolescents to feel free to disclose as they choose without concern that their confidentiality will be broken.

While different circumstances are presented in each case involving breaking confidentiality in counseling minors, Remley & Herlihy (2014) offer the following guidelines when responding to parents who demand confidential information. A counselor's first step should be to discuss the adult's inquiry with the minor and see if the minor is willing to disclose the content of the counseling session to the adult. Many times counselors are more concerned about privacy than a child is. First, discuss with the adult how it is not serving the child's best interest to disclose the requested information. Use this time as an opportunity to educate the inquiring adult about the nature of the counseling relationship, while assuring that he or she will be notified in circumstances that require the counselor to break confidentiality (i.e., in cases of abuse or neglect or harming self or others). However, if this is not successful, counselors make take the next step and conduct a joint meeting with the adults and the minor. As the counselor, your role would be to serve as a mediator and hope that the adult changes his or her perspective about wanting the information or that the minor will be willing to disclose enough information to satisfy the adult's concerns. If at this point you have not reached a successful solution, you have a few options. You may inform the child ahead of time and then disclose the content of the session to the inquiring adult. If the adult is not a parent or guardian, inform the parents or guardian before disclosing the information. Or, you may decide to refuse to disclose the information to the inquiring adult. If this is the decision you make, it is important to secure approval from your direct supervisor(s) before proceeding. In both of these options, it is important for you to remember that the caregiver may have a legal right to the information.

Remley and Herlihy (2014) suggest the steps outlined in Table 2.3 when caregivers demand confidential information.

Ethical Decision-Making Models

When making ethical decisions as professional counselors, most often, there is not one right or wrong answer. Rather, when faced with an ethical dilemma, it is a matter of deciding what the best option(s) may be for the particular situation. Using a decision-making model can be especially helpful when aspects of the situation seem rather ambiguous.

Remley & Herlihy (2014) suggest the following general steps, however, they warn that although they appear linear in fashion, seldom do legal and ethical situations occur in such a progression:

 a. Identify and define the problem

 b. Consider the principles and virtues

 c. Tune in to your feelings

 d. Consult with colleagues or experts

Table 2.3 Responding to Parents' Demand for Confidential Information

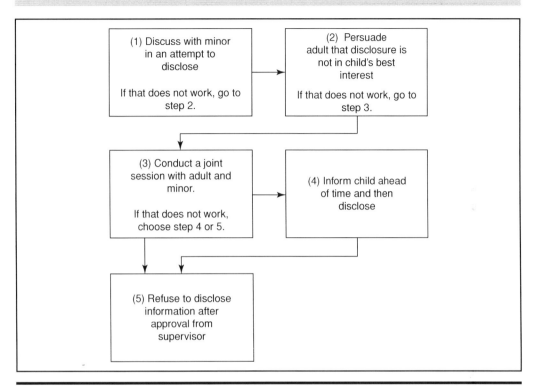

Source: Adapted from Remley, T., & Herlihy, B. (2014). *Ethical, legal, and professional issues in counseling* (2nd ed.). Boston, MA: Pearson.

   e. Involve your client in the decision-making process

   f. Identify desired outcomes

   g. Consider possible actions

   h. Choose and act on your choice

These general steps need to be taken into consideration, along with policies or protocols within your particular work setting. Further, this may require you to use steps of this process multiple times.

Sileo and Kopala (1993) provide the Assessment, Benefit, Consequences and Consultation, Duty, Education (A-B-C-D-E) worksheet as a means for taking abstract ideas and making them more concrete and practical while aiming to promote beneficence when considering ethical issues. While this approach does not help counselors in identifying a dilemma, an advantage is that counselors, regardless of their training, knowledge, or familiarity of the ethical codes that guide their profession, can use it.

For those that are working in a school setting, Stone (2013) has developed the following 9-step process, Solutions to Ethical Problems in Schools (STEPS):

1. Define the problem emotionally and intellectually

2. Apply the *ASCA Ethical Standards* and the law

3. Consider the students' *chronological* and developmental levels

4. Consider the setting, parental rights, and minors' rights

5. Apply the moral principles

6. Determine your potential course of action and its consequences

7. Evaluate the selected action

8. Consult

9. Implement the course of action

Case Illustration 2.1 illustrates how Stone's ethical decision-making model might be used by a counselor.

Case Illustration 2.1

In the following story, we apply the Stone (2013) ethical decision-making model to using a case example.

Barbara Cox is a new school counselor working in an elementary school. In the third week of her new job, she meets Catherine, a fifth-grade student who was sent by her classroom teacher. Catherine is having trouble getting along with her classmates this year. According to the teacher, this peer group problem is a new one for Catherine. Her friends from last year do not seem to be accepting her into their new friendship circle. Catherine has been sad for these first few weeks of class, withdrawn, and on the day that her teacher sent her to Ms. Cox, she had cried for part of the morning's lesson. When Ms. Cox sees Catherine, she learns that Catherine feels lonely and disconnected from her friends and school. Catherine also confides that she has seen magazines about people who cut themselves. She tells Ms. Cox that she has read about it but would not ever do anything to herself. In this first session, Ms. Cox makes a plan with Catherine that she will not harm herself. She is satisfied that Catherine is not hurting herself. When Catherine steps out of her office, Ms. Cox wonders to herself, "Should I call her mother? Should I refer her for community counseling services?"

Using Stone's (2013) nine-step process, Solutions to Ethical Problems in Schools (STEPS), Ms. Cox thinks this dilemma through.

Define the problem emotionally and intellectually. Ms. Cox is a new counselor. She graduated from her degree program just a few months ago. She is confronted with her own insecurities about her professional competencies. She also is deeply concerned about Catherine. She is personally touched by the story she hears and wants to help Catherine feel more comfortable with herself and her friends. She knows that she must provide appropriate counseling services to Catherine and protect her from harm. Though she does not feel like Catherine is harming herself, she also realizes that Catherine is distressed, and this could become a more serious problem. Barbara sits with her thoughts and feelings for a few minutes and then reaches out to a colleague.

Apply the ASCA Ethical Standards and the law. First, there are issues of counselor competence (ASCA E.1). Barbara reasons that she is competent to address Catherine's sadness and peer relationships but may want to refer her to a mental health counselor in the community if any signs emerge that she is cutting herself. ASCA codes A.5. (appropriate referrals) will guide her in the referral decision. Most urgently, Barbara must decide whether or not Catherine's disclosure about reading about cutting herself reflects her intent to harm herself. ASCA Code A.2.c. (confidentiality) states that information should be kept confidential unless legal statutes or the prevention of foreseeable harm require it to be breached. According to the ethical code, serious or foreseeable harm is different depending on the student's age, the setting, parental rights, and the nature of the harm.

Considering Catherine's chronological and developmental level. She is 11 years old and seems to be at a normal level of cognitive and social-emotional development for her age. Though she has insight for her age, she is at a young age and is experiencing a difficult emotional time in her development. Barbara considers that Catherine would really benefit from having a strong support system right now.

Consider the setting, parental rights, and the minor's rights. Catherine has a right to privacy in her counseling session with Ms. Cox. However, the child's parents also have a right to know if Catherine is at risk for harming herself. Given the circumstances, Ms. Cox and her supervisor have a conversation about confidentiality and making disclosures to parents.

Applying the moral principles and an ethic of care in this situation is intuitive for Barbara. While she has an ethical responsibility to protect Catherine's confidentiality, she has a moral responsibility to protect her from harm. When she focuses on her own moral guide, she also wants to make sure that Catherine feels connected and protected in her relationships.

Determine your potential course of action and its consequences. Barbara and her supervisor decide to let Catherine know the importance of relying on her trusting relationships at this time. Ms. Cox decides to talk to Catherine about informing her parents about the sadness she feels. The positive outcome of this course of action is that Catherine is empowered and gets the support she needs. The consequence related to this course of action is that Catherine might feel Ms. Cox betrayed her confidence compromising their therapeutic relationship. This is a consequence that can be mitigated if Ms. Cox and Catherine determine together that this is a best option for managing the distress that Catherine feels.

In implementing and evaluating her decision, Barbara determined that there might not have been an imminent risk of harm, but the seriousness of the potential harm could not be overlooked. There are no perfect answers to dilemmas that involve confidentiality. In this case, Barbara found that she could help Catherine inform her parents. Together they determined that an outside referral would be helpful.

Consulting with each other as professional counselors is an imperative, but school counselors, especially in elementary schools, can be isolated. Ethical decision making is not an individual but a team activity. Barbara was able to discuss her course of action with a colleague who was knowledgeable about counseling professional's ethics. Make sure that when you consult, as Barbara did, that you seek out professionals who are knowledgeable about legal or ethical issues in counseling.

PROFESSIONAL ORGANIZATIONS

Although understanding legal and ethical considerations is of paramount importance to professional counselors, quite often there is no *one* right answer. Rather, it is up to professional counselors to use their professional judgment in conjunction with the codes and standards set forth by their professional organizations and associations, as well as their work setting. When working with minors, one should refer to the 2014 ACA *Code of Ethics and Standards of Practice*, ASCA's *Ethical Standards for School Counselors* (2010), APA's *Ethical Principles of Psychologists and Code of Conduct* (2010), NASP's *Principles for Professional Ethics* (2010), or NASW's *Code of Ethics* (2008), as appropriate to your specific helping profession.

- American Counseling Association. (2014). "2014 ACA code of ethics." Retrieved from http://www.counseling.org/resources/aca-code-of-ethics.pdf (These standards lend very little direct guidance when it comes to counseling children and adolescents. Yet, many state licensure boards have adopted these standards.)
- American School Counselors Association. (2010). "Ethical standards for school counselors." Retrieved from http://www.schoolcounselor.org/asca/media/asca/Resource%20Center/Legal%20and%20Ethical%20Issues/Sample%20Documents/EthicalStandards2010.pdf
- American Psychological Association (APA). (2010). "Ethical principles of psychologists and code of conduct." Retrieved from http://www.apa.org/ethics/code/principles.pdf
- National Association of School Psychologists (NASP). (2010). "Principles for professional ethics." Retrieved from http://www.nasponline.org/standards/2010standards/1_%20Ethical%20Principles.pdf
- National Association of Social Workers (NASW). (2008). "Code of ethics." Retrieved from https://www.socialworkers.org/pubs/code/code.asp

In Guided Exercise 2.7, compare and contrast the ethical codes for these different mental health professions. Though for the most part, the ethical guidelines for these helping professionals are similar, you will find some differences too.

Guided Exercise 2.7

Compare and contrast the ethical codes for the helping professions listed in the previous section, Professional Organizations. Find corresponding ethical codes for one or more of these professional organizations (ASCA, ACA, NASP, or NASW) and compare the ethical perspectives for the different organizations. For example, how are the ethical guidelines for these organizations the same or different concerning boundary issues, breaking confidentiality, and counselor competency? What are the implications for working with helpers from these related disciplines?

COUNSELING KEYSTONES

- Although our clients may be minors and thus have less legal protections, it is the responsibility of adults in the children's lives to make decisions that are most beneficial for them.
- An effective counselor will consider his or her own values and ethics when dealing with child and adolescent clients.
- Understanding aspects of consent and confidentiality are of paramount importance when working with minors.
- Unique to each state, there exists legal statutes related to children's welfare, including abuse and neglect, foster care, custody, and adoption. It behooves you, as the professional counselor, to keep abreast to the latest laws pertinent to your state of practice.
- Two of the main federal statutes related to a client's privacy are HIPAA and FERPA. While HIPAA primarily deals with the protection of medical records, FERPA specifically addresses procedures related to educational records.
- Two federal laws provide provisions to specialized educational and support services to youth with disabilities: IDEA and Section 504.
- Counseling children and adolescents is a specialty area within the counseling profession; as such, professional counselors should practice only within the boundaries of their competence.
- While making ethical decisions is never a simple process, it can be helpful to use a decision-making model when aspects of the situation seem especially ambiguous.
- Counselors need to be aware of, and advocate against, discrimination problems faced by racial, sexual, and other minority groups within the child and adolescent populations.

ADDITIONAL RESOURCES

In Print

Cohen, L., & Mandelbaum, R. (2006). Kids will be kids: Creating a framework for interviewing and counseling adolescent clients. *Temple Law Review, 79*, 357–1387.

Crespi, T. (2009). Group counseling in the schools: Legal, ethical, and treatment issues in school practice. *Psychology in the Schools, 46(3)*, 273–280. doi:10.1002/pits.20373

Del Mauro, J. M., & Jackson Williams, D. (2013). Children and adolescents' attitudes toward seeking help from professional mental health providers.

International Journal for the Advancement of Counselling, 35(2), 120–138. doi:10.1007/s10447-012-9172-6

Dishion, T. J., & Stormshak, E. A. (2007). *Ethical and professional standards in child and family interventions* (pp. 241–264). Washington, DC: American Psychological Association. doi:10.1037/11485-014

Froeschle, J., & Moyer, M. (2004). Just cut it out: Legal and ethical challenges in counseling students who self-mutilate. *Professional School Counseling, 7(4),* 231.

Hermann, M., Remley, T., & Huey, W. (2010). *Ethical and legal issues in school counseling* (1st ed.). Alexandria, VA: American School Counselor Association.

Jacob, S., Decker, D., & Hartshorne, T. (2011). *Ethics and law for school psychologists* (1st ed.). Hoboken, NJ: J. Wiley & Sons.

Mitchell, B. (2007). *Documentation in counseling records* (1st ed.). Alexandria, VA: American Counseling Association.

Perfect, M. M., & Morris, R. J. (2011). Delivering school based mental health services by school psychologists: Education, training, and ethical issues. *Psychology in the Schools, 48(10),* 1049–1063. doi:10.1002/pits.20612

Shumaker, D., & Medoff, D. (2013). Ethical and legal considerations when obtaining informed consent for treating minors of high-conflict divorced or separated parents. *The Family Journal, 21*(3), 318–327. doi:10.1177/1066480713478786

Wilcoxon, S., Remley, T., & Gladding, S. (2013). *Ethical, legal, and professional issues in the practice of marriage and family therapy* (5th ed.). New York, NY: Pearson.

Online

Building the Legacy, IDEA: http://idea.ed.gov

Center for Law and Education: http://www.cleweb.org

Child Welfare Information Gateway: https://www.childwelfare.gov

Child Welfare Information Gateway, Mandatory Reporters of Child Abuse and Neglect: https://www.childwelfare.gov/systemwide/laws_policies/statutes/manda.pdf

Children's Bureau: http://www.acf.hhs.gov/programs/cb

Ethics and Boundary Issues in Counseling: https://www.youtube.com/watch?v=lxp7YqJ7n5Q

Family and Advocates Partnership for Education: www.fape.org

Legal and Ethical Issues for School Counselors with Dr. Carolyn Stone: https://www.youtube.com/watch?v=WLBhieDhrL4

National Center for Learning Disabilities: www.ncld.org

National Information Center for Children and Youth with Disabilities: www.nichcy.org

School Law: www.schoollaw.com

Street Law Online: www.streetlaw.org

United States Department of Education FERPA: http://www2.ed.gov/policy/gen/guid/fpco/ferpa/index.html

United States Department of Health & Human Services—HIPAA: http://www.hhs
.gov/ocr/privacy

Working with Young People Part 1: Your Duty of Care: http://youtu.be/
LqA6sZk3xus?list=UUhmzsNLxCLVW_Mvg9-v8hcQ

Working with Young People Part 2: Privacy and Confidentiality: http://youtu.be/
tqJ_yyKm12k?list=UUhmzsNLxCLVW_Mvg9-v8hcQ

Working with Young People Part 3: Reporting Child Abuse: http://youtu.be/
e4KFBOdeZhg?list=UUhmzsNLxCLVW_Mvg9-v8hcQ

REFERENCES

American Counseling Association (ACA). (2014). *2014* ACA code of ethics.
Alexandria, VA: Author. Retrieved from http://www.counseling.org/resources/
aca-code-of-ethics.pdf

American Mental Health Counselor Association. (2010). AMHCA code of ethics.
Retrieved from http://amhca.site-ym.com/?page=codeofethics

American School Counselor Association (ASCA). (2010). Ethical standards for
school counselors. Alexandria, VA: Author. Retrieved from https://www
.schoolcounselor.org/asca/media/asca/Resource%20Center/Legal%20and%20
Ethical%20Issues/Sample%20Documents/EthicalStandards2010.pdf

Child Abuse Prevention and Treatment Act of 2010. 42 U.S.C. 5101 et seq.; 42
U.S.C. 5116 et seq.

Child Welfare Information Gateway. (2013a). Online resources for state child welfare law and policy. Washington, DC: U.S. Department of Health and Human
Services, Children's Bureau. Retrieved from https://www.childwelfare.gov/
topics/systemwide/laws-policies/state

Child Welfare Information Gateway. (2013b). Mandatory reporters of child abuse
and neglect. Retrieved from https://www.childwelfare.gov/systemwide/laws_
policies/statutes/manda.pdf

Child Welfare Information Gateway. (n.d.). Child abuse and neglect. Retrieved
from https://www.childwelfare.gov/topics/can

Civil Action for the Deprivation of Rights, 42 U.S.C. § 1983.

Children's Defense Fund. (2014). Each Day in America: The state of America's
children. Retrieved from http://www.childrensdefense.org/library/state-of-
americas-children/each-day-in-america.html

Cohen, L. J., & DeBenedet, A. T. (2012, January 24). Why is the U.S. against
children's' rights? *Time*. Retrieved from http://ideas.time.com/2012/01/24/
why-is-the-us-against-childrens-rights

Donovan, M. S., & Cross, C. T. (Eds.). (2002). *Minority students in special and
gifted education*. Washington, DC: National Academies Press.

Family Educational Rights and Privacy Act of 1974 (FERPA or Buckley Amendment), 20 U.S.C § 1232g, See also regulations at 34 C.F.R. § 99 (2010).

Florida Department of Juvenile Justice. (n.d.). Delinquency in Florida's schools: 2009–2010 through 2013–2014. Retrieved from http://www.djj.state.fl.us/research/reports/delinquency-in-schools/school-delinquency-profile

Gershoff, E. T. (2008). *Report on physical punishment in the United States: What research tells us about its effects on children.* Columbus, OH: Center for Effective Discipline.

Griffin, P., Adams, S., & Firestine, K. (2011). *Juvenile offenders and victims: National report series. Trying juveniles as adults: An analysis of state transfer laws and reporting.* Washington, DC: U.S. Department of Justice.

Hansen, S. (2009). Confidentiality guidelines for school counselors. Retrieved from http://www.school-counseling-zone.com/support-files/confidentiality-guidelines-for-school-counselors-long-version.pdf

Hendrix, D. H. (1991). Ethics and intra-family confidentiality in counseling with children. *Journal of Mental Health Counseling, 13,* 323–333.

Hunt, J., & Moodie-Mills, A. (2012, June 29). The unfair criminalization of gay and transgender youth: An overview of the experiences of LGBT youth in the juvenile justice system. *Center for American Progress.* Retrieved from https://www.americanprogress.org/issues/lgbt/report/2012/06/29/11730/the-unfair-criminalization-of-gay-and-transgender-youth

Individuals With Disabilities Education Act (IDEA), 20 U.S.C. § 1400 (2004).

Indian Child Welfare Act of 1978, 25 U.S.C., Ch. 21.

Klingner, J. K., Artiles, A. J., Kozleski, E., Harry, B., Zion, S., Tate, W. . . . Riley, D. (2005). Addressing the disproportionate representation of culturally and linguistically diverse students in special education through culturally responsive educational systems. *Education Policy Analysis Archives, 13*(38). Retrieved from http://epaa.asu.edu/ojs/article/view/143/269

Kunkel, T. (2012). Substance abuse and confidentiality: 42 CFR Part II. Retrieved from http://www.ncsc.org/sitecore/content/microsites/future-trends-2012/home/Privacy-and-Technology/Substance-Abuse.aspx

Lawrence, G., & Kurpius, S. E. R. (2000). Legal and ethical issues involved when counseling minors in nonschool settings. *Journal of Counseling and Development, 78*(2), 130–136.

Leadership Conference on Civil and Human Rights. (2014). Summary: Racial discrimination within the U.S. criminal justice system for review of U.S. compliance with CERD–August 2014. Retrieved April 3, 2015 from http://www.civilrights.org/press/2014/2014-08-06-CERD-Leadership-Conference-Issue-Summary-Criminal-Justice-FINAL.pdf

Legal Information Institute. (n.d.). Children's rights overview. Cornell Law School. Retrieved from http://www.law.cornell.edu/wex/childrens_rights

MacKenzie, M. J., Nicklas, E., Waldfogel, J., & Brooks-Gunn, J. (2013). Spanking and child development across the first decade of life. *Pediatrics.* doi:10.1542/peds.2013-1227

Moyer, M., & Sullivan, J. (2008). Student risk-taking behaviors: When do school counselors break confidentiality? *Professional School Counseling, 11(4),* 236–245.

Myers, J. (2004). *A history of child protection in America.* Bloomington, IN: Xlibris Corporation.

National Association of School Psychologists (NASP). (2013). Racial and ethnic disproportionality in education (Position statement). Bethesda, MD: Author. Retrieved from http://www.nasponline.org/assets/Documents/Research%20and%20Policy/Position%20Statements/Racial_Ethnic_Disproportionality.pdf

National Board of Certified Counselors (NBCC). (2014). National certification and state licensure. Retrieved from http://www.nbcc.org/Certification-Licensure

National Dissemination Center for Children with Disabilities (NICHCY). (2012). Categories of Disability under IDEA. Retrieved from http://www.parentcenterhub.org/wp-content/uploads/repo_items/gr3.pdf

Office for Civil Rights (2015). Protecting students with disabilities. Retrieved from http://www2.ed.gov/about/offices/list/ocr/504faq.html

Parsons, R. D., & Zhang, N. (2014). *Counseling theory: Guiding reflective practice.* Thousand Oaks, CA: Sage.

Remley, T., & Herlihy, B. (2014). *Ethical, legal, and professional issues in counseling* (2nd ed.). Boston, MA: Pearson.

Sileo, F., & Kopala, M. (1993). An A-B-C-D-E worksheet for promoting beneficence when considering ethical issues. *Counseling & Values, 37(2),* 89–95.

Skiba, R. J., Simmons, A. B., Ritter, S., Gibb, A. C., Rauch, M. K., Cuadrado, J., & Chung, C-G. (2008). Achieving equity in special education: History, status, and current challenges. *Exceptional Children, 74*(3), 264–288.

Stone, C. (2013). *School counseling principles: Ethics and law* (3rd ed.). Alexandria, VA: American School Counselor Association.

Stopbullying.gov. (2014). Policies and laws. Retrieved from http://www.stopbullying.gov/laws

Stuart-Cassel, V., Bell, A., & Springer, J. F. (2011). Analysis of state bullying laws and policies. U. S. Department of Education. Retrieved from https://www2.ed.gov/rschstat/eval/bullying/state-bullying-laws/state-bullying-laws.pdf

Trusty, J., & Brown, D. (2005). Advocacy competencies for professional school counselors, *Professional School Counselor, 8(3),* 259–265.

U.S. Department of Education. (2009). Q and A: Questions and answers on disproportionality. Retrieved from http://idea.ed.gov/explore/view/p/,root,dynamic,QaCorner,9,

U.S. Department of Health and Human Services and U.S. Department of Education. (2008). Joint guidance on the application of the Family Education Rights and Privacy Act (FERPA) and the Health Insurance Portability and Accountability Act of 1996 (HIPAA) to students' health records. Retrieved from http://www.hhs.gov/ocr/privacy/hipaa/understanding/coveredentities/hipaaferpajointguide.pdf

U.S. Department of Health and Human Services, Office of the Assistant Secretary for Planning and Evaluation. (2004). Statutory rape: A guide to state laws and reporting requirements. Summary of current state laws. Retrieved from http://aspe.hhs.gov/report/statutory-rape-guide-state-laws-and-reporting-requirements-summary-current-state-laws

U.S. Department of Health and Human Services, Office of Civil Rights. (n.d.). Health Information Privacy. Retrieved from http://www.hhs.gov/ocr/privacy/index.html

U.S. Department of Justice. (n.d.). Constitutional protections afforded juveniles. Retrieved from http://www.justice.gov/usam/criminal-resource-manual-121-constitutional-protections-afforded-juveniles

United Nations Children's Fund (UNICEF). (n.d.). Convention on the rights of the child. Retrieved from http://www.unicef.org/crc

United Nations Children's Fund (UNICEF). (2005). Frequently asked questions. Retrieved from http://www.unicef.org/crc/index_30229.html

United Nations Children's Fund (UNICEF). (2010). *Facts for Life.* Retrieved from http://www.factsforlifeglobal.org/resources/factsforlife-en-full.pdf

Wheeler, A., & Bertram, B. (2012). *The counselor and the law* (6th ed.). Alexandria, VA: American Counseling Association.

Chapter 3

Attachment, Trauma, and Repair From Infant to Adolescent Development: Counseling Implications From Neurobiology

Mary Vicario and Carol Hudgins-Mitchell

> *... in a direct way, experience shapes the structure of the brain.*
>
> —Siegel, 2012, p. 47.

INTRODUCTION

Daniel is struggling in his fourth-grade class at school. He is about year and a half below grade level in reading and math. He has difficulty interacting socially with the other children. He appears anxious and frequently says, "Someone is looking at me." During free time, Daniel is encouraged to write or draw in his journal. His teacher angrily sends him to the principal when he discovers Daniel drawing inappropriate pictures of a sexual nature during his free time.

Thirteen-year-old Tina gets into fights with peers, has had frequent suspensions, and has a history of cutting herself. At school and around town, she claims to be proud of her tough attitude. She has been through a series of foster placements. Her present foster mother says she is committed to parenting her but is very tired of her stealing, lying, and manipulation.

Casey, a first grader, had a history of neglect and abuse before coming to live with his grandparents. His family experiences intergenerational poverty, and with it a lack of access to health care, inadequate housing, and toxic stress. He has trouble paying attention in class. His teacher says he is always trying to get attention, even negative attention. Casey's body appears tense and anxious, while his sense of personal space and boundaries is poor. He has trouble with transitions from activity to activity, in the hallways, at lunch, and at recess. While he is frequently in trouble at school, when disciplined, he appears sad and lost, as if he is not fully present. Casey's grandmother reports that he still wets the bed at night and recently began soiling himself.

Valerie, 17 years old, was diagnosed with autism spectrum disorder (ASD) at an early age. She has limited expressive language to explain her understanding of removal from her biological home or what she may have experienced in a home where it is known there was severe neglect and abuse of at least some of her siblings. Usually described as "sweet and calm," she has bouts of rage, when "she is like someone else," according to her caregivers. Given her developmental delays and limited ability to communicate, many would wonder how helpful counseling might be.

Counselors working with children and adolescents help young people like these every day. Expect to encounter clients who have difficulty with executive functioning tasks such as organization, problem solving, ability to recall information, sequencing, turning thoughts into action, and learning from consequences. Other problems are not limited to but may include the following:

- Intrusive thoughts
- Being easily overwhelmed
- Lack of emotional regulation
- Being angry and aggressive
- Self-harming behaviors
- Running away

- Attention-seeking behaviors
- Anxiety
- Poor self-esteem
- Difficulty with transitions
- Dissociation
- Poor proprioception (the awareness of one's own body and personal space)

What do all of these young clients have in common? Each of the young people in the vignettes has experienced some sort of trauma or toxic stress. The observable behaviors that bring children into counseling are vital communications of their inward experiences, yet many clinicians and school personnel have little understanding of childhood stress or trauma or their effects on the growing brain. This frequently leads to misunderstandings, and unfortunately, misinformed interventions. Teachers and other adults might view a child's rebellious attitude as disrespectful when it is an important survival skill in a dangerous or chaotic home. Survival skills that are crucial in abusive or neglectful homes often persist after a child is in school or in a safe home. These old survival skills, in the context of a safe environment, often look like antisocial and acting-out behaviors. In order to help the child shed these now maladaptive behaviors in favor of more prosocial ones, counselors need to understand the impact of trauma on the growing brain.

The treatment of trauma is undergoing a rapid evolution due to technical advances in neuroimaging and biochemistry. Our knowledge of the short- and long-term effects of trauma and toxic stress on the brain, human development, and human relationships is moving forward daily. These discoveries, coupled with a new understanding of neuroplasticity (the ability for the brain to grow and heal itself) (Doidge, 2006; Chapman, 2014) hold more hope than ever for helping traumatized children and adolescents heal, grow, and learn.

After reading this chapter, you will be able to

- explain some of the ways that early relational trauma can harm healthy brain development;
- discuss the Adverse Childhood Experiences (ACE) research and explore the impact of adverse life events on child and adolescent development;
- offer an explanation of mood regulation in children and adolescents using interpersonal neurobiology;
- examine counseling implications of brain research and neurobiological underpinnings of regulation;
- explore the relational/social brain and opportunities the educational system has in supporting and maximizing this healthy development; and
- share research, ideas, and best practices toward creating trauma-informed and trauma-responsive counseling practices for children and adolescents.

In this chapter, we explore how the social and physical environment and key relationships shape brain development (Cozolino, 2006). We, then, examine the intentional use of counseling interventions to facilitate growth and change. Eliana Gil (1991) states, "Everything an abused child does after the abuse is designed to give them a sense of safety" (p. 3). According to the Sanctuary Model of trauma-informed care, the effect of trauma on behavior can be reframed this way: "The question is, not what's wrong with you, but what has happened to you?" (Bloom, 2010). If counselors in school and mental health settings begin to see children's behavior through this lens, then they can bring the child's experience into sharper focus and begin a journey toward understanding the centrality of human connection, an ability to feel safe, to attach, and to regulate affective states. To understand more about how toxic stress and trauma impact brain development, it is first necessary to understand a bit about the developing brain and its basic structures and functions.

Understanding the brain's structure and function is a very complex and challenging task that we have still not mastered. In 2013, President Barrack Obama launched BRAIN (Brain Research through Advancing Innovative Neurotechnolo-gies), a broad initiative of the U.S. government, institutions of higher education, and the private sector to create a "dynamic understanding of brain function" (White House, 2014). According to the National Institute of Health (NIH), "With nearly 100 billion neurons and 100 trillion connections, the human brain remains one of the greatest mysteries in science and one of the greatest challenges in medi-cine (National Institute of Health, 2014)."

Given the intricacy and complexity of the study of the brain, it should be noted that the information provided in this chapter has been simplified. What follows is, therefore, best understood as a metaphor of the brain that enables us to discuss and conceptualize more complicated neurobiological structures and interactions. We describe the functions of these major areas of the brain: the cortexes, limbic system, brain stem, neurons and neuronal networks, and neurotransmitters.

As we map the human brain, we examine implications for counseling approaches that are based on brain functioning. Keeping this idea of mapping the brain in mind,

Figure 3.1   Simple Map of the Human Brain

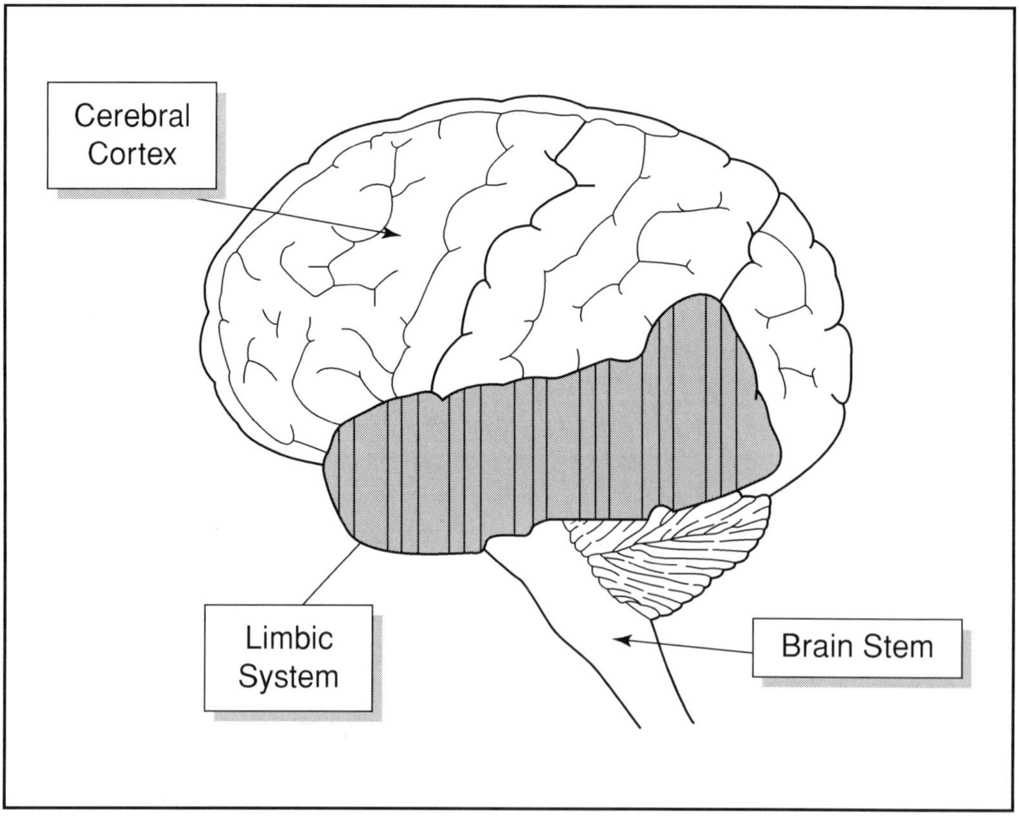

we turn our efforts to learning about the developing brain. For students who would like a more in-depth coverage of the implications of brain research for counseling interventions, we recommend the following books:

- Cozolino, L. (2010). *The neuroscience of psychotherapy: Healing the social brain* (2nd ed.). New York, NY: Norton.
- Porges, S. (2011). *The polyvagal theory: Neurophysiological foundations of emotions, attachment, communication and self-regulation*. New York, NY: Norton.
- Siegel, D. J. (2010). *The mindful therapist: A clinician's guide to mindsight and neural integration*. New York, NY: W.W. Norton & Company.

BRAIN DEVELOPMENT

Early in life, mammals are totally dependent upon others for access to resources and survival. Human infants cannot access food, water, shelter, or anything else they need without help. Because of this biological imperative for assistance from caregivers, the human brain and physiology have been hardwired for connection (Lieberman, 2013; Cozolino, 2006). Researchers in the social sciences have long highlighted how personal belief systems come from the extent to which early needs are met (Bowlby, 1988). John Bowlby's (1969) famous theory of attachment first emerged in 1951 in his report on homeless children in postwar Europe. Since that time, Bowlby and many other researchers have refined his theories, but the basic idea that human behavior and emotion is dependent on how people are treated as infants and young children remains prominent (Whelan & Stewart, 2015; see Chapter 5 for further discussion of attachment theory). Findings from brain research have supported Bowlby's theory by providing concrete evidence for much of what he believed to be true, that children's healthy development is impacted by early relationships (Kestly, 2014).

Daniel Siegel (2010) designed a very simple learning tool for understanding three primary areas of the brain; the cortex, the limbic system and the brain stem using his own hand as a model. This model of the brain is so simple; it can be used to explain brain functioning with children as well as adults. See Figure 3.2.

To use the hand to describe the brain and its function, Siegel (2010) begins by introducing the spinal column, which connects the brain with the rest of the body. He represents this part of the neural system as analogous to the wrist. Next, moving up the hand-brain is the brain stem, which is represented by the base of the palm of the hand. To represent the limbic system, the thumb is then placed against the palm of the hand. Finally, wrapping all of the fingers around the thumb illustrates the

Figure 3.2 Hand-Brain Model

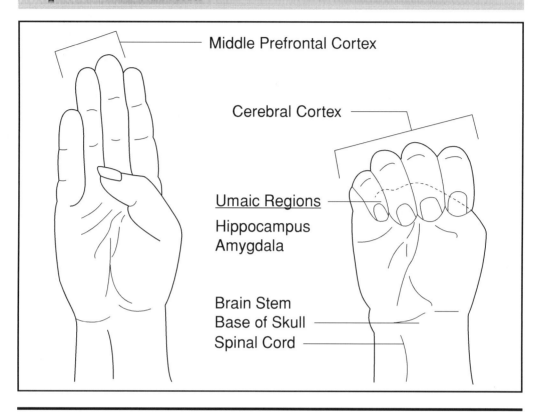

Middle Prefrontal Cortex

Cerebral Cortex

Umaic Regions
Hippocampus
Amygdala

Brain Stem
Base of Skull
Spinal Cord

cortex. Equipped with your own hand-brain we can now look more closely at each of these areas and their functions. In Guided Exercise 3.1, explore Dr. Siegel's hand-brain model and the parts of the human brain.

Guided Exercise 3.1

View Siegel's description of the hand-brain at https://www.youtube.com/watch?v=G0T_2NNoC68. Follow along and do the actions for the hand-brain until you feel like you have it. Now, show and explain the hand-brain to a classmate. For even more fun with the hand-brain, use it to help yourself to monitor your brain states and take a few calming breaths when you are feeling stressed before you flip your lid. It will all make sense when you see the video!

THE CORTEXES—EXECUTIVE CONTROL CENTER

As the executive control center, the cortexes control our executive functions such as working memory, organization, planning, problem solving, and sequencing. The cortex is represented in our hand-brain by the four fingers folded over the thumb. The Harvard Center on the Developing Child (Yeager & Yeager, 2013) compares this executive function to a busy air traffic control system, which works to "filter out distractions, prioritize tasks, set and achieve goals and control impulses" (p. 9). The cortexes also control executing action, which is the ability to turn thoughts into actions. People often take what seems like a simple step for granted, but putting thoughts into action is a complex neurological process that can be affected by traumatic stress, age, and developmental ability (Yeager & Yeager, 2013).

The cortexes also help people to read nonverbal cues like facial expression, tone of voice, body language, and posture. Importantly, together with the limbic system, the cortexes aid with affective regulation, which is our ability to mediate emotional arousal in order to accomplish a task or tolerate unpleasant emotional stimuli, helping with mood stability, frustration, tolerance, and impulse control (Schupp, 2004; Siegel, 2012). Because the cortexes are not fully developed until approximately 25 years of age, most researchers who study adolescents now consider adolescence to end later than age 18, nearer to age 25. Because people are not born with executive functioning skills; but rather, learn them over time from others and within our environment, it is clear that the function of the cortexes is impacted by relational and other environmental experiences, both positive and negative, across the lifespan. In the following case illustration, we illustrate what problems in executing action look like and how an intervention might work to help a young client self-regulate.

Case Illustration 3.1

A brain-based family intervention—Dorothy, age 19, and her child were referred for counseling by child protective services. Dorothy had a mild intellectual disability, which meant that she functioned in concrete operational thought. Concrete operational thought is marked by the inability to use abstractions to make sense of your world. Traditional talk therapy would be difficult for her because she made sense of her world, her life, and her problems by acting upon them rather than thinking about them. Dorothy's child was in the stage of preoperational thought. Aware of the way Dorothy and her young child made sense of their worlds, the counselor used art, play, dance, music, social stories, and other expressive media to work with them as a family.

Dorothy and her child progressed well, and she was on the threshold of completing her reunification plan and receiving her child back into her home. Her final hurdle was attending

(Continued)

(Continued)

her job regularly and on time. Dorothy was "over the moon" (her expression for ultimate happiness) with excitement when she landed a job at the library, a job she had been dreaming of since she was a young child. To everyone's surprise, including Dorothy, she was frequently late and only showed up for work about 2 or 3 days a week. When confronted about this, she clearly stated how motivated she was. When asked, "Why, then, can't you get to work every day?" Dorothy would break down into tears and shake her head and say, "I don't know. It just doesn't happen." In exasperation, her child protective services worker said, "You must not want your child back as much as you say you do." Dorothy was devastated by that statement, and it made her wonder if she was going to be like her own mother who said she loved her children but did not meet their needs adequately. Dorothy's counselor, who really believed Dorothy was motivated to get her child back, asked if Dorothy's hurdle might be that her brain was struggling to turn her motivation into action. She then asked Dorothy about her morning routine. Dorothy said she wakes up when the alarm goes off and starts getting ready for work. "Please walk me through or show me what 'getting ready for work' looks like, Dorothy," said her counselor. Dorothy explained that sometimes after the alarm went off, she would get showered and sometimes she would make breakfast and sometimes she was not sure what happened, but the next time she looked at the clock she had missed her bus or it was much later in the day than she thought it to be. The counselor shared that she, too, was not a morning person, and that it helped her to have a checklist to make sure she did not forget anything and to keep her focused on getting out of the door on time. At Dorothy's next session, a camera was brought in, and they role-played the morning routine Dorothy wanted. The counselor pointed out that this would allow Dorothy to help her child learn how to organize and get going in the morning. When asked later on what she wanted to pass onto her child to help him in life, Dorothy responded, "I want to teach him things, so his life can be easier than mine." Dorothy was lifting her head and showing interest at this point.

"Do you think we could take pictures of your child doing the tasks you want on your morning list?" the counselor inquired. Dorothy liked that idea, and it also worked to remind her how close she was to having her child home again. At the next therapy session, Dorothy taught her child the importance of getting up and off to work or school, and her child acted it out while Dorothy took pictures of him. Dorothy never missed another day of work and was on time as well. Dorothy's child was excited to know that these pictures of their fun "play" time would be hanging on the walls waiting for him when he returned home.

Dorothy was not resistant, oppositional, or unmotivated to attend the job she always wanted or to return to parenting her own children in her own home. She had a brain that needed concrete assistance (pictures that were fun, reminded her of those she loved) and help with executing action. Find fun and concrete ways to assist clients in executing action instead of labeling their actions as oppositional, defiant, resistant, or unmotivated. Similar interventions can be used with any task-oriented goal such as getting to school on time, getting homework done, and setting personal goals.

THE LIMBIC SYSTEM—WELCOMING CENTER OR GUARDHOUSE

As the welcoming center or guardhouse of the brain, the limbic system processes all of the information (stimuli) coming into the brain to determine whether it is safe or not safe and, depending on how the information is interpreted, where to send it (Porges, 2011). In your hand model, the limbic system can be represented by your thumb resting on your palm. If the entering information is seen as safe, it is sent on to the cortex to receive further attention and thought. It is the amygdala that identifies threat or nonthreat and filters the information to the brain stem or cortex respectively. If it is seen as unsafe, it is sent to the vagal nerve, in the brain stem, so that a warning can be sent from the vagal nerve to all of the other organs of the body. If there is a threat, it sets into motion the fight or flight response, deciding between the need for aggression (fight) or escape (flight) from fear. When this message is received, it is often called a visceral response because it is felt in your viscera, or the organs of your body (Porges, 2011). Everyone has experienced this feeling, which is generated by this early-warning system of danger. For example, when you go into a dark cellar, you are quite likely to get "the creeps."

The limbic system's main components are the hippocampus and the amygdala. The amygdala houses our emotional memories, both those that are tied to biographically recalled events and our earliest nonbiographical, or "felt" memories. The amygdala begins developing prenatally at 6 months gestation and continues until 18 months of age (Porges, 2011; Schupp, 2004; Siegel, 2012). The hippocampus helps calm the amygdala by accessing short-term memory in the cortex, and in this way, plays a role in self-soothing and emotional regulation. The hippocampus tracks memory and time and helps to consolidate short-term memory into long-term memory storage in the cortex. The hippocampus also helps to maintain our circadian rhythms, which are our physical, mental, and behavioral changes in response to light and darkness over a 24-hour cycle. As part of the circadian cycle, the hippocampus also helps to regulate sleep, appetite, digestion, and blood pressure. Importantly, the hippocampus also helps to control consciousness and maintain a sense of identity. Therefore, experiencing physical or emotional trauma early in life may disrupt one's sense of consciousness and a cohesive sense of identity. The hippocampus is completely developed by about 36 months of age, which explains why infants and toddlers frequently need the help of a caregiver to calm them.

The amygdala and hippocampus, which help to regulate a sense of safety and emotions, develop in the first years of life in relationship to the care provided by caregivers. When children grow up in a safe environment, the limbic system allows them to develop safe, secure attachments to caregivers and a congruent sense of self (Cozolino, 2006). If the attachment and reward centers properly develop in the limbic system, children are able to develop the regulation centers that will work with the cortex to pull positive relational memories forward to help them become physically and emotionally calm (Siegel, 2010). In Guided Exercise 3.2, examine your own experiences with self-regulation.

Guided Exercise 3.2

The Building Your Life Raft Activity is used for self-care and asks the following questions:

1. What activities soothe you?
2. What activities bring you joy or lift you up?
3. What music soothes you?
4. What music gives you joy?
5. What gives you a sense of play?

Interview a classmate, and have a classmate interview you using the Building Your Life Raft Activity. When describing your personal preferences in this exercise (likes and dislikes, for example, music or activities that soothe you or bring you joy), follow those activities to the first time you remember them. What positive relational memory (PRM) is attached to the activities you engage in to soothe yourself?

The brain structures needed for emotional regulation grow out of positive relational experiences (Siegel, 2010; Cozolino, 2006). As infants' limbic systems are developing and growing, positive relational experiences allow them to develop the circuitry to soothe themselves and manage stress (Siegel, 2010; Cozolino, 2006; Banks, 2015). When early relationships do not allow for repeated positive interactions, the child's limbic system is not able to adequately develop the pathways required for fully functioning regulatory mechanisms. This can often manifest in dysregulated behavior later in childhood, in which children cannot seem to calm down after exciting activities, have trouble managing transitions during the day, become easily overstimulated by the environment, and tantrum for long periods of time (Chapman, 2014; Solomon & Siegel, 2003). In Case Illustration 3.2 (Jayla), you will read about a counseling intervention that focuses on the regulation of feelings through fostering connectedness in the parent-child relationship.

Case Illustration 3.2

Emotional regulation through relationship—Jayla was a child who was described by her caregiver as "tantruming for hours until she just wears herself out." At the age of 3, she had already "blown through several foster homes," and while her new foster mother wanted to be committed to her, she was not sure "how much more I can take." The foster mother described how Jayla would come home from preschool tired and in need of a nap but would demand to watch television. The foster mother wanted TV to be a reward for taking her nap, but this restriction only led to hours of screaming. The counselor explained to the foster mother how children learn to calm and regulate affect in relationship with their caregivers. Given that Jayla had been removed from a home in which biological parents had been charged with neglect and heavy drug use, Jayla likely missed out on that primary and early experience of a calming connection with a caregiver. Alternatively, she had often used television as a source of connection and calming. Her foster mother was instructed to rock with Jayla each afternoon while she watched cartoons, gently cuddling, talking, and singing to her, while also letting her have her sippy cup and a blanket or doll. This intervention was designed to help smooth the transition to naptime by associating calm connection with a caregiver with watching the TV, which Jayla had previously used in an attempt to regulate herself.

Allan Schore (2005) describes how mutual interactions (e.g., gazing, smiling, cooing) between an infant and caregiver regulates the infant's arousal and affective (feeling) states in right brain to right brain, visual, auditory, tactile, gestural, and emotional nonverbal communications. The communications going on between caregiver and infant are direct, nonverbal communications from the right side of the brain of one member of the dyad to the right brain of the other. The right side of the caretaker's brain and the right side of the infant's brain engage in a dance of nonverbal interactions: the eye contact, the gentle play and facial mimicry, the lilting cadence of voice, the rhythmic movement, and reciprocity of caregiving and calming. According to neuroscientists, the right side of the brain holds body sensations, unconscious processing, emotions, perceptions, and mental models of preverbal memories (Chapman, 2014; Siegel; 2012; Cozolino, 2010).

The right brain holds memory in the body and unconscious processes before young children build biographical, personal stories, or a sense of self. It is in these early interactions that children begin to form a sense of self, self-worth, and an ability to regulate affective states (Siegel, 2012; Cozolino, 2010). As their brains are forming, infants need an adult to help with calming and soothing until about age three and sometimes longer, depending on their experiences and developmental abilities (Siegel, 2012; Cozolino, 2010). For example, at about age three is when toddlers often take a transitional object of soothing, like a blanket, stuffed animal, or other object to help carry the calming of the caregiver with them.

For 60% to 65% of children, this transition happens well enough for them to develop a secure attachment style (Beebe, 2005). This does not mean that for secure attachment to take place, the parent or caregiver needs to be responsive to the child 100% of the time; in fact, estimates are that caregivers of securely attached children get it right about 30% of the time, but they also are aware of their attunement to their child or catching disconnection (insecurity) and correcting it (Beebe, 2005). This process of miscuing and repair actually helps the child to grow the neural pathways needed for emotional regulation. As the child experiences a need for being attended to, and receiving loving attention, then they learn that their needs will be met, which gives them the basic sense of safety that is required to modulate stress (Siegel, 2010).

Children who do not receive safe, loving, attention, and care may experience toxic levels of stress or trauma that affect the developing brain. This could be due to a lack of attunement between child and caregiver, or young inexperienced parents, but more often it is due to insidious relational or environmental stressors (Garner et al., 2012). These toxic stressors are known as Adverse Childhood Experiences (ACEs) (Felitti et al., 1998). ACEs and the effects of toxic stress are explored further later in this chapter.

Children who experience chronic high levels of stress, especially when those high levels of stress are accompanied by inattentive caregiving, develop brains and behaviors needed to survive in that environment. For example, they may have come from families where the most violent person in the room appears to be the safest person in the room because that person is doing the hitting rather than being physically hurt themselves. When outside of their violent environments, these children may be safe but may not feel safe, and their attempts at safety seeking, coupled with decreased hippocampal volume and fewer neuronal pathways for soothing, can lead to behaviors that are frequently labeled as defiant, angry, and aggressive (Cozolino, 2013).

In a revolutionary reversal from the accepted wisdom of the brain as incapable of repair, neuroscientists have discovered that the human brain can, in fact, regrow some damaged neurons (Siegel, 2010) and connections (Doidge, 2006). Although major damage, such as what occurs in a stroke or serious head injury, may not heal completely, the human brain does have the capacity to generate new neurons and wire new neural pathways, throughout the life span (Siegel, 2010; Schore, 2003). This means that children from harmful environments literally need to grow new neuronal connections for experiencing, feeling, and creating safety. To help with this process, a safety script can be used in counseling (and with parents). A sample safety script follows:

"This is a safe place. I am not going to let anyone (use offending behavior here such as 'hit' or 'push' or 'curse at') you. So I can't let you ('hit' or 'push' or 'curse'). Because this is a safe place" (Vicario, Hudgins-Mitchell, Corbisello, 2012, pp. 10–11).

This statement, when used in the moment of the unsafe behavior (or as close to it as possible) and in the order in which it is written, is calming to the limbic system (puts safety first) and puts the rules for interpersonal relationships in the context of safety. The opening sentence is designed to calm the limbic, the place in the brain where all information is received so it can be processed as safe enough to allow the cortex to receive it (Schupp, 2004; Porges, 2011; Siegel, 2012). Next we put the protection of the child, from the very behavior they are doing, first because hurt children are focused on their own safety and second because children are developmentally more egocentric, so they need to hear immediately how we are going to protect them. The third sentence sets the limit. The final sentence connects that limit with safety, as it begins by reiterating the safety of the environment and the therapeutic relationship. It is important that this safety script is said in a calm manner. We have found this safety script to work well when used by a variety of caregivers such as parents (birth, foster, adoptive, and kinship care), teachers, counselors, therapists, case managers, direct support professionals, and psychiatrists.

The first time we use the above safety script we usually receive from the child a look of perplexed curiosity that is often demonstrated by tilting the head to one side. That is okay because curiosity is the beginning of learning. In our experience, it takes on average 6 months for a child to respond consistently to this safety script. At the same time, caregivers are also learning a new behavior and may not always remember to use the safety script. We find that mentally walking the caregiver back through the experience and having him or her imagine the script with the counselor and then discuss the difference it might have made in the parent-child relationship actually strengthens the new habit.

BRAIN STEM—BASIC SURVIVAL

As the oldest part of the brain, by evolutionary standards, the brain stem is responsible for all the body functions we do not have to think about such as arousal, bladder and bowel control, digestion, perspiration, breathing, and startle responses. When we work with those who are caring for children, like daycare workers, school personnel, caseworkers, and those in the parenting role, we make sure to talk with them about the brain stem's fear response that triggers wetting (enuresis) and soiling (encopresis). These are two brain stem functions connected with the vagal nerve (fear) response we discussed earlier (Porges, 2011). Often children who wet or soil themselves are punished for this behavior. It is viewed or experienced by adults as a willful way to be lazy, oppositional, to demonstrate anger, or to seek attention. While these brain stem responses may be present at the same time as a strong emotion, it is important to know that the brain stem is in charge, not the fully aware child who is experiencing the strong emotion. We have found that as we can help the child feel safe, the behavior decreases.

For nighttime enuresis, we use counseling interventions that focus on helping the child and primary caregiver to talk about the successes of the child's day. Sometimes, we use a success calendar where they can write or draw on the calendar to make it more concrete. We also ask the parents to work with the child to imagine the dreams they would like to have. When nightmares occur, we have children rework the nightmares with a safe person, to help them come up with more empowered endings. Children may want to draw or paint or sculpt the nightmares and the new endings in order to make the new endings and resulting experiences of safety more concrete. In Case Illustration 3.3, we provide an example of a counseling intervention for nightmares.

Case Illustration 3.3

Storytelling to retell nightmares—Casey, the first grader from the introduction, was having nightmares that were affecting his ability to pay attention in school. He and his counselor used storytelling to rework his nightmares. Casey's imagination was put into action. He decided he could "have a Ghost Busters' pack to suck up the ghosts that chase me or maybe I could shrink them like 'Honey I Shrunk the Kids,' and then I could just squish them." Casey dictated his new dream to his counselor, and together they made drawings to illustrate his story. His grandmother read his story to him each night for a few nights, and his nightmares stopped.

Now that you know how the cortexes, limbic system, and brain stem function, see what you can apply. In Guided Exercise 3.3, partner with a classmate and do some brainstorming about the brain and its functions and its role in counseling children and adolescents.

Guided Exercise 3.3

Make a table with a column for each of these three brain regions (cortexes, limbic system, and brain stem), and under each heading, list the kinds of behaviors you think a child might exhibit if his or her cortex, limbic system, or brain stem were damaged by trauma or toxic stress. What implications might this have on diagnosis or the counseling process?

NEURONS—THE BUILDING BLOCKS OF THE BRAIN AND NERVOUS SYSTEM

A neuron, or nerve cell, is a cell that processes and transmits information by electrical and chemical signaling (Cozolino, 2006, p. 38). This signaling occurs via synapses, which are specialized connections with other cells. Each of the billions of neurons in the nervous system has 10 to 10,000 synaptic signaling stations connected with it

(Cozolino, 2006, p. 39). If you do the math, multiplying the number and different patterns of connection (also known as neuronal networks) that can develop, you begin to understand the complexity that allows humans to be capable of so much more brain activity than any other species. By watching neurons interact with each other, we can see that even on a cellular level we are hardwired for connection. In Guided Exercise 3.4, explore the complexities of human connection after watching a brief video.

Guided Exercise 3.4

Take a few minutes to watch a YouTube video, "How Your Brain Looks When You Think New Thoughts," which shows neurons connecting, growing new neuronal networks, and even disconnecting and pruning away at https://www.youtube.com/watch?v=wl388XoCp48.

After watching the video, reflect on the admonition made to counselors by Judith Jordan, a pioneer in Relational Cultural Therapy (RCT), when she recommends for counselors to honor the complexity of relationships or stay in the complexity (Jordan, 2012). In RCT, a primary focus is on the healing nature of relationships. What does this quote mean to you? What relevance does this quote have for those in the counseling profession both in schools and clinical settings?

Humans, who have the most intricate brains and social networks of all primates, also have the longest duration of dependency on their caregivers for survival (Cacioppo & Bertson, 2002; Cozolino, 2006). This extended period of dependency serves to give the human brain the time it needs to develop the complex neuronal networks required to communicate needs, learn to understand others and predict their actions, attach, develop frustration tolerance, and acquire the ability to work in complex social groups from families to schools to communities (Cozolino, 2006).

Our Social Brains

In his book, *The Neuroscience of Human Relationships: Attachment and the Developing Social Brain*, Louis Cozolino (2006) describes the communication between brain cells well when he states, "Neurons are, by their nature, social; they shun isolation and depend on their neighbors for survival. If they aren't sending and receiving messages from other neurons on a constant basis, they literally shrink and die (p. 39)." Now research is showing how environment and relationships interact to shape brain development and genetics (Cozolino, 2006). Research has suggested that roughly one third of babies in orphanages who are simply fed and changed, but not fully nurtured, may actually die from a lack of human interaction, while half of those who survive will double the rate of mental illness found in the general population (Szalavitz & Perry, 2011). This finding may offer a neurobiological basis for the conventional wisdom that humans will settle for negative attention over no attention at all. A child's survival for the first dozen or so years of life depends on an ability to appeal to the adults in the community to feed, shelter, and comfort him or her when he or she is frightened. When these things do not happen regularly enough, negative cognitive, emotional, and physical outcomes are likely.

In fact, Sandra Bloom's research (2010) suggests that the use of isolation to shape human behavior can result in increased self-harm and suicidality. You may have heard stories of animals that bite off their paws when stuck in a trap or the climber who cut off his hand to free himself. Self-injury happens when someone feels trapped. People do not have to physically be trapped to *feel* trapped mentally. Just as people can physically be safe and still feel unsafe, those who have experienced trauma or toxic levels of stress can especially feel trapped from experiences of physical or emotional isolation such as, being physically isolated (e.g., time out, seclusion, sent to one's room) or socially isolated (e.g., being bullied, ignored, left out). Feeling misunderstood and unable to express our thoughts or feelings or being in a place where thoughts or feelings are not accepted can also result in feeling trapped. While feelings of isolation can occur without resulting in self-injury, in our brains, these experiences can trigger a sense of feeling trapped. Consider the case of Tina, who we introduced at the beginning of the chapter. In Case Illustration 3.4, we describe an art intervention for Tina that helps to stop her self-injurious behavior.

Case Illustration 3.4

Sugar scrub to reduce self-injurious behavior—Tina was introduced in the opening of this chapter as a young girl who had been injuring herself. When Tina entered the art room for the first time, she was invited, like all first time clients to that room, to paint her hand and leave her handprint on a wall covered with butcher-block paper. She chose red as the color for her handprint, and as she painted her hand, she also began to paint up her arm. "This is what it feels like when I cut," she said with a sigh of relief, as if to herself. Tina was sent home with the large, soft paint brush (not the paint), so she could engage in this sensory integration technique of brushing for self-soothing, which worked as an initial step to beginning a sensory diet that would lead to the replacement of her cutting behavior. The next step in the development of her calming sensory diet was the making of sugar scrub. The counselor brought to session, sugar, olive oil, and several scents such as lavender, pine, and vanilla extract. Combining one cup of sugar, a few drops of oil until the sugar began to clump, and a couple of drops of the scent of Tina's choice, she and her counselor made sugar scrub that they put in a small airtight container like a baggie that zips. At first, Tina and her caregiver were encouraged to have her use the sugar scrub whenever Tina felt like cutting. Over time, it was discovered that the scrub was even more powerful as part of a sensory diet that included using it at times of the day that were challenging for Tina, like the transition home from school. Making and using the sugar scrub with someone she trusted also gave Tina sensory self-soothing and a sense of increased connection. She was no longer alone in her pain.

Several publications over the past 20 years from different disciplines have documented the impact that social exclusion has on our bodies. For example, Candace Pert (1997), in her Nobel Prize–nominated work, *Molecules of Emotion*, estimates that each act of social exclusion increases a risk of coronary artery disease by 2.6% because of the long-term effect of stress chemicals released into our blood stream. In a similar way, Claude Steele (2010), in his book *Whistling Vivaldi*, takes this notion to a cultural level and shows how the perceived possibility of social exclusion releases stress chemicals in a manner that deters learning and interrupts retrieval of information. On the other side of this human equation, Lieberman, (2013) in his book *Social: Why Our Brains Are Wired to Connect*, demonstrates how positive connection with others actually increases the ability to learn. Taken together, research shows that when people generally feel safe in their environment, learning, problem solving, and overall productivity occur at a quicker rate than in areas where people feel socially isolated, threatened, or unsafe (Lieberman, 2013; Bloom, 2010). This may seem like a rather obvious conclusion, but the science that clearly links the increase of threat and the decrease of ability is recent and has only just begun to impact how human services professionals work.

As noted above, research now demonstrates that humans, on a basic neurological level, shun isolation, which makes sense for a species that is dependent upon one another for survival. This means that when children feel unnoticed and unimportant, they may show it through negative attention seeking, especially if their brains have developed in an environment where seeking attention in positive ways has been ignored. To help children develop neural networks for seeking attention in positive ways, they need opportunities to receive positive attention, to experience being important to someone else, to be told and shown that they matter. Like adults, children need to feel productive socially, as in a job, task, a way to help someone, or contribute to the greater good. In Case Illustration 3.5, we present Casey, a first grader, and an intervention related to planned positive attention.

Case Illustration 3.5

Planned positive attention—Casey, the first grader who was seen as attention seeking at school, was given special little jobs by his teacher such as cleaning the white board, taking a note to the office, or helping to water plants. The teacher also recommended him for a social skills play group where he was able to experience positive connection with peers and have fun doing it. His grandmother found ways for him to help out at home, such as helping to make scrambled eggs or setting the table, and soon discovered that he loved to take out the garbage! As he made more positive social connections, he got to do his "special jobs" and received recognition for his tasks, and the incidence of his inappropriate attention seeking diminished and his school performance improved.

Neuronal Networks

New research is showing how environment and relationships shape the brain and genetics (Cozolino, 2006). To help better connect with others and the environments in which we live, humans have evolved two ways in which genes work to help neurons connect to each other to form neuronal networks. One way is the genetic template that requires the nervous system to have a uniform structure. A second way that our genetics contribute to the growth of neuronal networks is through genetic transcription. Much like court transcribers record what is happening in the courtroom, genetic transcription allows the brain to be initially shaped and changed over time by experience (Cozolino, 2006, p. 40). What this means is that early negative experiences can often be rescripted by new experiences and importantly, within our significant relationships. Schore (2010) notes that transcription into neural structures can account for as much as 70% of the brain's structure after birth. This experience-dependent maturation of neuronal systems, also known as synaptogenesis, or the birth of the synapses, increases dramatically after birth and is dependent upon environment-stimulated activity (Putnam, 2006). This process allows the human brain to be adapted by and for the environment in which it finds itself. It can also mean that corrective experiences are not just psychologically meaningful for children, but they can also be brain changing.

What appear to be two random facts, actually, may not be random at all. First, humans are the only creatures on Earth that have half of their brain development happen after birth, and second, we are the only creatures on Earth that you can see the "whites" of our eyes (Cozolino, 2006; Porges, 2011). Having white sclera and the largest horizontal area of exposed sclera of all animals allows human infants to be drawn to the eyes of their caregivers. Eye contact, in turn, helps humans be better able to read the intentions of their caregivers and vice versa. Through this caring interaction, the infant's neocortex grows. The neocortex is the part of the brain that has the most influence over social interactions, inhibitory control of impulses, attention, learning, and lays the groundwork for the growth of other areas of the brain that control abstract thought, self-evaluation, and empathy (Cozolino, 2006, p. 22).

MIRROR NEURONS

In a 2006 *New York Times* article, researcher Giacomo Rizzolatti was quoted as follows: "We are exquisitely social creatures. Our survival depends on understanding the actions, intentions and emotions of others. Mirror neurons allow people to grasp the minds of others not through conceptual reasoning but through direct stimulation. By feeling, not thinking" (Blakeslee, 2006).

Years ago, while observing macaque monkeys, Rizzolatti, Fadiga Gallese, and Fogassi (1996) found that the same neurons that fired when a monkey grasped an object also fired when a monkey watched another monkey grasp an object. This stumbled-upon discovery led researchers to closely examine how humans' social behavior may have evolved in various parts of the nervous system and brain (Keysers, 2011). Mirror neurons are also connected to language development. In fact, the mirror system may be involved in the development of facial expressions and the muscles needed for speech (Keysers, 2011). People and many higher mammals, like monkeys, unconsciously mimic the facial expressions of those around them, especially those that look the most similar to them (Keysers, 2011; Porges, 2011).

Although questions remain as to whether mirror neurons "learn" or begin with these particular properties (Catmur, Walsh, & Heyes, 2007), what is clear is that mammals have deeply embedded biological mandates to attune to the emotions of others in their immediate vicinity. When trauma or toxic stress occur, these innate capacities can be reduced, often placing the person in peril of limiting the ability to accurately assess the emotions of others (Doidge, 2006; Porges, 2011). In Guided Exercise 3.5, take a moment to review a video on the relevant work of Beatrice M. L. deGelder.

Guided Exercise 3.5

To get a very visceral sense of what our mirror neurons take in and respond to, watch the video on the work of Beatrice M. L. de Gelder, professor of cognitive neuroscience and director of the Cognitive and Affective Neuroscience Laboratory at the Tilburg University (Netherlands) from the program *Through the Wormhole* as narrated by Morgan Freeman at https://www.youtube.com/watch?v=GwQe_FH1i1w. Every time Morgan Freeman says "blindsight," think mirror neurons.

Below are some activities that may help children improve the plasticity (growth) of the neuronal system, and therefore, exercise the brain connections needed for attachment and learning. (These activities are adapted from Vicario, et al., 2012):

- Peek-a-boo
- Ball tossing or rolling
- Making a collage of faces or eyes from magazine pictures or drawings
- Looking at pictures of you (parent, teacher, or counselor) at their age (this builds connection in their brain and with you)
- Using a disposable camera to take pictures to show you family events or the world through their eyes

These activities can be adapted for use with young children as well as adolescents. In Case Illustration 3.6, you will read about a "peek-a-boo" play intervention to foster parent-child attachment.

Case Illustration 3.6

Peek-a-boo playtime intervention—Jayla from Case Example 3.2 took her TV play even further by pretending to "be a TV" and have her foster mother pretend to "be the TV." As her foster mother playfully pretended to turn on and off the TV (opening and closing her eyes) while saying, "turning on the TV and turning off the TV," Jayla was delighted, laughing, and engaging in this modified game of "peek-a-boo." As seen in the earlier vignette, as Jayla experienced the rocking and cuddling rhythms of attuned caregiving, she began to be able to have fewer and shorter tantrums. This sense of connection was enhanced further by her playful game of "peek-a-boo TV" with her caregiver, which helped her to grow in relationship and self-worth, as she experienced being truly seen. In this simple intervention, Jayla was developing the neuronal and social-emotional connections that she had missed in her early development and that are needed for regulation through relationship (Cozolino, 2006; Siegel, 2010).

Similarly, Casey, who did not wear glasses, one day wanted to make paper eyeglasses, "like you have," he said to his counselor. Following his lead, he and the counselor made pretend glasses. Casey would turn away from the counselor, put on his pretend glasses and then turn back grinning with utter delight when the counselor said, "I see you!" Casey would giggle like a toddler and say, "Do it again! Do it again!" Casey's grandmother who had wonderful instincts about him, remarked, "Sometimes he is a lot like a 2-year-old. He probably missed playing peek-a-boo." She took the pretend glasses home and continued to playfully engage in his glasses game. Shortly after that, he wanted to play "hide and seek," often hiding in simple places, like a much younger child would, and delighting when his grandmother looked for him. As she would call out how much fun they had together and how many places she was looking, she would hear him begin to giggle. She would then "find" him with a surprised, "There you are!" and a warm, excited sense of reunion. Soon she was remarking on "how much more connected and settled he seems." These simple games, peek-a-boo, and hide and seek, are the perfect choice for relational interventions for children who need to be "seen" and "found." Though they are thought of us preschool games, they can be modified for people of all ages to replicate the early experiences with caregivers that help us to emotionally regulate.

Researcher Sandra Bloom (2010) explores what she calls "the counselor and emotional work" done by helping professionals and the effect it has on their own emotions, as does the emotional atmosphere of the environments in which they work. She found, for example, that when working with clients who are feeling overwhelmed, that emotion exists not only within that person but also could be transmitted to the work environment as a whole. Interestingly, when working with individuals who are depressed, she found that workers often begin to feel helpless, and that the work environment can become directionless. Figure 3.3 illustrates some of Bloom's findings on parallel process.

Imagine yourself in a counseling setting with one of the children discussed at the opening of this chapter. Imagine how you might be feeling. Then imagine how the child might be feeling. How many of these feelings are similar? If mirror neurons endow us with a natural ability to attune to the emotions of others, how do you think this might fit with Bloom's idea that the emotions of our clients affect the counselor and the organization? Over our many years of practice, we have seen too many compassionate and enthusiastic child counselors leave the field. Frustrated by working with children who have minimal control over their environment, they become disillusioned with their work. Look at the chart above again. When clients are overwhelmed, counselors also naturally feel a sense of being overwhelmed in relation to them. When clients are aggressive, as children and adolescents often are in counseling, acting out their insecurities and fears, the tendency of those who work closely with them is to become punitive. These parallel processes can then influence counselors' experiences within the counseling session, in their work environments, and in life.

Figure 3.3 Table for Bloom's Findings

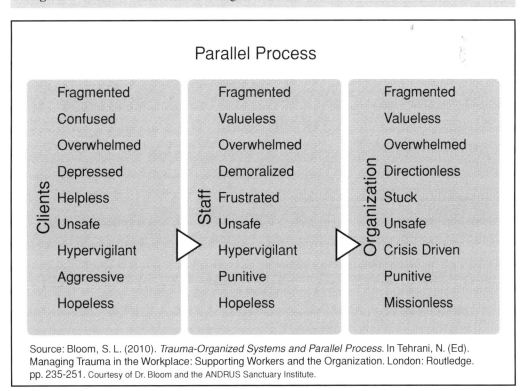

Parallel Process

Clients	Staff	Organization
Fragmented	Fragmented	Fragmented
Confused	Valueless	Valueless
Overwhelmed	Overwhelmed	Overwhelmed
Depressed	Demoralized	Directionless
Helpless	Frustrated	Stuck
Unsafe	Unsafe	Unsafe
Hypervigilant	Hypervigilant	Crisis Driven
Aggressive	Punitive	Punitive
Hopeless	Hopeless	Missionless

Source: Bloom, S. L. (2010). *Trauma-Organized Systems and Parallel Process.* In Tehrani, N. (Ed). Managing Trauma in the Workplace: Supporting Workers and the Organization. London: Routledge. pp. 235-251. Courtesy of Dr. Bloom and the ANDRUS Sanctuary Institute.

The good news is, because neural pathways are plastic, if counselors make a conscious effort to refocus after working with individuals experiencing strong emotions, we believe they can regulate their emotional response to young clients. To do this, we often recommend the *life raft activity*, presented to you earlier in the chapter. At the end of every workday or at the end of difficult sessions, counselors are asked to refer to the list of things that comfort them or bring them joy. We ask them to visualize the experiences using as much sensory detail as possible in order to regulate the emotional response they are having. Having pictures related to those experiences can also be helpful. We believe that this helps calm the distress they feel in relationship to their work. Moreover, we believe that this sort of brain-focused self-care frees counselors to impact the environment in a positive way. Carol Hudgins-Mitchell, one of the authors of this chapter, likes to remind the parents, counselors, and teachers with whom she works, "We *are* the environment." As counselors, we become part of the emotional environment in which children can learn and grow.

NEUROTRANSMITTERS—BRAIN CHEMISTRY

Neurotransmitters are chemicals released by nerve cells to send signals to other nerve cells. *Dopamine* is released for actions connected with survival, like eating, drinking, reproduction, and nurturance (Doidge, 2006). Dopamine provides a feeling of euphoria. It is the most powerful neurotransmitter in the brain.

Guided Exercise 3.6

Hershey's Kisses activity—Try this. Take a piece of plain chocolate. In our work we use Hershey's Kisses, but you can use any type of plain chocolate that you like. It can be dark or light. This will not work with white chocolate or chocolate that has something else with it or in it. Once you have your piece of plain chocolate, eat it slowly, and notice what feelings and emotions you have as you eat it. Write them all down. There are no wrong answers here. When you have your list, hold onto it, we will revisit your list and share with you the emotions we hear most often when we use this activity.

Reflect on your list of emotions that you felt while eating the chocolate. These are emotions associated with the neurochemical, dopamine. Many studies have shown that when you eat the chocolate, you raise the amount of dopamine in your brain through the cocoa in the chocolate. When eating chocolate, people offer the following words: "yum, happy, contented, more, cravings, guilty, smooth, joy," and even "disappointed" from those who do not enjoy chocolate. If dopamine's job is to reward us, then why do we also feel guilty at times? The guilty feelings come with the cravings. Our brains actually crave dopamine, so that we will crave what we need for survival. We are often socialized to feel guilty about things we crave, so that is where the mixed messages enter. Since we need food and water for survival, we receive dopamine for eating and drinking (not just chocolate).

Counseling strategies can be designed for the intentional release of positive neurochemicals. These strategies help children learn to calm themselves, both for their general well-being and also because cognition and memory work more effectively when we are calm. As counselors, we sometimes provide a beverage like herbal tea, juice, or water for some clients who arrive hungry or have attachment problems. We encourage parents (birth, kinship, or foster) to find ways to cook with the children in their care to help the child reexperience sustenance and nurturance in a safe and positive way. Having children help out in the kitchen represents to them that they have a sense of empowerment over their own survival (and helping a safe adult in the kitchen represents a positive attachment relationship). It conveys that the child is capable, and the adult can be trusted with the child's survival and nurturance. When we use this simple strategy, the more parents and children cook together, the more there is a decrease in overeating, stealing, or hording of food or other objects—behaviors that are often related to childhood attachment problems. Both food and connection are needed for survival, as are laughter and fun. All of these activities also help young brains heal. The release of dopamine helps heal the damage done by trauma and adversity.

In Case Illustration 3.7, we illustrate another dopamine-stimulating activity for children.

Case Illustration 3.7

Raining candy intervention—This intervention is a dopamine-stimulating activity for generating soothing and calming emotions. This intervention derives its name from Daniel's experience of using it for finding things that soothe and calm him. You will need a body shape (like a gingerbread person), markers, a pen or pencil, and chocolate-covered berry candy.

1. Have the client suck on a chocolate covered berry with the instruction to keep on letting the candy melt in his or her mouth until he or she gets to the berry in the center.

2. Ask the client to tell you about where he or she feels it in his or her body. Just repeat wherever he or she tells you he or she feels it, and ask if it has a size, a shape, or a picture. Daniel said, "Yeah, it's like I am laying on a hill, and it is raining candy." Again just repeat what the client says. When Daniel's raining candy sentence was repeated he added, "and I can go inside and get a great big bowl and put it on my tummy so it fills up with candy, and I can just have candy

(Continued)

(Continued)

whenever I want." He and the counselor drew a picture of this together and then the counselor asked if anything else happened when it was raining candy, and Daniel added, "It is like it is in my heart and makes me feel happy." They then drew the picture of raining candy in his heart and he added smiley faces.

3. Now ask, "What other things give you that feeling?" With Daniel, the counselor was careful to use his words, "what other things give you that raining candy feeling?" This response helps to stay in his metaphor and reinforce that he has been heard.

Being heard and developing new images and metaphors for safety is an important part of healing from trauma. When Daniel was asked what things gave him the "raining candy feeling," he replied, "Sucking on candy, smelling mint or chocolate, a pat on the back, when someone praises me, and a small, smooth, cool stone." Daniel had been really struggling in his foster placement. At first, his foster mother was unsure when asked if there was anything they could praise him for but soon remembered that he kept his room really tidy. As she thought about it further, there were several little things he really liked to do to be helpful, and she decided to have him help out doing those things so she could praise him even more. The counselor showed Daniel's foster mother how to do this by using descriptive rather than evaluative praise. For example, instead of saying "good job," which is an evaluative praise, use descriptive praise, by enthusiastically and colorfully describing all the things that were done to clean the room or keep it tidy. "You spent so much time making your bed, putting your clothes away, and putting things just like you like them." Another way to use descriptive praise is to attach it to a statement of gratitude that lets the child know exactly what he or she did for which you are grateful. It can be as simple as "Thanks for opening the door for me." Daniel's foster parents made an effort to pat him on the back more and got him a few small glass beads used for flower arranging that he could keep in his pocket. Fortunately he was not a child who threw things. All of these simple interventions came out of the "raining candy" experience and helped Daniel to get the connection he so craved and to find calm and soothing.

Other neurotransmitters include serotonin, which helps with regulation of mood, appetite, and sleep; and endorphins, which are released to reduce pain. These neurotransmitters also are present for parent-child bonding, and after 20 minutes of aerobic exercise, endorphins start to help decrease stress. Try this for yourself in Guided Exercise 3.7.

Guided Exercise 3.7

Engage in 20 to 30 minutes of aerobic activity before class. See how much you retain from that class. Attend the same class without engaging in aerobic activity, and see how much you retain from that class. Use a mandala to color, draw, or doodle in during class. See how much you retain from that class. See how much you retain from a class when you do not use the mandala and just focus on the verbal information. Record your reactions in a brief journal. Which techniques help you retain more information from class?

Oxytocin is an affiliative hormone that seems to support human connection (Moberg, 2003). It intensifies the effect of dopamine. Oxytocin is released in mother and child during nursing, gentle stroking, and cuddling. Oxytocin is released in couples following sexual intercourse, which triggers couple bonding. When humans interact with companion animals, both animal and human release small doses of oxytocin, which explains some of the effectiveness of animal-assisted therapies.

ADVERSE EVENTS AND CHILD DEVELOPMENT

Kaiser Permanente, a health insurance company, conducted the initial Adverse Childhood Experience (ACE) Study in collaboration with the Centers for Disease Control and Prevention (CDC) from 1995 to 1997, enrolling over 17,000 participants (Felitti et al., 1998). Most participants were White, middle-class, white-collar workers. The study participants filled out a confidential survey that contained questions about their current health status and behaviors along with questions about childhood maltreatment and family dysfunction. This survey information, combined with the results of a physical examination, formed the baseline data for the study. The CDC has continued to track the medical status of these baseline participants for almost 20 years. Table 3.1 and 3.2 show some of the startling results of this study. All facts and figures related to prevalence and health outcomes are taken from the CDC website, at http://www.cdc.gov/violenceprevention/acestudy.

The ACE score is calculated by adding one point for each category of exposure to child abuse and/or neglect, which adds up to a score ranging from 0 to 10. Higher ACE scores indicate greater exposure to adversity and therefore the greater

Table 3.1   ACE Prevalence Rates

ACE Factors Abuse	Prevalence %	ACE Factors Household	Prevalence %
Psychological/Emotional	10.6%	Substance Abuse	26.9%
Physical	28.3%	Mental Illness	23.3%
Sexual	20.7%	Loss of a Parent, Separation, Divorce	24.5%
Emotional Neglect	14.8%	Mother Treated Violently	12.7%
Physical Neglect (Includes food insecurity	9.9%	Imprisoned Household Member (AKA a stigmatized loss)	5.2%

the risk of associated negative behavioral and physical health consequences. Felitti et al. (1998), a coprinciple investigator in the ACE study, found "[a] person with an ACE score of 4 is 1,350 times more likely to become an injection drug user, and a person with an ACE score of 6 points is 4,600 times more likely to become an injection drug user. Ninety percent (90%) of those in the public mental health system have experienced childhood trauma. Eighty-five (85%) of girls in the juvenile justice system have experienced physical or sexual abuse as children."

Below in Table 3.2 are the long-term health results of adverse childhood experiences.

Table 3.2 ACE Long-Term Health Outcomes

Behavioral Health Effects	Physical Health Effects
Smoking	Fractures
Re-victimization	Chronic Obstructive Pulmonary Disorder (COPD)
Teen Pregnancy	Heart Disease
Poor Job Performance	Diabetes
Violent Relationships	Obesity
Alcoholism/Substance Abuse	Hepatitis
Depression	Sexually Transmitted Diseases (STDs)
Suicide	Early Death

High ACE scores are a public health epidemic, and they start with children who have experienced toxic stress and complex trauma. Unfortunately, school administrators, medical professionals, and even mental health clinicians too often look at observable behaviors rather than underlying trauma, and, as a result, children are misdiagnosed or given multiple misdiagnoses. Van der Kolk (2014) has framed this unfortunate circumstance for many young people in this way, "Before they reach the age of twenty, many patients have been given four, five, six or more impressive but meaningless diagnoses (p. 157)."

DEVELOPMENTAL TRAUMA AND DIAGNOSIS

"If children are exposed to unmanageable stress, and if the caregiver does not take over the function of modulating the child's arousal, as occurs when children exposed to family dysfunction or violence, the child will be unable to organize and categorize its experiences in a coherent fashion" (van der Kolk, 2005, p. 6).

In 2001, the National Child Traumatic Stress Network (NCTSN) was created by the U.S. Congress with the mission "To raise the standard of care and improve access to services for traumatized children, their families and communities throughout the United States" (NCTSN, n.d.). Out of the work of the NCTSN centers around the country, Bessel van der Kolk, MD, and Robert S. Pynoos, MD, led a task force of leaders in the field of child trauma to put forth a new diagnosis that would more appropriately address the impact of complex trauma on the deveolping brain. After 4 years of collecting research from over 130 studies with over 100,000 children and adolescents from around the world, the task force submitted their results to the American Psychiatric Association in 2009 and asked for inclusion of a new diagnosis in the DSM-V (van der Kolk, 2014). The outcome of this effort is that the DSM-V includes a new subtype of post traumatic stress disorder (PTSD) specific to preschool-aged children. However, this does not go far enough in acknowledging how expressions of trauma and toxic stress in latency age children, adolecents, or individuals with developmental disabilites contribute to maladaptive behaviors. The consequence is that many children, teens, and indivdiuals with developmetal disabilites receive diagnoses based on behavior rather than the underlying cause of those behaviors. In fact, according to van der Kolk (2014), "Eighty two percent of the traumatized children seen in the NCTSN do not meet the criteria for PTSD" (p. 157). Because these older individuals may be hypervigilant, lack affective regulation, or have difficulty with personal boundaries and relationships, they are instead labeled with attention deficiet hyperactivity disorder (ADHD), oppositional defiant disorder (ODD), or reactive attachment disorder (RAD), which might fit their behavioral presentation but also means any underlying trauma is going undetected and unaddressed.

You can follow a wealth of research findings related to the impact of trauma at the website for the trauma center at the Justice Resource Institute (JRI) at http://www.traumacenter.org. For example, read information on trauma-sensitive yoga for children and adolescents. While research continues on the effects of trauma and child outcomes, for counselors in schools and agency settings, it is imperative that every effort is made to learn children's stories and take a very thorough history that captures both the toxic stressors and trauma that may have impacted clients' developing brain resulting in the behaviors that are now being exhibited.

Counselors in schools and clinical settings are often called upon to advocate for young clients by sharing information concerning the impact of adverse experience. For example, because of new research findings that show changes in brain structure based on adverse experiences, some schools have been willing to use the category of other health impaired (OHI) instead of the more stigmitizing label of emotionally disturbed (ED) on a student's Individualized Education Plan (IEP). Because trauma can alter how one perceives and processes sensory information, those who have been subjected to trauma or toxic stress may experience their senses or body differently, resulting in problems in sensory processing. In young clients, this could look like an inability to sit still; engaging in self stimulatory behaviors for calming; clumsiness; bumping, pushing, running, or crashing into objects or people; being messy or being anxious about things perceived as messy; or a host of other sensory-seeking or sensory-avoiding behaviors that disrupt learning and regulation.

Counselors can advocate for a thorough occupational therapy evaluation for sensory integration that can lead to interventions that can be implemented both at school and in the home. Having this evaluation and program written into the IEP or 504 plan assures that the client will get the services needed. Sensory-focused interventions can help build a sense of calm and regulation as well as a sense of proprioception (where the body is in space) that assists with grounding and feeling safe (van der Kolk, 2014). Using these resources helps make sure that therapy is relationally and culturally respectful and interventions are trauma responsive.

PLAY COUNSELING FOR COMPLEX TRAUMA

Throughout this chapter, the authors have offered interventions grounded in the neurobiology of attachment and trauma, but many of these are also examples of relational and sensory-focused play therapy (Vicario, Tucker, Smith-Adcock, Hudgins-Mitchell, 2013). Relational and sensory play activities can be applied to clients of all ages with developmental disabilities, preverbal trauma, or early trauma that continues to limit the language expression of those entering treatment. All three of these conditions can limit the brains' functioning to preoperational or concrete operational thought (Gentile & Gillig, 2012; Siegel, 2012). When the brain functions in pre- or concrete operational thought, people understand and interact with the world in more sensory-based responses (direct interaction through the senses) rather than in abstract thought and language. Complex trauma affects and often occurs in intimate relationships (Cloitre et al., 2009), therefore, the use of sensory based and relationally based interventions provides an approach for working with young clients who might otherwise be difficult to treat and who do not benefit from more traditional forms of talk therapy (e.g., externalizing behaviors, developmental delays).

The interventions in the next section are examples of relationally and sensory-based treatment. These are interventions that combine the brain-focused ideas we have already explored in this chapter with developmentally appropriate sensory activities. Then, we illustrate these interventions using the case study of Valerie.

EXAMPLES OF RELATIONALLY AND SENSORY-BASED INTERVENTIONS

Peel the Anger Onion

Since sadness and fear take more energy, anger is often leading the emotional charge. In counseling with children and adolescents, we call this the *anger onion* and show children and parents and teachers how to peel the anger onion. On the outside of the onion is the anger, which gives you energy, protects you, and often gets you in trouble, but when you are brave enough, you can peel back that anger layer of the onion and see the sadness underneath. Just like with a real onion, peeling back the layers may make you cry. We tell clients and their caregivers this, "People who cry more, hit less." We may also note that there are other layers (feelings and behaviors) in the anger onion, and at its core is fear. Because fear is the core emotion in post-trauma or toxic stress, it is much more effective to ask a child who is upset, "How can I help you feel safe?" than a directive such as "Calm down."

Make a Worry Box

Remember Daniel from the vignettes at the beginning of the chapter? Daniel is a fourth grader who got in trouble for drawing sexually explicit pictures during free time at school. What his teacher did not know is that Daniel was experiencing intrusive memories, something that frequently happens when children who have experienced trauma are bored. He needs a calming activity that helps him contain and manage his troubling thoughts. Having a "worry box" is helpful in giving children and teens a place to leave the things that trouble them or have been brought up in counseling so that they do not go home or to school and act them out. A worry box is constructed from a shoebox or other sturdy box, decorated on the outside with pictures, which can be illustrated or cut from magazines, of things the child or teen likes. As the child decorates the box, the counselor puts the worry into perspective for the child by stating, "What we love is stronger than what worries us." Inside the box, the child may put pictures of what worries them or write the things down on slips of paper. It can be a good practice to use the worry box at the end of each counseling session and teach children how to mentally send their worries to the box between sessions. Alternatively, children can also have a worry box for home or school.

As counselors, we also need to learn to let go of troubling thoughts. In Guided Exercise 3.8, follow the directions to make your own "Counselor's Worry Box."

Guided Exercise 3.8

It can be helpful for therapists to have ways to let go of the difficult material and stresses of the day. Follow the directions above to make your own worry box. Try putting pictures or notes of the things that worry or stress you into your worry box, put the top on it, and let it go. Practice sending worries to your worry box using mental imagery.

Collect Items for a Calming Box or Bag

Children and adolescents may also benefit from having ready access to a variety of calming activities when they are feeling anxious. A multisensory or calming kit can be used at school or at home. Counselors can also help parents or teachers to make up a calming kit to be kept in a quiet corner or cupboard. Teachers of young children often have a "quiet area" where reading and/or sensory items are available so this would fit nicely there. The calming items need to be easily accessed but not intrusive to the class or embarrassing to the student. One teacher used the soft, nubby side of adhesive backed Velcro strips to tack under each child's desk so that they all could use it for calming. She said it worked so well that she decided she needed one for her desk!

Here are some ideas for items that children have found calming:

A journal	Bubbles	Sugar scrub	Mandalas	Play-Doh and/or clay	Squeeze balls	Shaving Cream
Coloring pages	Art supplies	Small container of sand or rice	Scented lotion or body spray	Rain stick	Picture of loved ones/safe people	Picture of a calming/ safe place
Pieces of fabric that feel good to touch	Fuzzy pipe cleaners	Personal CD or MP3 player	Playing cards for shuffling sorting	Magnetic toys, Etch A Sketch	Kaleido-scope	Small Magna Doodle
Slinky	Pin art	Drinking from a straw	Stuffed animal	Soft blanket or piece of fabric	Puzzles	Fidgets

Use Mindfulness and Guided Imagery

Many children and teens respond well to learning breathing techniques, mindfulness practices, and using guided imagery. These techniques are easy to use in school, at home, or in clinical settings. These are just a few of the ways we have used mindfulness activities. These basic activities can be modified and adapted to fit the needs of each child or teen.

1. Teach the child how to do "belly breathing" imagining that he or she is breathing in and blowing the belly up like a balloon so the belly goes out as one breaths in and down as one breaths out. Have the child place his or her hands on his or her abdomen to feel this up and down breathing.

2. Find a quiet time to sit with the child and ask them to take a few deep belly breaths. Using a soothing tone, prompt the child to imagine a time or place when he or she felt good and calm (this can be real or imagined). As the child imagines this calm place, help him or her connect to this place with all five senses. Ask the child to look around and notice what is in the special place. What does he or she hear? What special smells are there? Is it cool or warm? What does he or she feel? Taste? Is there anything else that would make this place just right or even more comfortable? Drawing the calm place can add another dimension to the experience. It should be fun to do so, but if a child is anxious about drawing, they can do it as a collage, swirls of color, stick figures, or diorama.

3. Enhance the calming place guided imagery by having the child or teen tap alternately on his or her knees or tap his or her feet alternately as he or she imagines walking through the comforting place. Remind the child that he or she can connect to this feeling of calm just by doing this action.

In Case Illustration 3.8, we return to the case of Valerie, a 17-year-old with a developmental disability. This case illustrates how to use relationally and sensory-focused interventions to help Valerie communicate more expressively. Read the case, and identify the relational and sensory interventions used.

Case Illustration 3.8

Developmental, relational, and sensory intervention: The case of Valerie—Valerie, the 17-year-old from the chapter's introduction, has autism and was removed from her biological home where there was severe neglect and abuse of at least some of her siblings. Valerie is an example of how brain-based interventions can assist in identifying and addressing early trauma. For the first 17 years of Valerie's life, she was considered to have severe autism, with little use of expressive language. Many would say she was not able to benefit from counseling, but with sensory and relational approaches, Valerie was able to gain communication and interpersonal skills that would probably not have been considered possible by previous evaluators of her disability.

(Continued)

(Continued)

Valerie's initial interactions with her counselor included Valerie making lists and repeating her lists both verbally and in writing. For example she listed the people in her birth family. She then read the list. As she read each name on the list, her counselor repeated them back to her. When her counselor repeated the first name on the list after her, Valerie stopped and made eye contact for the first time. She rewrote the list and read it a second time with the counselor repeating her words to her. This time the counselor added the reflection, "These are the people in your family." Valerie repeated, "family," and again made eye contact. This time her eye contact was fleeting and anxious. Each time she completed and read the list, the counselor repeated her words. This continued for the entire session. Knowing that all behavior is purposeful and a form of communication, the counselor was taking her time to allow a fuller meaning of the communication to emerge. For Valerie, she was establishing rapport and trust with her new counselor the only way she knew how.

At her second session, Valerie entered eagerly. She was clearly excited to start making her lists and having her words repeated back to her, so she knew they were being heard. After several rounds of list making and repetition, the counselor encouraged, by pointing to the first name on the list, and requesting, "Tell me about Daddy." Valerie did not respond. The counselor was not discouraged because she knew that individuals from environments where they have lost their personal power could not say *yes* to a request until they are allowed to say *no*. Both developmental disabilities and trauma can produce slower cognitive processing speed. When this need to refuse is not respected, oppositional and defiant behavior often erupts to compensate for the individual's inability to process quickly enough and agitation over having processing interrupted. Think about how frustrated you feel when people cut off your thoughts or finish your sentences. (We have found that teaching this simple skill of allowing for extra processing time has helped parents, teachers, therapists, and other professionals greatly decrease oppositional-defiant behavior in youth.)

Valerie's list making continued, as did the counselor's reflection and encouragement to tell her more about the first person on her list. Eventually, Valerie pointed to her sister's name on the list and said, "Sister." "Sue is your sister," the counselor repeated. The next time through the list, Valerie added the name of the town where she had lived with her family. "You lived in Mason with your sister, Sue," the counselor reflected. Valerie's one-word utterances continued, and over time, the counselor asked Valerie to make a picture of her family. Valerie did not immediately respond to this request either, but over time, she switched from making lists of her family member's names to drawing pictures of each of her family members repeatedly while the counselor reflected what she saw. In a subsequent session, Valerie drew a picture of a girl in a bed. As she drew Sue vomiting, she demonstrated intense concern, and the counselor reflected that, "Sometimes we worry when people are sick." Valerie moved onto saying, "Sue threw up." Valerie drew this scene repeatedly session after session. As the counselor gently added emotion words that matched Valerie's look and the content of her pictures, Valerie moved onto share more about her own pain.

To help Valerie with closure after each session, she would put her pictures in a folder. Each week Valerie would get her folder out, look at it, and be ready to draw again. One week, Valerie broke this pattern and came into session immediately requesting, "Paper, paper," with a sense of urgency. Upon receiving the paper, Valerie drew her first picture of herself outside of her repetitive family drawings. She pointed to the mouth on the picture and said, "Valerie mouth." The therapist immediately noticed that the mouth on this picture was different than any of the others. This mouth was open and looked frightened. The mouths in all of her other pictures had been straight lines. This time the counselor immediately encouraged, "Tell me about Valerie's mouth."

Without hesitation, Valerie responded, "Mouth bleeding," as she added blood to the mouth in the picture. The counselor gently requested, "Tell me about what happened to Valerie's mouth." Valerie returned to her repetitive drawing of herself with the bleeding mouth, and as she drew she became more agitated and started to rock (a self-soothing technique) while repeatedly saying, "Valerie mouth bleeding." This time as the counselor repeated Valerie's words, she added concern to her voice, "Valerie's mouth is bleeding. What happened to Valerie's mouth?" Valerie immediately replied, "Cane," and drew a picture of a cane. The counselor reflected with concern that Valerie's mouth had been hit with a cane. Valerie started nervously laughing. After reflecting Valerie's words, the counselor asked, "Who hit Valerie's mouth with a cane?" Valerie's anxious laughter increased as she responded and repeated, "Daddy Cane. Daddy Cane. Hit." The counselor reflected Valerie's revelation with "Daddy hit with cane." Valerie added, "Mouth bleeding. Mouth bleeding," as her nervous laughter increased. Then the counselor replied in a calm voice while shaking her head, "You're laughing, but I don't think it was funny." Valerie's face froze in a mask of terror so intense it concerned the counselor. Just at that moment, the terror broke, and Valerie began to cry. The counselor put her hand on Valerie's and reflected, "It hurt, and you are crying." Valerie replied, "Lip hurt crying," as she added tears to the picture. The counselor thanked Valerie for sharing her story of her hurt lip with her.

One day, Valerie entered the session with a picture of a monster with a tail shaped like a penis. She immediately put the picture in her "worry box." Valerie then "stared into space," unresponsive to her counselor and seemingly unaware of what was happening around her. To connect with her more fully in the here and now, the counselor asked if she could put her hand on Valerie's arm. Valerie nodded. The counselor put her hand on Valerie's arm and said, "Feel my hand on your arm. You are safe and here with me." Valerie looked at her counselor and looked at her arm. The counselor repeated, "Feel my hand on your arm. You are safe and here with me." This time Valerie said, "Hand on arm safe." Valerie then came back fully into the session by making and maintaining eye contact. The counselor then asked to bring Valerie's mother into the session and instructed, "When Valerie has memories that make her feel unsafe, she stares away from people and does not respond to them because her mind is somewhere else. It helps her to ask if you can put your hand on her arm and tell her she is safe and with you." When her mother followed this, Valerie started to rock softly, looked from her hand to her mother. When she made eye contact, Valerie said, "Safe." Her mother then reflected Valerie's words, "Yes, Valerie you are safe with me." To give them yet another coping skill for use at home the counselor taught both Valerie and her mother how to do deep breathing by placing their hands on their abdomens and inhaling like they were blowing up balloons. Valerie repeated, "belly balloons." Her mother added, "big belly balloons," and they both giggled. It took a few repetitions for them to get the belly breathing action, but they got it and went home to practice.

In subsequent sessions, the counselor worked with Valerie to draw and name what helps her feel safe. From a brain-based perspective, this helped Valerie to develop a neuronal network for this grounding technique. Each session, the counselor asked Valerie what helped her feel safe. One day Valerie responded with language first saying, "Hold a hand." She then drew a picture of people with whom she felt safe holding their hands. Weeks later, her mother shared, "Valerie started to have one of those temper spells, but I asked her if she wanted to sit and hold a hand, and she did it. She has come such a long way!"

Using sensory and relational interventions at a pace led by Valerie, the counselor learned how Valerie made sense of her world, joined her there, and walked with her through her traumatic life

(Continued)

(Continued)

experiences. In so doing, the results were improved functioning of the language centers of the brain, which are damaged from trauma (Carpenter & Stacks, 2009). We also saw the results of a limbic system that was healing and returning to its primary functions of felt safety (Porges, 2011). This basic neurological process of felt safety can either foster or inhibit attachment and regulation (Siegel, 2012).

Guided Exercise 3.9

Looking back at the Case Illustration of Valerie, name the relational and sensory-based interventions used in working with Valerie.

COUNSELING KEYSTONES

- Early trauma and toxic stress alters the architecture of the developing brain, but fortunately we have neuroplasticity and with brain-based counseling interventions we can help to heal the harm done by early trauma and toxic stress.
- Adverse childhood experience impacts behavioral and physical health; the more adversity one has, the more the health risks are compounded.
- Counselors are called to advocate for young clients whose toxic stress is often seen only as "behavior." We must also work across systems to help ameliorate toxic stress and foster resilience.
- Fifty percent (50%) of the brain's growth takes place after birth and is shaped by and for the environment in which it is being formed.
- When early relationships do not allow for repeated positive interactions, the limbic system is not able to adequately develop the pathways required for fully functioning regulatory mechanisms. This can often manifest in dysregulated behavior later in childhood and adolescence.
- Regulation, safety, and attachment occur together, so any time you work on one you strengthen the others.
- Developmentally, a child's feeling of safety (neuroception) is the starting point of regulation. When there has been trauma or toxic stress, one can be safe and not feel safe.
- Active listening and use of safety scripts allow the individual to feel understood and to connect and have coregulation through the therapist.

- Understanding the neurobiological underpinnings of regulation, therapists can help parents and other primary caregivers understand the importance of "time in," which develops the neuronal networks children need for regulation rather than "time out," which does not.
- Using guided visualization and teaching mindfulness helps build regulatory skills.
- It is important that counselors meet young clients where they are developmentally and emotionally, walk with them through their traumatic experiences whether expressed directly or in metaphor, help them release the trauma, and reorganize their lives.
- Counselors need to explore the relational/social brain with a focus on the opportunities the educational system has in supporting and maximizing healthy development that will in turn reduce unwanted behaviors and maximize learning potential.
- As we go forward to create trauma-informed and trauma-responsive counseling practices that are grounded in research and best practices, it is important to remember that what is easiest to measure and what is most effective is not necessarily the same thing.

It is crucial to stay current because the field of neurobiology is changing daily. The counseling field needs creative, young minds to help identify new ways to use the knowledge we are gaining, new ways to measure progress, and new ways to increase neuroplasticity, repair, and hope in those we serve.

ADDITIONAL RESOURCES

In Print

Cozolino, L. (2014). *Attachment-based teaching: Creating a tribal classroom.* New York, NY: W.W. Norton & Co.

Feinstein, S. (2009). *Secrets of the teenage brain: Research-based strategies for reaching and teaching today's adolescents* (2nd ed.). Thousand Oaks, CA: Corwin.

Gaskill, R., & Perry, B. (2014). The neurobiological power of play: Using the Neurosequential model of therapeutics to guide play in the healing process. In C. Malchiodi & D. Crenshaw (Eds.). *Creative arts and play therapy for attachment problems* (pp. 178–194). New York, NY: Guilford Press.

Kranowitz, C. S. (1998). *The out of sync child: Recognizing and coping with sensory integration dysfunction.* New York, NY: Peguin Group.

Perry, B. D. (2006). Applying principles of neurodevelopment to clinical work with maltreated and traumatized children. The neurosequential model of therapeutics. In N. B. Webb (Ed.), *Working with traumatized youth in child welfare.* New York, NY: Guilford.

Seigel, D. J., & Hartzell, M. (2003 & 2014). *Parenting from the inside out.* New York, NY: Penguin Group.

Online

Attachment Theory and the Brain: An Interview with Dr. Daniel Sonkin: http://neuronarrative.wordpress.com/2009/01/12/attachment-theory -and-the-brain-an-interview-with-dr-daniel-sonkin

National Child Traumatic Stress Network (NCTSN): http://www.nctsn.org

Neuroscience for Kids: https://faculty.washington.edu/chudler/neurok.html

Pediatricians Take On Toxic Stress: http://developingchild.harvard.edu/resources/ stories_from_the_field/tackling_toxic_stress/pediatricians_take_on_ toxic_stress/

The American Academy of Pediatrics (Technical Report) The Lifelong Effects of Early Childhood Adversity and Toxic Stress: http://pediatrics.aappublications .org/content/129/1/e232.full

Trauma Center at the Justice Resource Institute (JRI): http://www.traumacenter .org

In Film

Cain, L. (Director), & Stromer, T. (Producer). (2010). *Healing Neen* [Motion Picture]. United States: Maryland Disability Law Center and In the Hollow Films.

REFERENCES

Banks, A. (2015). *Four ways to click: Rewire your brain for stronger more rewarding relationships.* New York: Penguin.

Beebe, B. (2005). Mother-infant research informs mother-infant treatment. *Psychoanalytic Study of the Child, 60,* 7–46.

Blakeslee, S. (2006, January 10). Cells that read minds. *New York Times.* Retrieved from http://www.nytimes.com/2006/01/10/science/10mirr .html?pagewanted=all&_r=0

Bloom, S. L. (2010). Trauma-organized Systems and Parallel Process. In N. Tehrani (Ed.), *Managing trauma in the workplace—Supporting workers and the organization* (pp. 235–251)1. London, UK: Routledge.

Bowlby, J. (1969). *Attachment and loss*. New York, NY: Basic Books.

Bowlby, J. (1988). *A secure base: Clinical applications of attachment theory*. London, UK: Routledge.

Cacioppo. J. T., & Bernston, G. G. (2002). Social neuroscience. In T. J. Capcioppo, G.G. Bernston, R. Adolphs, C. S. Carter, R. J. Davidson, M. McClintock et al. (Eds.), *Foundations in social neuroscience* (pp. 1–10). Cambridge, MA: MIT Press.

Carpenter, G. L., & Stacks, A. M. (2009). Developmental effects of exposure to intimate partner violence in early childhood: A review of the literature. *Children and Youth Services Review, 31*(8), pp. 831–839.

Catmur, C., Walsh, V., & Heyes, C. (2007). Sensorimotor learning configures the human mirror system. *Current Biology, 7*(17), 1527–1531.

Chapman, L. (2014). *Neurobiologically informed trauma therapy with children and adolescents: Understanding mechanisms of change* (1st ed.). New York, NY: W. W. Norton & Company.

Cloitre, M., Stolbach, B. C., Herman, J. L., van der Kolk, B., Pynoos, R., Wang, J., & Petkova, E. (2009). A developmental approach to complex PTSD: Childhood and adult cumulative trauma as predictors of symptom complexity. *Journal of Traumatic Stress, Vol. 22*. No. 5, 399–408.

Cozolino, L. (2006). *The neuroscience of human relationships: Attachment and the developing social brain*. New York, NY: Norton.

Cozolino, L. (2010). *The neuroscience of psychotherapy: Healing the social brain*. (2nd ed.). New York, NY: Norton.

Cozolino, L. (2013). *The social neuroscience of education: Optimizing attachment and learning in the classroom*. New York, NY: Norton.

Doidge, N. (2006). *The brain that changes itself*. New York, NY: Penguin.

Felitti, V. J., Anda, R. F., Nordenberg, D., Williamson, D. F., Spitz, A. M., Edwards, V., Koss, M. P., Marks, J. S. (1998). Relationship of childhood abuse and household dysfunction to many of the leading causes of death in adults: The adverse childhood experiences (ACE) study. *American Journal of Preventive Medicine, 14*(4), 245–258.

Garner, A. S., Shonkoff, J. P., Siegel, B. S., Dobbins, M. I., Earls, M. F., McGuinn, L., . . . Wood, D. L. (2012). Early childhood adversity, toxic stress, and the role of the pediatrician: Translating developmental science into lifelong health. *Pediatrics 129*(224).

Gentile, J., & Gillig, P. (Eds.). (2012). *Psychiatry of intellectual disability: A practical manual*. Oxford, UK: Wiley-Blackwell.

Gil, E. (1991). *The healing power of play: Working with abused children*. New York, NY: Guilford Press.

Jordan, J. V. (2012). *Relational-cultural therapy*. Washington, DC: American Psychological Association.

Kestly, T. (2014). *The interpersonal neurobiology of play: Brain-building interventions for emotional well-being.* New York, NY: Norton.

Keysers, C. (2011). *The empathic brain: How the discovery of mirror neurons changes our understanding of human nature.* Groningen, Netherlands: Social Brain Press.

Lieberman, M. D. (2013). *Social: Why our brains are wired to connect.* New York, NY: Crown.

Moberg, K. U. (2003). *The oxytocin factor: Tapping the hormone of love, calm and healing.* Cambridge, MA: Perseus Books.

National Child Traumatic Stress Network (NCTSN). (n.d.). Retrieved from http://www.nctsn.org

National Institute of Health. (2014). The brain initiative. Retrieved from http://braininitiative.nih.gov/pdf/BRAIN_brochure_508C.pdf

Pert, C. (1997). *Molecules of emotion: The science behind mind—body medicine.* New York, NY: Scribner.

Porges, S. (2011). The polyvagal theory: Neurophysiological foundations of emotions, attachment, communication and self-regulation. New York, NY: Norton.

Putnam, F. W. (2006). The impact of trauma on child development. *Juvenile and Family Court Journal,* 1–11.

Rizzolatti, G., Fadiga, L., Gallese, V., & Fogassi, L. (1996). Premotor cortex and the recognition of motor actions. *Cognitive Brain Research, 3,* 131–141.

Schore, A. N. (2003). *Affect dysregulation and disorders of the self.* New York, NY: Norton.

Schore, A. N. (2005). Attachment, affect regulation, and the developing right brain: Linking developmental neuroscience to pediatrics. *Pediatrics in Review, 26,* 204–217.

Schore, A. N. (2010). Relational trauma and the developing right brain: The neurobiology of broken attachment bonds. In T. Baradon, *Relational trauma of infancy: Psychoanalytic, attachment and neuropsychological contributions to parent-infant psychotherapy.* New York, NY: Routledge, Taylor, Francis Group.

Schupp, L. J. (2004). *Assessing and treating trauma and PTSD.* Eau Claire, WI: PESI, LLC.

Siegel, D. (2010). *Mindsight: The new science of personal transformation.* New York, NY: Bantam.

Siegel, D. J. (2012). *The developing mind: How relationships and the brain interact to shape who we are* (2nd ed.). New York, NY: W.W. Guilford Press.

Solomon, M., & Siegel, D. (2003). *Healing trauma: Attachment, mind, body, and brain.* New York, NY: Norton.

Steele, C. M. (2010). *Whistling Vivaldi: How stereotypes affect us and what we can do.* New York, NY: W. W. Norton and Company.

Szalavitz, & Perry (2011). *Born for love: Why empathy is essential—And endangered.* New York, NY: Harper and Collins.

The White House. (2014, September 30). BRAIN initiative. Retrieved from https://www.whitehouse.gov/share/brain-initiative

van der Kolk, B. A. (2005). *Developmental trauma disorder: Towards a rational diagnosis for children with complex trauma histories.*

van der Kolk, B. A., (2014). *The body keeps the score: Brain, mind, and body in the healing of trauma.* New York, NY: Viking.

Vicario, M., Hudgins-Mitchell, C., & Corbisello, G. (2012). *The foster parent survival guide.* Cincinnati, OH: Finding Hope Consulting.

Vicario, M., Tucker, C., Smith-Adcock, S., & Hudgins-Mitchell, C., (2013). Relational-cultural play therapy: Re-establishing healthy connections with children exposed to trauma in relationships. *International Journal of Play Therapy, 22*(2), 103–117.

Whelan, W., & Stewart, A. (2015). Attachment security as a framework in play therapy. In D. Crenshaw, & A. Stewart, *Play therapy: A comprehensive guide to theory and practice* (pp. 114–122). New York, NY: Guilford.

Yeager, M., & Yeager, D. (2013). *Executive function and child development.* New York, NY: Norton.

Chapter 4

The Counseling Process: Establishing a Therapeutic Alliance

SONDRA SMITH-ADCOCK AND JENN PEREIRA

Children who feel well behave well.

—Haim Ginotte

INTRODUCTION

Childhood is a time lived both in fast forward and in slow motion, a time of joy, confusion, hurt, sorrow, and defeat. Through these ups and downs, young people grow in relationship to those who care for them—family, teachers, friends, and counselors. In this chapter, we explore aspects of the developmental nature of children and adolescents to help counseling professionals relate well to them, create the kind of free and protected space in which they need to grow, and nurture the emerging self in relation to others and the environment. To do this, we ask you to first closely examine your own worldview, including your biases (when you were growing up as well as now), your own ideas about how children and adolescents should be raised or taught, and to reflect on these experiences. Then, we provide an overview of some basic therapeutic tools that will help you to relate well to young people and to help them navigate challenging developmental terrain. Though much of this chapter will seem like review of the microskills training you have already had in your counseling preparation program, we hope you will find in this chapter both a refresher course on your basic skills and a user-friendly overview of skills and dispositions for relating to a very special group of clients.

After reading this chapter, you will be able to

- describe why it is crucial for counselors to assess their current attitudes toward children and adolescents and develop attitudes that foster connection with diverse youth;
- explain why an understanding of developmental stages and issues is critical for successful work with children and adolescents;
- explain the importance of understanding client systems and how a problem focus has the potential to impede the therapeutic alliance;
- describe ways of working and specific skills that are consistent with child and adolescent development, norms, and worldview; and
- suggest ways that counselors can actively engage child and adolescent clients in ways that foster creativity and connection.

THE CULTURE OF CHILDHOOD AND ADOLESCENCE

Childhood and adolescence are life stages that are not only unique from the world of adults in developmental scope but also in values, norms, and customs. Reflect on this for a minute. When have you last looked at the world from a child's point of view? What about teens? Put yourself in "their shoes." Chances are, when you reflect back, you will remember a time in your life when things were different than they are now in your adulthood. For example, can you remember what it felt like to tie your shoes for the first time, to ride your bike without training wheels, or to go to a movie without an adult tagging along? How about the first time your curfew was later than usual or the first time you broke up with someone? At that time, how did you perceive the adults around you? How did you experience your interactions with them? Did you feel seen and heard? Now, also consider the daily interactions you see around you—between parent and child, teacher and student, counselor and young client. What dynamics do you observe between youth and between youth and the grown-ups in their lives? Do you notice differences based on the cultural backgrounds of the people involved? Consider this perspective as you imagine your future as a counselor in school or clinical settings.

A SURVEY OF ATTITUDES TOWARD CHILDREN

Reflect on your beliefs about children, your current understanding of child development, the process and purpose of counseling, and your own willingness to challenge your beliefs about children and adolescents. In Guided Exercise 4.1, survey your own and your classmates' attitudes.

Guided Exercise 4.1

Review the following questions for a moment, and give some thought as to how you would respond. Pick a partner to discuss or write a reflection.

- Do you feel that children/adolescents possess an innate capacity to overcome obstacles and circumstances in their lives?

- Do you feel that children/adolescents know within themselves what they need from the therapeutic process and the counselor?

- Do you believe that children can grow and change when provided room to direct their therapeutic process?

- Do you believe that children/adolescents need specific direction from the counselor to work out solutions to their issues?

After your discussion, reflect on this:

- How would you summarize your beliefs about working with young clients, and how do you see your role as counselor?

- Are there beliefs you hold currently that may not be as conducive to working successfully with children and adolescents as you might like?

- Have you thought very much about where these beliefs come from?

- What sort of attitudes toward children are part of your individual dispositions or familial or cultural background?

- What steps will you take to adapt your current ideas to allow for deeper understanding and relationship building with young clients?

- Interview one or more of your classmates about their childhood. How are their experiences similar or dissimilar to yours?

The counselor impacts and is impacted by the child (Jordan, 2012; Tucker, Smith-Adcock, & Trepal, 2011). Though it seems clear how counselors affect children, how do our young clients teach us about ourselves? Our own personal responses can facilitate deep connections with our young clients, or they can get in our way. Many counselors take client reactions personally, whether they are aware of this or not. Counselors' reactions can be varied depending on the child, the situation, and their own experience. Our reactions can be positive or negative. They can reflect our own biases and our own psychological needs. In our experience, we find that this reaction can be of particular importance when we are learning to counsel young people. We frequently tell students that "no one can make you feel more helpless than a 5-year-old having a bad day." When you feel stuck or helpless, "remember that your feelings are about you, not the child." In working with young people, make sure you are constantly taking inventory of your own insecurities, negative thoughts, and unrealistic expectations, and how you bring those into your interactions with your young clients.

Depending on the ethnic, racial, gender, sexuality, and ability background of your clients and their families, their beliefs may be very similar to or very different from your own beliefs about how children and adolescents act and think. Counselors need to be aware of how their own cultural and personal background and experiences inform their ideas about child development, what is considered normal and what is not. For example, European-American counselors often describe frustration when their adolescent clients from collectivist cultures, such as most cultures of Asia, Latin America, and Africa, insist on attending a college near home to meet family obligations rather than applying to higher status universities further from home. Whereas White, middle-class, U.S.-based counselors are usually raised to believe that the priority of the client should be about himself or herself rather than the entire family or community, most of the world's population does not share these individualistic beliefs. Counselors need to carefully examine the beliefs ingrained in them by their native cultures and how those beliefs may differ from the beliefs of their clients. When we combine this multicultural and developmental perspective, we are freer to meet clients where they are rather than where the counselor feels they should be. We also are more likely to begin to see alternative and fuller explanations for their behavior, which can lead to a deeper understanding of their inner experiences.

RELATING TO THE WORLD OF CHILDREN

Rules such as "finders-keepers," "even-steven," belief in all things magical, egocentric thinking, and behaviors that can be puzzling to adults, such as singing loudly in public, nose picking during conversations, a fascination with bodily functions, and stating what you feel at any time regardless of the situation are examples of the culture of childhood. Adults tend to have a very different orientation to the world, which can contribute to frustration and misunderstanding, or what could be considered a cultural conflict between adults and the young people they care about. As adults, our hearts are usually in the right place as we work to guide and shape our youth in ways that we think will prepare them to function appropriately in an adult-oriented world. Adults often react, "Don't pick your nose!" "Things in life aren't always fair." "Say excuse me!" These directives can be important. However, basic differences in worldviews can also lead adults to unintentionally disrespect the culture of children, resulting in unwanted disconnection to the healthy relationships we are trying to build.

As adults, childhood is often a distant memory. Have you forgotten what childhood and adolescence felt like? Most people do, to some extent. As a result, we frequently unintentionally disrespect the culture of the young people in our lives. We interrupt children midthought and midsentence, while simultaneously chastising them for doing the same thing during an adult conversation. We often make decisions for them based on how we feel, such as their hunger (e.g., "How can you be hungry, you just ate?"), bodily functions (e.g., "Are you sure you don't have to go?), and body temperature (e.g., "It's cold in here; go put your sweater on"). Lastly, adults too often discuss a child's behaviors, thoughts, and feelings with others while the child is standing next to them, showing little regard for the child's privacy or feelings about having his or her personal information shared. A teacher shares with a parent, "His behavior is much better these days. I only have to tell him to sit down about three times a day now (shaking her head slightly)." A mother and father sit at the table quietly discussing the son or daughter's grades without talking directly to the child. "Well, if she got her homework done on time, we wouldn't be dealing with this."

As adults, our behaviors toward children can stem from culturally based attitudes and beliefs that children need constant guidance and direction to successfully navigate their lives; they need our help (Axline, 1969; Landreth, 2012). While young persons do often need our guidance, or protection, this belief can cause us to overlook and underestimate the ability children have to be responsible and self-directing. A competent counselor, then, is one who relies on both his or her own therapeutic skills to direct children as needed and a deep trust for the wisdom of his or her child clients (Landreth, 2012).

In Case Illustration 4.1, we share an example from our own experiences as school counselors.

Case Illustration 4.1

The following case illustration draws on one of the author's personal experiences working in an elementary school:

Routinely, I would engage in conversations with children in the hallways, classrooms, and lunchroom. These conversations, as those with children routinely do, ranged from the serious events of their lives, to jokes, to their thoughts on the cute new boy in class, to the latest theory about a particular superhero. Also routinely, during these conversations I always made a point of kneeling or bending down to meet the children where they were height-wise so that we could maintain eye contact while talking. Invariably, during one of these conversations, another adult would need to speak with me and would abruptly interrupt my conversation with the child. My typical response, from my crouched position, was something like, "Hello, Mrs. Peco, I see you have something to discuss with me. I'm in a conversation right now and will find you when I'm through," followed by an apology to the child for the interruption. Typically, this would cause consternation on the part of the adult who would continue speaking to me, insisting we have the conversation right then (the implication being that my conversation with the student was less important). As one would imagine, this was often not well received. In one incident, a teacher seemed to feel I was not appropriately acknowledging her need to speak with me and attempted to physically pull me to a standing position. At this point I should note that the adult was not interrupting due to an emergency but rather for an everyday general topic. As adults, we teach children not to interrupt. We teach children that interrupting is rude, making statements like "Don't interrupt when adults are talking; wait your turn," or "It's rude to interrupt; you'll need to wait." We typically do not, though, afford this same respect to our conversations with children. We do not apologize for interrupting, saying something like "David, I'm so sorry to interrupt you and Mikey, could I just let you know something quickly?" As adults, we usually do not wait our turn when children are talking, and in the end, we model the idea that our thoughts and conversations are more valuable than theirs.

Throughout the latter part of this text, the chapter authors emphasize cognitive, emotional, and physical development and its implications for counseling with specific age groups. Guided Exercise 4.2 is a structured activity to remind counselors, parents, and teachers how the world might look from a child's view.

Guided Exercise 4.2

Reflection activity: Getting on a child's level. Have you recently thought about how it feels to be small? Or young? Or to be dependent on others for your care? This activity is used to begin discussion of the ways in which we relate to children on various levels, the simplest being the physical space we occupy in relationship to each other. For this activity, choose a partner and have a conversation on a topic of your choice for 3 minutes per person. Take turns standing and sitting during the conversation. First one partner and then the other stands, while the other sits. At the conclusion of the 3 minutes, discuss the following: What was your experience as the person sitting? What about as the person standing? What dynamics did you notice during the conversation? Who led the conversation? How does this activity relate a better understanding of meeting children at their level?

Was there physical discomfort at the need to look up at a standing partner? Often, the sitter takes on a passive role in the conversation, while the person in the standing position generally takes a lead role in directing the conversation. Engaging in this activity and discussion allows us to begin thinking about the ways in which adults typically interact physically with children and how this might then impact the relationship-building process with child clients. Setting the tone at the outset of the relationship that the counselor is working to be a partner on for the child's therapeutic journey will engage the child in ways that are appropriate and comfortable for the child. The counselor acknowledges, by getting on a child's level physically, that this is a reciprocal relationship ruled by fairness and respect for the child in all ways.

RELATING TO THE WORLD OF ADOLESCENTS

Adolescents also have distinct rules, values, beliefs, and norms that are reflective of their development (Martin, 2003; Roaten, 2011). Their worldview, often a mixture of both the cultures of childhood and adulthood, causes some confusion for them and others, as they are at times childlike and dependent on others and other times, mature and insightful. In working with adolescents, as counselors, we are again faced with the need to honor their unique perceptions of the world and respect their opinions and views (Fitzpatrick & Irannejad, 2008; Roaten, 2011). A primary task of adolescence is learning to adapt to novel situations and meet new expectations and challenges, while also dealing with peer pressure, self-doubt, and conflicts of interest between peer groups and family systems (Skudrzyk et al., 2009). These various demands can cause adolescents to feel overwhelmed with the nuances of relationships and the personal choices they face each day. In navigating these demands, they may "experience disequilibrium as they strive to establish some sense of independence while also remaining close to their family roots" (Skudrzyk et al., 2009, p. 251).

Another critical task faced during adolescence is the development of identity, which means that counselors cannot treat this group as they would adults (Roaten, 2011) but rather must find treatment strategies that allow for these cognitive and emotional tasks. Treatment strategies that honor the adolescent experience are critical to building successful relationships and facilitating growth. Adolescents must feel a sense of safety and belonging to participate in counseling (Eyrich-Garg, 2008; Roaten, 2011). The counselor must work to engage adolescent clients through the creation of a strong therapeutic alliance and empathetic relationship (Fitzpatrick, & Irannejad, 2008; Martin, Garsky, & Davis, 2000; Roaten, 2011). Additionally, research has shown that experiential methods for relationship building are of great value in working with adolescents as "experiential input is critical to the development of both executive function and social cognition" (Blakemore & Choudhury, 2006; Roaten, 2011, p. 299). That is, providing a safe and creative space for adolescents helps them to develop self-regulation and social competencies.

As counselors, many times, we have experienced firsthand how challenging it can be to form a strong working alliance with adolescent clients. We also meet many beginning counselors that seem to believe that teens will reflexively trust them, be honest with them, and confide their deepest worries and fears to them. When this does not happen, beginning counselors can be perplexed, even though it is simply a matter of helping the young client to see that the counselor can be trusted with their deepest worries and fears. Imagine yourself as an adolescent, how likely would you have been to disclose to someone whom you did not know, whether a school counselor, mental health counselor, or a family counselor? In Case Illustration 4.2, we tell a story about how a counselor developed rapport with an adolescent who was shutting others out.

Case Illustration 4.2

Creating a strong working relationship with teens often takes a lot of care and time. In working with a teen boy who had been referred for cutting and suspected drug use, the counselor worked diligently for weeks just to assure the client that his opinions and the details of his personal story would be respected. His one-word responses were met with a smile and a nod, and a simple response, "You're not ready to talk about that." A few jokes were shared. A connection was made when the teen boy wore a favorite t-shirt to session. These assurances needed to come before the client felt safe enough to share the wounded parts of himself and required patience, unconditional regard, humor, honesty, and communication of a genuine liking of the client. Providing these essential conditions created an environment that allowed the client to display, in his perception, the worst parts of himself without the need for his typical tough-guy facade. In our work with adults, engaging clients in this way is seen as essential. Building an alliance with teens requires not only the usual skills but also a deeper understanding of the perceptions, needs, fears, and longings that are more specific to the world of the adolescent.

Guided Exercise 4.3

Reflection Activity: Understanding the World Through Adolescent Eyes. A complaint we often hear from adolescents in our work is "no one gets me" or "no one understands me." The idea of establishing an identity and having others value and accept them seems to be paramount to the lives of adolescents. As counselors, our role is to understand, value, and find meaning in the ways in which adolescents carry themselves in the world as well as determine how they can better communicate and interact successfully in that world.

Participate in the following intervention. Collages are helpful for exploring issues related to identity. Create a picture collage of all things meaningful and impactful in your life. Using your cell phone camera or a regular camera, take pictures during 1 week of anything that brings you meaning, frustration, joy, hurt, interest, and so on. Then, create a hard copy or digital collage, and share your work with peers, along with any related background information that feels important. In small debriefing groups, talk about your collage. This small group activity will also help you and your classmates to better practice facilitative listening skills with each other while sharing the collage. This activity can then be processed with the entire class, with students relating their own experiences and how they might mirror the experiences of adolescent clients. Discuss the ways in which this activity might be structured for use with clients of various ages or with specific presenting concerns. This activity, when used in a therapeutic setting, provides an element of fun and a level of interest and investment from the adolescent rather than traditional methods of collecting personal and background information. The counselor and client then also have a visual documentary of the presenting issue (usually), client strengths, interests, struggles, and support systems.

RELATING TO CHILDREN AND ADOLESCENTS: "WHAT WORKS"

Most theoretical orientations to counseling children are based on the importance of a therapeutic alliance, an understanding that successful outcomes are dependent upon the counselor's ability to connect to the child's experience and to build rapport (Landreth, 2012; Halstead, Pehrsson, & Mullen, 2011). In fact, research studies suggest that the therapeutic alliance is instrumental in change, no matter which technique or treatment the counselor uses (Shirk & Karver, 2011). Counseling children requires that counselors honor children's experiences, perceptions, and realities as they are presented (Pereira & Smith-Adcock, 2013; Ray, 2011), which allows us a glimpse into their inner worlds and to assist them in making lasting change.

In addition, with the current emphasis on evidence-based practices in counseling (Carey & Dimmitt, 2008), many counselors are persuaded to use brief and directive approaches and to overlook the essentials of a therapeutic alliance. What works in counseling children and adolescents is a balanced approach, one that relies both on the primacy of the counseling relationship as well as emerging science on interventions that work. More information about evidence-based practices for children and adolescents is provided at the end of this chapter and throughout this text. However, a comprehensive resource for counseling practitioners is provided by the Society of Clinical Child and Adolescent Psychology (SCCAP), a division of the American Psychological Association (APA), at http://effectivechildtherapy.org/content/ebp-options-specific-disorders.

Throughout this chapter thus far, we have emphasized the importance of relating to children and adolescents "as they are." Working with diverse children and teens requires that counselors respond to them in ways that respects their uniqueness and strengths. This work, then, can require a paradigm shift for many counselors: a shift in attitudes away from guiding and advising young clients toward a belief that they are self-directing and capable of making decisions (Landreth, 2012; Pereira & Smith-Adcock, 2013). Making this shift can be difficult, as much of the preparation we receive as counselors is focused on counseling adults (Van Velsor, 2004). We enthusiastically agree with Van Velsor (2004) who concluded, "It is then the counselor's responsibility to become fluent in children's 'language' whether they communicate in words or actions. What may be most critical, however, is for counselors to value the special qualities that children bring to counseling and to respond to each child client as a unique individual (p. 317)."

FOCUS ON THE CHILD, NOT THE PROBLEM

Young people often come to the attention of counseling professionals because their symptoms are problematic for the grown-ups in their lives. This means that treatment for children and adolescents might not only be problem-focused, but moreover, can be focused on someone else's view of the problem. For example, when a teacher brings a child to the school counselor, the presenting problem might be expressed as "Ryan is always shoving other children at recess." Focusing specifically on this problem, the counselor might quickly go to task helping the child empathize with the other children, which could be helpful or harmful, depending on what really happened from Ryan's perspective. Commonly, children are asked a variation on these queries: "What were you thinking? or Why did you do that?" which are both leading and evaluative questions. These missteps can lead to misguided or maybe even harmful interventions unless the counselor gives the child an opportunity to share his or her own perceptions of the problem. When we take time to talk to children or consider the context in which the behavior occurs to really understand what is happening, we often discover a new perspective on the problem. Ryan might be feeling lonely, or he might have been on the receiving end of days of bullying behaviors before he finally said, "Leave me alone," and shoved away the other child.

Garry Landreth (2012) has stated, "When you focus on the problem, you miss the child." Regardless of their setting, counselors are often expected to focus on their client's problematic or maladaptive behaviors (Halstead et al., 2011). Though this is a necessary part of our work, when we do this, we can become focused on the child's problem rather than his or her strengths and capabilities. If we unintentionally overlook the child's experiences, we run the risk of invalidating his or her point of view, misdiagnosing the presenting problem, and ultimately underestimating the child's ability to be an active participant in his or her own treatment. While focusing on the problem can be a necessary cornerstone of therapeutic work, helping to alleviate symptoms, create goals, and measure change, as counselors, we also want to be cautious about accepting the behaviors we see on the surface or that are reported to us by others, as this could cause us to miss the child and fail to meet his or her needs.

RELATING THE CHILD'S VIEW TO OTHERS

One way we understand our role as counselors who work with young people is that of *translator*. This metaphor can guide our thinking about the therapeutic relationship we create with young people. Counselors are uniquely positioned to help interpret both the worldviews of young people and that of adults and transmit the information between the groups in a way that allows for understanding and relationship building. Counselors need to engage in interpersonal interactions that not only meet young clients where they are, but also, aid the significant adults in their lives to do the same.

For example, one of the authors recently worked with a 15-year-old adolescent girl, who was struggling to deal with a recent relationship breakup. The girl wanted her emotions to be understood and validated by her parents, and when her parents did not respond in the way she hoped, it caused discord in their relationship. The client's parents, unknowingly, were communicating to their daughter that the breakup was not a big deal and that her emotional reaction was an overreaction. When her parents said, "You'll get over it; you're only 15, and these relationships aren't serious," their daughter heard something like, "Your feelings are not serious, and you should get over it." Though the parents meant to be helpful, their advice was not well received. The girl's counselor worked to validate her feelings of loss and hurt while also working with the parents to understand that her relationship experiences were wonderful opportunities to teach their daughter about self-esteem, self-respect, and to honor her emotions and ways to work through difficult situations.

When we are working with a child who is verbally and physically aggressive, we often hear from his or her caregivers how frustrated they feel and how taxing it can be to spend time with their child. During these conversations, we want to work to give them a new perspective on the child and his or her behaviors. We often assist caregivers in understanding that all behaviors are ways the child has developed to meet a need. When children act out in an angry or aggressive manner, there is often an underlying fear or anxiety. This fear could be related to the children feeling detached from their caregivers, anxious about their roles or places in their families, it could be a response to stressful events happening in the environment, or it could be due to a lack of a sense of safety or autonomy. Understanding how we see children in counseling and reframing their behaviors to caregivers can help caregivers cope with feelings of frustration and increase empathy and understanding. In a later section, we explore the technique of *assigning positive intent* to help with this.

Another way we help parents and teachers is assigning them the task of noticing "firsts" (Landreth, 2012). Counselors are alert for any small changes made by clients (e.g., an increase in self-confidence, setting new goals). Similarly, we ask caregivers to pay close attention to signs of change. We do this by informing parents and caregivers of changes to look for in their everyday lives, in a general way that does not break the child's confidentiality. The caregiver then attentively watches and listens for firsts or the first glimpse of change they see. For example, a parent can look for the first time a child responds with feeling words instead of having a tantrum or the first time a teen listens to the parent's opinion first and then shares his or her own. Teachers might pay attention to and reinforce the first time the child uses a new coping technique learned in counseling (e.g., using a refocusing strategy in class). The caregiver and counselor can then collaborate on documenting and reinforcing the child's progress.

USING THERAPEUTIC RESPONSES

Counseling diverse children and adolescents successfully depends on the counselors' ability to use developmentally appropriate interpersonal skills. Counselors must be able to communicate empathy, genuine regard, respect, reflective listening skills, questioning and challenging, insight, boundaries, and limit setting (or choice giving) (Ray, 2011) in a manner that is easily understood by young clients.

Recognizing Feelings

Young people often lack the verbal ability to articulate their inner worlds (Landreth, 2012). While young clients experience a wide range of emotions, they may struggle to communicate them. Therefore, a challenge emerges in counseling to sufficiently understand children's perceptual worlds and to provide information back to the children at a cognitive and emotional level that is accessible to them. As counselors, we learn to use tone, inflection, body language, facial expressions, and verbal expression to make reflective statements to a child. Communicating feelings with children, or adolescents, who have limited vocabulary or emotional expression means we have to communicate in a language they can understand.

In the next activity, we teach counselors to translate more sophisticated (adult-level) emotional vocabulary into reflective statements that can be made to child clients. This activity is adapted from the work of Dr. Jodi Mullen and colleagues (Mullen & Rickli, 2013).

Guided Exercise 4.4

The purpose of the activity is to allow the reader to gain a better understanding of how to engage in active listening with children to provide empathy, understanding, and insight for both child and counselor. Get into teams and translate each of the following emotion words into reflective statements appropriate for children. Here is an example to get started: How do you convey the emotion word, *excited* to a child? When working with children, reflections can be both verbal and nonverbal statements of understanding and emotion. Examples of excited could be "WOW!," "WooHoo!," or "YES!" (with a fist pumped in the air), with an additive reflection being "WOW! WooHoo, you're SO excited about that!" This developmentally appropriate language and action provides validation and understanding of the child's expressed emotion as well as an opportunity to teach the emotion word. By conveying the feeling in ways that children can understand paired with the emotional label, the child can assimilate the word into their emotional vocabulary, providing them with additional ways to communicate the feeling. Examples of some of the words provided are listed below:

1. Frustration
2. Enthusiastic
3. Courageous
4. Determined

(Continued)

(Continued)

5. Cooperative	16. Apprehensive
6. Daring	17. Gratified
7. Insecure	18. Malicious
8. Vulnerable	19. Unpopular
9. Frail	20. Overwhelmed
10. Defective	21. Embarrassed
11. Annoyed	22. Competent
12. Obstinate	23. Satisfied
13. Vindictive	24. Bored
14. Lonesome	25. Suspicious
15. Helpless	

Adults, sometimes even their counselors, seem to have a tendency to want to instruct or advise teens on numerous life issues. As counselors, we want to empathize rather than advising them or providing advice in the *guise* of reflection. Therefore, in the following guided exercise, we ask you to revise common advising statements into accurate and empathetic reflective statements. Using empathetic responses allows the child to discover his or her inner strength and resilience. Guided exercise 4.6 provides some practice in empathizing instead of advising.

Guided Exercise 4.5

Begin this activity by thinking about some of the statements that we make to children or adolescents every day that are evaluative or advising. For example, how often do you hear a grown-up say to a child, "Life is sometimes unfair." What does this statement really communicate to the child or adolescent? What actions or emotions displayed by the child would lead adults to make this or similar statements? Our hearts, as adults, are usually in the right place. We make these statements to help youngsters.

The following statements are some common things that adults say to children. For each of the following, write an alternative response that is more reflective of the child's experience (samples are provided). The following are examples with possible alternative reflections:

1. Don't worry = You're very worried about how this will go
2. Everything will be all right = You're afraid that things just won't be ok
3. It's not a big deal = This feels like a really big deal to you, and you're nervous about what will happen
4. You can't win them all = You are feeling disappointed and sad that you didn't do well
5. It could be worse = Right now you just can't imagine that anything could be worse than this; you're very angry
6. It's for your own good = You feel so mad when people make choices for you! You just want to be able to make some choices for yourself!
7. Sometimes life just isn't fair, and you have to deal with that = Ugh, life feels so unfair right now, and you're so upset about that!

Questions

In her famous book *Dibs: In Search of Self*, Virginia Axline (1967) writes, "Asking questions in therapy would be so helpful if anyone ever answered them accurately. But no one ever does" (p. 120). Like Axline, many counselors consider how questions are used in counseling and believe questions can actually hinder the relationship-building process and the counseling process (Landreth, 2012). Questions tend to direct the therapeutic process away from the child's agenda to what the counselor believes is important and focuses the child on thoughts rather than on his or her feelings (Sweeney & Homeyer, 1999). However, questions can also be helpful when they are used intentionally (e.g., examining thoughts about a situation). We caution counselors to be careful in their use of questions. Questions can create a situation where the client feels he or she is required to answer, often fostering feelings of defensiveness. When questions are meaningful and creative, children will respond more openly. Consider the following two interactions between a school counselor and a student:

Interaction One:

Counselor: Joey, who pushed Margie off the swing?

Joey: I don't know.

Counselor: Well, she said you hurt her, and she feels sad. What do you think you should do about that?

Joey: I don't know. Say I'm sorry?

Interaction Two:

> Counselor: Joey, Margie got hurt. What happened? How did Margie get hurt?
>
> Joey: I wanted the swing next, and she wouldn't get off.
>
> Counselor: So you and Margie both wanted the swing?
>
> Joey: Yes. And it was my turn so I got mad.

What is different about these two exchanges? Which question(s) puts Joey more on the defensive? Why?

With younger children, creative ways to elicit responses to questions include using puppets to answer incomplete sentences (e.g., "I am happiest when _____, Mommy is _____, my biggest problem is _____" (Knell & Beck, 2000) or projective questions like "If you had three wishes, what would you wish for?" (Webb, 1996). Use of expressive media and projective techniques increases psychological comfort and decreases defensiveness for child clients (Knell & Beck, 2000). When puppets speak for the child or the counselor, most children become amused, comfortable, and more open to revealing their inner world.

Similarly, in working with adolescents, it is most helpful to avoid a question-and-answer approach because adolescents frequently enter counseling already on the defensive and looking for empathy and understanding. Consider the following two interactions between an adolescent and her mental health counselor.

Interaction One:

> Mandy: I told you I don't drink! I don't care what my mom said.
>
> Counselor: So why did your mom find an empty beer can in your car?
>
> Mandy: It wasn't mine.

Interaction Two:

> Mandy: I told you I don't drink! I don't care what my mom said.
>
> Counselor: It's important for you to set the story straight. What is it you want to clear up about this situation?

Limits and Boundary Setting

In working with children and adolescents, although it is crucial to allow them the ability to make decisions, setting appropriate limits is also an important skill. Providing a list of rules up front can be off-putting and can get in the way of building the relationship. We agree with Garry Landreth (2012) that limits are not needed until they are needed. Setting limits as they are needed allows for exploration, therapeutic limit testing, and an opportunity to have meaningful conversations about choices and lifestyle with clients (Landreth, 2012). In his seminal work, *The Art of the Relationship*, Landreth (2012) outlines a limit-setting approach called the ACT model. Though you will read about how the ACT approach to limit-setting is used in play therapy in later chapters, we find it a useful way to set limits across settings and age groups. Counselors, teachers, and parents can use this simple model to establish healthy boundaries. The ACT model can also be taught to young people to help them communicate limits to others. The steps are as follows:

1. *Acknowledge the feeling.* Let the child or teen know that you see what he or she wants. Examples include the following: "I know you really want to run real fast right now." "I see that you are angry and want to throw that." For older children or adolescents, this can be modified. An example is "You really want your space right now." Reflecting feelings is important sometimes, too. "You're feeling so frustrated, you really want to call her bad names."

2. *Communicate the limit. State the limit.* Usually, these are limits set for reality or safety as we discussed earlier. Examples include the following: "Remember that running is not something you can do in here. You must be safe." Or, "But I am not for hitting." For older youth, consider the following: "But you have to stay in the room with me right now." Or, "remember that calling names is not something you can do."

3. *Target alternative.* When you set a limit, set an alternative choice. Examples include the following: "You can jump on the trampoline instead." Or, "We can take a walk instead." For a child who is threatening to hit you (or another child), you can offer the alternative "What you can do is hit this beanbag chair." For the older child, specifying an alternative or a choice such as "You can choose to talk or not talk in here." Or, "You can sit over there and rest, or you can put your head down right here." Using choice language means the counselor is always making space for the clients to feel that they have some autonomy in their lives. It models decision making and dealing with the consequences of those decisions. It also provides the counselor with opportunities to help clients understand the deeper or far-reaching impacts of their choices. When we provide clients with choices we provide them with opportunities to build competence, self-confidence, and responsibility (Bailey, 2000; Pereira & Smith-Adcock, 2011).

Limit setting can be one of the more difficult skills to master, causing discomfort and concern that setting limits will compromise the counselor client relationship (Smith-Adcock, Pereira, & Shin, 2015). Limits should be reality and safety-based. Therefore, the authors generally have the following specific limits: clients cannot throw things that might break, purposely break or damage materials, or shout derogatory things at people outside the room; private parts will never be shown or touched; nor will either the counselor or client engage in aggressive behavior toward the other. These limits are reality and safety based for the protection of client and counselor. Most of the other situations that arise are used as moments for the clients to learn about themselves and how they would like to handle themselves in their environment. For example, letting go of anger in a way that is not hurtful to others (e.g., throwing punches at a soft pillow) is an appropriate expression of feelings within the safety of the counseling setting. Young people should not feel as if they need to suppress difficult feelings so as not to offend their counselor.

With young children, we say, "Your words are safe in here." For adolescents, we might say, "This is a safe place where you can share your thoughts and feelings freely." For many counselors, especially those in schools where there is a set of institutional rules to be followed, this may be a difficult concept to work though. Sometimes counselors feel it is inappropriate to allow clients to use foul language in session. However, many children come to counseling with different ideas about what constitutes inappropriate language. Unfortunately, for some children, what someone else might consider a "bad" word can be the anatomical name for their private parts, and they have been warned not to talk about what happens to their private parts. Bad words can also be anything that is negative regarding a parent or caregiver, the names they have been called in school, or the names they have heard during a domestic violence altercation. Sometimes bad words are all the names the child would like to call someone who has hurt them deeply. These stories need to be told and heard for the client to heal, and we maintain that it is not our place to tell a young person how they should tell their story. By doing so, counselors risk overlooking the child's basic emotional needs. Challenge yourself to acknowledge your own comfort level with certain topics and the words associated with them. Make sure when you choose to set limits with a child, it is for the child and not your own preference or comfort.

In Case Illustration 4.3, we share a humorous story about how a young client understood the statement, "And, you can say anything in here."

Notice that the counselor's and the child's perceptions of what word is considered to be a bad word can be quite different. Although this is a humorous example,

---

Case Illustration 4.3

A session with a 4-year-old boy began in my typical fashion by running through my standard session opening, which ends with "and you can say anything in this room!" The exchange between us went as follows:

Client: (incredulously) "What? I can say anything? Even the F-word?"

Pereira: "Hmm, it seems really weird to you that a grown-up is telling you that you can say anything in here."

Client: "I really want to say the F-word; you're sure I can say it?"

Pereira: "You're still not sure about this, you're wondering if you'll get in trouble. This is a special room. You decide what to say in here."

Client: "Okay! Woohoo! Fart!"

---

it illustrates the need for the counselor to be open to client perceptions of the world and for children to be able to express themselves in the ways that best convey the thoughts and emotions they are struggling with. This may be particularly important for teens, who often feel that they are not able to express themselves in ways that are truly heard by others.

Assigning Positive Intent

When counselors respond to children's behaviors by assigning positive intent, they have the opportunity to create interactions that shape children's understanding of themselves as well as how others see them (Pereira & Smith-Adcock, 2011). Often, we assign negative intent to clients' behavior. For example, when working with a client who engages in bullying behavior or acts in ways that offend us, we tend to see the behavior as maladaptive and problematic and assign a negative intent: The child is using coercive power to intimidate others. To assign positive intent, we might reframe his behavior as intent to show us his insecurity and fear of rejection, so he communicates with his actions that he does not care about others. By seeing the client's behavior as a communication of his need to be accepted, the counselor is better able to respond in supportive ways. For example, the counselor can express that an offensive or rude manner of speaking to the counselor is letting her know that the client may feel worried about whether or not she will truly like him and want to help him. When we are able to reframe the client's behavior as meeting a need or asking for help, we are better able to act with compassion and support versus irritation and reprimand (Pereira & Smith-Adcock, 2011).

Assigning positive intent can also be used with caregivers (i.e., parents, teachers, foster parents, etc.) to respond constructively to young people's behaviors (Bailey, 2000). Consider the young child who is acting out at home. Tired and grumpy after a long day at school, the child responds to his mother with grunts and groans when confronted about homework. Exasperated, his mom communicates to a school counselor that arguments about homework are taking their toll on everyone. By assigning positive intent, the counselor helps the parent to problem solve. Instead of suggesting that the child is engaging in a power struggle over homework, the school counselor talks to the child's mother about what her son is trying to communicate to her. Together, they go over the events of the day and discuss the child's positive intent. After a long day away from his family, perhaps he is communicating that he needs some contact with his parent and some downtime.

One of the best ways to ensure longer lasting changes in children's lives is to work closely with parents, teachers, and others who are in the young person's life every day. To do so, we need to confidently navigate the concerns, frustrations, and fears of caregivers and validate their perspective, while also helping them to respond to their children or students in assertive but positive ways. To do this, counselors may provide parents or teachers with information on reflective listening, appropriate and positive limit setting, and assigning positive intent to behaviors.

CONCLUSION

Working with diverse children and teens can feel like a daunting task for counselors. One primary reason for this is that many counselors enter the field with little to no specific training to work with either population. Working with young clients may require a shift in beliefs and attitudes on the part of the counselor, as well as knowledge of child development and how young clients process and perceive the world around them. All of these components are important to successful counseling and are built on the foundation of a therapeutic alliance. The counselor also should examine his or her core beliefs about working with children and adolescents, and engage in personal and professional development to ensure he or she is meeting the clients where they are. It is the love we share and the respect we show that helps our young clients experience themselves as fully capable and to trust others to help them.

COUNSELING KEYSTONES

- Children and adolescents can be considered their own distinct cultural groups, with their own rules, norms, values, and perceptions.

- To work with children and adolescents successfully, we must understand that their reality, perceptions, and worldview are different from that of adults.
- When building a therapeutic alliance, it is important to meet child clients where they are cognitively, developmentally, emotionally, and physically.
- A problem focus can cause us to overlook the child's perception of the issue and focus instead on reports from caregivers, ultimately underestimating the child's ability to be an active participant in his or her own treatment.
- Relationship building requires counselors to use therapeutic responses that meet children at their developmental level.
- Teaching therapeutic skills to caregivers in the young person's life (e.g., teachers and parents) may lead to better long-term outcomes.

ADDITIONAL RESOURCES

In Print

Chesley, G. L., Gillett, D. A., & Wagner, W. G. (2008). Verbal and nonverbal metaphor with children in counseling. *Journal of Counseling & Development*, *86*(4), 399–411.

Jones, R. M., Vaterlaus, J. M., Jackson, M. A., & Morrill, T. B. (2014). Friendship characteristics, psychosocial development, and adolescent identity formation. *Personal Relationships*, *21*(1), 51–67. doi:10.1111/pere.12017

Siegel, D. J., & Bryson, T. P. (2011). *The whole-brain child: 12 revolutionary strategies to nurture your child's developing mind, survive everyday parenting struggles, and help your family thrive*. New York, NY: Delacorte Press.

Spies Shapiro, L., & Margolin, G. (2014). Growing up wired: Social networking sites and adolescent psychosocial development. *Clinical Child & Family Psychology Review*, *17*(1), 1–18. doi:10.1007/s10567-013-0135-1

Lin, Y., & Bratton, S. C. (2015). A meta-analytic review of child-centered play therapy approaches. *Journal of Counseling & Development*, *93*(1), 45–58. doi:10.1002/j.1556-6676.2015.00180.x

Online

American Counseling Association: http://www.counseling.org
American School Counselor Association: http://www.schoolcounselor.org
Association for Play Therapy: http://www.a4pt.org
The National Center for Traumatic Stress Network: http://www.nctsn.org
The National Child Traumatic Stress Network (NCTSN)—Empirically Supported Treatments and Promising Practices: http://www.nctsn.org/resources/topics/treatments-that-work/promising-practices

REFERENCES

Axline, V. M. (1967). *Dibs in search of self.* New York, NY: Ballantine Books.

Axline, V. M. (1969). *Play therapy.* New York, NY: Ballantine Books.

Bailey, B. A. (2000). *Conscious discipline.* Oviedo, FL: Loving Guidance.

Blakemore, S. J., & Choudhury, S. (2006). Development of the adolescent brain: Implications for executive function and social cognition. *Journal of Child Psychology and Psychiatry, 47*, 296–312. doi:10.1111/j.1469-7610.2006.01611.x

Carey, J., & Dimmitt, C. (2008). A model for evidence-based elementary school counseling: Using school data, research, and evaluation to enhance practice. *Elementary School Journal, 108*(5), 422–430.

Eyrich-Garg, K. M. (2008). Strategies for engaging adolescent girls at an emergency shelter in a therapeutic relationship: Recommendations from the girls themselves. *Journal of Social Work, 22*, 375–388. doi:10.1080/02650530802396700

Fitzpatrick, M. R., & Irannejad, S. (2008). Adolescent readiness for change and the working alliance in counseling. *Journal of Counseling & Development, 86*(4), 438–445.

Halstead, R., Pehrsson, D., & Mullen, J. (2011). *Counseling children: A core issues approach.* Alexandria, VA: American Counseling Association.

Jordan, J. V. (2012). *Relational-cultural therapy.* Washington, DC: American Psychological Association.

Knell, S. M., & Beck, K. W. (2000). The puppet incomplete sentence completion task. In K. Gitlin-Weiner, A. Sandgrund, & C. Shaefer (Eds.), *Play diagnosis and assessment* (2nd ed.). New York. NY: John Wiley & Sons.

Landreth, G. L. (2012). *Play therapy: The art of the relationship.* New York, NY: Routledge, Taylor & Francis Group.

Martin, D. G. (2003). *Clinical practice with adolescents.* Pacific Grove, CA: Brooks Cole–Thomson Learning.

Martin, D. G., Garske, J. P., & Davis, M. K. (2000). Relation of the therapeutic alliance with outcome and other variables: A meta-analysis review. *Journal of Consulting and Clinical Psychology, 68*, 438–450.

Mullen, J. A., & Rickli, J. M. (2013). *Child-centered play therapy workbook: A self-directed guide for professionals.* Champaign, IL: Research Press.

Pereira, J. K., & Smith-Adcock, S. (2011). Child-centered classroom management. *Action in Teacher Education, 33*, 254–264. doi:10.1080/01626620.2011.592111

Pereira, J. K., & Smith-Adcock, S. (2013). The effects of a training on school counselor trainee's attitudes, knowledge, and skills, and self-estimate of ability. *International Journal of Play Therapy, 22*(3), 129–142.

Ray, D. (2011). *Advanced play therapy: Essential conditions, knowledge, and skills for child practice.* New York, NY: Routledge.

Roaten, G. K. (2011). Innovative and brain-friendly strategies for building a therapeutic alliance with adolescents. *Journal of Creativity In Mental Health, 6*(4), 298–314. doi:10.1080/15401383.2011.630306

Shirk, S. R., & Karver, M. S. (2011). Alliance in child and adolescent psychotherapy. In J. C. Norcross (Ed.), *Psychotherapy relationships that work: Evidence-based responsiveness* (2nd ed., pp. 70–91). New York, NY: Oxford University Press.

Skudrzyk, B., Zera, D. A., McMahon, G., Schmidt, R., Boyne, J., & Spannaus, R. L. (2009). Learning to relate: Interweaving creative approaches in group counseling with adolescents. *Journal of Creativity in Mental Health, 4*(3), 249–261. doi:10.1080/15401380903192762

Smith-Adcock, S., Pereira, J. L., & Shin. S. M. (2015). Critical incidents in learning child-centered play therapy: Implications for teaching and supervision. *International Journal of Play Therapy, 24*(2), 78–91.

Sweeney, D. S., & Homeyer, L. E. (Eds.). (1999). *The handbook of group play therapy: How to do it, how it works, whom it's best for.* San Francisco, CA: Jossey-Bass.

Tucker, C., Smith-Adcock S., & Trepal, H. (2011). Relational-cultural theory for middle school counselors. *Professional School Counseling 5*(14), 310–316.

Van Velsor, P. (2004). Revisiting basic counseling skills with children. *Journal of Counseling and Development*, 82, 313–318.

Webb, N. (1996). *Social work practice with children.* New York, NY: Guilford Press.

Section II

Chapter 5

Psychodynamic Theories

CATHERINE TUCKER AND ELAINE WITTMAN

I was always looking outside myself for strength and confidence,
but it comes from within. It is there all the time.

—Anna Freud

INTRODUCTION

Although the psychodynamic theories have fallen out of favor since the introduction of quicker, less complex approaches like cognitive behavior therapy (CBT) and brief therapies, new research in brain science is causing many therapists and professors to take a new look at these older ways of conducting therapy. An article in the annual health issue of the *New York Times Magazine* (June 28, 2015), titled "Tell It About Your Mother: Can Brain Scanning Save Freudian Psychoanalysis?" shows a white-haired analyst sitting in front of an MRI machine, ready to take notes. Freudian analysts are talking about merging new findings about how the brain and body work to process information with theories first written down by Sigmund Freud in the early 1900s. If successful, the merger of new science and older theories may well usher in a new period of interest in new models of psychodynamic analysis. In this chapter, we examine the origins and ideas behind these theories and how they are used with children and adolescents. Where relevant, we have added in new findings from science that support the ideas from these early theorists.

These chapters on theories of counseling children and adolescents are intended to enrich your knowledge of theories, not to replace a basic theories course or text. Our exploration of theory in this text highlights how theories designed for adults have been adapted for use with younger clients. Before attempting to use any of the theories discussed in this book, the reader needs to carefully read and study original source texts and locate appropriate supervision.

SOCIOHISTORICAL CONTEXT

The world of the early psychiatrists, during the period from about 1880 until about 1910, was quickly changing from rural societies not much changed from ancient times to one of rapidly growing cities needing thousands of employees for new industrial, machine-driven manufacturing plants. Cities were experiencing rapid growth as workers moved in from the countryside to take jobs in the new factories. In Europe, monarchies were being challenged by republican, socialist, and communist workers-rights groups, which was causing great instability and sometimes riots and revolutions (Kidner, Bucur, Mathieson, McKee, & Weeks, 2013).

In the United States, the rights of workers, women, and former slaves were all being challenged. The country was still recovering from the deprivations and horrors of the Civil War and was working hard to rebuild cities and farms (Hakim, 1999). Universities had lost many students and faculty members to the war and were struggling to regain stability, perhaps slowing scientific innovation during the immediate postwar years. The rights of women, children, and ethnic/racial minorities still lagged far behind those of White men but did make significant gains during this period (Heywood, 2001).

As psychiatrists and neurologists began to more effectively apply the scientific method to their work with the adult mentally ill, much was learned about the course of mental illness in adults and how it might best be treated. Sigmund Freud, who trained as a neurologist, spent 5 months learning from Jean-Martin Charcot and Pierre Janet at the famous Salpetriere asylum in Paris (Berrios & Porter, 1995). (*n.b., All comments about sociohistorical context are limited to North American and Europe. This is not due to a lack of important events in the rest of the world but because the psychodynamic orientations we are describing in this chapter were born in the West.*)

It was during this time that Freud was introduced to the idea that uncovering unconscious material in the patient's memory could help the adult patient recover from his or her symptoms. It is possible that the notion of "partial insanity," (Appingnanesi, 2008, p. 65) meaning that madness can be cured, was the greatest mental health innovation of the era. Prior to the late 19th century, insanity was largely considered to be a permanent and hopeless malady (Grob, 1994).

As the 20th century began, mental illness was reframed from a lifelong, sinful, debilitated state to diseases of the brain and nerves requiring kind, attentive care

(Berrios & Porter, 1995). Another nominee for the most important innovation of this era is the creation of theories to guide the treatment of the mentally ill. Although the earliest counseling theories were not applied to children until long after adult treatments were first specified, the treatment of children and adolescents later benefitted from the genesis of these theories. Precisely what ingredients this care should consist of in order to most effectively treat mental illness is a debate that continues to this day.

While adults were making great strides in terms of human rights during this period, children remained largely at the mercy of their parents. Children as young as five or six often worked alongside adults in factories and on farms, usually for much less pay than adults (Heywood, 2001; Hindman, 2002). The United States did not have a federal child labor law until 1938. Child neglect was first made illegal in the United States in 1825, but the legal system did not mandate state coordination of care for dependent children until 1930 (Myers, 2004). Until the mid to late 20th century, children's mental health care was largely relegated to families, schools, and sometimes orphanages (Heywood, 2001).

In this chapter, we explore these early psychodynamic theories that emerged during the early 20th century, as well as current versions of these approaches as they relate to counseling children and adolescents.

After reading this chapter, you will be able to

- describe the basic principles common to all psychodynamic theories;
- explain how the social and cultural context of the late 19th and early 20th centuries affected the ideas of Freud, Jung, and Adler;
- compare and contrast the major theories included in this chapter; and
- describe at least one specific intervention from each theory outlined in the chapter.

THEORISTS

The various individuals who gave us psychodynamic theories harbored quite an array of beliefs about the nature of human beings, their problems, and how problems should be addressed in therapy. For example, Sigmund Freud was generally regarded as a pessimist who believed that human nature was determined and fixed by early experiences and environment (Wallerstein, 1995). On the other hand, Carl Jung and Alfred Adler saw human nature as malleable into adulthood and heavily influenced by social connections (Adler, 1964; Jung, 1964). What all of the psychodynamic theories do have in common is the belief that people's problems exist at least in part in the un- or subconscious mind (Murdock, 2013).

Freud and the attachment theorists, including John Bowlby and Mary Ainsworth, created theories based largely on the neurobiological understanding of the human brain (Karen, 1998). Attachment and psychoanalytic theorists also share a belief in the power of early experiences to influence behavior throughout the lifespan. While the attachment theorists studied how the trauma of inappropriate caregiving of young children caused later problems in the organization of a child or adult's emotions and actions, psychoanalysts looked to problems in a person's psychosexual development for the causes of neurosis or psychosis. Both groups believe that much of the motivation for a person's behavior is not within his or her conscious awareness and must be carefully uncovered in order to identify the source of the trouble and move past it (Wallerstein, 1995). The methods of reaching and treating these hidden memories and impulses were matters of great debate among the early theorists (Murdock, 2013).

Sigmund Freud, Anna Freud, and Melanie Klein

Although Sigmund Freud only saw perhaps one child for one session of therapy, Little Hans, whose treatment is outlined in his 1909 publication, *Analysis of Phobia in a Five-Year-Old Boy,* his daughter Anna focused her work on the analysis of young clients. Most psychoanalysts in the early 20th century helped child clients primarily by indirect observations of their behavior and consultation with parents (Merydith, 1999). Few, if any, specific techniques for child analysis existed in published writings until at least the late 1920s (Landreth, 1991). Anna Freud greatly expanded her father's ideas on human development and became very interested in how a child's ego develops to control his or her irrational drives (Freud, 1965). Anna Freud pioneered methods of psychoanalysis for use with children, including the use of toys and art media to help children express free associations and dreams (Freud, 1965). She emphasized the crucial nature of the child's relationship to the therapist and believed that without a warm and inviting relationship, therapy with a child could not be successful (Landreth, 1991).

Also working with children in the early 20th century, Melanie Klein developed object relations theory (Klein, 1955). Klein was a Freudian analyst who developed her own theory to explain how children develop the capacity for creating a sense of self. Klein stated that children internalize cognitive templates of caregivers, and that over time, these templates become the blueprints for how the child views relationships with others and develops a sense of who he or she is in relation to these templates (Klein, 1955). This concept is one that has gained support in the 21st century. Studies of memory storage and retrieval show that early attachment relationships build patterns for how to interact in social settings, and that early trauma can cause problems with this crucial process, leading to interpersonal problems across the lifespan (Perry, 2002).

Unlike Anna Freud, Klein did not place strong emphasis on the child-therapist relationship. She used play techniques with children in order to help the child communicate his or her unconscious needs and desires so that the analyst could then interpret the material and facilitate catharsis in the client (Klein, 1955). Klein and Freud believed that the understanding and exploration of unconscious material, especially traumatic memories, was necessary for the client to heal. The use of play was unique to work with children, adults therapy involved free association, dream analysis, and sometimes hypnosis to uncover unconscious material.

More recent innovations in psychoanalytic therapy for children involve using child-directed play in order for the child to express his or her inner conflicts (Esman, 1983). As the child plays, the therapist may make interpretive comments about the meaning of the play. However, the purpose of this interaction is not to achieve what Freud called "abreaction" or an emotional release but rather to assist the child in achieving an understanding of his or her inner conflicts so that he or she might eventually come to a more helpful solution to the conflict (Esman, 1983). An example of this type of play therapy may be found in Case Illustration 5.1.

Case Illustration 5.1

George, age 9, an only child of affluent parents, was brought to therapy for "his lack of respect for authority." According to his mother, George was very destructive at home, often purposefully breaking things and claiming that the damage was accidental. He also often argued with his parents and other adults.

During the first play session, George chose to play with the plastic army figures. He made two lines of soldiers, and for 15 minutes, the two sides rammed into each other and had quite a battle, complete with sound effects. The therapist watched quietly for the first several minutes, weighing various options. She thought it could have been a display of an Oedipal conflict, but it was too early to tell. Instead, the therapist said, "Wow, it looks like those guys are really mad at each other." This comment indicated to George that the therapist was paying close attention to his play and was trying to understand what was going on in the play scene. Although she thought the play scene was probably a reflection of the anger the child felt at being ignored by his too-busy parents, she also knew it was too early to offer this interpretation. Timing is very important in offering interpretations—too early in therapy they might be brushed off or incur a response of "You don't understand!" and too late might miss the moment when change is most possible.

George's response to this statement was, "Yeah, they really hate each other. The green guys are always trying to tell the blue guys what to do." This statement gave the therapist a solid clue about the origin of George's anger and shaped how she responded to the next part of the play scene.

Carl Jung

Carl G. Jung founded depth psychology, or analytical psychology, as a theory of the psyche after a split from Freud (Jung, 1964). While Freud saw the driving force of individuals as psychosexual traumas and repressed disturbances coming from childhood conflicts, Jung understood the origins of personality as coming from a universal, almost spiritual, psychic energy (Jung, 1964). Both Freud and Jung agreed on the concepts of the conscious and unconscious, but Jung included the collective unconscious in which archetypes reside. Jung proposed that archetypes are inherited from the collective memory of all humanity's past. These themes or patterns of energy are imprinted on our psyche, sensations, and feelings and were experienced through our dreams and fantasies (Jung, 1964).

Jung's concept of the child was not that they were blank slates but products of a collective unconscious and many generations of their family's history. According to Jung, children are able to pull from a deep well of shared human experience, even from birth, primarily through dreams, archetypal stories, and other unconscious material. Jung did not work with children specifically but saw problems in childhood as related to the "shadow" of the parents and family, related to this notion of a shared store of unconscious material. The major goal of Jungian therapy is individuation through the integration of the ego and the shadow. Jung saw individuation as a lifelong process and not only development in childhood. Jung was optimistic about children and the potential for growth and wholeness (Jung, 1983). One frequently used technique in Jungian analysis is the creation of a mandala. In Guided Exercise 5.1, experiment with this method with a peer or on your own.

Guided Exercise 5.1

The creation of a mandala is a very flexible project. There are hundreds of premade patterns available in various books and websites. Originally used in Buddhist and Hindu meditation sessions as representations of the cosmos, mandalas are usually drawn as circles to represent wholeness and integration. Within the circle, a square is often drawn, the four corners of which generally represent various forces of the universe or parts of the psyche. The corners of the square usually represent the integration of opposites, such as masculine and feminine, active and passive, or internal and external processes. A center point is drawn to represent the self. Before beginning this drawing, take a few seconds to breathe deeply and relax. You might dim the lights and play some soft music. Eliminate as many distractions as you can. Gather a piece of paper of whatever size and color you like and some colorful pencils, markers, paints, or pastels. In this drawing, use a circle, which encompasses most of your paper, with a square drawn immediately inside it, and create a center (this does not have to be a dot, it can be a smaller drawing). As you create the mandala, try to visualize your inner state in the moment, and transfer that vision to the paper. Don't worry about how good it looks, this is an exercise about process, not products. When you complete the drawing, as Carl Jung did daily from 1916 to 1920, reflect on what the drawing can tell you about your current inner state. Is it an orderly, balanced drawing, or is it chaotic and fractured? Is it bright on one side and dark on the other? What emotions does it elicit from you? If you enjoyed this exercise, consider creating a series of daily mandala drawings to watch your inner processes evolve and change across time. You can see Dr. Jung's drawings in *The Red Book*, a compilation of his private artwork and writing published in 2009.

Adler and Individual Psychology

Adler's theory of human nature and human problems developed directly to work with children rather than having to be adapted (Adler, 1964). Adler held many beliefs that diverged from both Freud and Jung, while still holding to the basic psychodynamic belief that much of the material key to solving problems resides in the sub- or unconscious mind. Adler believed that people are socially embedded creatures whose choices in life are made to reflect their feelings about their own unique contexts and circumstances (Adler, 1979). Family constellation, birth order, and early memories all contribute to a person's sense of self, or lifestyle, and the lifestyle in turn contributes to how a person acts in the world. Adler was very concerned with encouraging clients to become interested in the well-being of others and to take part in community work (Adler, 1964).

Adler also often saw clients with their families, which was a new and revolutionary way of conducting therapy (Adler, 1979). His family therapy model emphasizes encouragement and education of clients so that they may better attend to the basic life goals: love, community, and work (Bitter, 2008). Adler and his colleague, Rudolph Driekurs, developed many techniques suitable for work with children, including building partnerships with schools to provide counseling and consultation services on site (Murdock, 2013). The Adlerian model of counseling remains influential in school counseling today and has informed prevention and academic success programs (Brigman, Villares, & Webb, 2011). In more recent years, Terry Kottman (1995) and others have delineated specific play therapy techniques for use with Adler's theory.

Guided Exercise 5.2

An interesting technique often used with children in Adlerian therapy is the "Typical Day" (Bitter, 2008). When working with adults or older children, the therapist might simply ask, "What is a typical day like for you?" and prompt the client to tell about a typical day in detail, beginning with waking up and ending with falling asleep. With younger children, the therapist might use a dollhouse to facilitate the conversation. Using a dollhouse and people figures, the counselor can ask the same question but add "Show me a typical day using the house and people here." It can be helpful to also have a play school and school bus when using this intervention with young children. To try out this technique, find a peer, a friend, or a child to interview. Using either the play technique or the talking version, ask the person to tell you about a typical day. You might follow up with questions like "What is your favorite part of the day? Least favorite?" or "What one thing would you most want to change in the day you just told me about?" After the interview is complete, reflect on how it felt to ask this question. What kind of information did you learn about the person with whom you spoke? Do you think this assessment might be helpful in your counseling practice? Why, or why not?

Attachment Theories

After World War II, psychiatrist John Bowlby became very interested in the reasons behind the growing problems with juvenile delinquents in London. He began working with young offenders and quickly discovered that almost all of the adolescents in the juvenile justice system had suffered the loss of, or separation from, one or both parents during the war (Bowlby, 1982). This discovery, along with his own personal history with distant, cold parents, sparked Bowlby's curiosity about the mechanisms by which babies emotionally attach to their caregivers and how this attachment process affects later life (Karen, 1998). Unlike Melanie Klein, with whom he studied, Bowlby did not believe that children's misbehavior was related to unconscious material and fantasies but rather related to actual experiences with caregivers and other significant people (Karen, 1998). Over time, Bowlby developed attachment theory, which put forth the idea that much of people's adult behavior is rooted in very early experiences with caregivers. If a child experiences consistent, warm care, he or she generally develops a secure attachment style, which is charac- terized by a pattern of trusting, confident, and emotionally stable behavior. On the other hand, if the child experiences inconsistent, harsh, frightening, or anxious care, he or she will likely form an insecure attachment style.

Mary Ainsworth's research showed that insecure attachment is further broken down into categories: anxious/avoidant, ambivalent/resistant, and disorganized (Ainsworth, Blehar, Waters, & Wall, 1978; Main & Solomon, 1990). The disorganized category was recognized by Mary Main in the late 1980s and represents the most severe and troubled of the insecure categories. It is this most severe form of insecure attachment and is most descriptive of the reactive attachment disorder diagnosis.

Bolstered by the research work of Mary Ainsworth, Harry Harlow, and many others, attachment theory is now based on a large body of scientific inquiry. Recent work using advanced technologies, such as functional MRI scans and cortisol measurements, have supported most of the earlier theoretical work (Schore, 2001). Attachment theorists have primarily focused on identifying healthy and unhealthy attachment styles, the causes of insecure or unhealthy attachment, and factors that may protect children from developing severely insecure patterns. However, only in recent years have therapists and scientists begun to study how to assist children and adults who have insecure attachments in changing their parenting behavior so that they do not pass insecure attachment styles on to their own children (Slade, 2007).

Application and Techniques

Dream Analysis

Carl Jung reported vivid dreams as a child and came to rely on his dreams and fantasies to find solace and solutions to problems (Jung, 1983, 2008). Jung did not work with the dreams of children directly but looked at the childhood memories of dreams reported by adults and the impact of the lingering images from the dreams on their lives. Childhood dreams, according to Jung, originated in depths of the personality and were of the highest importance. Dreams could give hints of what is to come in a lifetime (Jaffe, 1989).

For Jung, dreams came directly from the collective unconscious in symbolic form as messages for the conscious (Jaffe, 1989). The collective unconscious, coming from all of history and nature, is reflected in the stories of myths and fairy tales across cultures. In the spirit of dreams telling the ego what the unconscious already knows, Jung and his students and colleagues used the metaphors of these traditions to interpret the dreams remembered by adults. While the power of the dream's message may not need interpretation (Jung, 2008), Maria Von Franz stated that in looking at these symbolic messages, the ego is able to remember and use the images to influence everyday life. Despite careful examination of a dream, "the meaning of a dream is never exhausted" according to Von Franz (1994).

When working with children or adolescents, the counselor might make the process more concrete by having the client draw, paint, or build the main events of the dream. Dreams may also be acted out in a role play or with puppets or miniatures. Adolescents may also enjoy writing about dreams in a journal they can bring to the session each week.

Jungian Sandplay

Jungian sandplay has roots not only in the prodigious writing and teaching of Jung himself but also in the unlikely source of the science fiction author H. G.Wells (1975). As Wells observed his sons playing with small figures on the floor, he theorized that children's play was meaningful and had purpose, which was a major departure from the general understanding of children's play as frivolous and without deeper meaning. Wells's ideas, combined with the teachings of Carl Jung, influenced several of his contemporaries who were interested in the mental health of children, including Dora Kalff and Margaret Lowenfeld.

Lowenfeld, a child psychiatrist and pediatrician, used small figures in the sand as an assessment tool that she referred to as the "world technique" (Lowenfeld, 1935). This assessment is still used by Jungian sandplay therapists today. Counselors who want to use this technique should seek out in-person training and supervision.

Kalff integrated Jungian psychology and Eastern philosophy to develop a technique known as "sandplay," in which a story could be developed when small figures were placed in a tray of sand (Kalff, 1980). Archetypes from the collective unconscious were revealed as the story developed (Kalff, 1980; Turner, 2005). In this silent process of *temenos*, a "free and protected space," the witness or counselor holds the space for the client toward the goal of the birth of a healthy ego (De Domenico, 1988, personal communication, 2008; Turner, 2005). Individual sandtrays are tracked over time and only then are they verbally interpreted. (Turner, 2005; Amatruda & Helm, 2007).

Adlerian Play Therapy

Play therapy is a large field of inquiry and practice that encompasses many theoretical approaches to working with clients (Schaefer & O'Connor, 1983). Most forms of play therapy share the belief that play is the natural language of children, and that play allows children in counseling to more easily express concerns (Schaefer & O'Connor, 1983). When a play therapist layers the theories of Adlerian or individual psychology onto the basic ideas of play therapy, Adlerian play therapy emerges.

Adler believed strongly that the first task in any counseling or teaching relationship is to establish a sense of mutual respect and understanding (Murdock, 2013). When working with children, Adlerian counselors make an effort to ensure that the child feels that he or she is being heard and understood (Kottman, 1995). This may be accomplished in early sessions with basic reflective listening skills and attention to the details of a child's stories.

Once the therapeutic relationship is established, the Adlerian therapist usually then embarks on an extensive assessment of the child, the family constellation, the child's lifestyle, and the child's motivations for misbehavior (Kelly, 1999). Reasons for misbehavior, or causes of discouragement, are keys to understanding why the client is misbehaving. Adler believed that people behave the way they do, no matter how destructive it may seem, in order to meet their basic needs, and that their behavior reflects their best ideas for achieving those goals at a given time (Adler, 1964). According to Adler, there are four basic goals of misbehavior: attention-seeking, power, revenge, and proving inadequacy (Kottman, 1995).

In play therapy, following the general assessment process with the family, the therapist observes the child's play in order to solidify his or her ideas about which of the four goals the child's misbehavior is striving to meet. Once this is established, the therapist may chose directive techniques or may guide the child's imaginative play to help him or her find ways to better achieve the goal (Kottman, 1995).

Adlerian play therapists may employ a wide range of techniques, including structured games, imaginative play, role plays, creative writing exercises, visual arts techniques, family and sibling sessions, and homework assignments in order to encourage the child to meet his or her goals (Kottman, 1995). Adolescents may be more comfortable with art supplies and more directive activities, while younger children are often happy to express their needs and ideas through play with toys and imaginative play schemes. An example of Adlerian play techniques with a 12-year-old can be found in Case Illustration 5.2.

Case Illustration 5.2

Lindsey is a 12-year-old girl from a middle-class family in a rural area. She is the second of three children who live with their single mother. Lindsey was referred to the school counselor because of her recent misbehavior in class. According to the teacher, Lindsey is often rude to the teacher, refuses to follow directions or turn in work, and acts like she doesn't care when the teacher assigns her extra work or detention for this behavior. The teacher also reports that Lindsey appears to be the "Queen Bee" of a group of sixth grade girls and is often seen being mean to some of the younger or less attractive girls in the group.

During the first two sessions with Lindsey, and a call to her mother, the school counselor gathers information about Lindsey and her family. It appears that Lindsey is attempting to gain power by misbehaving in class and at home. Her mother reported that this behavior got much worse after her grandfather was diagnosed with cancer last year. Although he is doing well, Lindsey appears to be taking out her feelings of frustration and powerlessness in the face of his illness on authority figures she encounters.

One of the strategies the counselor plans to use with Lindsey to help her find ways to express her need for power constructively is to allow Lindsey to initially control all of their interactions in the sessions. The counselor will allow Lindsey to choose what they will do each time, how the activity will be completed, make any decisions about rules, and so on. After a few sessions, the counselor will gradually introduce the idea of sharing power with Lindsey. At the point where decision making is about equally split between the counselor and Lindsey, they will begin having explicit discussions about taking turns, sharing supplies, and so on. Meanwhile, the counselor will also invite Lindsey's mother in to talk about ways she might help Lindsey feel like she has more control at home. This might entail choosing between two chores, deciding what they will make for dinner on certain nights, and the like. The counselor may also ask the teacher to give Lindsey a leadership position in the class.

These techniques, all adapted from Terry Kottman's (1995) work, are designed to encourage Lindsey to feel competent and capable, while at the same time helping build up her social support system. Adlerian theory views people holistically, as existing within social systems, not as separate from their families or friendship systems, so including the family and teacher is critical to the success of counseling.

Attachment-Based Approaches

Unlike most of the approaches outlined in this text, the attachment-based approaches do not have single techniques that can be easily pulled out and used as examples of how to work with clients. Instead, each of three of the most common of these approaches, parent-child interaction therapy (PCIT), dyadic developmental psychotherapy (DDP), and Theraplay*, have complex, integrated systems for assessment and treatment of problems. Readers who are interested in using these approaches should visit the webpages associated with the approaches and learn how to access appropriate training. These pages are listed at the end of this chapter.

However, it is possible to give the reader a brief overview of each of these three approaches. All three are designed to assist children (and sometimes adolescents or adults) who have attachment disturbances. All three accomplish this task by

Note: Theraplay is a registered trademark of Theraplay Institute.

working with the client and his or her caregiver, and all use some degree of play. Beyond these basic similarities, the three approaches begin to differ.

In PCIT, the therapeutic process is divided into two primary stages, child-directed interaction and parent-directed interaction (McNeil & Hembree-Kigin, 2010). In the first phase of counseling, the child leads interactions and is allowed to choose play materials and the direction of play. During this phase, the therapist coaches the parents in how to interact responsively to the child. This phase is designed to enhance the parent-child relationship. In the second phase, parent-directed interaction, the parent learns techniques to improve the child's compliance with directions (McNeil & Hembree-Kigin, 2010). PCIT is designed for use with children between the ages of about 3 and 6 and their parents. The usual course of therapy takes about 12 sessions to complete but may be extended as needed (PCIT.org).

Dyadic developmental psychotherapy is also designed to help children, especially those who have experienced trauma, become more securely attached to their caregivers. In DDP, the therapist assumes a patient-accepting stance as the child and parent work to deepen their understanding of each other. This is accomplished through what Hughes (2014) calls the "affective-reflective" dialogue. In the A-R dialogue, the parent and therapist reflect back to the child their internal experiences of the child. The child experiences this while exploring his or her life story, including the stories of traumatic experiences. At times, the therapist may assist the child in this storytelling by supplying words for the story. This mutual storytelling and reflection allows the child to experience the trauma in a safe place, which helps him or her to gain a greater internalized sense of safety and reduces anxiety.

Theraplay, on the other hand, uses relatively few words to accomplish the goals of improving the parent-child relationship and reduce the child's symptoms of discomfort. Theraplay was first developed for use in the Chicago Head Start program in the 1960s. The intent of the program at that time was to help the young children to learn coping and self-soothing skills for the stressful environments in which they lived (Booth & Jernberg, 2010).

Over the past 50 years, Theraplay has evolved to include an observation-based assessment, the Marshack interaction method (MIM), a four-part guide for therapy, an extensive listing of therapeutic activities and games for each of the four dimensions, and a classroom-based group intervention program (Booth & Jernberg, 2010). Most Theraplay clients are children under about the age of 12 and their caregivers. Although this approach can be used for a wide variety of common problems, including autistic spectrum disorders, it is often used to help foster and adoptive children settle into their new families.

Family Theraplay is conducted with the child who has the presenting problem and the caregiver(s). After assessing the functioning of the family using the MIM, the therapist creates a treatment plan based on the four dimensions (structure, nurture, challenge, and engagement). Each session consists of a range of short, playful, developmentally appropriate activities in each of the targeted dimensions. Play is directed by the therapist and is light-hearted and joyful. Caregivers are asked to join most activities and are often given activities to do at home with the child (Booth & Jernberg, 2010). After several sessions, or when caregivers begin to see positive changes at home, the MIM is repeated, goals are adjusted, and therapy continues until the goals are met. This cycle may be repeated as many times as needed depending on the severity of the child's problems and the level of engagement of the family. However, many families experience significant relief in about 12 sessions (Booth & Jernberg, 2010).

Outcome Research

Outcome research on most forms of counseling, including psychodynamic therapies, is scarce at best, even for adults with common mood disorders. There is a large body of anecdotal evidence from therapists writing about clients they have treated, but large-scale, well controlled studies are few and far between, especially for those approaches most closely identified with Freudian, Jungian, and Alderian concepts. Outcome research regarding the efficacy of approaches for children and adolescents is even more difficult to locate (Forman-Hoffman et al., 2013).

What evidence is available for effective counseling practices with children most often involves cognitive or cognitive-behavioral interventions, which are generally easier to manualize and study than some of the more complex interventions (Forman-Hoffman et al., 2013; Ramchandani, & Jones, 2004). There is more evidence for the effectiveness of attachment-based therapies such as Dyadic Developmental Therapy (Becker-Weidman, 2006), Parent-Child Interaction Therapy (Lanier et al., 2011; Nieter, Thornberry, & Brestan-Knight, 2013), and Theraplay (Wettig, Coleman, & Geider, 2011) than for the other psychodynamic approaches with children and adolescents.

There is outcome research that points to the effectiveness of psychodynamic approaches in working with adults. In a review of randomized controlled trials, Leichsenring and Klein (2014) found these approaches to be helpful for adults with a variety of mood disorders, including depression and anxiety, as well as complicated grief. However, much more research is needed to determine the effectiveness of psychodynamic approaches, especially with children and adolescents, in counseling.

As with all types of intervention in clinical practice, counselors are encouraged to track the effectiveness of various approaches with their own clients. Evidence may be built even within one counselor's caseload for the use of specific interventions. By using simple techniques to chart results, counselors can compare the effectiveness of interventions across clients. For example, scaling questions may be added to any counseling session to give a rough idea of the client's experience of symptoms over time. The answers to the scaling questions can then be transferred to a simple graph for each client, allowing the counselor to view a person's progress over time.

Application in Schools and Clinics

Although any of the approaches described in this text may be used with children and adolescents, some may be more appealing to individual counselors than others based on time and space constraints and the needs of the population served. For example, Adler's individual psychology approach, with its emphasis on psychoeducation and encouragement, has long been a popular approach with school counselors (Meany-Walen, Bratton, & Kottman, 2014).The growing evidence that programs based on these principles are effective in boosting student performance (Brigman et al., 2011) adds interest for busy school counselors who need to implement interventions that allow for a great deal of impact in a short space of time.

For example, school counselors might work on identifying the reason behind the misbehavior and design interventions that encourage more prosocial behavior in its place. A child who is acting out in class in order to gain attention might be given one-on-one time with a student teacher or older student or be allowed to tutor a younger student as pathways to gaining appropriate attention. A child who acts out in order to gain power might be given a job in the classroom, such as taking papers to the office or leading the line to lunch in order to help fill his or her need for feeling powerful.

On the other hand, counselors who work in community mental health settings and have a large number of clients with complex trauma issues may be better served by one of the longer-term, more wide-ranging models. Although all psychodynamic theories have been used to treat people with trauma-related problems, the largest body of current outcome research belongs to the newer attachment-based therapies, such as dyadic developmental therapy, parent-child interaction therapy, and other similar family-based approaches. Counselors who primarily see clients who are able to sustain longer term therapy may wish to explore some of the neo-Freudian or neo-Jungian approaches, which have limited evidence for effectiveness but a great deal of anecdotal evidence from over a century of practice (Leichsenring & Klein, 2014).

All of the psychodynamic theories are benefitting from recent brain research, which points toward the crucial nature of early experiences in shaping adult behavior, the need for in-depth therapies for PTSD, and evidence supporting the idea that survivors of trauma often cannot tell the story of their experiences in a narrative fashion (van der Kolk, 2014). This new work may spur a resurgence in interest from the therapeutic community about psychodynamic approaches. At the same time, these findings are also altering the vocabulary and techniques within the psychodynamic methods.

COUNSELING KEYSTONES

- All of the psychodynamic theories do have in common the belief that people's problems exist at least in part in the un- or subconscious mind.
- During the 20th century, while adults were making great strides in terms of human rights, children remained largely at the mercy of their parents or other custodians.
- Anna Freud and Melanie Klein were among the first to work directly with children. Both saw the advantage of using play and toys, but they disagreed on the primacy of the therapeutic alliance between counselor and child.
- Adlerian counseling with children focuses on social belonging, goals for behavior and misbehavior, and parenting strategies. Adlerian approaches for children remain popular today, especially in school settings.
- Attachment theorists focus on identifying healthy and unhealthy attachment styles, the causes of insecure or unhealthy attachment, and factors that may protect children from developing severely insecure patterns. In recent years, many have begun to study how to assist children and adults who have insecure attachments (e.g., theraplay). Advances in neuroscience appear to be supportive of attachment theories.
- Some recent psychodynamic approaches are showing effectiveness in outcome studies. These include dyadic developmental therapy and parent-child interaction therapy.

ADDITIONAL RESOURCES

In Print

Oppenheim, D., & Goldsmith, D. (Eds.). (2007). *Attachment theory in clinical work with children: Bridging the gap between theory and practice.* New York, NY: Guilford.

Online

Dyadic developmental psychotherapy: http://ddpnetwork.org
Jungian sandplay training: http://barbaraturner.org
Parent-child interaction therapy: http://PCIT.org
The Theraplay Institute: http://Theraplay.org

REFERENCES

Adler, A. (1964). *The individual psychology of Alfred Adler.* H. L. Ansbacher and R. R. Ansbacher (Eds.). New York, NY: Harper Torchbooks.

Adler, A. (1979*). Superiority and social interest: A collection of later writings.* H. L. Ansbacher and R. R. Ansbacher (Eds.). New York, NY: W. W. Norton.

Ainsworth, M. D., Blehar, M., Waters, E., & Wall, S. (1978). *Patterns of attachment: A psychological study of the strange situation.* Hillsdale, NJ: Lawrence Erlbaum.

Amatruda, K., & Helm, P. (2007*). Sandplay: The sacred healing: A guide to symbolic process.* Taos, NM: Trance-Sand-Dance Press.

Appingnanesi, L. (2008). *Mad, sad, and bad: A history of women and the mind doctors.* New York, NY: Norton.

Becker-Weidman, A. (2006). Treatment for children with trauma-attachment disorders: Dyadic developmental psychotherapy. *Child & Adolescent Social Work Journal, 23*(2), 147–171. doi:10.1007/s10560-005-0039-0

Berrios, G., & Porter, R. (Eds.). (1995). *A history of clinical psychiatry.* London, UK: Athlone Press.

Bitter, J. R. (2008). *Theory and practice of family therapy and counseling.* Boston, MA: Cengage.

Booth, P., & Jernberg, A. (2010). *Theraplay* (3rd ed.). San Francisco, CA: Jossey-Bass.

Bowlby, J. (1982). *Attachment and loss, Vol. 1: Attachment.* New York, NY: Basic Books.

Brigman, G., Villares, E., & Webb, L. (2011). The efficacy of individual psychology approaches for improving student achievement and behavior. *Journal of Individual Psychology, 67*(4), 408–419.

De Domenico, G. S. (1988). Sand tray world Play. Vol 1–3. In *Sand tray world play: A comprehensive guide to the use of the sand tray in psychotherapeutic and transformational settings.* Oakland, CA: Vision Quest into Symbolic Reality.

Esman, A. (1983). Psychoanalytic play therapy. In C. Schaefer, & K. O'Connor (Eds.), *Handbook of play therapy* (pp. 11–12). New York, NY: Wiley.

Forman-Hoffman, V. L., Zolotor, A. J., McKeeman, J. L., Blanco, R., Knauer, S. R., Lloyd, S. W., & Viswanathan, M. (2013). Comparative effectiveness of interventions for children exposed to nonrelational traumatic events. *Pediatrics, 131*(3), 526–539. doi:10.1542/peds.2012-3846

Freud, S. (1909). Analysis of phobia in a five-year-old boy. In J. Strachey (Ed., & Trans.), *Standard edition of the works of Sigmund Freud* (Vol. 10, pp. 3–149). London, UK: Hogarths.

Freud, A. (1965). *The psychoanalytic treatment of children.* New York, NY: International Universities Press.

Grob, G. (1994). *The mad among us: A history of the care of America's mentally ill.* Boston, MA: Harvard University Press.

Hakim, J. (1999). *A history of the US: Book 7: Reconstruction and Reform (1865–1896)*. New York, NY: Oxford Press.

Heywood, C. (2001). *A history of childhood*. Malden, MA: Blackwell.

Hindman, H. D. (2002). *Child labor: An American history*. New York, NY: M.E. Sharpe.

Hughes, D. (2014). *Dyadic developmental psychotherapy*. Retrieved from http://ddpnetwork.org/backend/wp-content/uploads/2014/03/DDP-Toward-a-Comprehensive-Treatment-Dan-Hughes.pdf

Jaffe, A. E. (1989). *Jung, C.G. memories, dreams, reflections*. New York, NY: Random House

Jung, C. (1964). *Man and his symbols*. New York, NY: Dell.

Jung, C. (1983). *The essential Jung*. A. Storr (Ed.). New York, NY: MJF Books.

Jung, C. (2008). *Children's dreams: Notes from the seminar given in 1936–1940*. Princeton, NJ: Princeton.

Kalff, D. M. (1980). *Sandplay*. Boston, MA: Sigo Press.

Karen, R. (1998). *Becoming attached: First relationships and how they shape our capacity to love*. New York, NY: Oxford University Press.

Kelly, D. (1999). Adlerian approaches to counseling with children and adolescents. In H. Prout, & D. Brown (Eds.), *Counseling and psychotherapy with children and adolescents* (pp. 108–154). New York, NY: Wiley.

Kidner, F., Bucur, M., Mathieson, R., McKee, S, & Weeks, T. (2013). *Making Europe: The story of the west since 1300*. Boston, MA: Cengage.

Klein, M. (1955). The psychoanalytic play technique. *American Journal of Orthopyschiatry, 25*, 223–237.

Kottman, T. (1995). *Partners in play: An Adlerian approach to play therapy*. Alexandria, VA: American Counseling Association.

Landreth, G. (1991). *Play therapy: The art of the relationship*. Levittown, PA: Associated Development Press.

Lanier, P., Kohl, P. L., Benz, J., Swinger, D., Moussette, P., & Drake, B. (2011). Parent–child interaction therapy in a community setting: Examining outcomes, attrition, and treatment setting. *Research on Social Work Practice, 21*(6), 689–698. doi:10.1177/1049731511406551

Leichsenring, F., & Klein, S. (2014). Evidence for psychodynamic psychotherapy in specific mental disorders: A systematic review. *Psychoanalytic Psychotherapy, 28*(1), 4–32. doi:10.1080/02668734.2013.865428

Lowenfeld, M. (1935). *Play in childhood*. London, UK: V. Gollancz Limited.

Main, M., & Solomon, J. (1990*)*. Procedures for identifying infants as disorganized/disoriented during the Ainsworth strange situation. In M. T. Greenberg, D. Cicchetti, E. M. Cummings (Eds.), *Attachment in the preschool years: Theory, research, and intervention* (pp. 121–160)*.* Chicago, IL: University of Chicago Press.

Meany-Walen, K. K., Bratton, S. C., & Kottman, T. (2014). Effects of Adlerian play therapy on reducing students' disruptive behaviors. *Journal of Counseling & Development, 92*(1), 47–56. doi:10.1002/j.1556-6676.2014.00129.x

Merydith, S. (1999). Psychodynamic approaches. In H. Prout, & D. Brown (Eds.), *Counseling and psychotherapy with children and adolescents* (pp. 74–107). New York, NY: Wiley.

McNeil, B., & Hembree-Kigin, T. (2010). *Parent-child interaction therapy* (2nd ed.). New York, NY: Springer.

Murdock, N. (2013). *Theories of counseling and psychotherapy.* Thousand Oaks, CA: Sage.

Myers, J. E. B. (2004). *A history of child protection in America.* Bloomington, IN: Xlibris Corporation.

Nieter, L., Thornberry, T., & Brestan-Knight, E. (2013). The effectiveness of group parent-child interaction therapy with community families. *Journal of Child & Family Studies, 22*(4), 490–501. doi:10.1007/s10826-012-9601-5

Perry, B. D. (2002). Childhood experience and the expression of genetic potential: What childhood neglect tells us about nature and nurture. *Brain and Mind, 3,* 79–100.

Ramchandani, P. P., & Jones, D. H. (2004). Review: Psychological therapies can improve psychological symptoms in children who have been sexually abused. *Evidence Based Mental Health, 7*(3), 73.

Schaefer, C., & O'Connor, K., (Eds.). (1983). *Handbook of play therapy.* New York, NY: Wiley.

Schore, A. (2001). The effects of early relational trauma on right brain development, affect regulation, and infant mental health. *Infant Mental Health Journal, 22*(1–2), 201–269.

Schwartz, C. (2015, June 28). Tell it about your mother: Can brain scanning save Freudian psychoanalysis? *New York Times Magazine* (pp. 39–43, 69–73).

Slade, A. (2007). *Disorganized mother, disorganized child.* In D. Oppenheim, & D. Goldsmith (Eds.), *Attachment theory in clinical work with children: Bridging the gap between theory and practice* (pp. 1226–1250). New York, NY: Guilford.

Turner, B. A. (2005). *The handbook of sandplay therapy.* Cloverdale, CA: Temenos Press.

Wallerstein, R. S. (1995). *The talking cures.* London, UK: Yale University Press.

Wells, H. G. (1975). *Floor games.* New York, NY: Arno Press.

Wettig, H. G.; Coleman, A. R.; Geider, F. J. (2011). Evaluating the effectiveness of Theraplay in treating shy, socially withdrawn children. *International Journal of Play Therapy,* Vol. 20(1), pp.26-37.

Von Franz, M. L. (1994). *Dream.* Boston, MA: Shambala.

van der Kolk, B. (2014). *The body keeps the score: Brain, body, and mind in the healing of trauma.* New York, NY: Viking.

Chapter 6

Humanistic Approaches

CATHERINE TUCKER AND SONDRA SMITH-ADCOCK

*We are all personalities that grow and develop as a result of our experiences,
relationships, thoughts and emotions. We are the sum total of all the parts
that go into the making of a life.*

—Virginia Axline

INTRODUCTION

Humanistic approaches to counseling children and adolescents focus on the holistic experience of living. It's hard to imagine a time when we are more full of life than in childhood or more examining of our human existence than in adolescence. These are periods of life that are critical to our development, our present and our future, and to the very nature of our existence. Carl Rogers (1961), whose work we examine later in this chapter, viewed children as having two basic needs in order to grow and achieve. He saw these fundamental lifelines as *positive regard* and *self-worth*. The essence, therefore, of the work of the humanistic counselor is to offer the child or adolescent a safe place in which to grow, a safe place that allows the child to experience himself or herself as whole person who is capable. According to humanistic counselors, prizing and empowerment of the individual is the essence of change.

After reading this chapter, you will be able to

- describe the basic ideas behind all humanistic theories and relate these ideas to the nature of change for children and adolescents;

142 COUNSELING CHILDREN AND ADOLESCENTS

- compare and contrast each of the humanistic approaches described in the chapter;
- explain how humanistic theories can be modified to apply to children and adolescents; and
- describe in detail at least three interventions based on the theories that are appropriate for use with children or adolescents.

SOCIOHISTORICAL CONTEXT

The cluster of approaches often labeled humanistic began to gain popularity around the end of World War II. Western Europe and the United States were shaking off the horrors of death, disease, hunger, and fighting to begin the optimistic second half of the 20th century. The United States' economy was now fully recovered from the Great Depression of the 1930s. Full employment, low interest rates, affordable homes, and a booming stock market were converging to create a powerful middle class and a growing sense of well-being among a large portion of the population (Brinkley, 2009).

Meanwhile, in Western Europe, rebuilding from the devastation of war was also beginning to repair a ragged economic system. Europeans had experienced the war in much closer quarters than U.S. citizens, and much of the infrastructure had to be rebuilt from rubble. Eastern Europe was now behind the Iron Curtain of the Soviet Union, often splitting families apart. The resulting Cold War between the United States and the U.S.S.R. constructed a new environment of distrust, spy networks, and fears of nuclear war for the next 50 years (Brinkley, 2009).

After the war, psychiatry, and psychology in the United States were experiencing expansion due in part to the first national policy on mental health, the National Mental Health Act of 1946, which established federal funding for mental health research, the training of mental health professionals, and the establishment of treatment centers (Grob, 1994). The demand for services by returning veterans, along with the discovery of the first effective antipsychotic medications and emerging research showing the effectiveness of psychotherapy all converged to create an apparent need for more mental health professionals able to deliver services in an outpatient setting. Prior to this time, most mental health services had been delivered within the hospital setting (Grob, 1994).

The two primary systems of thought in psychiatry and psychology before and during World War II were the psychodynamic theories of Freud and his followers and the strict behaviorism of B. F. Skinner (Grob, 1994). Although these theories remained popular for many years, mental health professionals and clients began to seek another way to address the problems of ordinary people, without the judgment and long-term analysis required by psychodynamic practitioners and with more emphasis on thoughts and feelings than behaviorism. In 1964, James Bugental published the five basic principles of humanistic psychology, which ushered in a new "third force" in psychology. All of the theories we explore in this chapter are based on these five principles:

1. Human beings, as human, supersede the sum of their parts. They cannot be reduced to components.

2. Human beings have their existence in a uniquely human context, as well as in a cosmic ecology.

3. Human beings are aware and are aware of being aware—that is, they are conscious. Human consciousness always includes an awareness of oneself in the context of other people.

4. Human beings have some choice and, with that, responsibility.

5. Human beings are intentional; aim at goals; are aware that they cause future events; and seek meaning, value, and creativity.

THEORISTS

Humanism represents a diverse array of approaches to people and problems. Although all of the theorists we discuss here agreed with the five basic principles of Bugenthal, they had varied ideas about how to best treat clients. All of these theories of counseling remain popular today and are in wide use across the globe.

Carl Rogers and Virginia Axline

Carl Rogers was a prolific author and master counselor who first developed the humanistic orientation to counseling, called person-centered counseling. Virginia Axline, who was a contemporary of Rogers, adapted the person-centered approach to children, in the form of play therapy. According to Rogers (1961, 1980), the three primary conditions for change in therapy are unconditional positive regard by the therapist for the client, empathic understanding, and therapist congruence within himself or herself. Congruence, as described by Rogers, is a state of accepting oneself without judgment and being aware. In other words, congruence means *being you* and being okay with whatever *being you* means.

Being out of congruence is the primary cause of suffering according to Rogers (1980). Incongruence between who you are (the real self) and who you want to be (the ideal self) can cause anxiety, depression, and other forms of psychic distress. Rogers believed that one of the main causes of incongruence is that those who are close to people place conditions of worth on them (Rogers, 1961). Conditions of worth imply that someone will only be loved and accepted *if*. For example, *if* he or she has a high-status job, *if* he or she is attractive, follows the rules, or is pleasing to the other in some way, he or she may earn the love and acceptance of the other. For children, conditions of worth might include whether or not they make good grades or behave in particular ways that are pleasing to the adults in their lives. When people experience conditions of worth rather than an unconditional positive regard from those about whom they care, they may develop incongruencies between how they are in the world and how they pretend to be. For an illustration of this inauthenticity people sometimes experience, we offer the following case illustration.

Case Illustration 6.1

Sarah is a 17-year-old biracial high school junior. She lives with her mother and stepfather, who are White, and her two younger brothers, who are also White in a middle-class suburb of a large city. She is a good student at her high school and is active in several arts groups. Her biological father, who is African-American, and her mother divorced when Sarah was four. Her mother remarried a year later, and Sarah sees her father regularly on weekends.

Sarah's mother referred her to counseling because she says Sarah has become "moody and impossible" at home. She says she knows some of this behavior may be due to normal adolescent development, but says, "I'm so tired of arguing with her about every little thing, something has to change." Sarah agrees that things are tense between her mother and herself but denies any symptoms of more serious disorders.

As a person-centered counselor, Beth begins by asking Sarah how she feels about her mother and her home life, in order to try and understand Sarah's world view. She then asks Sarah to describe how she feels when she's with her family and how she feels when she's with her friends. Sarah responds that when she is at home, she feels "incompetent, like I can't do anything right," while with her friends, she feels "smart and responsible." Beth quickly sees an incongruence between these statements. Over the next few weeks, Sarah and Beth work together to explore Sarah's real and ideal self. After identifying several conditions of worth Sarah feels her mother sets for her, Beth helps Sarah tell her mother about these feelings in a joint session. Sarah's mother is not happy to hear this information but agrees that she is placing a great deal of pressure on Sarah. With Beth's help, the dyad completes several relationship-building activities, and after four joint sessions, both Sarah and her mother feel as if they have met their original goal.

Becoming more congruent within oneself is a prerequisite for the ultimate goal of human development: the fully functioning person (Rogers, 1961).

Becoming a fully functioning person is not a state to be achieved but is an ongoing, dynamic growth process (Rogers, 1961). When people are fully functioning, they are able to live what Rogers termed "the good life," which includes a growing openness to experience, living each moment fully, trust in oneself to do the right thing in a variety of circumstances, full freedom to choose actions and words, increased creativity, increased reliability and constructiveness, and a rich, full life (Rogers, 1961).

In order to help adult or older adolescent clients become more congruent between their real and ideal selves, Rogers advised an active, engaged approach within the therapy room (Rogers, 1980). Using a wide range of basic active listening skills and well-timed questions to the client about his or her beliefs about self in relation to the world, Rogers believed that he could help clients move significantly toward "the good life." For an excellent example of Carl Rogers using the three conditions and very skilled questions and challenges to help a client, visit YouTube and watch him with "Gloria." This is one part of a three-part film series on psychotherapy, which has become a classic. Though Gloria is an adult, this film gives you a vivid depiction of how Carl Rogers embodied the core conditions essential to counseling.

Guided Exercise 6.1

Watch Dr. Carl Rogers work with Gloria on YouTube (https://www.youtube.com/watch?v=24d-FEptYj8). Before you watch, write down Rogers' core conditions for counseling: (1) empathy, (2) congruence or genuineness, and (3) unconditional positive regard. As you watch the film, find examples of how Rogers facilitates each of these conditions. Pay attention to what he says, how he responds nonverbally, and what sort of effect his intentional responses have on Gloria. How do you think Gloria feels? How do you think change might occur for her?

After you watch the video, imagine how counselors show this level of acceptance to children and adolescents. How do you fully accept children's experiences? Can you accept children just as they are, or do you want to change them in some way? Imagine these core conditions in schools and clinical settings. What are barriers to showing children unconditional positive regard? What are your personal views on this humanistic philosophy? How person-centered are the settings in which you work (schools, hospitals, clinics, agencies)?

Rogers' ideas have been adapted for many uses, including group therapy, consultation, and teaching and learning environments (Murdock, 2013). Virgina Axline, a colleague of Rogers's at the University of Chicago, revised his theory for use with children. She called her approach nondirective play therapy (Axline, 1969). Nondirective play therapy is based on the idea that children naturally strive toward growth and are capable of making choices and taking responsibility for change. Dr. Louise Guerny, Dr. Gary Landreth, Dr. Rise Van Fleet, and many others have continued Axline's work. The play therapy model outlined by Axline is now generally referred to as child-centered play therapy (CCPT). CCPT is used with individual clients, with small groups, and in parent-child and family play settings. Currently, the Center for Play Therapy at the University of North Texas is the world's largest training center for play therapists and generally uses the approach first described by Axline (Crenshaw & Stewart, 2015). There is an extensive discussion about this approach in Chapter 11.

Fritz Perls and Violet Oaklander

Gestalt therapy was first developed by Fritz and Laura Perls. Fritz and Laura Perls were among the thousands of people of Jewish descent who fled Germany just before the outbreak of World War II. Although Perls was a practicing psychiatrist and had already begun thinking about ideas that eventually became Gestalt theory before leaving Europe, it was not until he and Laura moved to New York after the war that the theory coalesced (Bernd, 2010). Like the other humanist theorists, Perls believed that people could generally solve most of their own problems given the right environment. For him, the right environment included the capacity and willingness of a person to be in "contact" with his or her senses and emotions, to be present, "in the moment," and authentic (Perls, 1969).

For Perls, being in contact with the world meant not shutting off painful or embarrassing emotions or thoughts but rather fully experiencing, using all five senses, the inner and outer worlds. Perls believed that being in contact leads people to the ability to examine and understand their own motivations and behaviors (Wheeler & Axelsson, 2014). Perls also talked about unfinished business, or unresolved conflicts, as being at the root of many human problems (Perls, 1969). Being in contact with the world and examining any unfinished business can help people become fully aware of their environments, which then allows them to choose how and when to act, rather than reacting to situations and people out of habit or experience (Perls, 1969). In Gestalt therapy, the counselor forms a warm, respectful relationship with the client. Once the relationship is established, he or she develops experiments with the client to assist the client in coming in greater contact with the world, examining unfinished business, and becoming more self-regulating (Wheeler & Axelsson, 2014). Probably the most well-known of these experiments is the empty chair technique, in which the client is asked to perform a conversation between himself or herself and someone with whom there is a conflict. The resulting conversation leads to increased contact with hidden feelings and sometimes resolves unfinished business (Wheeler & Axelsson, 2014). However, there is much more to Gestalt theory than the empty chair. There are dozens of training institutes for Gestalt therapy worldwide, and it remains a popular way of working with clients.

Gestalt therapy's emphasis on the here and now and sensory experiences makes it a natural fit for the expressive therapeutic approaches, including play (Oaklander, 1978). Violet Oaklander, an author, trainer of therapists, and Gestalt therapist, has written extensively about the use of Gestalt therapy with children and adolescents (Oaklander, 1978, 2006). Her work incorporates various art media, dance and movement, play, sand tray, and nature modalities to reach young people. In the introduction to her 2006 book, *Hidden Treasure*, Oaklander states,

> When a child comes into therapy I know that she has lost what she once had, was entitled to have, as a tiny baby: the full and joyful use of her senses, her body, her intellect, and the expression of her emotions. My job is to help her find and regain those missing parts of herself. (p.18)

Oaklander devises creative, spontaneous sensory experiences for her young clients to remove impediments to full contact with the inner and outer worlds. She directs clients to smell, taste, touch, move, play, and talk through emotional pain and barriers (Oaklander, 2006). She employs a variety of creative and playful media to engage children, including clay (or Play-Doh), art supplies, and soft toys (boxing gloves or soft bats). Her two books, listed in the references section of this chapter, give detailed descriptions of many of these experiments. Additionally, the application section of this chapter outlines two of Oaklander's techniques.

For a beginning idea of CCPT and an introduction to Garry Landreth and Violet Oaklander's work, go to YouTube.

Guided Exercise 6.2

1. Watch a brief clip of Garry Landreth (published by Routledge) at https://www.youtube.com/watch?v=JlMWOOlR_9g.

2. The Association for Play Therapy has a number of videos available on YouTube: Garry Landreth at https://www.youtube.com/watch?v=SOYhs593-kE.

3. See Violet Oaklander at https://www.youtube.com/watch?v=tpATTNleCAQ.

Irving Yalom and Clark Moustakas

Although existential psychotherapy generally focuses on the most abstract and philosophical of life's problems, such as the meaning of life, the inevitability of death, and the anxiety caused by having freedom of choice and responsibility for its consequences, existentialism can be adapted for work with younger clients and may be especially indicated for adolescents. There are many existential theorists and therapists, including Victor Frankl (1959), who wrote *Man's Search for Meaning* based on his experiences in a concentration camp during World War II. If you have never read this work, we highly recommend it. In his seminal work, Frankl also articulated an approach to therapy, called *logotherapy*, which is based on finding personal meaning. Like other existential therapists we will study, Frankl described the core elements of counseling as fostering self-discovery through creativity; fully experiencing oneself, others, and the environment; and realizing your personal agency (Frankl, 2006). These basic goals of therapy are wonderfully consistent with the work we do with young people. In the remainder of this text, we expand on Frankl's ideas by examining the work of two of the most prolific writers on existential therapy, Irving Yalom and Clark Moustakas.

Dr. Irvin D. Yalom has published dozens of books about the application of existential theory to counseling. Unlike most other authors of books on psychotherapy, he has used both fiction and nonfiction formats to help his readers learn more about what he calls the *four givens* of human experience: isolation, meaninglessness, mortality, and freedom (Yalom, 1980). According to Dr. Yalom, people often feel anxious, confused, or depressed when faced with navigating one or more of these *four givens* of life. These feelings of worry can occur at any point in life but often begin in the unsettled period of middle to late adolescence, when people often question their basic identities and reasons for living. Though existential crises are often prominent in adolescence, these worries can happen at any age. A common example of early existential experiences might include a young child who loses a grandparent or pet and faces the reality of death. However, also keep in mind that some young children also encounter tragic loss early in their development and must navigate these fears early on in their development. In Guided Exercise 6.3, relate these existential themes to childhood and adolescent experiences.

Guided Exercise 6.3

How do you make meaning of your own existential experiences in childhood and adolescence? Using the following list of main sources of anxiety (death, meaning, isolation, and freedom), reflect on your own early existential experiences. Respond to this activity in a small group, if possible. Do you believe existential approaches are applicable for young clients? Why, or why not? How do you think the existential experience of children and adolescents is different from that of adults?

Existential themes are life themes. Freedom and responsibility, life and death, belonging and isolation are universal experiences (Yalom, 1980). The child faced with bullying from his peers must decide how he will act. A young child whose parents are divorcing experiences a deep sense of loss. As she transitions to middle school, a sixth grader faces a strong sense of isolation. Just because they are young does not mean that the essence of life does not affect them. To examine these childhood existential stories more closely, we recommend watching films. Films are helpful ways to encounter the existential realities of young people. In Guided Exercise 6.4, we have provided a short list of films about children and adolescents who are dealing with existential matters. We invite you to watch one or more of these films and complete a brief reflection activity.

Guided Exercise 6.4

IFC Productions, & Linklater, R. (2014). *Boyhood* [Motion Picture]. United States: IFC Films.
This recent film tells the story of Mason from early childhood until college.

Cinereach, & Zeitlin, B. (2012). *Beasts of the Southern Wild* [Motion Picture]. United States: FoxSearchLight.
Six-year-old Hushpuppy faces her hot-tempered father's health problems and a flood of her bayou home with courage and love.

Red Crown Productions, & McGehee, S., & Siegel, D. (2013). *What Maise Knew* [Motion Picture]. United States: Millennium.
In this film, 7-year-old Maise is caught in the middle of her parents' bitter divorce.

Momentum Pictures, & Lasse Hallstrom (1985). *My Life as a Dog* [Motion Picture]. United States: Skouras Pictures.
A boy and his brother, who do not get along, are sent to separate homes when their ill mother cannot care for them.

A&M Films, Channel Productions, & Hughes, J. (1999). *The Breakfast Club* [Motion Picture]. United States: Universal Pictures.
Five high school students, all from different stereotypical adolescent groups, connect and related to each other's experience in detention hall.

Paramount Pictures, Wildwood Productions, & Redford, R. (1980). *Ordinary People* [Motion Picture]. United States: Paramount.
Conrad, a high school senior, deals with his own despair and his strained family relationships in the wake of the death of his older brother.

Yalom, like most of the existentialist therapy writers, generally eschews techniques beyond the use of interpersonal verbal exchanges in counseling. In his 2002 book *The Gift of Therapy*, Yalom explains his beliefs about the crucial importance of the therapist-client relationship and its power to help clients lead more meaningful lives, stating that "the establishment of an authentic relationship with patients, by its very nature, demands that we forego the power of the triumvirate of magic, mystery, and authority" (p. 124). This abiding belief in the sanctity of the therapist-client relationship requires that existential therapists be genuine, fully present in the here and now, and able to connect with client thoughts and emotions. Yalom often employed group therapy to help clients achieve their goals, believing that several people exchanging ideas about life and meaning were more effective at times than two people engaged in such dialogue. He also occasionally asks clients to recount their dreams in order to more clearly identify deeper issues causing the presenting problems (Yalom, 2002). Yalom's highly abstract, thoughtful approach can work very effectively with older adolescents who are able to think abstractly and with clients whose cognitive functions lie within the typical or normal ranges.

Clark Moustakas (1923–2012) was a leading proponent of humanistic psychology from the 1960s to the 1990s. Early in his career, Dr. Moustakas was a pupil of Virginia Axline, the creator of CCPT (Moustakas, 1997). During his long career, Dr. Moustakas worked for the longest spans at the Merrill-Palmer Institute for Child and Family Development (http://mpsi.wayne.edu/about/history.php) and later as the cofounder of the Michigan School for Professional Psychology (http://mispp.edu/about/founders). His humanistic and existential approach to psychology, combined with his work with children, led him to create what he called "relationship play therapy" (Moustakas, 1997), which bears a strong resemblance to the work of Dr. Axline, with an existential twist. In this form of play therapy, the therapist emphasizes the values of "faith in the child's unique potentials for directing his or her life, acceptance of the child's silent and verbal expressions, and respect for the child" (1997, p. 21). Moustakas, like Yalom, was a strong believer in the importance of the therapist's presence and believed that it was the strength of the child-therapist relationship that helped the child express emotions and make changes in thoughts, feelings, and emotions. He believed that the therapist should not intrude on the child's freedom of expression, except to provide limits for the sake of safety, and that, "diagnosis, cause-effect inferences, manipulations and controls, pre-determined and directed by the therapist undermine the tenets, values, and meanings inherent in relationship therapy" (1997, p. 14). Like Axline's nondirective play therapy, Moustakas's relationship therapy relies heavily on the creation of a permissive, safe, and caring atmosphere; reflective listening; and occasional limit setting to accomplish its goals. Unlike Axline, however, Moustakas wrote about making comments on the emotions behind actions (wow, you must be mad!) and focused his internal dialogue about the sessions on existential needs common to all people, such as love and belonging (Moustakas, 1997).

APPLICATION TO COUNSELING SETTINGS

Humanistic approaches to counseling children and adolescents are both a philosophy and a set of practices. Humanistic counselors adhere to a set of beliefs and attitudes toward children that include (but may not be limited to) the following: (1) children are innately good and capable, (2) children can make developmentally appropriate choices and self-govern, (2) children are capable of insight, (3) children are resilient, (4) children are worthy of love and acceptance, and (5) children grow and thrive in relationship to others (Landreth, 2012). Yalom (1980), for example, proposes that we, as humanistic counselors, aim to know and to fully experience others. Scalzo (2010) suggests that the counseling process creates an existential dialogue between the child and the counselor. This client-counselor interaction promotes an opportunity for the young person to explore his or her experience, awareness, choice, and responsibility. Scalzo suggests that deeper philosophical interpretations are not the goal but rather the examination of our daily lives, ourselves, and our worldview. As humanistic counselors, one way we understand our role is to help others feel seen, heard, and valued for who they are. The focus is not on the counselor. We do not ask "What can I do for this child?" or "How can I help him or her?" Indeed, our appraisal of the person or his or her situation is not forefront. Instead, we ask, What does this person understand about himself or herself? How does her or she understand his or her situation?

The practice of humanistic counseling with children and adolescents employs varied techniques to help bring the children's and adolescents' experiences into sharp focus and to build a counseling relationship. Skills related to listening and responding, "reflective listening" or "reflecting feelings," are principal to effective counseling from this orientation. "Reflective listening" is often misunderstood (Arnold, 2014). Reflective listening is not a simple way of parroting back what a client says or even yet, "And, how does that make you feel?" It is a deeper and a more complex interpersonal exchange than that; it is a way of checking the counselor's understanding of the client's experiences. Rogers also called this process *testing understandings*, or a counselor to client negotiation of meaning and experience (Rogers, 1986). In Case Illustration 6.2, we provide an example of what this dialogue might look like with a child or an adolescent.

Case Illustration 6.2

Reflective Listening

In the following examples, we illustrate Rogers's ideas on reflective, or empathic, listening. The first example is a conversation with a young child, at about 6 years old, and the second is with an adolescent, at about 14 years old. Notice in each of these examples that the counselor does not evaluate or direct. She focuses on the child's experience and trusts both young people to direct the problem solving that takes place. Active, reflective, empathic listening is a core skill for the humanistic counselor working with children and adolescents. Good listening and reflecting the child's experience is an essential skill no matter what the approach.

Example 1: Donovan is a first grader who is talking to his school counselor (Ms. E.) after an argument on the playground resulted in pushing, shoving, and hitting.

D: *He hit me first!*

Ms. E: *You want me to know he hit you first.*

D: *(Crying) It's not fair. I get blamed for everything!*

Ms. E: *You're pretty mad right now because you feel like you got blamed today and that wasn't fair.*

D: *Yeah. I told him to leave me alone, and he wouldn't. He just wouldn't. I yelled at him to get back, and he pushed me. I had to push him back.*

Ms. E: *When he pushed you, you pushed him back. You want me to know that you pushed him because he pushed you. Sometimes it's hard to get people to listen to you.*

D: *Yeah. I just wanted him to leave me alone.*

Ms. E: *So Donovan, you tried to solve the problem by using your words, but that didn't work. You were angry that he didn't listen to you and pushed you. You're so upset right now it's making you cry.*

D: *I feel like I got in trouble, and he didn't get anything; I'm always in trouble! I told him stop!*

Ms. E: *It feels like this is just one more time when you are in trouble, and you don't feel like you should be. You tried to make a good choice and because he didn't listen to you, you two ended up fighting. That's frustrating!*

D: *(Sniffs) Yeah.*

Ms. E: *You feel like he should have a consequence also; that would feel more fair to you since you were both fighting.*

D: *Yeah, that would be better because we were both fighting even though we aren't supposed to.*

Ms. E: *So even though you are frustrated by it, you understand why you're in trouble, and you just want it to feel fair.*

Example 2: Sarah is a 14-year-old girl who is not getting along with her parents, who are currently going through a divorce. She is seeing a mental health counselor (Dr. J.) because she has recently shown some signs of depression.

Sarah: *I'm not going to talk to her. She makes me crazy. You can't make me do it.*

Dr. J:	You don't feel like talking to her about this. You feel frustrated when you try to talk about this with your mom.
Sarah:	It's because she doesn't listen to what I'm telling her, she just keeps talking at me.
Dr. J:	You really want your mom to hear how you feel, and it's hurtful to you that she isn't listening.
Sarah:	Why are they doing this to me anyway? This is ruining my life; I don't even have a family anymore!
Dr. J:	This whole situation feels overwhelming to you. You feel like everything is changing way too fast, and you aren't able to stop any of it; that's really scary.
Sarah:	Everything is different, and I don't know what it's going to be like. Mom and Dad are always mad now.
Dr. J:	It's scary when you think of what this new life will look like, and you're not sure how to deal with all the changes. You've been trying to get your mom to understand how scared and unsure you are, but you feel like she isn't hearing you.
Sarah:	Yeah . . .
Dr. J:	It sounds like you would feel better if mom could explain a little about what's happened and what life will be like for you with mom and dad being divorced. Things might feel less overwhelming.

Person-centered and related counseling interventions are commonly used in both schools and clinical settings. In fact, Rogers advocated for applications of person-centered approaches that extended far beyond the one-to-one setting of the individual psychotherapy session and into educational settings (Rogers, 1989). In addition to seeing the importance of child-centered approaches in educational settings, he was a great proponent for humanitarian and social change. Rogers viewed education as a means to develop the "holistic, fully functioning person, who is a leader in a democratic society" (Cornelius-White, 2007). Today, humanistic approaches are widely used in schools to promote social skills (Villares, Lemberger, Brigman, & Webb, 2011), student-teacher relationships (Cornelius-White, 2007; Ray, 2007), school violence and bullying prevention (Carney, Jacob, & Hazler, 2011; Stanley, Small, Owen, & Burke, 2012), and counselor advocacy (Lemberger & Hutchison, 2014). Many of these approaches are covered in more detail in Scholl, McGowan, and Hansen's (2012) comprehensive review of contemporary humanistic counseling.

Humanistic approaches also are used to promote parent-child relationships. For example, filial therapies such as child-parent relationship therapy (CPRT; Landreth & Bratton, 2006) teach child-centered skills to parents and have been shown to reduce parenting stress and improve children's outcomes (Ray, 2008). In

CPRT, counselors employ the basic relational skills of CCPT to help parents relate well to their children and improve the parent-child relationship. These approaches are not focused on problem solving or on changing the child's behavior but rather are intent on facilitating experiences that empower both parent and child. In Guided Exercise 6.5, participate in an interactive "follow the leader" activity.

Guided Exercise 6.5

Follow the Leader

In CPRT, the goal is to teach parents the basic relational skills of humanistic, child-centered counselors. In this way, the parent becomes the therapeutic agent of change. This interpersonal process increases trust, security, warmth, and playfulness between parent and child (Landreth and Bratton, 2006). This filial approach involves parents and children in structured, nondirective play sessions.

Do you remember playing *follow the leader*? How does it feel to be in the lead? This is a very empowering feeling. Letting children lead the way is an optimal way for counselors, or parents, to approach children if they hope to learn about them, help them learn what they are capable of, and let them know that they can make their own decisions.

Pick a young person in your life (or any person) to practice this with (keep it simple because you're still learning). Following the recommendations of Landreth and Bratton (2006) in the CPRT treatment manual: A 10-session filial model for training parents. Give the person a small bag of toys (Play-Doh, crayons, and a few miniatures will do). Or, just play *follow the leader*. For several minutes (at least 10), allow the person to lead and you follow. Do not ask any questions or make any suggestions. (Pay close attention, as these behaviors can sneak up on you.) Empathize with the other person. Describe what the person is doing/playing. Reflect what the child is saying/feeling.

What does it feel like to lead/follow? How do you believe anyone (child or adult) feels when they are followed this way? What can you learn about them? What do you learn about yourself? Are you comfortable following, or do you want to direct?

Humanistic counselors also use a wide variety of expressive techniques and modalities. Because of their emphasis on affective experience and self-expression, the use of play (e.g., Landreth, 2012) and creative arts in counseling children and adolescents, such as art, music, dance, and drama (e.g., Malchiodi, 2008) has its roots in a humanistic tradition. Though a review of all these creative approaches is beyond the scope of this single chapter (and many are reviewed in other sections of this text), we strongly recommend Malchiodi's (2008) *Creative Interventions With Traumatized Children*, Vernon and Barry's (2013) *Counseling Outside the Lines: Creative Arts Interventions for Children and Adolescents—Individual, Small Group, and Classroom Applications*, and Green and Drewe's (2013) *Integrating*

Expressive Arts and Play Therapy with Children and Adolescents. We also provide examples of two humanistic creative arts approaches in the techniques sections. Though creative approaches are powerful ways to connect to and treat children, they should be used with care for individual, social, and cultural differences (Malchiodi, 2008). While creative approaches to counseling children are widely used, they are not as often studied and validated as evidence-based treatments (Ray, 2006).

Both Rogers (1970) and Yalom (1970) were strong proponents of group therapy for promoting healthy interpersonal relationships. In the text, *The Theory and Practice of Group Psychotherapy*, Yalom and Leszcz (2005) define *therapeutic factors* of group work:

Installation of hope	the belief that things will get better
Universality	a sense of having common experiences as others
Imparting information	gaining helpful information and confronting misconceptions
Altruism	belief in the benefit of giving to others
Corrective recapitulation of primary family group	group reflects a family for resolving conflicts
Development of socializing	basic social skills practice
Imitative behavior	group members learn from each other and the group leader
Interpersonal learning	the experience of productive relationships
Group cohesiveness	closeness that facilitates communication
Catharsis	emotional expression and cognitive change
Existential factors	existential anxieties (e.g., death, isolation)

Group work, as we know it today, is based on these fundamental humanistic ideas about group dynamics. Group work is common in school and mental health settings and is widely used for children and adolescents, particularly in schools (Prout & Brown, 2007). A humanistic orientation to group work has been applied to a multitude of populations and conditions, such as trauma (Shen, 2010), learning disabilities (Danino and Shechtman, 2012), at-risk adolescent girls (Smith-Adcock, Webster, Leonard, & Walker, 2008; Zinck & Littrell, 2001), building confidence in African-American boys in elementary school (Baggerly & Parker, 2005), and improving parent-child relationships with toddlers (Proulx, 2002). Although many humanistic counseling groups embrace the verbal exchange as their primary mode of intervention, other humanistic groups might use play, art, or other creative means to reach client's goals (Baggerly & Parker, 2005). This expansion into the creative and expressive therapies makes the humanistic group model flexible and adaptable, allowing it to encompass an almost limitless array of issues.

EXISTENTIAL–HUMANISTIC COUNSELING TECHNIQUES

The following techniques illustrate humanistic counseling in action. These are examples and are not meant to be a comprehensive representation of humanistic-focused activities. To review, humanistic techniques allow for optimal expression of the child's experience, contact with the counselor, and ultimately with the environment and world. The counseling process remains focused on the child and not on the therapist, although some of these interventions are somewhat structured and directed by the counselor. The interventions described here are applicable to both schools and clinical settings and are relevant for varied age groups.

Drawing Out the Real and Ideal

This technique can be used with most children above age 5, up through the adult years. It illustrates in a very concrete manner Carl Rogers's idea of the conflict between a person's actual life and their idealized vision of what they would like life to be like. Supply the client with a large blank piece of paper, preferably white or buff in color. Offer them whatever type of drawing tools you have available; colored pencils, crayons, markers, pastels, charcoal, and paint pens are all good options. Ask the client to draw his or her "real life" on one side of the paper. When that drawing is completed, turn the paper over and ask the client to draw "what you wish your real life" looked like. Drawings can be realistic depictions of one or more aspects of a client's life, or he or she may use symbols to describe his or her ideas.

Once both drawings are complete (which may take more than one session depending on how quickly the client works), discuss the drawings with the client. Questions like "What is the single biggest difference between the two pictures?," "What is one way you can make the real side more like the ideal side?," "What's stopping you from being like the ideal side all of the time?," focus on areas within the clients' control, empowering them and using this realized personal agency to guide future sessions.

Rosebush Strategy

This Gestalt-related technique is described in detail, complete with case examples in Violet Oaklander's book *Windows to Our Children* (1978) and also elaborated by Ray, Perkins, and Oden (2004) as an intervention for elementary school counseling. The rosebush strategy can be used with children as young as 5 or 6 and also is appropriate with adolescents and adults. In the rosebush strategy, following a guided imagery (which we will describe next), the child is asked to draw a picture of himself or herself as a rosebush. This simple projective becomes a metaphor for the child's inner world. As Oaklander (1997) suggests, "The child then can look at it, examine it, and, when ready, own it" (p. 11).

The activity begins with a progressive muscle relaxation activity. The intent is to clear any intervening thoughts so that the child can focus on the visualization. This is followed by a guided imagery of life as a rosebush (Ray et al., 2004). When the child is ready, the counselor states,

> "Now, I want you to close your eyes and imagine yourself as a rosebush." Specific questions help a child to define the self as the rosebush. For example, as the child's eyes remain closed, the counselor will continue, "What kind of rosebush are you? Are you small? Are you large? Do you have flowers? What are your stems and branches like? Do you have thorns? What are your roots like? Look around you . . . are you in a yard? In a park? Are you in a pot or growing in the ground? Are you alone? Does someone take care of you? What's the weather like?" (Ray et al., 2004, p. 279)

With art media made available before the visualization begins, the child draws the picture of the rosebush. Ray et al. (2004) recommend a choice of art materials, ranging from a simple 8x10 piece of paper and a pencil to more extensive supplies, such as crayon, markers, or paint. Postprocessing of the rosebush activity reveals the inner world of the child or adolescent. To stay in the metaphor of the "life of the rosebush," the counselor only asks about the rosebush, often focusing on the use of the first-person pronoun, "As a rosebush, I am . . ." According to Ray et al. (2004), the counselor may also say,

> "Describe your rosebush for me. Tell me about your leaves, your branches, your flowers. Tell me where you live. Who takes care of you? How does it feel to be a rosebush?" The counselor may also choose to engage the child in storytelling. For example, the counselor may ask the child to talk about what happens next, or ask for one part of the drawing to talk to another part, "If this fence could talk, what would it say to the roses?"

The stories that emerge from the child's "life as a rosebush" drawing are often very enlightening about their everyday lives. Again, with this and other creative approaches, the counselor must be prepared for the intensity of feelings that are revealed. Oaklander (1978) proposes asking the child questions based on his or her readiness to examine the life situations that emerge. In some cases, it is acceptable and helpful to ask, How, if anything, is living like a rosebush like your everyday life?

Sandtray

Homeyer and Sweeney (2011) have developed a humanistic sandtray model. In their manual, *Sandtray Therapy: A Practical Manual* (2nd ed.), these authors outline a relatively simple to follow, but highly expressive, approach to the use of sandtray in counseling. Sandtray is a versatile medium that is appropriate for use with clients of almost any age (Homeyer & Sweeney, 2011; Shen & Armstrong, 2008). Sandtray makes use of a tray, approximately 20" × 30" and 3" deep, filled with sand, and a set of miniature figures with which to build a scene or a world in the tray. The miniatures are intentionally collected to represent a variety of themes (e.g., people, nature, transportation, spiritual, fantasy). Homeyer and Sweeney recommend a collection of 300 miniatures. Miniatures should be of varied sizes (a large reptile and a small reptile). Like many of the expressive techniques we use in humanistic counseling approaches, the sandtray focuses on the metaphor of the sand world, which increases a sense of safety and emotional distance for the young person. According to Homeyer and Sweeney, the prompt to create the world can take a variety of approaches, including those that are more directive (e.g., create your world at school) or nondirective (e.g., build a scene or build a world). During the creation of the sand world, the therapist is a witness to the child's process. Through this creation process, the child can project aspects of self and his or her experience on the objects and metaphor of the projective world. It is important when processing that the focus is on the metaphor in the sandtray and not directly on the child.

Common ways to process the sandtray include (1) giving the world a title (e.g., If you were to name your world, what would you call it?), (2) describing the scene or telling a story (e.g., Tell me what's happening in this world.), (3) describing sections of the world (e.g., How would you describe this part of the world?), or (4) giving action to the scene or giving certain miniatures a voice (What does the little bear say to the big bear? Who has power in this world?). Staying in the metaphor is important for emotional expression and safety (e.g., Where is the safest place in this world, instead of Where do you feel safe?). An exception to this, according to Homeyer and Sweeney (2011), is when the child makes a connection between the sand world and their everyday world.

OUTCOME RESEARCH

Outcome research related to humanistic counseling approaches with children and adolescents could be considered limited relative to other approaches because of the nature of the approach, the practitioners who use it, and the settings in which it is practiced (Ray, 2006). Because of their adherence to humanistic philosophies, many practitioners and researchers who apply humanistic approaches are uncomfortable with categorizing children into groups or using randomized controls that exclude some children from potentially helpful treatments. By today's rigorous standards for evidence-based practices, humanistic counseling is often not recognized as a research-supported treatment (Cain, 2001). However, a few studies offer some support for humanistic counseling in general (Elliot, 2002; Shechtman & Pastor, 2005), and other studies are beginning to show positive outcomes for young clients using counseling approaches that are based in humanistic theory, including play therapy (Bratton, Ray, Rhine, & Jones, 2005), art therapy (Eaton, Doherty, & Widrick, 2007), and person-centered education (Cornelius-White, 2007).

There are a number of meta-analytic studies to support the use of humanistic approaches with children. A recent meta-analysis on child psychotherapy outcomes (Shirk & Karver, 2003, 2011) reported that the counseling relationship was shown to be an important factor in positive changes for children. In a meta-analysis of studies that compared different treatments for youth with depression, anxiety, and behavior disorders, Miller, Wampold, & Varhely (2008) found that the difference in effectiveness across studies was small. When differences were found, it seemed that they were more related to the researchers' allegiance to the approach rather than true treatment differences. What does this mean? It means that it is probable that counselors' strong allegiance to their counseling techniques is a factor that affects counseling.

Meta-analyses of play therapy outcome studies (Bratton et al., 2005) and CCPT in schools (Ray, Armstrong, Balkin, & Jayne, 2015) have documented the basic effectiveness of CCPT in schools and clinical settings. Bratton, Ray, Rhine, and Jones (2005) reported a strong treatment effect for children who participated in play therapy, compared to those who did not, and humanistic, nondirective, approaches were among the most effective of all of the approaches studied. In their recent meta-analysis of CCPT interventions in schools, Ray et al. (2015) conclude that decades of research findings point to the effectiveness of CCPT in schools. These authors echo those of Bratton et al. (2005) that CCPT is clearly better than no intervention. Furthermore, there is beginning evidence to demonstrate that CCPT might be effective in addressing myriad childhood issues such as attention deficit hyperactivity disorder (ADHD; e.g., Schottelkorb & Ray, 2009), aggression (e.g., Schumann, 2010), teacher-child relationships (e.g., Ray, 2007), and academic achievement (e.g., Blanco & Ray, 2011).

The effectiveness of person-centered education programs for school settings has been examined. In a meta-analytic study, Cornelius-White (2007) investigated teacher-student relationships based on Rogers's work, finding that person-centered or learner-centered teacher behaviors were linked to both affective and behavioral outcomes. Teachers' person-centered beliefs were associated with increases in students' participation, satisfaction with school, and motivation to learn. These findings are consistent with recent outcome studies based on a person-centered teacher consultation (PCTC) model (Ray, 2007; Schottelkorb & Ray, 2009). Person-centered teacher consultation has been shown to affect teachers' empathy, positive regard, and congruence and to decrease stress (Ray, 2007). Schottlekorb and Ray (2009) found that PCTC together with CCPT worked to decrease ADHD symptoms. These findings are promising, but further research is needed to confirm that PCTC is effective as a school-based counseling intervention, especially when used with other child-centered interventions. For those of you studying in other countries, please consider that school-based humanistic counseling approaches have been as widely studied elsewhere as in the United States, especially in Europe (Cooper et al., 2010; Ho"lldampf, Behr, & Crawford, 2010).

COUNSELING KEYSTONES

- Humanistic approaches focus on the holistic experience of living.
- Humanistic approaches emerged after World War I and II, when psychiatry and psychology in the United States were experiencing expansion due in part to the first national policy on mental health, the training of mental health professionals, and the establishment of treatment centers.
- The five basic principles of humanistic psychology are
  - human beings, as human, supersede the sum of their parts;
  - human beings exist in a human, as well as in a cosmic ecology;
  - human beings are aware and are aware of being aware;
  - human beings have some choice and, with that, responsibility; and
  - human beings are intentional and seek meaning, value, and creativity.
- Virginia Axline translated Carl Rogers's humanistic counseling approach into counseling children using play.
- Violet Oaklander used Gestalt therapy with children and adolescents (Oaklander, 1978, 2006). Her work incorporates various art media, dance and movement, play, sand tray, and nature modalities to counsel young people.
- Both Irving Yalom and Clark Moustakas explored existential counseling approaches focused on life's meanings, which is just as important to children as to adults.

- Moustakas's relationship therapy emphasizes the emotions behind actions and focuses on existential needs common to all people, such as love and belonging.
- Because of their emphasis on affective experience and self-expression, play counseling and creative arts have their roots in a humanistic tradition.
- Group counseling, based on Yalom's existential therapeutic factors, is helpful for children and adolescents but maybe particularly beneficial for adolescents.
- Though less conclusive than research related to directive interventions, outcome research in humanistic-existential counseling with children and adolescents suggests the importance of the therapeutic alliance, and child/learner-centered individual, parent, and school interventions.

ADDITIONAL RESOURCES

In Print

Rogers, C. R., & Freiberg, H. J. (1994). *Freedom to learn*. Columbus, OH: Charles Merrill.

Online

Association for Humanistic Counseling, a division of ACA: http://afhc.camp9.org

Center for Play Therapy at the University of North Texas (mainly Child Centered): http://cpt.unt.edu

Dr. Victor Daniels, professor emeritus at Sonoma State University, maintains a list of Gestalt Training Institutes: http://www.sonoma.edu/users/d/daniels/gestaltinst.html

Dr. Irvin D. Yalom's website: http://www.yalom.com

REFERENCES

Arnold, K. (2014). Behind the mirror: Reflective listening and its tain in the work of Carl Rogers. *Humanistic Psychologist, 42*(4), 354–369. doi: 10.1080/08873267.2014.913247

Axline, V. (1969). *Play therapy*. Boston, MA: Houghton-Mifflin.

Baggerly, J., & Parker, M. (2005). Child-centered group play therapy with African American boys at the elementary school level. *Journal of Counseling and Development, 83*(4), 387–396.

Blanco, P., & Ray, D. (2011). Play therapy in elementary schools: A best practice for improving academic achievement. *Journal of Counseling and Development, 89*, 235–243.

Bratton, S. C., Ray, D., Rhine, T., & Jones, L. (2005). The efficacy of play therapy with children: A meta-analytic review of treatment outcomes. *Professional Psychology: Research and Practice, 36*(4), 376–390.

Brinkley, A. (2009). *The unfinished nation: A concise history of the American people, Vol. 2.* New York, NY: McGraw-Hill.

Bernd, B. (2010). *Fritz Perls in Berlin 1893–1933. Expressionism-Psychoanalysis-Judaism* (p. 292). Bergisch Gladbach, Germany: EHP Verlag Andreas Kohlhage.

Bugental, J. (1964). The third force in psychology. *Journal of Humanistic Psychology, 4*(1), 19–26. doi:10.1177/002216786400400102

Cain, D. J. (2001). Defining characteristics, history, and evaluation of humanistic psychotherapies. In D. J. Cain & J. Seeman (Eds.), *Humanistic psychotherapies: Handbook of research and practice* (pp. 34–54). Washington, DC: American Psychological Association.

Carney, J. V., Jacob, J. J., & Hazler, R. J. (2011). Exposure to school bullying and social capital of sixth grade students. *Journal of Humanistic, Counseling, Education, and Development, 50*(2), 238–253.

Cooper, M., Rowland, N., McArthur, K., Pattison, S., Cromarty, K., & Richards, K. (2010). Randomised controlled trial of school-based humanistic counselling for emotional distress in young people: Feasibility study and preliminary indications of efficacy. *Child and Adolescent Psychiatry and Mental Health, 4*(1), 1–12.

Cornelius-White, J. (2007). Learner-centered teacher-student relationships are effective: A meta-analysis, *Review of Educational Research, 77(1),* 113–143. doi: 10.3102/003465430298563

Crenshaw, D. & Stewart, A. (2015). *Play therapy: A comprehensive guide to theory and practice.* New York, NY: Guilford.

Creswell, J. W. (2008). *Research design: Qualitative, quantitative, and mixed methods approach.* Thousand Oaks, CA: Sage.

Danino, M., & Shectman, Z. (2012). Superiority of group counselling to individual coaching for parents of children with learning disabilities. *Psychotherapy Research, 22*(5). 592–603. doi: http://dx.doi.org/10.1080/10503307.2012.692953

Eaton, L. G., Doherty, K. L., & Widrick, B. A. (2007). A review of research and methods used to establish art therapy as a treatment method for traumatized children. *The Arts in Psychotherapy, 34,* 256–262. doi: 10.1016/j.aip.2007.03.001

Elliot, R. (2002). The effectiveness of humanistic therapies: A meta-analysis. In D. J. Cain & J. Seeman (Eds.), *Humanistic psychotherapies: Handbook of research and practice* (pp. 57–81). Washington, DC: American Psychological Association.

Frankl, V. (1959). *Man's search for meaning.* New York, NY: Pocket Books

Frankl, V. (2006). *Man's search for meaning.* Boston, MA: Beacon Press.

Green, E., & Drewes, A. (2013). *Integrating expressive arts and play therapy with children and adolescents.* Hoboken, NJ: John Wiley & Sons.

Grob, G. (1994). *The mad among us: A history of the case of America's mentally ill.* Cambridge, MA: Harvard.

Hölldampf, D., Behr, M., & Crawford, I. (2010). Effectiveness of person-centered and experiential therapy with children and young people: A review. In M. Cooper, J. C. Watson, & D. Ho¨lldampf (Eds.), *Person-centred and experiential therapy works: A review of the research on counselling, psychotherapy and related practices* (pp. 16–44). Ross-on-Wye: PCCS.

Homeyer, L. E., & Sweeney, D. S. (2011). *Sandtray therapy: A practical manual* (2nd ed.). New York, NY: Routledge.

Landreth, G. L. (2012). *Play therapy: The art of the relationship* (2nd ed.). New York, NY: Brunner-Routledge.

Landreth, G. L., & Bratton, S. C. (2006). *Child parent relationship therapy (CPRT): A 10-session filial therapy model.* New York, NY: Routledge.

Lemberger, M. E., & Hutchison, B. (2014). Advocating student-within-environment: A humanistic approach for therapists to animate social justice in the schools. *Journal of Humanistic Psychology, 54*(1), 28–44. doi: 10.1177/002216781246931

Malchiodi, C. A. (Ed.). (2008). *Creative interventions with traumatized children.* New York, NY: Guilford Press.

Miller, S., Wampold, B., & Varhely, K. (2008). Direct comparisons of treatment modalities for youth disorders: A meta-analysis. *Psychotherapy Research, 18*(1), 5–14. doi: 10.1080/10503300701472131

Moustakas, C. (1997). *Relationship play therapy.* Northvale, NJ: Aronson.

Murdock, N. (2013). *Theories of counseling and psychotherapy.* Thousand Oaks, CA: Sage.

Oaklander, V. (1978). *Windows to our children: A Gestalt therapy approach to children and adolescents.* Lafayette, CA: Real People Press.

Oaklander, V. (1997). The rosebush. In H. Kaduson & C. Schaefer (Eds.), *101 favorite play therapy techniques* (pp. 11–13). Northvale, NJ: Jason Aronson.

Oaklander, V. (2006). *Hidden treasure: A map to the child's inner self.* London, UK: Karnac.

Perls, F. (1969). *Gestalt therapy Verbatim.* Lafayette, CA: Real People Press.

Proulx, L. (2002). Strengthening ties, the parent-child-dyad: Group art therapy with toddlers and their parents. *American Journal of Art Therapy, 40,* 238–259.

Prout, H. T., & Brown, D. T. (2007). *Counseling and psychotherapy with children and adolescents: Theory and practice for school and clinical settings.* Hoboken, NJ: John Wiley & Sons.

Ray, D. (2006). Evidence-based play therapy. In C. Schaefer & C. Schaefer (Eds.), *Contemporary play therapy* (pp. 136–157). New York, NY: Guilford.

Ray, D. (2007). Two counseling interventions to reduce teacher-child relationship stress. *Professional School Counseling, 10*(4), 428–440.

Ray, D. (2008). Impact of play therapy on parent-child relationship stress at a mental health training setting. *British Journal of Guidance and Counseling 36(2),* 165–187.

Ray, D., Armstrong, S. A., Balkin, R. S., & Jayne, K. M. (2015). Child-centered play therapy in the schools: Review and meta-analyses. *Psychology in the Schools, 52,* 107–123. doi:10.1002/pits.21798

Ray, D., Perkins, C., & Oden, S. R. (2004). Rosebush fantasy technique with elementary school students. *Professional School Counseling, 7(4),* 277–282.

Rogers, C. (1961). *On becoming a person: A therapist's view of psychotherapy.* London, UK: Constable.

Rogers, C. R. (1970). *Carl Rogers on encounter groups.* New York, NY: Harper and Row.

Rogers, C. (1980). *A way of being.* Boston, MA: Houghton Mifflin.

Rogers, C. (1986). Reflection of feelings and transference. *Person-Centered Review, 1,* 375–377.

Rogers, C. R. (1989). Resolving intercultural tensions. In H. Kirschenbaum & V. L. Henderson (Eds.). *The Carl Rogers reader* (pp. 438–445). Boston, MA: Houghton Mifflin.

Scalzo, C. (2010). *Therapy with children: An existential perspective.* London, UK: Karnac.

Scholl, M. B., McGowan, S., & Hansen, J. T. (2012). *Humanistic perspectives on contemporary counseling issues.* New York, NY: Routledge.

Schumann, B. (2010). Effectiveness of child centered play therapy for children referred for aggression in elementary school. In J. Baggerly, D. Ray, & S. Bratton's (Eds.), *Child-centered play therapy research: The evidence base for effective practice* (pp. 193–208). Hoboken, NJ: Wiley.

Schottelkorb, A. A., & Ray, D. C. (2009). ADHD symptom reduction in elementary students: A single-case effectiveness design. *Professional School Counseling, 13,* 11–22.

Shechtman, Z., &Pastor, R. (2005). Cognitive–behavioral and humanistic group treatment for children with learning disabilities: A comparison of outcomes and process. *Journal of Counseling Psychology 52,* 322–336.

Shen, Y. J. (2010). Trauma-focused group play therapy in the school. In A. A. Drewes and C. E. Schaefer (Eds.). *School-based play therapy* (2nd ed.). Hoboken, NJ: John Wiley & Sons.

Shen, Y. P., & Armstrong, S. (2008). Impact of group sandtray therapy on the self-esteem of young adolescent girls. *Journal for Specialists in Group Work, 33,* 118–137.

Shirk, S., & Karver, M. (2003). Prediction of treatment outcome from relationship variables in child and adolescent therapy: A meta-analytic review. Journal of Consulting and Clinical Psychology, 71, 462–471.

Shirk, S. R., & Karver, M. S. (2011). Alliance in child and adolescent psychotherapy. In J. C. Norcross (Ed.), *Psychotherapy relationships that work: Evidence-based responsiveness* (2nd ed., pp. 70–91). New York, NY: Oxford University Press.

Smith-Adcock, S., Webster, S., Leonard, L. G., & Walker, J. L. (2008). Benefits of a holistic group counseling model to promote wellness in girls at risk for delinquency: An exploratory study. *The Journal of Humanistic, Counseling, Education, and Development, 47(1),* 111–126. doi: 10.1002/j.2161-1939.tb00051.x

Stanley, P. H., Small, R., Owen, S. S., & Burke, T. W. (2012). Humanistic perspectives on addressing school violence. In M. B. Scholl, S. McGowan, & J. T. Hansen (Eds.). *Humanistic perspectives on contemporary counseling issues.* New York, NY: Routledge.

Vernon, A., & Barry, K. L. (2013). *Counseling outside the lines: Creative arts interventions for children and adolescents—Individual, small group, and classroom applications.* Champaign, IL: Research Press.

Villares, E., Lemberger, M., Brigman, G., & Webb, L. (2011). Student success skills: An evidence-based school counseling program grounded in humanistic theory. *Journal of Humanistic Counseling, 50,* 42–55.

Wheeler, G., & Axelsson, L. (2014). *Gestalt therapy.* Washington, DC: APA.

Yalom, I. D. (1970). *The theory and practice of group psychotherapy.* New York, NY: Basic Books.

Yalom, I. D. (1980). *Existential psychotherapy.* New York, NY: Basic Books.

Yalom, I. (2002). *Gift of therapy: An open letter to a new generation of therapists and their patients.* New York, NY: HarperCollins.

Yalom, I. D., & Leszcz, M. (2005). *The theory and practice of group psychotherapy* (5th ed.). New York: Basic Books.

Zinck, K., & Littrell, J.M. (2001). Action research shows group counseling effective with at-risk adolescent girls. *Professional School Counseling, 4*(1), 50–59.

Chapter 7

Cognitive–Behavioral Approaches

TINA SMITH-BONAHUE AND KAITLYN TIPLADY

There is nothing either good or bad but thinking makes it so.

—Shakespeare, Hamlet, Act 2, Scene 2

INTRODUCTION

The idea that how we experience the world is more influenced by how we *think* than by what happens to us was described by philosophers, scholars, and scientists long before cognitive behaviorism was articulated in the 1960s and 1970s. Psychologists such as Beck, Ellis, and Meichenbaum advocated a framework for understanding psychopathology that de-emphasized history, genetics, and underlying diagnostic conditions, focusing instead on individuals' cognitions, emotions, and behaviors. As the name suggests, at its most basic, cognitive behavioral therapies (CBT) can be considered a fusion of behavioral and cognitive approaches. From this foundation, CBTs have exploded in number and include a myriad of techniques. Despite the number and variety of CBT approaches and paradigms, all share a few basic assumptions:

1. Individuals respond to their cognitive representations (i.e., perceptions) of the circumstance and events rather than to the circumstance and events themselves.

2. Learning is mediated by cognitions.

3. Thoughts, behaviors, and emotions are causally interrelated.

4. Cognitions, including schemas, processes, and structures, must be taken into account when planning and evaluating counseling interventions.

5. Thoughts and feelings can be understood through observable and testable means and addressed actively, through behavioral interventions.

6. Within a CBT framework, the counselors's roles include consultant, educator, and diagnostician in order to help the individual identify and remediate cognitive distortions, skill deficits, and patterns of maladaptive behavior.

(Kendall, 1992)

This chapter begins with a description of cognitive behaviorism in general, then summarizes contributions of individual theorists and approaches to counseling youth. Next, we describe how different approaches can be used within a cognitive behavioral framework to improve outcomes for children. Specific strategies and techniques are described, and case examples are provided.

After reading this chapter, you will be able to

- articulate the underlying rationale for CBT;
- explain how CBT can be used to address a wide range of childhood concerns and psychopathology;
- describe specific techniques that enhance the CBT therapists' effectiveness with children and adolescents; and
- outline the empirical support for CBT techniques to promote positive coping and adjustment for children.

SOCIOHISTORICAL CONTEXT

This section begins by describing the context in which CBT was originated as a counseling approach. Then we provide a brief overview of the seminal work of behavioral theorists, Skinner and Watson, followed by cognitive therapists, and concluding with a description of the pioneers who pulled together the two approaches to articulate CBT.

The foundations of the behavioral aspects of CBT were laid during the early 1900s, while the refinement of CBT continues today. Some of the important influences on the behaviorists in the early 1900s were the industrialization of the United States, the creation and spread of the factory model where the assembly line became a dominant feature, and World Wars I and II, which vastly increased the need for improved sorting and training methods for the armed forces.

On the cognitive side of CBT, later movements, such as the existential turn in Europe between the Great Wars and the increasing popularity of self-help methods in the United States in the 1960s and 1970s created an interest in mental processes and their impact on the daily lives of ordinary people. Additionally, following World Wars I and II, Korea, and Vietnam, the United States Veteran's Administration and other mental health providers were searching for quicker and more immediately helpful methods for helping soldiers returning from wars reintegrate with civilian life.

Today, CBT continues to be a popular counseling approach for people of all ages, including children. CBT emphasizes the existential role of cognitions, perceptions, and beliefs in our understanding of the world. At the same time, CBT is action oriented, with the goal of helping clients learn to problem solve. Psychoeducational in nature, with strong emphasis on data-based decision making and observable behavioral changes, CBT is often associated with brief, solution-focused therapies. And, while

Figure 7.1   Cognitive–Behavioral Connections

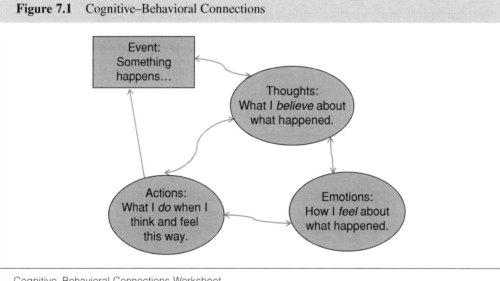

Cognitive–Behavioral Connections Worksheet

1. Describe the event. What happened?

2. What did you think at the time that it happened? Try to remember your exact thoughts and complete the following sentences:

   a. When it was happening, I thought . . .

   b. Right after it happened, I thought . . .

   c. Now I think . . .

4. How did you feel when you were thinking about the event?

5. How did you act? What might other people have seen you do? How do you think they thought you felt?

CBT tends to be more behavioral and reliant on discreet, observable behavior changes than other approaches described in this text, theorists who claim this approach range considerably, falling on a continuum from behavioral to cognitive.

In Guided Exercise 7.1, examine *Thinking-Feeling-Behaving* connections in your own life.

Guided Exercise 7.1

Thinking–Feeling–Behaving Connections

Think about a time in recent memory when you felt upset (e.g., a lower-than-expected grade, another driver cut you off in traffic, etc.). Complete the Connections Worksheet in Figure 7.1. Turn to a classmate, and share your own "connections." Our reactions don't occur in a vacuum. Depending on how you responded, the consequences of your reaction could have made the situation improve or deteriorate. How did your reaction to the event contribute to the consequences? Reflect for a moment on how these thinking-feeling-behavior connections were different for you at varying stages of your life.

THEORISTS

Watson and Classical Conditioning

John B. Watson is the father of behaviorism, which is one of the most influential theories in psychology. In 1913, Watson (1994) challenged the field of psychology through his seminal piece "Psychology as the Behaviorist Views It," where he coined the term *behaviorism* and challenged the existing emphasis on internal, subjective experiences (Schneider & Morris, 1987). Specifically, Watson shocked his colleagues by claiming that for behaviorists, psychology is an objective science based upon measurable and observable characteristics. He famously claimed that if he were give a dozen children, he could raise each one to take on a specific profession (artist, lawyer, doctor, thief, etc.) based on the environment he provided (Schneider & Morris, 1987). This illustrates Watson's approach to his work as well as the radical nature of his theory. Watson denied the significance of cognition in creating behavior and believed that all behaviors could be manipulated by environmental factors (Watson, 1925).

Watson read the work of Ivan Pavlov early in his career, and Pavlov's groundbreaking work with animals greatly influenced his work and led to the development of Watson's theory of classical conditioning (Schneider & Morris, 1987). Classical conditioning is the application of behaviorism where two stimuli are paired together until an association is made. For example, a child may refuse to eat chocolate after an instance when chocolate led to a stomachache because he now associates chocolate with the feeling of nausea. Watson's application of behavioral theory to human behavior may be best illustrated through his seminal case study, "Little Albert" that was originally published by the *Journal of Experimental Psychology* in 1920. While the study is now regarded as highly unethical, it is a powerful example of how the environment can be purposefully manipulated to produce desired results. The intention of the study was to provide evidence for the effectiveness of classical conditioning in changing human behavior by inducing a phobia in a child who previously displayed no phobia behaviors (Watson, Rayner, Jones, & Webb, 2013). Watson established baseline data by exposing Albert to a variety of stimuli including objects and animals like rabbits, dogs, and rats. Initially, Albert was not scared of any of the items or animals (neutral stimulus). During the experimental stage, Albert was continually presented with a rat, and when he attempted to touch the rat, a loud noise (unconditioned stimulus) was made which caused Albert to cry and show fear (unconditioned response). After a few trials, Albert stopped trying to play with the rat, and he became distressed when the rat was introduced (conditioned response). Albert also demonstrated stimulus generalization after the experiment because similar animals, like the bunny and dog, also caused Albert to become distressed (Watson et al., 2013). Watson's experiment with Little Albert demonstrates the core principle of behaviorism—when properly manipulated, the environment can be used to produce specific behavioral responses.

Skinner and Operant Conditioning

Like Watson, B. F. Skinner did not believe that humans have free will or that human cognitions have great influence over behaviors (Skinner, 1953). B. F. Skinner expanded upon the behaviorist principles outlined by Watson and extended those principles into applied practices (Schneider & Morris, 1987). Not only is he responsible for the development of operant conditioning and behavioral analysis, but Skinner is also the father of radical behaviorism (Modgil & Modgil, 1987). Skinner's theory of operant conditioning is built upon the idea that behaviors operate on schedules of reinforcement based on prior experiences that shape the current production of behavior (Skinner, 1953).

Skinner highlighted the concepts of reward and punishment as reinforcement tools for increasing or decreasing the occurrence of specific behaviors. According to Skinner (1953), something is considered a reinforcer only if the frequency of the target behavior increases once the reinforcer is introduced. This means that reinforcers can be both positive (e.g., the introduction of another variable like food, water, free time) and negative (e.g., removing a preexisting aversive stimuli like bright lights or a high-pitched tone) (Skinner, 1953). On the contrary, punishment is the introduction of an aversive stimulus (e.g., spanking, additional chores) or the removal of a preferred variable (e.g., food, videogames), which decreases the likelihood of a future behavior. It is important to note that punishments often occur naturally. For example, a small child may run at the pool and slip and fall in a puddle. The pain is the immediate punishment, but the child also becomes conditioned to walk at the pool.

Skinner, like Watson, did not work directly with children, but his work exerted a strong influence on the design of instruction for them (Murdock, 2013). His theory of operant conditioning remains popular among education professionals who value its efficiency and ease of adaptation to many environments and situations.

Ellis and REBT

Albert Ellis was a contemporary of both B. F. Skinner and Carl Rogers. However, his methods of working with clients differed a great deal from both of them. While psychoanalysis was a popular therapeutic model at the time, Ellis was not satisfied with the slow progress his clients made in resolving their problems in therapy. In response, he began challenging his clients by taking a problem-solving approach that challenged the beliefs of his clients in a rationale and systematic way (The Albert Ellis Institute, 2014).

This lead to the development of rational emotive behavior therapy (REBT), in which the therapist takes an action-based approach to promote rapid positive change in the lives of clients (Ellis, 1995). REBT is an early form of cognitive behavioral therapy, blending the teaching methods of the behaviorists with the challenge of irrational thinking favored by the cognitive theorists.

Because the model is fairly simple to use and understand, it is easy to adapt to the needs of older children and adolescents (Vernon, 2009a). Ann Vernon (2002, 2009b) has written extensively about modifying the basic principles of the theory to work with children and adolescents, often using creative and expressive activities to enhance understanding.

REBT is based on the premise that clients have goals in their lives that contribute to a sense of purpose. As a client attempts to pursue a goal, he or she may encounter an "activating event," which introduces an obstacle in achieving the goal (Ellis, 1994, p. 12). When this obstacle is introduced, individuals either choose to respond positively or negatively, which is the ultimate "consequence" (Ellis, 1994, p. 12). The consequence can result in adaptive feelings like disappointment or maladaptive feelings like anxiety and depression (Ellis, 1994, p. 12). According to REBT, the "beliefs" about the activating event actually shape the consequence the individual experiences (Ellis, 1994, p. 12). By employing rational beliefs about activating events, maladaptive consequences can be avoided. Rational beliefs tend to surround individuals' preferences for specific outcomes, but these beliefs recognize that things are not absolute (Ellis, 1994). For example, a parent who believes that children absolutely must listen to their parents at all times may experience heightened anxiety In comparison to a parent who believes that children should listen to their parents at all times, but also recognizes that children may attempt to assert their independence through defiance. The difference in the absolute nature of their beliefs significantly influences the consequences of the activating agent. To challenge irrational beliefs, clients and therapists must "dispute" those beliefs (Ellis, 1994, p. 13). Ellis considered dispute to be a mainly cognitive process that clients must undergo to achieve "effective new philosophies, emotions, and behaviors" (Ellis, 1994, p. 14). According to Ellis (1994), the effective new philosophy is logical and leads to decreases in neuroticism among clients.

Beck and Cognitive Therapy

Aaron Beck is known as the father of cognitive therapy and is considered to be one of the most influential figures within the field of psychotherapy (Beck, 2011). Like Albert Ellis, Beck was originally trained as a psychoanalyst and became frustrated by the slow progress his clients made (Beck, 1993). His frustration led him to develop a new method for working with clients based on identifying and eliminating irrational thoughts.

Cognitive therapy seeks to change the way that individuals process information by challenging negative thoughts about themselves, the world, or the future (Beck, 1993). It operates on three main assumptions surrounding human cognition. The first assumption is that an individual's thoughts and beliefs will influence his or her behaviors (Beck, 1993). The second assumption is that maladaptive behaviors are the result of irrational thoughts held by individuals (Beck, 1993). Finally, cognitive therapists assume that behaviors are modified when individuals challenge the validity of their thoughts and face the reality of their misconceptions (Beck, 1993).

According to Beck (1993), most individuals can combat negative thoughts by using logic and reasoning, but a person with psychopathology experiences those thoughts so frequently that his or her perception of reality begins to reflect those maladaptive thoughts. By uncovering the content of those thought patterns, cognitive therapists can then determine whether clients are experiencing anxiety, depression, or other psychological disorders (Beck, 1993). Once appropriately identified, they can be successfully treated. Ultimately, the goal of cognitive therapy is to reduce symptomology by teaching clients to directly challenge the legitimacy of their maladaptive thoughts (Beck, 1993).

Many clinicians have adapted Beck's ideas for use with younger clients. Judith Beck has developed an array of training materials for counselors to use with children and adolescents. Cognitive therapy has been used with young clients for a wide variety of problems, including anxiety, trauma, depression, and autism (Beck Institute, 2015).

Compare and contrast the interrelated ideas of cognitive, behavioral, and CBT theorists in Guided Exercise 7.2. Whose ideas resonate for you personally and professionally?

Guided Exercise 7.2

1. Draw a Venn diagram to illustrate the overlapping and differing beliefs of Skinner and Watson. Compare your diagram to a classmate's, and discuss how the therapeutic approach of a counselor relying on Watson's theories might differ from that of a counselor relying on Skinner's theories.

2. Repeat the activity using Beck and Ellis.

3. With a small group of classmates, using the example of specific phobia, discuss ways in which behavioral and cognitive behavioral therapists are similar and different in their approaches to counseling. Consider, for example, a child who has an extreme fear of dogs. How might behavioral counselors explain this? How might cognitive behavioral counselors explain it?

MERGING COGNITIVE AND BEHAVIORAL INTO CBT

From the time of Watson's first writings in the early 1900s until the 1990s, a controversy raged within psychology between the followers of radical behaviorism and the followers of cognitive and psychoanalytic factions (Murdock, 2013). On the behaviorist side, theorists such as Watson, Skinner, and Wolpe argued that all behavior is learned and can be changed through systematic learning situations and experiences. On the other hand, theorists like Alfred Adler, Aaron Beck, and Albert Ellis stated that thinking and feeling are also important to human existence and need to be considered by clinicians (Murdock, 2013).

Along with other clinicians who were active in the 1970s and 1980s, Donald Meichenbaum (1993) sought out a common ground between the two camps. He used Albert Bandura's social learning theory (Bandura, 1969) as a first step toward connecting thoughts and behaviors in counseling. By the late 1980s, many counselors were using a wide array of approaches that integrated aspects of both cognitive and behavioral therapies.

There are now many forms of therapy that combine cognitive and behavioral elements. Reality therapy, REBT, CBT, trauma-focused CBT, multimodal, acceptance and commitment therapy, and dialectical behavioral therapy all have common roots (Trull, 2001). As described in previous sections, different approaches within CBT emphasize different explanations for the relationship between thoughts, feelings, and behaviors. However, CBT sessions tend to be fairly predictable.

Therapists using different CBT approaches (e.g., REBT) use different vocabulary to describe the stages of therapy. However, all CBT therapists typically proceed according to the following general phases: (1) goal-setting, (2) development of a therapeutic alliance, (3) identifying cognitive distortions, (4) disputing and modifying those distortions, (5) skill development, and (6) practice and generalization of new skills. To learn about and apply these phases in greater detail, please see Guided Exercise 7.3.

Guided Exercise 7.3

Phases of Treatment in CBT

Goal setting. CBT is goal directed, with specific, behavioral goals identified at the beginning of the counseling relationship. To identify the goals for counseling, the therapist meets with the child's parents, teachers, or other important figures in his or her life. To identify the issues of concern, therapists use interviews and possibly naturalistic or structured observations, checklists, and other assessment techniques. Diagnostic information (e.g., presence of attention-deficit hyperactivity disorder [ADHD]) may be important for understanding how the child is likely to approach the counseling session. However, neither history nor diagnoses will drive the goals for the counseling. Only current behaviors, thoughts, and feelings will be the focus of the counseling, and therefore, the focus of the assessment. Once the issues are fully understood, the therapist and the child's caregivers work collaboratively to identify measurable goals.

Development of the therapeutic alliance. The importance of a strong therapeutic alliance is well supported in the counseling literature (Karver, Handelsman, Fields, & Bickman, 2006). *Therapeutic alliance* refers to the strength of the relationship between the child and the therapist. Because CBT requires collaboration between the therapist and the client, a strong, respectful, and trusting alliance is particularly important.

Identifying cognitive distortions and deficits. Once the therapeutic alliance has been established; the "problem" has been identified; and the child's preferences, strengths, and interests identified, the focus of the CBT moves into helping the child understand the thought processes that are interfering with the issue of concern. In CBT, in this phase of counseling, the therapist seeks to help clients identify the errors in their thinking and understand the relationship between these errors and their feelings and behavior. This process is best described as "educational" and is heavily verbal (Seligman & Reichenberg, 2014).

When working with children, "cognitive distortion" must be viewed through a developmental lens. The child's cognitive developmental level must not only be taken into account, but it may also require the therapist to conceptualize the construct of "cognitive distortion" differently (Drewes, 2009). Children may hold irrational or distorted beliefs that are maladaptive but developmentally appropriate. For example, it's common for children whose parents divorce to believe that the divorce is their fault (Knell, 2009). While such egocentrism is developmentally typical, without intervention, the inaccurate belief will likely interfere with adaptation. It's also important to note that when working with very young children in CBT, they may lack the metacognitive ability to reflect on their own beliefs, or they may simply not have considered the issues yet. For example, Knell (1998) points out that preschoolers may not have thought about the issues they face at all. Rather than considering "distortions," often it is more helpful to think of addressing preschoolers' lack of understanding, reflection, or skills. Thus, rather than disputing irrational beliefs, the therapist's role is to build skills and knowledge to facilitate healthy adaptation.

Addressing cognitive distortions or deficiencies. Once the cognitive distortions or deficiencies are identified, therapists begin to help children adopt new ways of understanding their worlds. This stage generally involves the therapist verbally challenging the irrational or erroneous beliefs of the client. Depending on the specific approach taken, CBT might include inductive questioning, games or activities, or even tasks to be completed outside of therapy.

Central to this stage is facilitating problem solving for children or adolescents. The extent to which the therapist directs this process versus takes a more client-directed approach varies by technique and individual theorist. Knell (1998, 2009) advocates a more directive approach, pointing out that modeling is almost always used to help children develop more adaptive strategies. Numerous modalities can be used, including puppets, dolls, art, bibliotherapy, etc., but in this framework, the therapist identifies the strategy and uses models to teach the technique.

Skill development. Once the new cognitions or skills have been modeled, it is important to ensure that the child fully understands them and can apply them, initially in the safety of the therapy room. By this point, the therapist typically knows what kinds of materials the client is likely to prefer (Knell, 2009).

Practice and generalization of new skills. Unless clients use new skills and cognitions in their everyday lives, the therapeutic change stays in the therapy room. For this reason, CBT therapists almost always assign homework to their clients. For children, this homework must be facilitated by parents or family members; even for adolescents, homework must generally be monitored by parents. It is at this stage that the importance of collaboration between the therapist, the client, and the family is highlighted.

Homework assignments provide a structured way for the family to help the child or adolescent reinforce and practice new skills. In the spirit of collaboration, the client, and for younger children the client and family, should be invited to participate in developing the homework assignments. When working with children, at the beginning of each session, the therapist asks the parent and the child, if the child is developmentally able, to report on the success of the homework since the last session. At the end of each session, the therapist, parent, and child plan the next homework assignment.

Activity: Applying the Phases of CBT

Max is an 11-year-old boy who loves to play soccer, video games, and talk with his friends. While he excels socially, he struggles academically and, reportedly, hates school and his teachers. Yesterday, Max threw his notebook at his math teacher. As part of his behavioral intervention, you would like to teach him strategies to recognize his anger, relax, and build his academic self-esteem. But before you can teach him these skills, you must establish a therapeutic alliance. During your first session, Max refused to speak to you and avoided eye contact. Based on Max's interests, what strategies can you use to establish a therapeutic alliance?

In Case Illustration 7.1, examine how the connections worksheet and homework were used with an adolescent client.

Case Illustration 7.1

Ricky

Ricky is a 14-year-old ninth grader who asks to see the counselor because of concerns about bullying. Ricky reports that he has a few friends at school, but none are in his classes. He describes feeling left out and bullied in most of his classes, indicating that he looks forward to being old enough to drop out of school to avoid his peers.

Ricky is very verbal and willingly engages in conversations with Mr. Blake, the counselor. Mr. Blake notes that Ricky does not describe interests that are typical of high school freshmen and seems a bit immature. When he asks Ricky to describe the instances of "bullying," he is struck by Ricky's lack of social sophistication. To understand Ricky's perceptions of his peers' behaviors and his feelings about their teasing, Mr. Blake and Ricky work together to complete the CBT Connections worksheet. It becomes clear that Ricky interprets many ambiguous comments as being targeted at himself. Further, his interpretation of typical high school banter assumes that others are making fun of him.

Mr. Blake and Ricky work together to develop goals for counseling that include helping Ricky develop strategies for dealing with peers' teasing. To begin this process, Mr. Blake and Ricky identify comments that his peers frequently make during class and discuss possible interpretations of them. Once rapport is established, Mr. Blake begins to gently challenge Ricky's assumptions that the comments are all targeted at him by asking him to hypothesize about what else his peers might mean by their comments. They also work together to develop a "script" for Ricky to use when he feels like he's the target of peer teasing.

At the same time, Mr. Blake recognizes that Ricky's assumptions are in part fueled by his own perceptions of himself as "different" and somehow inferior to his peers. He and Ricky agree on a series of homework activities in which Ricky is asked to work with his parents to identify his own strengths, interests, and goals.

ADAPTING CBT FOR YOUNGER CHILDREN

While considerable research supports the effectiveness of CBT for adults, and to some extent adolescents, its application for children, particularly younger children, has not been studied as extensively. Of particular concern for application with children is CBT's heavy reliance on language and the need for metacognition and reflection that exceeds the cognitive capability of some children, particularly younger children. In order for CBT to be effective and practical with younger children, modifications to reduce the need for complex language must be made. Because younger children are less adept at expressing their thoughts and feelings and at solving problems verbally, play-based techniques can be very effective.

For children, many of the issues addressed in counseling are complex and abstract. The use of metaphors (e.g., in pretend play) can help make these abstract concepts more real for the child. Any number of techniques and modalities can be used within CBT to help clients understand these abstract issues, depending on the presenting problem, the child's developmental level, and interests of the child or adolescent. This section briefly provides an overview of how games, storytelling, puppets and drama, and super hero play can be used to teach metaphors and practice skills in CBT. Each of these techniques is both similar to and separate from the real world, enabling the child first to understand complex issues and concepts, then take risks and try out new ideas without danger of social consequences.

INTEGRATIVE AND COGNITIVE BEHAVIORAL PLAY THERAPY

Drewes combined traditional play therapy with cognitive-behavioral therapy and other techniques to produce an eclectic framework referred to as integrative play therapy (Drewes, 2009). Specifically, Drewes encourages practitioners to draw upon CBT techniques based on the plethora of empirical support provided by researchers (Drewes, 2009). A similar melding of techniques to make CBT approaches appropriate for children was described by Knell (1995) as cognitive behavioral play therapy (CBPT). In this approach, Knell advocates using play as a medium to accomplish the goals of CBT. Because CBPT does not rely on language, instruction in cognitive change is less direct and often accomplished through modeling. Other aspects of CBT, such as generalization and homework, are included in CBPT but modified to include parents and other important adult care providers.

As compared to approaches such as child-directed play therapy, CBPT is more directive and more structured. Goals for the counseling are agreed upon at the beginning of the relationship, and the individual sessions planned in a way that facilitates movement toward the goals. Similarly, in CBPT, unlike other forms of play therapy, play is assumed to be educational in nature, and the activities selected are chosen based on the therapists' judgment regarding what techniques will be most efficient in teaching the new thoughts and behaviors. Within both CBPT and play therapy, play is assumed to be the primary mode of communication with the child, a means for the child to be heard and understood (Foulkrod & Davenport, 2010). However, the CBP therapist adds verbal labels and teaches language associated with coping, making specific connections between the child's new understanding of links between thoughts, feelings, and actions (Drewes, 2009).

The role of the therapist varies within CBPT as well. Most commonly, the therapist assumes the role of an educator, explicitly teaching cognitive strategies and skills. How directive the CBP therapist is may vary, however, depending on the age and developmental level of the child, the presenting concerns, and the therapist's preferences and style.

CBPT also has similarities and differences with traditional, adult-focused CBT. Unlike CBT, CBPT minimizes demands on the child for talking and focuses on experiential learning. As a result of the nature of play, CBPT also tends to be more indirect in teaching new skills and thought processes (Knell, 1995). Further, the role of homework may be minimized (Pearson, Russ, & Spannagel, 2008). Using homework in counseling children and adolescents is explored in Guided Exercise 7.4.

Guided Exercise 7.4

Homework

Albert Ellis is famous for explaining the role of homework with the old joke "How do you get to Carnegie Hall? Practice, practice, practice." Changing beliefs and behaviors is no small task, and there's really nothing for it but hard work and practice. CBT is an educational approach, so it's probably not surprising that cognitive behavioral therapists assign homework to help clients acquire and generalize new skills. Homework in a CBT sense doesn't have to be academic in nature. In his workshops, Ellis described wildly creative homework activities, individualized to meet the specific therapeutic needs of clients.

Work with a small group of classmates to develop creative, nonacademic homework assignments to address the referral concerns and developmental levels of the following examples:

- 14-year-old with social anxiety
- 9-year-old with anger control issues
- 5-year-old with social skills deficits

TRAUMA-FOCUSED CBT

Trauma-focused CBT (TF-CBT) is a relatively short-term (12 to 18 sessions) treatment process designed to help children, adolescents, and their nonabusive parent or caregiver reduce the emotional impact of traumatic events (Cohen, Mannarino, & Deblinger, 2006). There is research supporting the effectiveness of TF-CBT across many diverse groups in reducing the symptoms of anxiety, sleep disturbance, depressed mood, irritability, anger, and other common problems that arise following one or more traumatic events (Child Welfare Information Gateway, 2012).

Counselors wishing to use TF-CBT with clients should seek out additional training, either online or in person. The Medical University of South Carolina offers free introductory online training at their website, https://www.musc.edu/tfcbt. In essence, the TF-CBT treatment protocol can be summed up by the acronym PRACTICE:

P: Psychoeducation and parent training

R: Relaxation training

A: Affective expression and regulation

C: Cognitive coping and processing

T: Trauma narrative and processing

I: In vivo experiencing

C: Conjoint parent and child sessions

E: Enhancing personal safety and growth

Within the basics of the PRACTICE model, counselors are able to modify how each goal is accomplished based on the developmental and cultural needs of the client. For example, *T*, trauma narrative and processing with a 4-year-old might take the form of sandtray play and finger painting, while with a 17-year-old, it might be a primarily verbal exchange enhanced by journaling or role plays.

DIALECTICAL BEHAVIOR THERAPY WITH ADOLESCENTS

Dialectical behavior therapy (DBT) was developed for use with clients who have borderline personality disorder by Marsha Linehan, a psychologist who has learned to cope with her own borderline personality disorder. DBT is a set of very structured and specific coping skills designed to help clients with borderline personality disorder and/or chronic suicidal ideation. Linehan's first book about DBT with adult clients was published in 1993 and since then has been adapted for use with other populations, including adolescents (Rathus & Miller, 2014). When used with modifications for adolescents, it is referred to as DBT-A.

DBT combines basic CBT ideas about reforming irrational thoughts with mindfulness training and very specific concrete skills to help clients learn to master emotional regulation, distress tolerance, and interpersonal effectiveness (Rathus & Miller, 2014). The course of treatment with DBT includes multiple modalities, including group, family, and individual sessions. Phone call coaching sessions are also suggested as part of treatment follow-up after the conclusion of therapy for a short period of time to encourage continued use of new behaviors and cognitive strategies (Linehan, 1993).

Several research studies to date have pointed to DBT-A as an effective treatment for adolescents with a variety of issues similar to those found in adults with borderline personality disorder. Some examples include Trupin, Stewart, Beach, and Boesky (2002), who studied the use of DBT-A with girls incarcerated in juvenile justice facilities, and James, Taylor, Winmill, and Adofari (2008) who found it to be effective with adolescent girls who had a history of self-harming behaviors. DBT-A appears to show promise in helping adolescents learn to better manage difficult emotions, reduce suicidal thoughts and gestures, and improve relationship skills.

However, more research is needed to show whether DBT-A is equally effective across gender, race, ethnicity, and other cultural variables. Counselors who want to use DBT-A should attend a formal training after reading the Rathus & Miller (2014) text. Dr. Linehan's website, https://dbt-lbc.org, offers online and in-person training information. To see an example of a DBT-A exercise for improving emotional regulation, see Guided Exercise 7.5.

Guided Exercise 7.5

DBT-A Skills for Emotional Regulation

In order to reduce the impact of negative emotions, adolescents are taught the following mnemonic device: ABC PLEASE

- A—Accumulate Positive Emotions: Be mindful of and remember positive experiences.
- B—Build Mastery: Do things that create a sense of accomplishment.
- C—Cope Ahead of Time With Emotional Situations: Figure out effective responses in advance of situations.
- Treat Physical Illness—Being sick lowers resistance to negative emotions.
- Balance Eating—Eat what helps you feel good.
- Avoid Mood Altering Drugs.
- Balance Sleep—Get the right amount of sleep.
- Exercise—Aerobic exercise, done consistently, is a powerful antidepressant.

CREATIVE TECHNIQUES FOR USING CBT WITH CHILDREN AND ADOLESCENTS

Games

In the context of CBT, games can be a rich teaching tool, particularly for elementary-aged children. Games are particularly useful in CBT for helping children develop and practice cognitive strategies. The therapist can structure tasks within the game to challenge children to realistically evaluate situations and interpret the consequences of their choices in a safe context.

Many games include risk and decision making. To successfully navigate them, children must pay attention and plan. In this way, games may simulate reality, affording opportunities for children to practice skills and new ways of thinking without suffering the consequences that occur in real life. Swanson and Casarjian (2001) state that games can help children practice social skills, particularly self-control and regulation.

Many types of games can be adapted to meet the therapists' needs. Numerous therapeutic games are commercially available, addressing a huge array of presenting concerns, such as anger-management, social skills, self-control, emotional regulation, and so on. However, counselors may find that adapting traditional board games to meet the specific needs of their clients is not only more economical, it is also more efficient. The counselor, working individually or with the child, can create rules to encourage skill development. For example, if a child enjoys playing Candy Land, the therapist could add a rule to the game that every time players land on yellow they must answer a card about feelings, while every time they land on blue, they must answer a question about thoughts. For younger or very active children, similar modifications can be made to locomotor games, such as hopscotch or catch. In Guided Exercise 7.6, brainstorm ways to use popular games in counseling children and adolescents.

Guided Exercise 7.6

Games in Counseling

Turn to a partner, and discuss how the following games could be adapted to a CBT framework and used with children: Jenga, Chutes and Ladders, and Trouble. What additional games could you use?

Storytelling

Stories provide a way to introduce new ideas and can help children and adolescents perceive the world differently through metaphor. Freidberg and Wilt (2010) describe how the use of stories can provide metaphors to help make complex psychological situations real for children. Stories can be therapist developed or based on popular media, depending on the particular issue being addressed. Depending on the age and developmental level of the child and the nature of the issues, metaphors and stories may be more or less abstract. In helping children understand issues, metaphors may be more abstract and taught through books or stories. For example, stories about pirates avoiding sharks and dangerous coastlines could be used to understand a socially anxious child's perceptions of a school lunch room and the demands for interacting with others. The therapist can use the story to help the child identify and reframe the dangers she perceives in her world. Once the issues are understood and reframed, therapy can shift to more concrete, realistic storytelling, complete with skills and scripts to be practiced.

Drama and Puppet Play

Seminal work by researchers and theorists such as Bandura (1969) and Meichenbaum (1971) highlight the power of social learning—that is, children and adolescents are much more likely to engage in a behavior if they see a peer or other role model engage in it first. The more concrete and attuned to the child's reality the story is, the more likely the child is to emulate desired behaviors (Freidberg & Wilt, 2010). Dramatic play can provide developmentally appropriate and enjoyable contexts for application of new ideas and behaviors through social modeling.

Knell (1995, 2009) describes how puppets, stuffed toys, or dolls can be used to model more adaptive responses to social situations. The therapist is an active participant in this role play. Depending on the phase of counseling, the counselor can act as the role model who gives the appropriate response or the antagonist who attempts to elicit a different, more adaptive, response.

Other forms of dramatic play have been found to promote social skill development in young children (Lillard et al., 2013). Working with one child or a group of children, a therapist can provide a script that sets up a vignette parallel to the real-life situation that poses a challenge for the children.

Consider the case of Jasmine. Her counselor used toys to help her transition to school and a new teacher.

Case Illustration 7.2

Jasmine

Jasmine is a 5-year-old kindergartner referred by her teacher, Ms. Johnson, to the counselor because of concerns about her "adjustment to school."

Assessment

Teacher Interview: Before she begins work with Jasmine, the counselor, Ms. Ramirez, wants to make sure she understands what Ms. Johnson means by "adjustment to school." Ms. Ramirez begins by interviewing Ms. Johnson in order to better understand her concerns as well as to collaborate with Ms. Johnson to operationally define the referral concern. As a result of the interview, Ms. Ramirez learns that Ms. Johnson sees Jasmine as a sweet little girl who is extremely shy and reluctant to participate in class. Ms. Johnson says that Jasmine keeps to herself and doesn't participate in class activities. Ms. Johnson worries that Jasmine's passivity will interfere with her academic achievement.

Parent Interview: Ms. Ramirez meets with Jasmine's mother, Ms. Adams. According to Ms. Adams, Jasmine met all developmental milestones within normal limits. An only child, Jasmine stayed home with her mother until she began kindergarten. Ms. Adams reports that Jasmine has had typical opportunities to interact with peers through play groups and soccer. She is very surprised to hear Jasmine described as passive. According to Ms. Adams, Jasmine is shy, but not excessively so, and eventually warms up to most adults.

Observation: Ms. Ramirez observes Jasmine during reading instruction and at lunch. During reading, Jasmine seemed to keep to herself, avoiding eye contact with Ms. Johnson and other children. Even when children are encouraged to work with a partner, Jasmine looks down at her book, avoiding other children's attempts to engage her in conversation. Ms. Ramirez also notes that Ms. Johnson is a loud and enthusiastic teacher. She frequently tells students that if they don't follow rules, they'll lose recess.

During lunch, however, Ms. Ramirez sees very different behavior. Jasmine sits between two other girls who talk, giggle, and share food.

First Meeting With Jasmine: During her first meeting with Jasmine, Ms. Ramirez immediately notices that Jasmine seems shy, reluctant to make eye contact or conversation. To help establish rapport and a therapeutic alliance, she encourages Jasmine to select a game that they can play together. Jasmine chooses Candy Land. While they play the game, Jasmine begins to relax and starts to respond to Ms. Ramirez's inquiries about her favorite foods, colors, activities, and so on. Ms. Ramirez concludes that Jasmine's social skills fall roughly within normal limits, and that temperamentally, she is best described as "slow-to-warm-up."

Second Meeting With Jasmine: To understand Jasmine's perceptions of school, without trying to force her to talk about her thoughts and feelings, Ms. Ramirez introduces a Fisher-Price toy school, with desks, child figures, and teacher figures. She encourages Jasmine to play with the figurines and notes that Jasmine's preferred play involves taking the small figures out of the school building and onto the "playground." Jasmine avoids playing with the adult figures, focusing instead on the child figures. Ms. Ramirez begins to prompt Jasmine to include the adult figure by making comments like "I wonder what the teacher is going to do now?" Gradually, Jasmine begins to give the teacher figurine a voice. Jasmine's "teacher voice" is loud and angry sounding, and the child figurines continue to avoid her.

Third Meeting With Jasmine: This week, Ms. Ramirez introduces art materials, asking Jasmine to "draw a picture of a child at school." Jasmine seems happy to comply and draws two figures, one very large, identified as the teacher, and one very small, identified as the student. When Ms. Ramirez asks how each person in the drawing is feeling, Jasmine responds that the smaller, student figure is "scared," and the larger teacher figure is "angry."

Hypothesis and Goal Setting: Ms. Ramirez hypothesizes that Jasmine interprets Ms. Johnson's loud voice as angry, and assumes that Ms. Johnson is angry with her. She plans a series of activities to challenge Jasmine's assumptions. At the same time, Ms. Johnson works collaboratively with Jasmine's mother and teacher to provide homework opportunities that reinforce the idea that *loud* is different from *angry*. She works with Ms. Johnson on strategies to improve her relationships with Jasmine, including opportunities for quiet conversations about Jasmine's interests and family.

When children and adolescents are first learning new skills, they will likely need more support through a more complete script. As children become more comfortable with the new skills, the vignette can become more open-ended, and children can be encouraged to improvise the resolution of the story. Children can also be asked to play multiple roles in the scenes, with children taking on the persona of adults such as teachers and parents while the therapist takes on the persona of the child. Such enactments enable the child to take the perspective of others as well as to practice possible reactions to different social situations. In addition to interventions created individually by counselors, there are many CBT-based manualized treatments available for purchase. Two of the more popular and effective such interventions, Coping Cat (for anxiety in children and adolescents) and the Penn Resiliency Program (for reducing depressive symptoms in adolescents) are described in Guided Exercise 7.7.

Guided Exercise 7.7

Manualized Programs to Treat Internalizing Disorders

Anxiety Disorders

One of the most widely used treatment paradigms for anxiety is the coping cat (Kendall & Hedtke, 2006). Coping Cat is a 16-session counseling program designed for children between the ages of 6 and 17 with generalized anxiety disorder, social phobia, and separation anxiety disorder. The manualized program builds upon rational CBT principles by teaching children how to recognize anxiety, minimize anxiety, and how to reinforce good behaviors. Simple terminology, pictures, and straightforward examples are used to communicate concepts to children in concrete ways. There is also a corresponding workbook that provides exercises, illustrations, and homework assignments.

Kendall and Hedtke (2006) describe Coping Cat as a "treatment manual" that is best used when therapists employ clinical judgment and individualize the program (p. v). The authors stress the importance of using Coping Cat flexibly to meet the developmental and contextual needs of the children and families they work with. Implementation fidelity research is presented to provide guidance regarding how to modify the Coping Cat to meet the specific needs of the clients, while still maintaining the validity and integrity of the program. Specifically, in addition to anxiety, the authors report research supporting the adaptation of Coping Cat for individuals with comorbidities, social skills deficits, and common problems like ADHD and depression. (See, for example, Beidas, Benjamin, Puelo, Edmunds, & Kendall, 2010).

Coping Cat is designed around the simple acronym, FEAR. This helps children remember how to recognize when they are "Feeling frightened" and "Expecting bad things to happen" as a result of that fear (Kendall & Hedtke, 2006, p. iii). The acronym helps remind them to form "Attitudes and Actions that can help," which leads to "Results and Rewards" (Kendall & Hedtke, 2006, p. iii). Throughout the first eight sessions, therapists introduce CBT strategies in developmentally appropriate ways. For example, they teach coping strategies, relaxation training, self-talk, and contingent rewards using role-play and visualization activities (Kendall & Hedtke, 2006, p. ii). Then in the next eight sessions, children practice the skills they have learned through exposure tasks. During sessions four and nine, parents are also encouraged to participate as this leads to better long-term results for children. At the end of the Coping Cat sessions, children actually tape a commercial, in which they summarize the strategies they have learned to reduce their anxiety (Kendall & Hedtke, 2006).

Depression

The Penn Resiliency Program for Adolescents (PRP-A; Gillham, Brunwasser, & Freres, 2008) addresses maladaptive thinking patterns. The PRP-A is specifically designed to reduce depressive symptoms in adolescents. The program has two components. In the first sessions of the intervention, adolescents learn about the relationship between their beliefs, their feelings, and their actions. They are encouraged to apply this understanding to their own thinking styles, particularly beliefs that result in feelings of hopelessness and pessimism. In the second half of the intervention, the focus shifts to skill building. The clients learn specific strategies to address problem-solving and social skills. An optional parent component, in which parents are taught to reinforce the skills learned during the adolescent sessions and to apply the skills to their own lives, can be added as well (Gillham, Hamilton, Freres, Patton, & Gallop, 2006).

OUTCOME RESEARCH

CBT is one of the most well researched intervention therapies, with "over 325 published outcome studies" and more than 270 meta-analytic studies of CBT approaches (Butler, Chapman, Foreman, Beck, 2006, p. 17; Hofmann, Asnaani, Vonk, Sawyer, & Fang, 2012). A great deal of empirical support suggests that CBT is effective to treat and prevent a wide array of presenting problems with many different client groups (Allen, 2011; Forman & Barakat, 2011), such as anxiety (Cohen, Edmunds, Brodman, Benjamin & Kendall, 2013; Crawley et al., 2013), depression (Gillham et al., 2012), academic problems (Schmitz & Perels, 2011), ADHD (Levine & Anshel, 2011), and externalizing disorders (Powell et al., 2011).

In 2006, a meta-analysis of cognitive-behavioral interventions was conducted and analyzed according to 16 different disorders. Researchers found that CBT produced the greatest positive change in populations with depression, generalized anxiety disorder, panic disorder, social phobia, posttraumatic stress disorder, and childhood depressive and anxiety disorders (Butler, Chapman, Forman, Beck, 2006, p. 17). Change was also recorded in populations with marital distress, anger, childhood somatic disorders and chronic pain, but the change was not as significant as those previously listed (Butler, et al., 2006, p. 17). In another analysis of over 100 meta-analytical studies, CBT produced positive change for individuals who struggled with anxiety, somatoform disorders, bulimia, anger control problems, and stress (Hofmann et al., 2012).

CONCLUSION

Cognitive Behavioral Therapy has received a great deal of attention in recent years as an empirically supported, effective, and efficient approach for addressing most psychosocial problems. Its applications for children, however, are limited by the heavy reliance on verbal instructions and the need to understand and reframe complex, abstract cognitions. Play offers a means of translating the underlying framework and constructs of CBT into a form that is helpful and understandable for children.

COUNSELING KEYSTONES

- CBT arose from combining behavioral and cognitive theories, which had existed since the early 1900s.
- CBT is an umbrella term for a large variety of treatments and techniques that combine elements of behaviorism and cognitive theory in some form.

- Although originally designed for use with adults, CBT has been modified to fit the needs of children and adolescents across a broad range of problems and cultures.
- CBT has the largest research base of all forms of counseling as of this date. Many approaches for use with children and adolescents have been researched, some extensively, and have been shown to be effective.
- Counselors should be cautious not to assume that any technique or intervention program is valid and reliable because it is labeled as CBT. Some programs and techniques work well only with certain populations or problems, and many have not been researched at all.

ADDITIONAL RESOURCES

In Print

Drewes, A. A., Bratton, S. C., & Schaefer, C. E. (2011). *Integrative play therapy.* Hoboken, NJ: John Wiley and Sons, Inc.
Knell, S. (1995). *Cognitive behavioral play therapy.* New York, NY: Aaronson & Sons.

Online

Coping Cat: http://www.workbookpublishing.com/coping-cat-workbook-2nd-edition-ages-7-13.html
Creative Therapy Store: https://www.creativetherapystore.com
National Child Traumatic Stress Network: http://www.nctsn.org
Penn Resiliency Program for Adolescents: http://www.ppc.sas.upenn.edu/prpsum.htm

REFERENCES

The Albert Ellis Institute. (2014). *About Albert Ellis.* Retrieved from http://albertellis.org/about-albert-ellis-phd
Allen, K. (2011). Introduction to the special issue: Cognitive-Behavioral Therapy in the school setting—Expanding the school psychologists' toolkit. *Psychology in the Schools, 48*(3), 215–222.
Bandura, A. (1969). *Principles of behavior modification.* New York, NY: Holt, Rinehart & Winston.

Beck, A. (1993). Cognitive therapy: Past, present and future. *Journal of Consulting and Clinical Psychology, 61*(2), 194–198.

Beck Institute. (2015). *What is CBT?* Retrieved from https://www.beckinstitute .org/get-informed/cbt-faqs

Beck, J. S. (2011). *Cognitive behavior therapy: Basics and beyond* (2nd ed., pp. 19–20). New York, NY: The Guilford Press.

Biedas, R. S., Benjamin, C. L., Puelo, C. M., Edmunds, J. M., & Kendall, P. C. (2010). Flexible applications of the coping cat program for anxious youth. *Cognitive Behavioral Practice, 17*(2), 142–153. doi: 10.1016/j.cbpra.2009.11.002

Butler, A. C., Chapman, J. E., Forman, E. M., Beck, A. T. (2006). The empirical status of cognitive behavioral therapy: A review of meta-analyses. *Clinical Psychology Review, 26*, 17–31.

Child Welfare Information Gateway (2012). *Trauma-focused cognitive behavioral therapy for children affected by sexual abuse or trauma.* Retrieved from https:// www.childwelfare.gov/pubPDFs/trauma.pdf

Cohen, J. A., Mannarino, A. P., & Deblinger, E. (2006). *Treating trauma and traumatic grief in children and adolescents.* New York, NY: Guilford.

Cohen, J. S., Edmunds, J. E., Brodman, D. M., Benjamin, C. L., & Kendall, P. C. (2013). Using self-monitoring: Implementation of collaborative empiricism in cognitive-behavioral therapy. *Cognitive and Behavioral Practice, 20*, 419–428.

Crawley, S. A., Kendall, P. C., Benjamin, C. L., Brodman, D. M., Wei, C., Beidas, R. S., Podell, J. L., & Mauro, C. (2013). Brief cognitive-behavioral therapy for anxious youth: Feasibility and initial outcomes. *Cognitive and Behavioral Practice, 20,* 123–133.

Drewes, A. A. (2009). *Blending play therapy with cognitive behavioral therapy: Evidence-based and other effective treatments and techniques.* Hoboken, NJ: John Wiley and Sons.

Ellis, A. (1994). *Reason and emotion in psychotherapy: A comprehensive method of treating human disturbances.* New York, NY: Citadel Press.

Ellis, A. (1995). Changing rational-emotive therapy (RET) to rational emotive behavior therapy (REBT). *Journal of Rational-Emotive and Cognitive-Behavior Therapy, 13*(2), 85–89.

Forman, S. G., & Barakat, N. M. (2011). Cognitive behavioral therapy in the schools: Bringing research to practice through effective implementation. *Psychology in the Schools, 48*(3), 283–293.

Foulkrod, K., & Davenport, B. R. (2010). An examination of empirically informed practice within case reports of play therapy with aggressive and oppositional children. *International Journal of Play Therapy, 19*(3), 144–158. doi .org/10.1037/a0020095

Freidberg, R. D., & Wilt, L. H. (2010). Metaphors and stories in cognitive behavioral therapy with children. *Journal of Rational Emotive Cognitive Behavioral Therapy, 28,* 100–113.

Gillham, J. E., Brunwasser, S. M., & Freres, D. R. (2008). Preventing depression in early adolescents: The Peen resiliency program. In J. R. Z. Abela, & B. L. Hankin (Eds.), *Handbook of depression in children and adolescents* (pp. 309–322). New York, NY: Guilford Press.

Gillham, J. E., Hamilton, J., Freres, D. R., Patton, K., & Gallop, R. (2006). Preventing depression among early adolescents in the primary care setting: A randomized controlled study of the Penn resiliency program. *Journal of Abnormal Child Psychology, 34,* 203–219.

Gillham, J. E., Reivich, K. J., Brunwasser, S. M., Freres, D. R., Chajon, N. D., Kash-MacDonald, V. M., Chaplin, T. M., Abenavoli, R. M., Matlin, S. L., Gallop, R. J., & Seligman, E. P. (2012). Evaluation of a group cognitive-behavioral depression prevention program for young adolescents: A randomized effectiveness trial. *Journal of Clinical Child and Adolescent Psychology, 41*(5), 621–639.

Hofman, S. G., Asnaani, A., Vonk, I. J. J., Sawyer, A. T., & Fang, A. (2012). The efficacy of cognitive behavioral therapy: A review of meta-analyses. *Cognitive Therapy Research, 36*(5), 437–440.

James, A. C., Taylor, A., Winmill, L., & Alfoadari, K. (2008). A preliminary community study of dialectical behaviour therapy (DBT) with adolescent females demonstrating persistent, deliberate self-harm (DSH). *Child and Adolescent Mental Health, 13*(3), 148–152.

Karver, M. S., Handelsman, J. B., Fields, S., & Bickman, L. (2006). Meta-analysis of therapeutic relationship variables in youth and family therapy: The evidence for different relationship variables in the child and adolescent treatment literature. *Clinical Psychology Review, 26,* 50–65.

Kendall, P. C. (Ed.). (1992). *Child and adolescent therapy: Cognitive behavioral procedures.* New York, NY: Guilford Press.

Kendall, P. C., & Hedtke, K., (2006). Cognitive-behavioral therapy for anxious children: Therapist manual 3. Ardmore, PA: Workbook Publishing.

Knell, S. (2009). Cognitive behavioral play therapy. In K. J. O'Connor, & L. D. Braverman (Eds.), *Play therapy theory and practice: Comparing theories and techniques* (pp. 203–236). Hoboken, NJ: Wiley & Sons.

Levine, E. S., & Anshel, D. J. (2011). "Nothing works!" A case study using cognitive-behavioral interventions to engage parents, educators, and children in the management of attention-deficit/hyperactivity disorder. *Psychology in the Schools, 48*(3), 297–306.

Lillard, A. S., Lerner, M. D., Hopkins, E. J., Dore, R. A., Smith, E. D., & Palmquist, C. M. (2013). The impact of pretend play on children's development: A review of the evidence. *Psychological Bulletin, 139,* 1–34.

Linehan, M. (1993). *Cognitive-behavioral treatment of borderline personality disorder.* New York, NY: Guilford Press.

Meichenbaum, D. (1971). Examination of model characteristics in reducing avoidance behavior. *Journal of Personality and Social Psychology, 17,* 298–307.

Meichenbaum, D. (1993). Changing conceptions of cognitive-behavior modification: Retrospective and prospect. *Journal of Consulting and Clinical Psychology, 61,* 202–204.

Modgil, S., & Modgil, C. (1987). *B. F. Skinner: Consensus and controversy.* Basingstoke, Hants: Taylor & Francis.

Murdock, N. L. (2013). *Theories of counseling and psychotherapy: A case approach* (3rd ed.). Columbus, OH: Prentice Hall.

Pearson, B. L., Russ, S. W., & Spannagel, S. A. C. (2008). Pretend play and positive psychology: Natural companions. *The Journal of Positive Psychology, 3,* 110–119.

Powell, N. P., Boxmeyer, C. L., Baden, R., Stromeyer, S., Minney, J. A., Mushtaq, A., & Lochman, J. E. (2011). Assessing and treating aggression and conduct problems in schools: Implications from the coping power program. *Psychology in the Schools, 48*(3), 243–253.

Rathus, J., & Miller, A. (2014). *DBT with adolescents.* New York, NY: Guilford.

Rubin, L. C. (2007). *Using superheroes in counseling and play therapy.* New York, NY: Springer.

Schmitz, B., & Perels, F. (2011), Self-monitoring of self-regulation during math homework behavior using standardized diaries. *Metacognition Learning, 6,* 255–273.

Schneider, S. M., & Morris, E. K. (1987). A history of the term radical behaviorism: From Watson to Skinner. *The Behavior Analyst, 10*(1), 27–39.

Seligman, L. W., & Reichenberg, L. W. (2014). *Theories of counseling and psychotherapy: Systems, strategies, and skills* (4th ed.). Upper Saddle River, NJ: Pearson.

Skinner, B. F. (1953). *Science and human behavior.* New York, NY: MacMillan.

Swanson, A. J., & Casarjian, B. E. (2001). Using games to improve self-control problems in children. In C. E. Schaefer, & S. E. Reid (Eds.), *Game play: Therapeutic use of childhood game* (pp. 316–330). New York, NY: John Wiley & Sons.

Trull, T. J. (2001). *Clinical psychology: Concepts, methods, and profession* (6th ed.). Boston, MA: Wadsworth.

Trupin, E., Stewart, D. G., Beach, B., & Boesky, L. (2002). Effectiveness of a dialectical behavior therapy program for incarcerated female juvenile offenders. *Child and Adolescent Mental Health, 7*(30), 121–127.

Vernon, A. (2002). *What works when with children and adolescents: A handbook of individual counseling techniques.* Champaign, IL: Research Press.

Vernon, A. (2009a). *Counseling children and adolescents* (4th ed.). Denver, CO: Love.

Vernon, A. (2009b). *More what works when with children and adolescents: A handbook of individual counselling techniques.* Champaign, IL: Research Press.

Watson, J. B. (1925). *Behaviorism.* New York, NY: People's Institute.

Watson, J. B. (1994). Psychology as the behaviorist views it. *Psychological Review, 101*(2), 248–253.

Watson, J. B, Rayner, R., Jones, M. C., & Webb, D. (2013). *The case of Little Albert.* Retrieved from http://www.all-about-psychology.com

Chapter 8

Family and Organizational Systems Approaches

ELLEN AMATEA AND DAYNA WATSON

I believe that a child's family is that child's primary resource for healing.

—Stern, 2002, p. 10

INTRODUCTION

There are few mental health professionals who would dispute the idea that the family is a major influence on all aspects of a child's development and adjustment. Yet many counselors who work with children and adolescents apply treatment approaches that either view the individual child as the container of his or her pathology (i.e., being, or having, the problem) or as the victim of uncaring, dysfunctional, or even exploitative family members. In contrast, family systems counselors believe that family members hold the key to helping both the counselor and the other family members to better understand a child or adolescent's difficulty and to creating solutions to resolve that difficulty. In family systems approaches, the involvement of family members is an essential element of the therapeutic process for counseling youth.

Since the 1980s, interest in family-based approaches for resolving children and adolescents' difficulties has been gaining popularity among a wide variety of mental health professionals. This interest in families has been part of a larger cultural and professional movement of mental health professionals who are rethinking the boundaries of their clinical work to include community settings and discovering not only how families affect children but also how larger community institutions such as schools and social service agencies impact children and their families.

After reading this chapter, you will be able to

- describe how systems theory has been used to explain how family members influence each other;
- describe how systems theory has been used to explain how family members both influence and are influenced by members of larger social institutions;
- explain and illustrate the specific skills and techniques used by family counselors working in schools and clinics; and
- summarize the outcome research assessing the effectiveness of this approach.

The chapter begins with a definition of family systems intervention and a discussion of the key theoretical principles of this approach. This section is followed by an explanation of specific skills and techniques used by family counselors working in schools and clinics. The final section summarizes the outcome research assessing the effectiveness of this approach.

DEFINING FAMILY SYSTEMS COUNSELING

Family systems counseling (a.k.a., family therapy) is defined as "any psycho-therapeutic endeavor that explicitly focuses on altering the interactions between or among family members and seeks to improve the functioning of the family as a unit, or its subsystems, and/or the functioning of individual members of the family" (Gladding, 2011, p. 125). In contrast to counseling approaches that focus only on helping a parent learn how to more effectively manage his or her child, family systems counseling approaches "(a) often involve meeting with the child and other family members conjointly, (b) focus on the needs of the parents (and other family members) as well as the needs of the child, (c) consider how the family's ways of interacting and thinking (i.e., the family processes) may contribute to the child's problematic behaviors, and (d) focus treatment on the child initially identified with the problem, as well as on any and all family members believed to be necessary to resolve the presenting problem or other problems that arise during the treatment process" (Northey, Wells, Silverman, & Bailey, 2002, p. 91). In addition to alleviating the presenting problem, the family counselor's goals often also include teaching parenting skills; enhancing family problem solving; managing negative family interactions; building family cohesion, support, and intimacy; and restructuring family relationships. Moreover, in recent years, many counselors also help families interact more productively with members of larger institutions such as schools or mental health agencies (Madsen, 2012).

THEORISTS

Although families have always been recognized as a central influence on children's emotional well-being, the training of most mental health professionals has often not given them systematic ways of assessing and working with families. Family systems theory gives us a focused lens for understanding human behavior and assessing and intervening with families. The central advantages of family systems theory are (a) that it offers more complex, nonblaming ways of understanding families experiencing difficulties; (b) it offers a way to understand the complex dynamics between members of families and larger systems such as schools or social service agencies; and (c) it provides useful ways to promote positive changes in children, their families, and in the larger systems that serve them. In the following section we describe seven basic premises about human systems that define family systems counselors' assessment and work with families. To do this, we draw from the work of several prominent family systems theorists (Bowen, 1978; Haley, 1976; Minuchin, 1974; White & Epston, 1990).

1. *People's behavior does not originate from within the individual who displays that behavior but from within the interaction between that individual and other individuals.*

Over time, the ways in which people interact with others repeat with some regularity and develop into a pattern of interaction that restricts the development of alternative ways of interacting. These interactional patterns can be seen as a series of mutual invitations in which the actions of one person invite a particular response from the other, and that response invites a counter response. Thus, rather than viewing individuals as independent and autonomous with A causing B to happen, from a systems perspective, causality is reciprocal (that is, A and B are understood to mutually influence one another). The idea of a set of interaction patterns that become the focus of treatment is the core of the theory. Families develop and maintain dozens of interaction patterns such as mealtime activities; ways of managing sad or angry feelings or conflict; ways of handling secrets and privacy; and ways of dealing with outside systems such as schools. The counselor who thinks systemically believes that we cannot understand a child's behavior by just searching within the individual child or adolescent for a singular cause or chain of causes resulting in a problem behavior. Instead, the family systems counselor "zooms-out" and views the cause of any instance of problem behavior as part of a cyclical pattern of actions and reactions between participants. Each event in an interactional cycle can be seen as both a cause of ensuing events and the effect of preceding events depending on where we choose to "punctuate," and change, the cycle.

> 2. *Members of a system are viewed as interdependent or interconnected so that a change affecting one member affects other members of the family.*

A family is viewed as a patterned *system* of mutually shaping influences. Simply stated, a system is defined as "any perceived whole whose elements hang together because they continually affect each other over time and operate toward some common purpose" (Minuchin, Nichols, & Lee, 2007, p. 4). For example, when a child in a family faces serious difficulty, that problem acts as a stressor for the whole family. Case Illustration 8.1 is an example of such a family situation.

Case Illustration 8.1

Seeing the "Chain of Events" Around Problem Behavior

Nine-year-old Tim was referred for counseling because of his teacher's concern with his inability to focus and attend to classroom tasks. Assessment by a psychologist revealed that Tim had attention deficit hyperactivity disorder (ADHD). As is often the situation, everybody in the family was affected. Tim's parents learned that Tim needed a highly structured environment in order to complete academic tasks, so Tim's mother assumed the job of supervising Tim's homework completion. However, she herself tended to have difficulty with staying organized and focused. As a result, Tim's father often criticized her for letting Tim "off the hook" in completing his homework. As a result, Tim's mother feels she is doing a bad job, his father feels that the mother is too soft and just needs to be more organized, and Tim feels misunderstood and unsupported, like a bad kid. Despite the fact that each member of the family may be trying hard, family members can feel exasperated, frustrated, demoralized, and misunderstood. The sense of competence of both parents and child can plummet, leading to more serious symptoms developing such as depression in the mother and acting out or aggression in the child. Cycles of negativity between parent and child and parent and parent add to a parent's sense of guilt and failure, which in turn affect the child's sense of belonging to his or her family. This may make the child act out even more. Hence, instead of viewing behavior as affecting only one person, family counselors look for the "chain of events" that depicts how other people in the family both affect and are affected by an individual's behavior.

> 3. *Family belief systems powerfully influence members' behavior and interactions.*

If interaction patterns represent behavioral sequences, family belief systems represent shared assumptions about the family and its relationship to the larger world. These beliefs involve implicit and explicit rules about how family members should behave both with each other and with the outside world. Researchers such as David Reiss and his colleagues (1981) and Larry Constantine (1999) have developed models for describing the different ways in which families view the larger social environment in which they live, along the lines of dangerous versus safe, predictable versus unpredictable, and controllable versus uncontrollable. These beliefs can be particularly salient around children and parenting. Families also have organized beliefs about their internal dynamics —"what kind of a family we are." For example, some families demonstrate strong beliefs about their children's sense of purpose and achievement potential. Studying how families responded to significant crises, Walsh (2003) reported that families who shared strong beliefs in having a sense of purpose and personal control were more able to cope with and "rebound" from serious crises than were families who did not share such beliefs. The family systems counselor takes note of these core family beliefs (and degree of agreement) inherent in the stories family members tell about coping with a child's current difficulty or with previous family difficulties. Helping families to share a consistent vision, or worldview, around which their members cohere, can help them create positive change.

4. *Family health requires clear family organization and boundaries—knowing who is responsible for what and who is in and out of the family and its subsystems.*

Minuchin (1974) describes a family as composed of three subunits: the marital subsystem, the parental subsystem, and the sibling subsystem. According to Minuchin, an appropriately organized family will have clearly marked boundaries. For example, the parental subsystem will have a clearly organized power hierarchy and clear boundaries between parents and children but not so impenetrable as to impair the relational warmth and closeness needed for good parenting. The boundary around the family will also be respected. Because healthy families are able to clearly decide how and by whom certain family responsibilities for nurturing and maintenance are to be performed, family therapists and researchers such as Pauline Boss (2006) use the term *boundary ambiguity* to describe the situation where family members are unsure who is in the family or how members belong or fit in. For example, in a postdivorce family, the children may regard their father as still a member of their family, while their mother may regard the family as a single parent unit. In remarried families, it is often not clear whether the mother's new husband should act like a father to the children or like a friend; if like a father, what then, is the status of the biological father? Family researchers like Boss (2006) have demonstrated that when individuals and families are unclear about the boundaries of their family, they experience a great deal of stress. This stress can be of particular concern for young people in the family.

5. *Healthy families balance their members' needs for emotional connection and individuation through the ways they interact.*

Families must continually balance their members' needs for group solidarity and individual autonomy. Is the family a place where members feel supported and nurtured and are able to communicate their needs and wants effectively? Families with too much connectedness—either in the family as a whole or in particular dyads or triads—raise children who are oversocialized to the family and have emotional difficulty leaving home. In contrast, families with too much separateness will raise children who are undersocialized and have difficulty trusting others. Minuchin (1974) developed the terms *enmeshment* to describe overinvolved families with excessive emotional bonding and insufficient individual autonomy and *disengagement* to describe underinvolved families with too little emotional bonding, with insufficient nurturing and monitoring. For example, parents with enmeshed ways of relating to their child may react with great anxiety to their son being snubbed by other middle school students in a new school and insist that teachers correct the behavior of the other children. Or, in contrast, parents who are disengaged may tell the school that their son's academic problems are not their problem and may fail to help him with schoolwork or provide encouragement to him.

6. *Healthy families are flexible and able to adapt to internal and external demands for change.*

A key family system theory principle is that healthy families are flexible systems— able to change their rules, interaction patterns, beliefs, and roles in response to the demands from inside the family or from the outside world (Walsh, 2012). For example, parenting often involves continually adjusting family patterns as children change developmentally. A parental monitoring style that is appropriate for a toddler is inappropriate for an adolescent. In the face of a family crisis brought on by illness or accident or divorce, some families rally and adapt their roles and routines, while other families stay stuck in patterns that no longer work. For example, in one family in which the mother returned to work after a divorce, she continued to assume all responsibility for care of her four children even though she was working the evening shift and not available to supervise them after school. In another family in which the mother returned to work after a divorce, she discussed the situation with her children and assigned the older children developmentally appropriate responsibilities for supervising the children after school and cooking dinner in the evenings. Therefore, stressful events and demands for change do not disable families; the family's flexibility or resiliency often determines whether the event has a positive, neutral, or negative outcome for the family and whether problem behavior develops.

7. *Families' beliefs and ways of interacting to solve a child's problem both shape and are shaped by members of the outside systems with whom the family interacts.*

Brofenbrenner (1979) was one of the first family theorists to emphasize how outside professionals who interact with families employ certain beliefs and ways of interacting that have important effects on how family members see themselves and others. For example, if a counselor thinks a mother in a family is "angry and overcontrolling," the counselor may feel protective of the children in the family and respond to the mother in an emotionally distant and judgmental way. As a result, the mother may feel criticized and unsupported and grow angrier and more strident in her demands for how the counselor should work with her family. In family systems counseling, counselors assume that the perceptions that counselors and stakeholders in outside institutions develop about a child or family in the course of interacting with them shape how these stakeholders respond to the family and how the family responds to the outside stakeholders (Madsen, 2012). Because children's behavior is created and maintained by social interactions with others outside the family as well as inside the family, counselors should consider how their own beliefs and perceptions are shaped by the family and how the family members' beliefs also shape the family's experiences of the counselor and the counseling process. Thus, to understand a child or adolescent's difficulty and intervene effectively, counselors in schools and clinical settings must examine all aspects of the context of the child's problem, starting with the family, then moving out to include important relationships outside of the home, such as interactions between the child and family and teachers and friends and then moving further out to examine the impact of larger systems and culture on these outside relationships. A counselor's experience with a child's difficult school behavior in Case Illustration 8.2 provides a poignant illustration of the need to look at the impact of larger systems on the family when examining children's behavior.

Case Illustration 8.2

Examining the Effects of the Family's Interaction With the School

Bobby, a vivacious 9-year-old boy came to the school counselor's attention through Mrs. Harden, Bobby's third-grade teacher, who contacted the school counselor regarding her concerns about Bobby's behavior and academic performance. The teacher noted that Bobby often wandered around the classroom and failed to complete any of his work. On the playground, Bobby seemed to have a difficult time making new friends. He also struggled to function in the classroom during group work and collaborative learning times. The teacher admitted she had difficulty understanding Bobby. He made

(Continued)

(Continued)

very little eye contact and seemed unable to communicate with peers. When feeling misunderstood, Bobby would have an outburst, including shouting and being physically aggressive toward his teacher and classmates. Both in the classroom and in the lunchroom, Bobby made noises that Mrs. Harden described as "bizarre" and "inappropriate." As a result, Mrs. Harden requested that the school counselor meet with Bobby to get to know him better. Bobby and the school counselor met during Bobby's lunch time. Initially, Bobby avoided eye contact with the school counselor and refused to answer any direct questions. The school counselor asked Bobby to draw a picture of school. After a few encouraging prompts, Bobby began working on the drawing. Bobby told the school counselor that he didn't think that Mrs. Harden liked him very much, and he explained that he was "always in trouble" in class. Bobby told the school counselor that the kids in his class were his friends, but he didn't like the way they played on the playground or the books they chose during reading time. Bobby stated that his old school was much better than his current school, and he hoped he and his mom would just move back to their old house.

The school staff members invited Bobby's mother to a meeting at the school to share their concerns about Bobby and propose that he be assessed to determine how best to meet his educational needs. In the meeting, Bobby's mother, Sharon, seemed quiet and reserved. As the school personnel began to address their concerns, his mother became defensive about Bobby's abilities. She described him as bright, energetic, and sweet natured. When asked about the school's concerns about Bobby's odd behavior, Sharon minimized the seriousness of his behavior. She admitted that he made inappropriate noises at times, but thought that this behavior was a relatively benign way for him to "blow off steam" when he was frustrated or misunderstood. Sharon seemed to grow increasingly upset as the meeting progressed. When asked whether other family members such as his father were involved in raising Bobby, she seemed to grow more guarded. She explained that Bobby's father had never been too involved with Bobby. He saw him every few months, but she was really the one fully responsible for all discipline and parenting decisions.

Questions

- Why do you believe Bobby's mother reacted the way she did during this meeting?
- What skills do you see the school counselor using to connect with Bobby and his mother?
- What additional information might you want to gather from the family?

APPLICATIONS IN COUNSELING SETTINGS

Counseling a family with children and adolescents present is frequently "messy" and is often characterized by frequent distractions, whining, interruptions, nagging, varying attention spans, and outbursts. It might be tempting for the counselor to exclude the child or adolescent from the session, yet much of what can be learned about how a child is affected by his or her family and how the family is affected by the child, can only be seen if the child or adolescent is included in the family session. To create a context for meaningful involvement of family members of all ages, Chasin (1999) has described a six-step process for interviewing the family and assessing the family context. In step 1, the counselor orients the family to the counseling process through making introductions of family members (e.g., what name would you like me to call you?); explaining the purpose of the family meeting; and establishing the rules about safety, about answering questions (e.g., children will not be coerced to answer), about who is to discipline children during the meeting (parents are in charge of their children in the session), and about who is in charge of the room and equipment (the counselor is in charge of the physical space). The purpose of step 2 is to join with the family and create the *counselor-family system*. Chasin (1999) explains that in family counseling, the counselor temporarily joins the family and becomes part of the new system, establishing rules, roles, and responsibilities for all members, including the counselor. In steps 3 and 4, the family goals and enactment of those goals are explored, and hopes and fears about the future are discussed. In step 5, problem exploration is undertaken. The sixth step serves as a time for the counselor to share impressions and offer recommendations.

In the following sections we look at the skills you might use in (a) deciding whom to work with and orienting them to the counseling process, (b) building relationships with family members and exploring their goals, (c) assessing the problem in its interactional context and the family's relational structure, and (d) formulating goals and intervening in helping a family change.

Getting Started and Orienting Family Members

Counseling a family of a child or adolescent demonstrating problem behavior typically begins with a parent's request for help. Ideally, this request should involve both parents. Together, they can provide the counselor with information about whether to begin by seeing the parents alone, with the whole family, or some other individual or subgroup. More often than not, the counselor meets with the parents (or other responsible adults) first. Sometimes, through support and advice, this first meeting is all that is needed. If so, the child will not be seen and thus will be spared the feeling that he or she caused the family to seek outside help. When problems are more complex, a preliminary meeting with parents can be used to gauge parents' commitment and competencies and to take a careful and extended history of the family and past attempts to solve the problem. Such a meeting also gives parents an opportunity to ask questions and express concerns about the counseling approach. However, there are exceptions to this parents-first rule. We often see the family first, without this preliminary meeting, if the initial referral has indicated that it is the family's wish to be seen first as a whole or if adequate background information has already been collected. We may see a child first if the child so requests or in an emergency situation when the parents are unavailable.

In the first session, orient the family to the purpose and process of counseling. This involves reviewing background information and establishing ground rules. It is just as important to engage young children in this phase as it is to engage older family members, so the counselor must take care to use language accessible to all family members. The counselor will introduce himself or herself first, and then have family members introduce themselves. Next, any background information should be reviewed by the counselor, including prior contacts with the parents or others (e.g., school personnel). Expectations for everyone's participation, including the counselor, should be discussed in a way that children can understand.

Defining the Purpose of Counseling for Children and Adolescents

While many adults come into counseling understanding what to expect, children may feel confused and wonder why the family is meeting with a stranger to discuss their problems. With young people, a noncoercion rule is in force, with some caveats. For example, we don't ask children, "Do you know why you are here today?" They often do not know what to say. Instead, we open by talking about the view of the parent and frame the concern in a way that promotes insight and change. For example, we might say something like, "Your Mom called me and told me that you two don't have as much fun together anymore because there is a lot of yelling at home. Your Mom called me because I help families decide how to have more fun together. She also mentioned that she yells too much, and she wants to change that. Do you think that you would like to have more fun in your family?" To a younger child, we might say that this is a special place where we talk together and play together and figure out how to work together as a family.

Establishing Ground Rules

Ground rules set the tone for family sessions and outline clear expectations for attentiveness and communication. While each family has the freedom to set their own guidelines, there are general guidelines that may be helpful for most families. There are three types of rules that must be established: rules of discipline, safety, and noncoercion. For example, it is important to make it clear that parents—not the counselor—are expected to take responsibility for disciplining their children. Parents should be asked to enforce the rules the family uses at home. By allowing parents to discipline, the counselor emphasizes the boundary between the parental and the therapeutic roles, reinforces the parents' role in the family hierarchy, and gives the counselor the opportunity to observe how discipline is conducted.

Safety is established as a joint responsibility of everyone to intervene to protect the physical safety of everyone else. A noncoercion or "pass" rule gives each person the right to decline to answer any question or follow any suggestion without giving a reason. This rule can be particularly comforting to children, who fear being put on the spot, unable to defend an intrusion by adults (Gammer, 2009). Other rules are made, depending on the family's patterns. For example, it may be important to establish with parents that no one is to be punished after the session for what is said and done in the session. Rules such as no name calling or use of disrespectful language or rules about taking turns speaking may also be necessary. Phrase ground rules in a positive way, and be clear and concrete with the concepts. For example, a ground rule of "be respectful" can be interpreted in many different ways. Instead, the family could establish a rule of calling family members by their proper names (i.e., first names or Mom or Dad) and letting a family member finish what he or she is saying before responding. These guidelines offer target behaviors rather than a vague concept such as respect. Using a talking stick or a piece of carpet to indicate who "has the floor" in session cues family members to listen to the speaker. Families may also be in the habit of communicating in accusing or argumentative ways. Establishing a guideline for all family members to use "I" messages during the family session not only sets a clear expectation for in-session behavior but also teaches a communication skill that can be practiced at home.

Getting Children to Participate

Children and adolescents may be reluctant to engage in counseling with their families. Small children may feel confused or afraid, while teenage clients may feel defensive or resistant to engaging with the counselor. As discussed earlier, it is necessary for each family member's viewpoint to be heard and valued in the family counseling process, regardless of how young the family member is. This can be accomplished by offering children and adolescents equal talk time during the counseling sessions or by offering other methods of communication, such as art or writing, to young people who struggle to communicate their viewpoint verbally. By employing playful and expressive activities, the counselor can successfully engage all family members in the process. Including parents in play and expressive arts is also a comfortable way to begin engaging the family in working and communicating together in a different way.

The counselor may ask a young person and parent to first draw an individual picture done from a scribble and then together draw a picture of their family doing something together (also known as a kinetic family drawing; Gammer, 2009; Gil, 1994; Kottman, 2002). Or a child and parent pair might be asked to complete a follow-the-leader type of drawing task. As the parent and child participate in these activities, the counselor can observe and assess relationship patterns such as how the parent attempts to control a child or how the parent allows the child to take the lead. The counselor can also assess whether the parent and child can communicate about the task and navigate conflicts. In Case Illustration 8.3, an art task was used to gain an understanding of a child's perspective on his family and on how his mother interacted with him.

Case Illustration 8.3

Using Art to Share a Child's Perspective on His or Her Family

As you read this case, consider what the counselor learned from the child's and the mother's drawing task?

- What position did this child perceive himself to have in the family?
- How did you notice the mother interacting with this child?

When asked to draw an individual picture of his family doing something fun together, a lonely and unresponsive 12-year-old boy drew his family visiting Disney World. In his individual drawing, his mother and father are holding his 8-year-old sister's hands and are moving away from him and leaving him behind. As his mother worked on her individual drawing, she drew her son watching TV while she and her husband and daughter made popcorn together. Moreover, during the drawing time, the mother seemed to react as if her son was not in the room. She admitted that their first-born child had died as an infant, and she and her husband had been fearful that this son would suffer the same fate. Consequently, both she and her husband had "kept their distance" and tried not to get over involved. When their daughter was born, they had felt less anxious and thus provided a more nurturing relationship to her.

Engaging the entire family in collaborative activities is as a way for the counselor to observe relationship patterns, as well as the overall functioning of the family. For example, asking all the members of a family to use puppets to role-play together how they would like their family to be or how family members are afraid they might become can be powerful and informative. Through such tasks, the counselor can get a clear picture of how each family member views his or her relationships; negotiates conflict; and understands roles, hierarchies, and power in the family.

Building Relationships With Family Members and Exploring Goals

Building rapport with a family begins at the counselor's first point of contact. Basic reflective listening skills, such as reflecting feelings and content communicate to the families that the counselor hears and understands what is being communicated. While building rapport and assessing the family, it is essential to connect with each family member individually, as well as the family as a whole. When joining with children it is important to avoid those well-worn questions (e.g., How old are you?) that children often suffer through with adults. One way to avoid this is to use an exercise that highlights the unique qualities or strengths of each family member. The counselor might say, "I would like to hear from each of you something good about yourself—something you are good at doing or something you are proud of." Ordinarily it is wise to ask the parent to comment first. If they boast (give them a wink and a nod), it will make everyone else less shy and establish an atmosphere of openness.

Many family counselors find it useful to ask the family about their goals first (and only later in the session to focus on the problem). Having family members think about their goals for change can be difficult because families are often quite focused on their distress. Some family members are eager to complain about another family member. However one of the benefits of starting with goals is its positive quality. Emphasizing the family's desires for the future, rather than the problems they are experiencing, tends to avoid blaming and discouragement. To do this, the counselor must give clear, simple instructions, such as "I am going to give each person a chance to tell me one or two ways the family can be better than it is now. Remember you don't have to say anything if you don't want to. But each of you will have a turn to talk if you want it. Who would like to start?" A follow-up to this discussion might be to ask the family to co-create a minidrama to demonstrate what these goals would look like to them.

Exploring the Problem and Assessing Family Structure

As we have discussed in prior chapters, most children and adolescents come to counseling because an adult in their life has identified a problem. Although it is tempting to take this one person's view of the problem as truth, it is essential that the counselor understand each family member's viewpoint to understand the extent of the problem.

While a traditional intake interview can gather a great deal of information about a family, there are other creative assessment activities that can be used with families. Family sculpting, for example, provides an opportunity for the counselor to observe the family working together while simultaneously gathering information about the structure and functioning of the family from the family members' viewpoints (Blatner, 1994). Creating a genogram collaboratively with the family may also give the counselor additional information about how each family member views relationship dynamics within the family (McGoldrick, Gerson & Shellenberger, 1999). Creating a family genogram on a large piece of butcher paper using miniature toys may interest the whole family in looking at current and generational patterns (Gil, 1994). Asking each family member to complete and share a family portrait is also a good way to keep children and adolescents involved while offering the counselor insight into how each member views their family (Gammer, 2009).

Examining the Interactional Patterns Around the Problem

Children behave in response to the people with whom they interact. When a family enters counseling with a "problem child," many counselors may adopt the view that the child's behaviors are intrapsychic. Instead, counselors should recognize the perhaps inadvertent role the family has in sustaining the troublesome behaviors. Is the family responding to the child's behavior in such a way that it maintains that behavior? Is the child's difficulty a result of the family's difficulty in adapting to a major life transition or stressor? Is the family responding to the influence of a larger system in such a way that the child's problem behavior is exacerbated? To answer these questions, the family systems counselor explores the interactional patterns around the problem behavior(s) by tracking sequences of interactions inside and outside of the family and inviting the family to enact certain family interactional patterns. Examine what the counselor did in Guided Exercise 8.1 to build relationships with each of the family members and to assess their potential for resolving the problem. What did you learn that will help you decide how to focus your intervention efforts with families?

Guided Exercise 8.1

After reading the following case, reflect on the roles that a family counselor might play in assessing and intervening directly with a family and helping them effectively connect with a child's school and with social services. After you read this case, please answer the following questions:

- What information you would you want to gather from the family?
- What you would be hoping to observe as Keisha and her father interact in session?

Keisha, a 4-year-old, African-American female, and James, her father, presented for counseling at a community counseling agency following alleged sexual abuse by her mother's boyfriend. Her father had learned of the abuse when Keisha made several comments to him about being hurt by her mom's boyfriend, and a physical examination by Keisha's pediatrician confirmed that she had experienced some type of sexual abuse. Family counseling had been recommended to the father after Keisha refused to speak during a forensic interview at the local child advocacy center.

During the initial counseling session involving both Keisha and her father, Keisha wandered around the room and did not respond to any of the counselor's efforts to become acquainted. When Keisha's father asked her a question, she responded with two or three words combined with grunting noises and pointing gestures. James told the counselor that Keisha is the oldest of four children; she has twin siblings who are 3 years old and a baby brother who is 18 months old. All four children live with their father and paternal grandparents. Keisha's mom abandoned the family when Keisha was 4 years old. Initially, mom took Keisha and her sisters with her. It was during that time that Keisha was sexually abused by mom's new boyfriend. After 2 months living with mom, Keisha and her sister came back to live with her father, and he was legally granted full custody of all four children. Since returning to be with her father, Keisha had shown aggression toward her siblings, defiance toward adults, emotional outbursts, and difficulty communicating with others.

Keisha's father, James, works hard at a local construction company, but he admitted that he struggled to provide financially for his large family. (The counselor observed that at times the family appeared dirty when they attended counseling, and their clothes often seemed very well worn.) James expressed some frustration with parenting four children without his spouse, but he was grateful for the help of his parents. Keisha's grandparents take care of all four children while James works, but according to James, they often felt overwhelmed by all the children's energy levels and behavior. James admitted that neither he nor his parents knew how to "discipline these babies." James reported that he especially felt unsure about how to discipline Keisha. He wonders whether he can really expect her to behave well since she seems "slower" than most other children her age. James also expressed deep regret and anger with himself at not being able to protect Keisha from the sexual abuse. He reported feeling very angry with the slow moving legal process and worried that justice would not be done for his daughter. When the counselor met with Keisha alone for a session, she invited Keisha to play with a family of dolls in a dollhouse and noted that Keisha repeatedly had a rubber alligator come into the dollhouse and attack the family aggressively. While Keisha seemed to enjoy the play session, she often resisted limits set by the counselor. Keisha communicated primarily through short strings of words and various grunting sounds. The counselor arranged for a session with Keisha and her father. Initially, the counselor observed that Keisha's father did not join in the dollhouse play with Keisha but instead seemed to alternate between a calm disengagement with Keisha's play and repeated attempts to correct Keisha's behavior through direct and somewhat harsh commands. The same style of parent-child interaction pattern continued during sessions with Keisha's father and his four children. During these family sessions, Keisha often acted aggressively toward her younger brother and sisters when she did not get her way. Her father yelled at her, did not provide any consequences, and turned back to the counselor saying, "You see what I mean. She doesn't listen to me."

Stern (2002) provides a useful set of questions to serve as a guide to evaluating how a family is defining, coping with, and adapting in response to a problem. The questions are provided below:

1. Who is defining the problem, and how is the problem understood?

2. What are different family members doing in response to the problem, and what do they see as the consequences. For example, who is most/least affected?

3. What choices have the family members made in regard to responding to the presenting problem, and what values, beliefs, or myths guide those choices?

4. How successful has the family been in responding to the problem, and how do they imagine they will continue this success in the future?

5. What within-the-family capacities (strengths, resources, coping strategies, resilience, supports across generations) have promoted this success? What is already working?

6. How has the family adapted to and managed other adversities and challenges?

7. In what ways has the family actively chosen to make or not make changes in response to living with the problem?

8. What assets, strategies, and resources do they have that can help them to change? How could family resources be supported or enhanced?

Not only can these questions help the counselor determine whether the problem is situational or pervasive, they can also reveal the various capacities of the family for resolving the child's problem.

Observing Family Structure and Family Patterns

Assessing how a family influences and is influenced by the child's problem also involves learning about the way family members have organized themselves to get the work of the family done. How do parents interact with each other? How does each parent interact with each child? How do siblings interact with each other? As the counselor listens to stories of the presenting problem and the family's efforts to resolve it, he or she identifies the interactional sequences around the problem (i.e., who does and says what to whom) and observes how family members respond to each other. As the story unfolds, the counselor begins to make inferences about family structure (e.g., alignments, coalitions, triangles); boundaries; and relationship quality with extended family and with broader systems such as schools, courts, or social agencies. Counselors define the family's current life cycle stage and how family members are adapting to meet the demands of this transition.

Examples of interactional sequences between children and their family include the following:

- When a child is feeling upset, who does the child go to?
- How do parents manage a difficult child? What kind of emotion is expressed when the parent disciplines the child? Is the parent overly solicitous or consistently critical toward a child who is engaging in a tantrum? Do the parents respond to a child in a way that reinforces the child's problematic behaviors?
- Is there an obvious conflict between the parents about how to deal with the child? What is the overall temperament of the family? Is this a markedly conflictual group who frequently argue or a cautious group who talks indirectly about conflicts?
- Are the child's problem behaviors an adaptive or coping function in the family? Do the child's symptoms distract the family from conflict between the parents?
- Do two family members pull in a third (often the child) to side against the other, or is there an overt or hidden partnership between two family members against a third family member?

- Are there cooperative alliances? Is there an alignment between one parent and a child that causes a split between the parents or other family members?

Gathering such information allows the counselor to formulate goals and to then share counseling recommendations.

Intervening in Helping Families to Change

By understanding a child or adolescent's difficulty from multiple perspectives, the counselor can work with the family to create a counseling plan. While the wording of counseling goals is specific to each family, family counseling goals often focus on four main areas: (1) building family emotional connection, (2) improving family functioning, (3) changing or reducing reactivity, and (4) improving family relationships with larger systems. Guided Exercise 8.2 asks you to consider whether the agreed upon goals with Keisha's family were appropriate.

Guided Exercise 8.2

Based on the information you have about Keisha and her family, what decisions would you make about intervening?

- Whom would you work with, and what are your goals?
- Are they the same as those described below?

Based on the counselor's observations of Keisha, of her interactions with her father, and between the four children with their father, several counseling goals were developed. First, the counselor wanted to enhance Keisha's sense of safety and security through creating a safe, warm parent-child connection with her father. Second, she wanted to assist Keisha's father in implementing parenting strategies in which he sets limits and proactively manages Keisha's behavior and that of her siblings. As part of this goal, Keisha's father also wanted to help his parents, who watch the children while he is at work, develop consistent routines with the children. Finally, the counselor and father agree that having a structured playtime, for the father to play with the children, will enhance the enjoyment of the father with the children and bring them closer. To address these goals, counseling with this family might include individual sessions with Keisha, sessions with just Keisha and her father, and family sessions with the father and Keisha and her siblings. Though Keisha's father and the counselor discussed the possibility of including Keisha's grandparents in the family sessions, problems with transportation prevented the grandparents from participating in the counseling process.

To address Keisha's individual needs, the counselor used play approaches to create an environment for Keisha to work through her sexual abuse trauma. Keisha was given free play time with the counselor where she had access to a range of toys. Often, Keisha gravitated

(Continued)

(Continued)

toward playing with the dollhouse and playing out family-related scenarios. At other times, Keisha would "arrest" the counselor, placing her in handcuffs and yelling that the counselor must go to jail because she did something very bad. During family sessions with Keisha and her father, the counselor used the dollhouse as a context for play experiences for Keisha and her father to reconnect. Initially, Keisha's father seemed to struggle with engaging in play, and at times, he seemed frustrated by Keisha's loud and active behavior. During free playtime, the counselor encouraged Dad to allow Keisha to lead the play and to give her simple choices rather than yelling or directing Keisha toward a specific behavior. During this playtime, Keisha's father connected with Keisha and maintained clear and consistent boundaries. Similarly, during family sessions with Keisha, her father, and her siblings, the counselor coached Keisha's father to interact with all four children, while maintaining clear limits and giving choices. On occasion, the counselor met individually with Keisha's father to address his specific concerns about parenting young children and to help him manage his own stress as a single parent.

Building emotional connections within families can be accomplished through a wide range of counseling interventions. As we have discussed previously, interventions that are playful and expressive help foster connection between family members. Also, playful interactions (playing with toys, sharing stories, drawing pictures, playing games, reading to each other) that are practiced in counseling can also be generalized to the home. Similarly, joint family tasks, facilitated by the counselor, such as creating family rules together or participating in collaborative problem solving, provide the family with opportunities to practice working together and negotiating differences. Each of these interventions has the potential to foster family connection while also improving family functioning. Approaches such as filial and family systems play therapy are discussed in greater detail in other chapters in this text. Additionally, many excellent texts on family-focused play counseling are available as supplemental resources to this text. (Of these, we highly recommend *Child Parent Relationship Therapy: A 10-Session Filial Therapy Model* by Landreth & Bratton, 2006 or *Filial Therapy: Strengthening Parent-Child Relationships through Play* by Van Fleet, 2013). However, we consider a primary source for bringing children and parents together in family counseling to be Eliana Gil's *Play in Family Therapy* (2014).

At times, roles and hierarchies in the family need to be restructured. Parent training or other psychoeducational interventions might be useful to help families navigate these changes in dynamics. For example, sometimes an appropriate level of power may need to be shifted back to the parents, so the counselor may work with the parents to implement new parenting and discipline practices (Eyberg,

Boggs, & Algina, 1995; Hood & Eyberg, 2003). In other cases, however, teaching parents discipline techniques is not indicated as much as is coaching them in relating to their children with warmth and consistency. Depending on the family's interactional patterns, it is just as likely that parents would benefit from help in relating to their children in more playful and less hierarchical ways (Hill et al., 2014). Improving parenting skills can be an important goal for families in counseling. Evidence-based parenting programs are discussed further in the Outcome Research section of this chapter.

Goals in counseling families may be reached through counseling the family as a whole, with individual family members, or with parts of the family. Sometimes the therapeutic goal is not situated within the family but in the broader ecosystem, and the goal becomes to help family members build connections and interact successfully, on behalf of their children, within schools and the larger community. In Guided Exercise 8.3, consider the counselor's approach to helping Keisha's family interact with larger systems and discuss whether these interventions are appropriate.

Guided Exercise 8.3

Assisting a Family in Interacting With Larger Systems

In the following case excerpt, please consider the role the family's counselor assumed in working with this family and the school.

- Do you consider this an appropriate role?
- What other roles might the counselor take?
- What additional supports might Keisha's family need?
- How might you understand Keisha's father's emotional experience as a parent?

Through working with Keisha's family, the counselor also learned of several material needs of the family. The counselor notified Keisha's father of the financial support for counseling provided by victims' services, but Keisha's father was unsure about how to apply for the support. The counselor attained all the necessary paperwork and assisted Keisha's dad in completing the forms. Keisha's family also needed support with food, so the counselor connected Keisha's father with a local food bank.

During the time the family was in counseling, Keisha began prekindergarten at a rural elementary school. Dad reported to the counselor that school personnel were concerned about Keisha's behavior and her verbal skills and had made a recommendation to evaluate Keisha for special education services. Keisha's father admitted that he was confused by the school's policies and procedures. He asked if the counselor would contact Keisha's school counselor and become

(Continued)

(Continued)

involved in decisions the school was making. When the family's counselor contacted the school counselor, the school counselor stated that she was hoping to expedite the psychological evaluation process so that Keisha could be placed in a self-contained special education prekindergarten classroom. The school counselor described Keisha's behavior as "young for her age" and "low functioning in a classroom setting." The family's counselor had a different perspective than the school counselor regarding Keisha's current abilities and potential for improvement, so the family's counselor shared her observations of Keisha's strengths and areas of recent growth and improvement. The family's counselor and the school counselor also discussed ways that Keisha's sexual abuse might have been impacting her behavior and functioning at school.

The family counselor suggested to Keisha's father that the father and she meet together with the school counselor to fully discuss the process of assessment at the school. In this meeting, the school counselor explained the process and paperwork to Keisha's father. Keisha's father and the family counselor both had an opportunity to ask questions about the process, as well as to address specific concerns about Keisha's experience at school. Keisha's father agreed to have her assessed by the school psychologist, and he requested that the results of the assessment be shared with the family's counselor. In addition to the original treatment goals and interventions, the counselor began to integrate interventions targeting Keisha's school behavior and performance. Specifically, the counselor worked with Keisha on following directions given by her teacher, managing conflict with peers, and asking for help when she felt confused or unsure. Keisha's father and the counselor also discussed ways Keisha could be supported at home by her father and grandparents. Together, the counselor and Keisha's father found ways that he could provide consistent, clear directions regarding behavior at home, as well as working school-related routines into the family's schedule, such as time spent quietly reading and time sitting at a table completing an art activity. These new family processes not only helped Keisha to develop new behaviors but also brought them closer as father and daughter. With time, Keisha became more verbal in counseling, at school and at home, and more amenable to direction from her father and teachers. She was calmer and less aggressive in her play with other children. Within a few months, Keisha's father became increasingly more comfortable in enjoying playtime and structuring his family to manage his small children's behavior.

School Counseling and Family Systems Approaches

While the role of a school counselor does not often include traditional family systems counseling, we believe that the school counselor is in a position to connect, assess, and work with the family to meet the student and parents' goals while helping to build a strong working relationship between the family and the school. The American School Counselor Association (ASCA) recommends that school counselors collaborate with families to enhance the educational success of students, addressing barriers to family involvement, including mistrust and miscommunication, and advocating for effective family-school partnerships (ASCA, 2010). Using a family systems approach, like the one we have described in this chapter, can help school counselors to develop strategies that help parents to become successfully involved in their child's schooling (Amatea, Smith-Adcock, & Villares, 2006; Bryan, 2005; Epstein, 2010; Nelson, 2006).

The importance of family involvement in children's academic success is widely touted (Epstein, 2004), and several authors have described counseling interventions that are systemic and target school-family partnership. School counselors can use a family systems model similar in many ways to the therapy model we have already discussed. For example, both Amatea, Daniels, Bringman, and Vandiver (2004) and Davis and Lambie (2005) have recommended strategies for school counselors, based on family systems theory, which can be used to facilitate improved family-school relationships. We include an overview of these strategies below:

Initial assessment—Davis and Lambie (2005) suggest an initial assessment in the form of a needs assessment. This involves understanding the current state of family-school partnerships from multiple perspectives (e.g., teachers, students, and families) from a systemic lens. What are the patterns between participants in the school community? Examining systematic barriers to family involvement in school is critical before implementing any strategies to involve families (Amatea et al., 2004; Amatea et al., 2006; Davis & Lambie, 2005). Some questions you might ask include the following (Davis & Lambie, 2005). (Comparable questions can be generated for assessing family-school partnerships from caregivers' and students' perspectives.)

1. What are the main reasons that school personnel contact families?
2. What are the school's current policies regarding contacting families?
3. What are school personnel's current feelings and thoughts about interacting with caregivers?
4. When (and where) are family-school meetings scheduled?

Educating school personnel—School counselors can take a key role in understanding and educating school personnel about the importance of teacher-student, parent-teacher, and other relationships from a systemic viewpoint (Davis & Lambie, 2005). Effective (inviting and informative) communication is the hallmark of effective family-school collaboration and fosters trust between caregivers and the school (Adams & Christenson, 2000; Amatea et al., 2004). Helping school personnel (and family members, too) examine the nature of the family-school partnership from a systemic lens (looking for patterns) helps to reduce blaming and isolation (Amatea et al., 2006).

Restructuring family-school interactional patterns (Davis & Lambie, 2005)— In an earlier section of this chapter, we presented in some detail how counselors observe for interactional patterns. In schools, the same tools can apply to the work of the school counselor. Similarly, school counselors might observe and develop strategies that structurally modify the working relationship of teachers, administrators, students, and families. For example, Amatea et al. (2004) recommended collaborative problem-solving meetings that were not problem focused as well as student-led parent-teacher conferences that put children in the lead role in communication between family and school. Ongoing evaluation of systemic interventions is important, especially in terms of how they meet children's social, emotional, and academic needs in school settings (ASCA, 2010; Davis & Lambie, 2005).

OUTCOME RESEARCH

There is now a substantial body of evidence describing the effectiveness of family-based intervention in alleviating many of the core symptoms of mental disorders that affect youth. In this section we briefly discuss evidence of the effectiveness of family treatment for four of these disorders: (a) oppositional defiant disorder/conduct disorder, (b) ADHD, (c) depression, and (d) anxiety. These disorders have been identified as "key problem domains" for which evidence-based treatments for children and adolescents exist (Kazdin, 2000, 2004; Nathan & Gorman, 2002).

The effectiveness of family-based interventions for treating oppositional defiant disorder (ODD) has been documented in several research studies. For example, Nixon, Sweeney, Erickson, and Touyz (2003) reported decreases postintervention in preschool-aged children's externalizing behaviors among families who participated in parent-child interaction therapy (Eyberg et al., 1995) with findings maintained over 2 years. In a more recent study, Scott et al. (2009) found that parent management training reduced the ODD symptoms of 6-year-old children by 50% compared to children with ODD in a nontreatment control condition. Family-based approaches have also been recognized as an essential component of the ecological treatment of adolescent conduct problems and delinquency. Ecological treatment approaches, such as functional family therapy (Sexton & Turner, 2010) and multisystemic family therapy (Henggeler, Schoenwald, Borduin, Rowland, & Cunningham, 2009), recognize the need to intervene in the peer group, school context, and larger social network as well as in the family of the delinquent adolescent. Both of these approaches have compiled extensive evidence of their effectiveness spanning 3 decades (Sexton & Turner, 2010; Henggeler et al., 2009).

There are also a significant number of studies documenting the effectiveness of family-based interventions in treating ADHD (Chronis, Jones, & Raggi, 2006). For example, a study by Nixon (2001) assessing the effects of parent-child interaction therapy with preschool children and their parents revealed that mothers reported less hyperactive behavior, and children were less likely to meet the diagnostic criteria for ADHD. Moreover, Barkley and his associates (Barkley, Edwards, Laneri,

Fletcher, & Metevia, 2001) reported that in addition to improving adolescent's organizational and social skills, family-based interventions improved the communication patterns between teenagers and their parents. Hence family programs are now viewed as an essential part of the treatment of youth with ADHD symptoms.

Although there are many more studies establishing the effectiveness of family therapy with externalizing disorders in children than internalizing disorders such as anxiety, inhibitions, shyness, immaturity, sadness, social withdrawal, there is a growing body of evidence documenting the efficacy of family counseling in addressing these types of disorders. In addition, several recent studies suggest that family therapy interventions are successful in treating depression in children and adolescents. For example, Diamond, Siqueland, and Diamond (2003) reported positive outcomes from using an attachment-based family therapy (ABFT) to treat depressed adolescents. ABFT was more successful in reducing depression and anxiety symptoms, hopelessness, and suicidal ideation and was linked with greater improvement in mother-adolescent attachment than a minimal contact control group. Fristad, Verducci, Walters, and Young (2009) also reported that families of 8- to 12-year-olds with depression and bipolar disorder who participated in a multifamily psycho-educational group (MFPG) reported greater gains in parents' knowledge about childhood symptoms, increased positive emotions and family interactions, more positive perceptions of parental and peer support from the children, and greaser use of appropriate services than those families in the waitlist control group. Similarly, Barrett, Farrell, Dadds, and Boulter (2005) noted that children with anxiety disorders (e.g., overanxious disorder, separation anxiety disorder, or social phobia) or obsessive-compulsive disorders who engaged in family cognitive behavioral therapy had significantly higher recovery rates than children involved only in individual cognitive behavioral therapy, particularly if these youth had an anxious parent.

To conclude, involving the whole family in working with a child or adolescent has many benefits. First seeing the child and his or her whole family provides the counselor with a "moving picture of family life" right before his or her eyes. It helps the counselor see firsthand what the family deals with daily. Second, meeting with the important figures in the child's life allows the counselor to (a) obtain multiple perspectives on the problem, (b) get a more comprehensive understanding of the interpersonal nature of the problem, (c) observe family structure and dynamics, and (d) see what the child learns from his or her siblings about how to relate and from his or her parents' marriage about how they treat each other. In essence, the counselor can get a better understanding of how the family shapes the child and how the child shapes the family. Third, being there with a family, whether there are two members or six, says to them that the counselor is willing to tackle their problem with them in the real-life context in which these problems take place.

COUNSELING KEYSTONES

- Family systems approaches assume that people behave in response to the behavior of the people with whom they interact.
- The family counselor assumes that members of a human system such as a family (or work group) are interdependent and interconnected so that a change affecting one member affects other members of that system.
- Family belief systems powerfully influence their members' behavior and interactions.
- To operate effectively, a family must develop a clear family organization and boundaries so family members know who is responsible for what and who is in and out of the family and its subsystems.
- Healthy families balance their members' needs for emotional connection and individuation through the ways they interact.
- Healthy families are flexible and able to adapt to internal and external demands for change.
- Family beliefs and ways of interacting to solve a child's problem both shape and are shaped by members of the outside systems with which the family interacts.
- Based on a referral, usually from a caregiver, the counselor decides whether to first meet with the parents alone, to first meet with the child alone, or to first meet with the entire family.
- In the first meeting, the counselor orients the participants to the meeting purpose and process by making introductions, explaining the purpose of the meeting (in terms everyone can understand), and establishing rules about safety
- To ensure that every family member's viewpoint is heard, family counselors often use various play therapy or expressive arts techniques with the family to engage children or adolescents in the counseling process.
- Whole family tasks also serve as a way for the counselor to observe the relationship dynamics in the family and to assess the structure and functioning of the family.
- The counselor must explore the interactional patterns around a child's problem behavior to determine whether family members are responding to a child's problem in a way that maintains it.
- The counselor must also assess how the family functions by assessing how people are aligned in the family and how they interact with larger outside systems.
- Most family counseling goals focus on four areas: (1) building family connection, (2) improving family functioning, (3) changing or reducing emotional reactivity, and (4) improving family relationships with larger systems.

- School counselors can apply the tenets and practices of family systems theory to improve family-school partnerships.
- Evidence is mounting concerning the effectiveness of family-based counseling in alleviating many of the psychological problems affecting children and youth such as (1) ODD, (2) ADHD, (3) depression, and (4) anxiety.

ADDITIONAL RESOURCES

In Print

Gladding, S. T. (2014). *Family therapy: History, theory, and practice* (6th ed.). Upper Saddle River, NJ: Pearson Education.

Goldenberg, I., & Goldenberg, H. (2012). *Family therapy: An overview* (8th ed.). Belmont, CA: Wadswoth/Thomson.

Online

American Association for Marriage and Family Therapy (AAMFT): http://www.aamft.org

International Association of Marriage and Family Counseling (IAMFC): http://www.iamfconline.org

The Incredible Years Training Program for Parents and Teachers: http://www.incredibleyears.com

American School Counselor Association (ASCA) Position Statement: https://www.schoolcounselor.org/asca/media/asca/PositionStatements/PS_Partnerships.pdf

REFERENCES

Adams, K. S., & Christenson, S. L. (2000). Trust and the family-school relationships: Examination of parent-teacher differences in elementary and secondary grades. *Journal of School Psychology, 38,* 477–497.

Amatea, E. S., Daniels, H., Bringman, N., & Vandiver, F. M. (2004). Strengthening counselor-teacher-family connections: The family-school collaborative consultation project. *Professional School Counseling, 8,* 47–55.

Amatea, E. S., Smith-Adcock, S., & Villares, E. (2006). From family deficit to family strength: Viewing families contributions to children's learning from a family resilience perspective. *Professional School Counseling, 9(3),* 177–189.

American School Counseling Association (ASCA). (2010). Position statement: The school counselor and school-family-community partnerships position statement. Retrieved from https://www.schoolcounselor.org/asca/media/asca/PositionStatements/PS_Partnerships.pdf

Barkley, R., Edwards, G., Laneri, M., Fletcher, K., & Metevia, L. (2001). The efficacy of problem-solving communication training alone, behavior management alone, and their combination for parent-adolescent conflict in teenagers with ADHD and ODD. *Journal of Consulting and Clinical Psychology, 69,* 926–944.

Barrett, P., Farrell, L., Dadds, M., & Boulter, N. (2005). Cognitive-behavioral family treatment of childhood obsessive-compulsive disorder: Long-term follow-up and predictors of outcome. *Journal of the American Academy of Child and Adolescent Psychiatry, 44,* 1005–1014.

Blatner, A. (1994). Psychodramatic methods in family therapy. In C. Shaefer, & L. Carey (Eds.), *Family play therapy* (pp. 235–246). London, UK: Jason Aranson.

Boss, P. (2006). *Loss, trauma and resilience.* New York, NY: W.W. Norton.

Bowen, M. (1978). *Family therapy in clinical practice.* New York, NY: Jason Aranson.

Bronfrenbrenner, U. (1979). *The ecology of human development: Experiment by nature and design.* Cambridge, MA: Harvard University Press.

Bryan, J. (2005). Fostering educational resilience and achievement in urban schools through school-family-community partnerships. *Professional School Counseling, 8(3),* 219–228.

Chasin, R. (1999). Interviewing families with children: Guidelines and suggestions. In C. E. Schaefer, & L. J. Carey (Eds.), *Family play therapy* (pp. 57–70). Northvale, NJ: Jason Aranson.

Chronis, A., Jones, H., & Raggi, V. (2006). Evidence-based psychosocial treatments for children and adolescents with attention-deficit/hyperactivity disorder. *Clinical Psychology Review, 26,* 486–502.

Constantine, L. (1999). *Family paradigms.* New York, NY: Guilford Press.

Davis, K. M., & Lambie, G. W. (2005). Family engagement: A collaborative systemic approach for middle school counselors. *Professional School Counseling, 9(2),* 144–151.

Diamond, G. S., Siqueland, L., & Diamond, G. M. (2003). Attachment-based family therapy for depressed adolescents: Programmatic treatment development. *Clinical Child and Family Psychology Review, 6,* 107–127.

Epstein, J. L. (2004). Meeting NCLB requirements for family involvement. *Middle Ground, 8(1),* 14–17.

Epstein, J. L. (2010). School counselors' role in developing partnerships with families and communities for student success. *Professional School Counseling 14(1),* 1–14.

Eyberg, S., Boggs, S., & Algina, J. (1995). Parent-interaction therapy: A psychosocial model for the treatment of young children with conduct problem behavior and their families. *Psychopharmacology Bulletin, 31*, 83–91.

Fristad, M., Verducci, J., Walters, K., & Young, M. (2009). Impact of multi-family psychoeducational psychotherapy in treatment of children ages 8 to 12 years with mood disorders. *Archives of General Psychiatry, 66*, 1013–1021.

Gammer, G. (2009). *The child's voice in family therapy*. New York, NY: W. W. Norton.

Gil, E. (1994). *Play in family therapy*. New York, NY: Guilford.

Gil, E. (2014). *Play in family therapy* (2nd ed.). New York, NY: Guilford.

Gladding, S. (2011). *Family therapy: History, theory, and practice* (5th ed.). Boston, MA: Pearson.

Haley, J. (1976). *Problem-solving therapy*. New York, NY: Harper Colophon.

Henggeler, S., Schoenwald, S., Borduin, C., Rowland, M., & Cunningham, P. (2009). *Multisystemic therapy for antisocial behavior in children and adolescents* (2nd ed.). New York, NY: Guilford.

Hill, J., Wren, B., Alderton, J., Burck, C., Kennedy, E., Senior, R., Aslam, N., & Broyden, N. (2014). The application of a domains-based analysis to family processes: Implications for assessment and therapy. *Journal of Family Therapy, 36*, 62–80. doi: 10.1111/j.1467-6427.2011.00568.x

Hood, K., & Eyberg, S. (2003). Outcomes of parent-child interaction therapy: Mothers' reports of maintenance three to six years after treatment. *Journal of Clinical, Child, and Adolescent Psychology, 32(3)*, 419–429.

Kazdin, A. E. (2000). *Psychotherapy for children and adolescents: Directions for research and practice*. New York, NY: Oxford University Press.

Kazdin, A. E. (2004). Psychotherapy for children and adolescents. In M. J. Lambert (Ed.), *Handbook of psychotherapy and behavior change* (5th ed., pp. 543–589). Oxford, UK: Wiley.

Kottman, T. (2002). Partners in play: An Adlerian approach to play therapy. Alexandria, VA: American Counseling Association.

Landreth, G., & Bratton, S. (2006). *Child parent relationship therapy: A 10-session filial therapy model*. New York, NY: Routledge.

Madsen, W. (2012). *Collaborative therapy with multi-stressed families* (2nd ed.). New York, NY: Guilford.

McGoldrick, M., Gerson, R., & Shellenberger, S. (1999). *Genograms: Assessment and intervention*. New York, NY: Norton.

Minuchin, S. (1974). *Families and family therapy*. Cambridge, MA: Harvard University Press.

Minuchin, S., Nichols, M., & Lee, W. (2007). *Assessing families and couples: From symptom to system*. New York, NY: Pearson.

Nathan, P. E., & Gorman, J. M. (Eds.). (2002). *Treatments that work* (2nd ed.). New York, NY. Oxford University Press.

Nelson, A., J. (2006). For parents only: A strategic family therapy approach in school counseling. *The Family Journal, 14* (2).

Nixon, R. (2001). Changes in hyperactivity and temperament in behaviorally disturbed preschoolers after parent-child interaction therapy (PCIT). *Behaviour Change, 18*, 168–176.

Nixon, R., Sweeney, L., Erickson, D., & Touyz, S. (2003). Parent-child interaction therapy: A comparison of standard and abbreviated treatments for oppositional defiant preschoolers. *Journal of Consulting and Clinical Psychology, 71*, 251–260.

Northey, W., Wells, K., Silverman, W., & Bailey, C. (2002). Childhood behavioral and emotional disorders. In D. Sprenkle (Ed.), *Effectiveness research in marriage and family therapy*, (pp. 891–121). Washington, DC: American Association for Marriage and Family Therapy.

Scott, S., Sylva, K., Doolan, M., Price, J. H., Jacobs, B., & Crook C. (2009). Randomized controlled trial of parent groups for child antisocial behavior targeting multiple risk factors: The SPOKES project. *Journal of Child Psychology and Psychiatry and Allied Disciplines, 51*, 48–57.

Sexton, T., & Turner, C. (2010). The effectiveness of functional family therapy with youth with behavioral problems in a community practice setting. *Journal of Family Psychology, 24,* 339–348.

Stern, M. (2002). *Child-friendly therapy: Biopsychosocial innovations for children and families.* New York, NY: Norton.

Reiss, D. (1981). *The family's construction of reality.* Cambridge, MA: Harvard University Press.

Van Fleet, R. (2013). *Strengthening parent-child relationships through play* (3rd ed.). Sarasota, FL: Professional Resource Press.

Walsh, F. (2003). Family resilience: A framework for clinical practice. *Family Process, 42*, 1–18.

Walsh, F. (2012). *Normal family processes: Growing diversity and complexity* (4th ed.). New York, NY: Guilford.

White, M., & Epston, D. (1990). *Narrative means to therapeutic ends.* New York, NY: W.W. Norton.

Chapter 9

Constructivist Approaches

Donna M. Gibson and Shajuana Isom-Payne

What we talk about and how we talk about it makes a difference.

—Berg & de Shazer, 1993, p. 7

INTRODUCTION

How profound to think that we are living what we communicate with others. Basically, how we perceive our own experiences is built around our communication within our relationships, community, and culture. Although it may seem like an abstract concept, meaning-making through language is a foundation of human development.

Because this process is developmental, understanding a child's process of meaning-making in counseling can be challenging. This chapter offers information on how constructivist counseling approaches evolved from the postmodern intellectual movement that acknowledges the importance of recognizing the subjective realities of clients.

After reading this chapter, you will be able to

- review the history of how constructivist approaches evolved to become recognized, effective counseling approaches today;

- describe the tenets of solutions-focused brief therapy, narrative therapy, and relational-cultural therapy,
- articulate specific interventions and applications of constructivist counseling approaches with children; and
- review outcome research related to the effectiveness of these approaches.

In order to understand constructivist approaches to counseling children, understanding the historical foundations of constructivism is warranted. Compared to many of the theories and approaches used in counseling children, the underlying philosophy behind constructivism represents a different kind of thinking. Born from postmodernism, constructivism represents a paradigm of counseling that includes clients' social and subjective realities, as opposed to the observed realities that are a foundation of modernist theories (Cottone, 2012).

The postmodern intellectual movement pertaining to science, history, and culture began in the late 20th century (Lyotard, 1992). The premise of the postmodern movement is that "what is known derives from social interaction within cultural contexts" (Cottone, 2012, p. 89). In essence, there are multiple ways to understand and "know" reality. There is no one way of knowing reality, and understanding reality around us should consider the social context of the reality we are learning to "know."

Postmodernism is a sharp contrast to the existing modernist theories that are built on assumptions that there is an objective reality that can be observed and tested systematically through scientific method (Corey, 2013). In 1966, Berger and Luckmann wrote about scientists' subjective experiences of the world in *The Social Construction of Reality: A Treatise in the Sociology of Knowledge*. George Kelly, creator of personal construct therapy, is one of the first theorists to apply social constructionist ideas to counseling. His theory purported that each person develops his or her own reality based on experiences and expectations (Kelly, 1955, 1963). Later, U.S. psychologist Gergen expanded upon Kelly's ideas to study the social nature of human meaning making (Gergen, 1992, 2001). As ideas about how "truth" is found within social contexts and how this shapes individuals' perceptions of reality grew, the term *social constructionism* evolved (Gergen, 1985). Therefore, social constructionism offered an explanation of the development of phenomena relative to social contexts. In comparison, traditional cognitive-behavioral therapies rely significantly on the behaviors and internal thoughts of the individual without much consideration of the reciprocal influence of social context on those behaviors and thoughts (Kalodner, 2011).

Maturana's (1978) work on human perception added another layer to understanding social constructionism. He found that there are limits to what humans can perceive biologically (i.e., sight, hearing, touch, smell, taste), which is defined by the individual's nervous system. Therefore, the "experience" of something is not dependent on the object perceived but is dependent on the relationship of the individual to what is being observed and perceived. For example, an adult enters a home and smells baking cookies and feels happy. She knows through smell that cookies are baking, but the happy feelings associated with coming home from school as a child to baking cookies meant that her family earned extra income to purchase the needed ingredients for cookies. If cookies are baking, then her family is less stressed economically, and her parents are happier and less stressed overall. Thinking or "experiencing" is a result of the nervous system being influenced by perceptual and social influences. How an individual makes meaning from these experiences is referred to typically as the psychological concept of social constructivism.

For counselors, the social constructivism paradigm grew out of postmodern ideas as a vehicle for understanding what "knowing" or "truths" clients bring to counseling (Cottone, 2013). It is still considered an emerging paradigm within the counseling arena because empirical evidence on the tenets and effectiveness of approaches and interventions is growing compared to the well-established modernist counseling approaches (e.g., cognitive-behavioral). However, differences between these approaches are notable. Interventions using modernist counseling approaches have focused traditionally on the problems presented by the client (e.g., irrational beliefs, inappropriate behavior), and problem solving is usually present oriented (Granvold, 1996). In counseling children using these approaches, interventions are less talk oriented and more focused on children's behaviors without much input solicited about the context for the children's needs for counseling. Hence, counseling and counseling interventions, using this approach, have corrective goals. Using a constructivist approach, historical, developmental, and cultural contexts of the client are considered in counseling. An exploration of the client's personal meanings of the experience that brought them to counseling will facilitate a transformation of these meanings that will allow the client to perceive the experience differently. Hence, a constructivist approach incorporates the goal of meaning making and psychological development.

As social constructivist theory has developed over the last century, a debate has emerged among the theorists who emphasize the individual's role in meaning-making and those who emphasize the extent that meaning resides in culture and language systems that influence an individual. Is the meaning of an experience constructed in an individual's culture and this influences the individual, or does the individual integrate culture and language into his or her own sense of understanding to create meaning within? Can it be both as human thinking is quite complex? The theory as a whole is inclusive of different populations due to its focus on familial, ethnic, and cultural systems and the meaning inherent in those systems. Implications for self-advocacy and counselor advocacy inherent in these approaches are applicable to clients of all ages, including children. Guided Exercise 9.1 encourages the reader to process how cultural contexts intersect with ethical dilemmas when counseling children.

Guided Exercise 9.1

Ethics and Culture

One of the main tenets of constructivist counseling approaches is built around understanding the client's "reality," which is based on his or her culture and social systems. However, ethical dilemmas may occur in counseling through this lens. What ethical dilemmas could occur specific to counseling children? Discuss with either a classmate or a small group how the American Counseling Association 2014 ethical codes apply to these dilemmas. Explain what social or cultural contexts could alter how the dilemma is resolved (e.g., child discipline being viewed as abuse depending on culture). Provide two alternative solutions to how these dilemmas could be resolved. Based on the child discipline example, would the counselor discuss discipline with the parents first, contact child services first, call the police first, or so on?

THEORISTS AND TENETS OF THEORIES

Although there have been several theorists who have influenced the development and application of constructivist counseling approaches, there are a few who have made a significant impact on the profession. According to Corey (2013), postmodern counseling approaches deconstruct established truths and evaluate their value in relationship to the individual's life and experience. The counseling relationship is, therefore, characterized by open dialogue and a collaborative relationship.

Among the pioneers of postmodern approaches to counseling are Insoo Kim Berg and Steve de Shazer, codevelopers of solution-focused brief therapy (SFBT), which has been used widely in both individual and family counseling (Corey, 2013). They developed this approach in the early 1980s at the Brief Family Therapy Center in Milwaukee, Wisconsin. It is a future-focused, goal-oriented therapeutic approach that works on the assumption that for every problem, there is a solution (George, 2008). Change is constant and inevitable. Based on the foundation of constructivist counseling, SFBT reframes "problems and dysfunction" to "successes and adaptation" (Cottone, 2013). Therefore, counselors take a non-pathologizing stance with clients (Neukrug, 2011). The assumption is that clients want to change, have the capacity to change, and are doing their best to make that change happen (Corey, 2013).

Through SFBT techniques, the counselor helps clients construct an understanding of their experiences from a positive perspective (Corey, 2013). It is assumed that clients are experts about their lives (Neukrug, 2011). If clients do not identify any problems, then counselors do not attempt to help them change any behaviors. However, they may help clients identify something that works for them that needs to be practiced more often. These are typically resources that feed clients' resiliency when there are issues occurring. Tapping into those resources will help clients' effect change, which can occur in very small steps that lead to bigger change in their lives. Sometimes, there is no logical connection between a solution and a problem. If the solution works for the problem, then the client is encouraged to use it. Solutions to problems are relative to different clients, so one size does not fit all in this therapy. However, there are always exceptions to problem situations, so counselors can help clients discover those exceptions and create solutions around them.

For children, SFBT enhances resiliency through a lens of understanding the child's culture and worldview. Due to its efficient nature, SFBT is optimal for use in school settings where small concrete changes can occur in a brief period of time (Corey, 2013). It also helps them learn how to find solutions to their own issues within group and school settings. However, focusing on the more positive aspects or exceptions to a problem runs a risk of invalidating the negative feelings the client may bring to counseling. This approach also assumes the clients will have the necessary skills and abilities to achieve their goals, which may be a challenge for children with intellectual, emotional, and physical disabilities.

Michael White and David Epston are the cofounders of the narrative therapy movement. Through his work in developing narrative therapy, White founded the Dulwich Centre for Narrative Therapy with his wife Cheryl in Adelaide, Australia (Neukrug, 2011). During the 1980s, White and David Epston, who lived in New Zealand at that time, developed a friendship based on shared beliefs and ideas about political systems. Subsequently, they wrote several books together that led to the development of narrative therapy.

Based on Bruner's (1990) view that humans give meaning to their lives from the social constructions in their world by organizing their experiences in a narrative form in a sequence over time, narrative therapy was developed. Hence, one individual's reality differs from another individual's reality. "Narratives are self-constructed and also constructed and adapted during interactions with others" (Hannen & Woods, 2012). These narratives reflect an individual's culture's social beliefs and can shape and reflect the individual's sense of identity. As White (1995) reflected, "We live by the stories that we have about our lives. These stories actually shape our lives" (p. 14). In essence, individuals engage in "storying" throughout their lives. These stories can change over time, and some stories will contradict themselves. The narrative therapist's role is to understand the many different stories an individual has and identify contradicting stories or stories that may be problem saturated and may cause problems in a person's life (Neukrug, 2011). In addition to listening for problem-saturated or contradictory stories, the narrative therapist is also listening for the times in an individual's life when he or she was resourceful. A significant impact of narrative therapy is how stories can change the client telling the story and can change the counselor who is part of the process of narrative therapy (Monk, 1997).

In working with children, the nondirective nature inherent in narrative therapy may be more helpful with children who are experiencing specific issues that promote defensiveness in the counseling setting. Additionally, stories can be "told" using a variety of mediums. For example, a child may be more willing to tell his or her story through play, drawing, acting, or music. It promotes a more creative counseling environment for the child and counselor. Guided Exercise 9.2 requires you to be creative in considering how to encourage children to tell their stories in a variety of ways.

Guided Exercise 9.2

Creative Storytelling

Directions: Work with a partner to complete this exercise. Each person will think of the story of how he or she decided to become a counselor. Individually and without the partner seeing, write out as much detail as possible about the story. Using creative methods, convey your story to your partner. For example, art, music, drama, lyrics, poems, or so on can be used. After each partner "tells" his or her story, discuss the following:

1. What were your initial feelings and thoughts about sharing your story?
2. What were the cultural and social contexts of your story? How did these influence your decision to become a counselor?
3. What were your thoughts about using a creative medium to convey your story?
4. How would children react to using this same medium to sharing their story?
5. What are some cautions to consider when doing a similar exercise with clients?

Relational-cultural theory (RCT) is an evolving constructivist counseling theory developed in 1978 by Jean Baker Miller, Irene Stiver, Judith Jordan, and Janet Surrey at the Stone Center at Wellesley College in Massachusetts (Jordan, 2008). In 1995, the Jean Baker Miller Training Institute was formed to further the development of the theory and clinical aspects of the work. Although the original work was focused primarily on college-age women, the work has been applied to males and children.

The basic premise of RCT is that people "grow through and toward connection" (Jordan, 2008). This is in contrast to many of the human development theories that posit humans strive from dependence to autonomy and implies that individuals grow stronger and healthier by being more independent, building firm boundaries, and having power over others. RCT posits that a sense of safety and well-being comes from developing good relationships and connections with others throughout the lifespan. Jean Baker Miller noted that these "growth fostering" relationships create "five good things":

1. A sense of zest

2. Clarity about oneself, the other, and the relationship

3. A sense of personal worth

4. The capacity to be creative and productive

5. The desire for more connection. (Jordan, 2008, p. 2)

Mutual empowerment and mutual empathy are products of growth-fostering relationships (Jordan, 2008). This encourages the individuals in the relationship to grow and support each other. If not connected, chronic disconnections can result in less energy, decreased sense of self-worth, less productivity, less clarity, and withdrawal from relationships. These disconnections not only occur at the individual level but also at the societal level where differences in sex, race, class, color, and sexual orientation can be used to promote disconnection.

The primary focus of the RCT counselor is to promote, help build, and sustain healthy relationships with their clients (Cannon, Hammer, Reicherzer, & Gilliam, 2012). Jordan (2009) reported that RCT therapy "is largely based on a change in attitude and understanding rather than a set of techniques" (p. 5). Counselors use RCT to encourage their clients to examine and revise, if necessary, their relational patterns and relational images. In essence, clients should gain a sense of relational awareness that will help them increase or deepen connections, which will give them the tools and capacity to develop new relationships.

RCT is a constructivist approach that focuses on the relationship and how it is perceived by the individuals in the relationship (Jordan, 2008). It incorporates the influence of culture and social systems on the individual and how this can promote disconnection. In applications with children, helping children learn how to self-empathize without criticism and blame not only promotes healthy development but also helps the child learn connections can be healthy and beneficial. Attention and education regarding social system dynamics and power encourages mutual empathy and empowerment. The counselor can explore this through different techniques, such as individual, group, large group, and creative counseling. Guided Exercise 9.3 requires you to conduct research on evidence-based methods that have been proven to work with children.

Guided Exercise 9.3

Evidence-Based Creative Counseling

Although constructivist approaches to counseling center around the client's sense of "truth" and "knowing," it may be difficult for the counselor to obtain information from children who are not able to verbally communicate this well. What creative methods could be employed with children, so their experiences and stories are "heard" correctly? Conduct a review of evidence-based research on creative methods that represent constructivist approaches that work with children (e.g., SFBT, narrative, RCT). What are the similarities among these? What are the developmental considerations?

TECHNIQUES AND APPLICATION OF CONSTRUCTIVIST COUNSELING APPROACHES

Although the underlying paradigm runs a common theme among constructivist counseling approaches, the techniques can vary among them. For each approach, the techniques specific to the approach will be provided with a description of how the techniques can be applied to counseling children and adolescents. Specific examples of application are provided.

Solution-Focused Brief Therapy

As a foundation of providing SFBT, the counselor approaches all clients with respect and appreciation (Neukrug, 2011). The counselor offers the client a collaborative working relationship in order to find exceptions and solutions to the client's issues that brought him or her to counseling. Without this collaborative working relationship, the results will be ineffective. The counselor needs to be flexible in the use of SFBT techniques as they should be tailored to the unique circumstances that the client presents in counseling (Murphy, 2008). The following are SFBT techniques that are applicable to use with children and adolescents:

1. Being tentative

When the counselor meets with the client, there should be an attitude of the client is the expert, and there should be no assumptions on the part of counselor about the issue that the client will present. De Jong and Berg (2008) explained that this type of attitude is part of a "not-knowing posture." The counselor can demonstrate this posture by being respectful and curious. Language also reflects this posture in how questions or inquiries are made of the client. For example, the counselor may test an exception out by saying to the client, "Let me know if I'm wrong about this, but it seems like you and your brother have played together well in the past?" Another example of collaborating on solutions with a not-knowing and tentative stance would be for the counselor to say, "I would guess you play best with your brother after dinner? Is that correct?"

2. Questions

In SFBT, asking specific types of questions is one of the most important and potentially effective techniques. For older children (ages 10 and up) and adolescents, counselors may want to include questions regarding their goals for counseling. Questions regarding their hopes for the session, determining when things are better for them, and how they will know when things are better for them are referred to as preferred goals questions (Bertolino & O'Hanlon, 2002). The questions are future oriented and not focused on the presenting issue.

When exploring the presenting issue with the client, exception questions may elicit times in the client's life he or she could identify with not having the issue or the issue was not as intense as he or she is experiencing it at the present time (Corey, 2013). The counselor will need to determine if exception questions are developmentally appropriate for the child client. However, school-age children should be able to respond to some form of an exception question. For example, a third-grade child may come to counseling because she cries at recess. An exception question to this child could be "Many people cry because they are sad or unhappy. Have there been times at recess when you didn't cry? Can you tell me about those times when you didn't cry at recess?" In order to coconstruct a solution with the child and find what resources she has, the counselor could asking a follow-up question, such as "What has to happen for you not to cry at recess?"

An additional type of question used in SFBT is the miracle question. The miracle question response helps the counselor and client construct therapy goals (de Shazer, 1988). It keeps the focus of counseling on the future and encourages clients to think about what they would most like to see changed about their situation (De Jong & Berg, 2008). For older children and adolescents, the question may be phrased as "If you went to sleep tonight and a miracle occurred so you would not feel so sad anymore, how would you know this, and what would be different?" For younger children, the question could be phrased as "If you had a magic wand and were able to use it to make you not feel so sad on the playground, how would you know that it really worked, and what would be different on the playground?"

If goals are constructed and the counselor and client are tracking progress in obtaining the goals through different interventions in and out of counseling, scaling questions provide a simple measurement of change in feelings, communication, or moods for the client to note progress (de Shazer & Berg, 1988). For example, the counselor can ask the child client, "On a scale of 1 to 10 with 1 being feeling so sad that you are going to run out of tears from crying to 10 being feeling so happy that your face is starting to hurt from smiling, what would you say your number is today?" For younger children that may not understand the abstractness of a Likert scale, a shorter scale of feeling faces (i.e., smiling, frowning, etc.) can be drawn out on paper for children to choose. Another option for children is to ask them to draw their own scales at the onset of counseling and have them draw a picture to represent their scaled response for each section. Follow-up questions to their responses could include "How did you move from that space to the one you chose?" or "What do you need to do to make it move to the next number or space?" Scaling questions and responses are also simple ways to document the effectiveness of the counseling relationship but not necessarily the specific session. Case Illustration 9.1 is an example of creating and using scaling questions with children.

Case Illustration 9.1

Scaling Questions

As a school counselor whose caseload includes pre-k through second grade, you believe that SFBT is the most appropriate approach to use with the population and setting. The following is an example of how scaling questions can be used to help students in your caseload identify their feelings about the experiences they discuss in counseling. How do you see yourself using scaling in your work with children? What are some pitfalls of using the scale?

1. Construct a five-point Likert scale.

Counselor: *Today we will draw some faces that show your feelings. Some of the faces will show sad feelings, and some will show happy feelings.* (Either you or the child draws five faces in a row, with varied expressions from happy to sad.)

2. Give simple directions to the child. Help them, as much as is needed, to know the meaning for each of the points on the scale. Often, children can make up their own scale.

Counselor: *We will use these pictures to help you tell me how you've been feeling today (or in your life). On this side, the picture shows someone who is very happy, and on this side, the picture shows someone who is pretty sad. The ones in between are happy but not-so-happy and sad but not-so-sad. The face in the middle is not happy or sad. Let's talk for a minute about how you've been feeling in class lately. Which picture shows your feelings? Tell me about that.*

3. Repeat the scaling activity as needed or to reflect change for the child.

Counselor: *We will use these pictures every time I see you so you can show me how your days have been going at school.*

Counselor: *What would change to make your face go from here (point to sadder picture) to here (pointing to next picture on the scale)?*

3. Amplification and complimenting

Amplification and complimenting are similar techniques with similar goals in SFBT. In order to reinforce the successes of clients, the successes of clients in attempting to achieve their goals in counseling are complimented (Neukrug, 2011). For example, a compliment for the child with the crying on the playground issue may sound like this: "I like how you decided to play with the new student in your class at recess. You really made an effort to play with someone new instead of waiting on the other children to ask you to play." In order to reinforce the solution the client used, the counselor would encourage the client to expand her discussion of how the solution worked. For example, "It sounded like you decided to play your favorite game at recess to make you happy. How did you come up with the idea to ask the new student to play with you?" or "It sounds like you and the new student had a good time playing together at recess. Tell me how playing with him has helped you with feeling less sad during recess."

Narrative Therapy

Initially, it may seem that narrative therapy techniques may be too abstract to use with young children. However, there are several techniques that work well with all children. With some creativity and modification, the use of some of these techniques can be very helpful to the counseling relationship.

1. Externalization of the problem

Externalizing the problem allows the client to not see himself or herself as the problem (Freedman & Combs, 1996). This can be key to working with children who are often identified as *the* problem, instead of examining behaviors, feelings, or language that has become problematic. When clients have been identified as the problem, it limits their ability to handle the issue effectively. In externalizing the problem, the problem is often named and referred to by that name within the counseling relationship. For example, the previous example of the child crying at recess could be either renamed "the crying at recess problem" or "the feeling unhappy on the playground problem." In naming the problem, the counselor works with the client to help the client name it in a co-construction process. Once named, the client can begin to construct solutions to the problem without conflicting feelings and emotions related to feeling like he or she is the problem. In the crying at recess scenario, the child may have feelings of shame, guilt, or anger related to thinking about himself or herself as the problem that needs to be assessed and processed within the child's social and cultural context.

2. Questions from a not-knowing stance

Questions are the most critical tools in narrative therapy (Neukrug, 2011). More importantly, questions should reflect the respectful curiosity of the counselor. Asking questions from a not-knowing stance demonstrates to clients that counselors do not have the answers to the questions they are asking. Counselors are relying on clients to educate and help them understand their experience (Monk, 1997). Questions help clients explain their experiences with the problem, cultural and system influences on the problem, and how clients have attempted to resolve the problem. This process deconstructs the problem-laden story and leads the counselor and client to externalizing the problem.

With older children and adolescents, talking through the story process and asking questions verbally may be appropriate. However, younger children may not have the ability to understand and use language to tell their stories. Some children may be able to draw a picture of their problem or make a sculpture of their problem to discuss in simpler language. Alternative techniques, such as play therapy and other storytelling techniques, can be used and will be described briefly as sub-areas to this section.

3. Play therapy and storytelling

One of the most unique methods to help young children communicate and express their emotions in counseling is play therapy (Russo, Vernam, & Wolbert, 2006). In play therapy, children's "narratives and reconstructions occur within the context of cognitive development" (Landreth, as cited in Russo et al., 2006, p. 230). Depending on the characteristics of the client's narrative, meaning-making may be reflected as occurring within specific stages of cognitive development (i.e., Piaget's stages). Specifically, sandplay can apply to specific stages of cognitive development with sandplay exercises involving the use of objects and figures that children can manipulate to make a sand picture or to tell a story about the figures.

There are several sandplay techniques that are applicable to narrative therapy, but storytelling through sandplay can help children engage in storytelling and make connections between their stories and their lives (Gil, 1991). In mutual storytelling, the counselor and client work collaboratively where the counselor interprets the client's story with the same characters and settings but offers healthier solutions and adaptations (Gardner, 1993). This reiterates the need for counselors to use clients' words, characters, and symbols to demonstrate understanding of their narratives.

4. Mapping the problem

Through the use of questions or other creative counseling methods, clients can be encouraged to describe the influence of the problem on their lives and relationships (Epston & White, 1995). In essence, the counselor is attempting to gain a richer narrative of the problem. When did the client notice that this was a problem? How does it affect his or her life? How does it affect his or her relationship with parents, friends, siblings, teachers, and so on? Asking younger children to draw pictures of what they look like with and without the problem in their lives may be helpful, but counselors are encouraged to give specific direction to young children. For example, for the child with the "crying at recess problem," the direction for drawing may be "Draw me a picture of you doing something at recess before the 'crying at recess problem.'" Guided Exercise 9.4 includes an activity that allows children and adolescents to map out significant events in their lives on a time line, which aids in telling their stories.

Guided Exercise 9.4

Life TimeLine

A time line of life events is often used in narrative therapy to map significant events in clients' lives. This can be a useful tool in working with children also. What are the considerations in using this with younger children? What direction would you provide? What materials would you provide? How would you process their time lines in counseling?

---

5. Search for unique outcomes and reauthoring stories

Questions can also be used to help clients acknowledge any actions, feelings, and language that contradict the dominant story (Wolter, Dilollo, & Apel, 2006). Similar to "exceptions" in SFBT, unique outcomes can be found in the past and present (Corey, 2013). However, some can be hypothesized for the future and can be developed into solution stories or new alternative narratives. Younger children may want to act out new solutions, and the counselor can role-play with them.

Older children and adolescents may want to journal and write out their new narratives as they "try them on." Sometimes, it feels safer for clients to prepare ideas and bring them to counseling before trying out a new narrative. This is relative to each client, and the flexibility offered through narrative therapy is conducive to the client in reauthoring his or her story.

Case Illustration 9.2 is an example of the application of SFBT to a 10-year-old male student who has been withdrawn in class. As you read through the case of Manuel, consider the following questions:

- How does the counselor orient Manuel to the SFBT approach?
- How does the counselor use active listening and problem identification (e.g., What feelings are associated with the problem? How would you rate those feelings on a scale of 1-10?)?
- How does the counselor help Manuel with goal setting (e.g., using miracle question, finding exceptions, or scaling improvements)?

Case Illustration 9.2

Manuel is a 10-year-old boy who is referred to the school counselor for being withdrawn in the classroom. Based on the teacher's referral information and school records, Manuel transferred to the school this year from another state. He identifies as a Hispanic-American with both parents working and is considered to have a lower-to-middle socioeconomic status (SES). The demographic characteristics of his current school are majority Caucasian, middle to upper-middle SES, and English is the primary language of the students.

When Manuel arrives at the school counselor's office, he appears to be apprehensive and tentative upon entering. The school counselor greets him and informs him that his teacher has referred him for a visit since he was quiet in the classroom. He displays some surprise in his facial expression when he hears this but simply nods his head affirmatively. Taking a "not-knowing stance" (SFBT), the counselor replies, "I wasn't sure if this was the case, but your head nodding makes me think this is true. Is that right?" Manuel nods again. The counselor says, "Since, I'm not in the classroom, can you tell me more about you being quiet?" This question is a way for the school counselor to remain respectful yet curious and to enlist Manuel in helping her understand the situation.

Manuel begins to talk about being new to the school and his fellow students. He explains that the family only arrived to the school community one week prior to the beginning of school, so Manuel does not know any of the children. The school counselor asks, "Have there been times when you were not so quiet in any classroom?" (Exception question) Manuel explains that he spoke up frequently at his former school where the majority of students were Mexican-American and with whom he attended church and other community-related events. Not knowing anyone at his new school, and with the majority of the other students being Caucasian, he reported that he was not sure of how he should make friends and was nervous in the classroom.

The school counselor asks, "On a scale of 1 to 10, with 1 being extremely calm and confident to 10 being extremely nervous and unsure, how would you rate yourself?" (Scaling question) Manuel answered with an eight. The school counselor also asked Manuel what he liked to talk about and participate in when he was involved more in his former classroom. Manuel reported that he enjoyed history and learning in teams. (Looking for solutions) The school counselor asked Manuel, "If a miracle happened when you went to sleep tonight, and you were less nervous and more confident in your classroom the next day, how would you know that a miracle had occurred?" (Miracle question) He said that he would be answering more history questions and volunteering to partner with a reading buddy in class more often.

Based on the information that he provided, the school counselor and Manuel coconstructed some initial goals. First, Manuel would start to answer more history questions in class. Second, he would volunteer to be a reading buddy for the next week. Third, he would ask another boy in class about sports opportunities in the community to learn more about the community and his classmates. Manuel and the school counselor agreed to meet the next week as a follow-up and to scale his nervousness/confidence level and determine if he met some of his goals.

Relational–Cultural Therapy

RCT is an inclusive constructivist approach in which techniques from other theoretical orientations can be applied when appropriate (Frey, 2013). Specific to RCT, Tucker, Smith-Adcock, and Trepal (2010) summarized five basic skills that are involved in putting RCT into practice: encourage, explore, educate, explain, and expand. These skills are explained and applied to counseling children.

1. Encourage

This skill is related to the counselor encouraging the client in order for him or her to develop self-empathy or self-acceptance (Tucker et al., 2010). Having empathy for one's self and understanding self in relation to other people is a prerequisite to developing the ability to empathize with others. Self-empathy is the process of developing empathy for one's own experiences without criticism and blame (Jordan, 1991). Although the ability to blame one's self is related to development, children develop this quickly. Younger children may externalize emotions and beliefs on a regular basis, but gradually children internalize responsibility fairly quickly whether it is self- or other-imposed.

Similar to techniques found in narrative therapy, encouraging the child to tell his or her story (verbally or through other means) in a nonjudgmental stance provides the counselor with information on where and when self-blame was associated with the experience. Specific to RCT, the counselor provides his or her own reaction to the story and expresses empathy and compassion for the student that demonstrates the counselor's authenticity in the relationship. For an 8-year-old crying at recess because nobody will play with her, the counselor could empathize by saying, "It must feel very lonely at recess with no one to play with you. I would feel sad and upset, too." If the child blames herself for no one wanting to play with her, then the counselor could ask, "What if it was your sister or brother at recess with no one playing with them?" This would be an attempt to get the client to think about it differently and develop compassion for her experience. During this time, the counselor can also explore the client's relationships with others who may be related to the experience (e.g., classmates, teachers, etc.) and examine those connections and disconnections. With an authentic counseling relationship, children begin to feel safe to recognize behaviors that may be promoting disconnections in their lives.

2. Explore relational images

Relational images are mental templates of relationships that are based on past relationships (Miller & Stiver, 1997). Counselors may assume that children would have limited past relationships to form these relational images, but caution should be used in making this assumption. Children's relationships can include family members, peers, authority figures (e.g., teachers, religious leaders, community leaders), and culture-specific figures. Counselors are encouraged to assess this before exploring the impact of relational images on the experience that is causing the client distress. For example, a genogram of family can provide more insight into how influential family members are and who and what are important to the client (Taylor, Clement, & Ledet, 2013). Younger children can be asked to draw their family doing something at home or their friends doing something at school. Counselors need to ask and assess to determine if there were once important people in the client's life who are no longer important to the child. Why is there this disconnection? How has the client processed this? If the 8-year-old child has no one initiating play with her at recess, has the child rejected these relationships because she has been abandoned by peers or family members in the past? Is she self-protecting through disconnecting before she is hurt again in what she assumes is future abandonment? Exploring the thoughts and feelings around these relationships helps in creating solutions for the situation that the child brings to counseling.

3. Educate

Educating clients about power and power differentials is a core aspect of RCT (Jordan, 2009). For children, power differentials are inherent in many of their relationships with adults. However, issues of abuse influence children's relational images negatively and provide an impetus for education about the role of power in relationships. Dominant culture also influences children's views of self and self in relation to others. Diversity in race, gender, physical ability, spirituality, learning, and social class can be explored with children in individual, small group, and large group counseling. Bibliotherapy can be used with all age groups of children with follow-up activities that are developmentally appropriate. As children begin to embrace their own differences and those of others, the ability to empathize with self and others is enhanced. This leads to the development of mutual empathy and empowerment of each other. Guided Exercise 9.5 is an exploration of mutual empathy or mutuality.

Guided Exercise 9.5

Mutuality

In RCT, mutuality speaks to both individuals involved in the relationship having mutual empathy for each other. This is also true of the counselor-client relationship. To have mutuality, the counselor is authentic with the client and shares reactions to the client's story. How would you determine what reactions should be shared? How do your own social systems and culture influence your reactions? Think about some potential issues that children may share in counseling (e.g., poor grades, friendship concerns, discipline issues at home). Did you have any of these issues as a child? If so, it may be easy to self-disclose your own experiences. Mutuality is different than self-disclosure. Take another look at those issues, and identify the feelings associated with them. The feelings are associated with empathy. How can you convey those appropriately? How would a child empathize with you?

Counselors need to assess the role of power in the experiences that clients bring to counseling. For example, if a client is being bullied or harassed or is bullying or harassing someone at school, there may be a need to reiterate limits of confidentiality due to emotional and physical safety issues related to these behaviors. If the counselor is working within the school setting, then there may be policies that direct the actions of the counselor.

4. Explain disconnections and conflict

One of the key tenets to RCT is the central relational paradox related to relationship disconnections (Miller & Stiver, 1997). Individuals can experience acute or chronic serious relationship disconnections. If they experience the latter, then they learn to keep their thoughts, feelings, and experiences out of their relationships to keep themselves emotionally and physically safe. In doing this, they do not allow for mutuality and authenticity within their relationships. For them, these "strategies of disconnection" are survival mechanisms, especially if they are survivors of abusive relationships (Miller & Stiver, 1997, p. 106). However, RCT is based on the construct that individuals are striving and yearning for these authentic relationships. If individuals yearn for this type of relationship but are protecting themselves with strategies of disconnection, this is referred to as a *central relational paradox*.

The 8-year-old in the recess example may have a central relational paradox occurring in her life. She is complaining that no one wants to play with her (and she desires for someone to play with her), but she may be using strategies of disconnection based on her past relationships. Examining her behaviors in the situations with classmates at recess and reframing these behaviors to explain how she is using them to protect herself from getting hurt again may allow for her to incorporate different behaviors with classmates. It is the role of the counselor to determine if these strategies of disconnection are related to routine disconnections or chronic and severe disconnections, as in the case of abuse, with appropriate intervention.

5. Expand

Once clients experience an authentic counseling relationship, explore their relational images, receive education about power and differences, and learn about their own disconnections and conflict with a specific experience, the counselor encourages them to apply this to subsequent conflicts and experiences. Expanding their understanding of self and self-in-relation can help them develop mutual relationships that empower each person in the relationship and to cope with routine disconnections that may occur. Tucker et al. (2010) recommend that counselors teach children how to use I-messages in communicating with others, social skills, and peer mediation skills to promote healthy relationships and positive relational templates.

OUTCOME RESEARCH

Although outcome research for constructivist counseling approaches is growing, there is still limited research available. The following information highlights research studies that have demonstrated the effectiveness of SFBT, narrative therapy, and RCT. As with both modernist and postmodernist counseling approaches, there is still a need for more outcome-based research.

Much of the research on the effectiveness of solution-focused brief therapy (SFBT) with children is based on work in the schools applied to different types of behavioral and academic problems (Kim & Franklin, 2009). In a review and analysis of the most rigorous outcome studies on SFBT conducted in schools, Kim and Franklin (2009) calculated effect sizes to examine the effectiveness of the approach. Using Gingerich and Eisengart's (2000) systematic review of SFBT components, Kim and Franklin (2009) determined that at least one of the core components of SFBT had to be used in the studies included in their analysis. These components included use of the miracle question; use of scaling questions; giving the client a set of compliments; assigning homework tasks; looking for strengths or solutions; goal-setting; and looking for exceptions to the problem. Mixed results were found. Positive outcomes indicated that SFBT helped students reduce negative feelings, improve academic outcomes, manage conduct problems, and impact behavioral problems and substance use in a positive direction. However, SFBT was found not to be successful in improving attendance rates or raising grade point averages (GPAs).

Overall, it appears that SFBT has a positive impact with children. It is an efficient counseling approach that school counselors find appealing. Additionally, it is positive and future oriented, which provides children and families a positive direction in intervention.

Narrative therapy. Although narrative therapy is a newer counseling approach, there are several outcome research studies that demonstrate its effectiveness with different populations and issues. Specific to working with children, Hannen and Woods (2012) conducted a study that examined the effectiveness of using narrative therapy with an adolescent who self-cuts. Using a case-study design, six sessions of narrative therapy were provided to a 12-year-old female who reported self-cutting behaviors. The *Beck Youth Inventories,* (2nd ed.), a narrative interview, and parent report were used to assess the effectiveness of the therapy. The results indicated that the client's emotional well-being, resilience, and behavior improved over the intervention period.

In Ramey, Tarulli, Frijters, and Fisher's (2009) outcome study, they wanted to validate narrative therapy founder Michael White's map of the externalizing process with children. Eight children, between the ages of 6 and 15 years old, received brief counseling services where they received narrative therapy for a variety of issues. Each session was videotaped to be transcribed for sequential analysis. The results supported White's map of scaffolding and concept formation in narrative therapy. Additionally, the results indicated that externalizing occurred in the sessions and was important in the therapy process with children.

In an outcome study with 10 children diagnosed with autism (ages 10–16 years), each child received five 1-hour sessions of narrative therapy conducted over 10 weeks (Cashin, Browne, Bradbury, & Mulder, 2013). Parents of the children completed the Strengths and Difficulties Questionnaire (SDQ) as the primary outcome measure while the Kessler-10 Scale of Psychological Distress, the Beck Hopelessness Scale, and a stress biomarker were also measured with the children. Although there were reductions on the emotional symptoms scale of the SDQ, there were no significant statistical differences. However, there were substantial reductions from baseline data to after completion of the therapy in psychological distress on the other measures.

Although there is a need for more outcome-related research to be conducted using narrative therapy, it is apparent that it is effective with children. Due to research consent issues with parents, guardians, and agencies/schools who serve children, research may be difficult to conduct with children. However, there is a need to continue to pursue this evidence.

There are limited studies on relational cultural therapy (RCT) and counseling outcomes (Frey, 2013). Since RCT was designed originally for work with adult women, two outcome studies were conducted with female adult participants. Oakley, Addison, and Piran (2004) applied a time-limited, manualized RCT model to women receiving counseling in a community setting. Qualitative and quantitative data were collected between the initial screening and 6 months posttreatment. On measures of depression, anxiety, alexithymia, self-silencing, self-esteem, and psychological well-being, participants reported significant improvement. Additional outcome results indicated significant treatment goals attainment, maintenance of gains at 3- and 6-month follow-ups, and strong satisfaction related to the RCT model and thera peutic relationship. In a second study that compared short-term cognitive-behavior therapy and RCT groups for women diagnosed with bulimia nervosa or binge-eating disorder, the results indicated that the groups were equally as effective as CBT but experienced higher levels of mutuality in the group (Tantillo & Sanftner, 2003).

Although several RCT model applications for counseling children on a myriad of topics (e.g., trauma, art, middle school) have been published (Cannon et al., 2012; Sassen, Spencer, & Curtin, 2005; Tucker et al., 2010; Vicario, Tucker, Smith-Adcock, & Hudgins-Mitchell, 2013), only one outcome-based study has been published to date. Lenz, Speciale, and Aguilar (2012) conducted a small series single-case study to assess the effectiveness of a nine-session RCT intervention with adolescent females incarcerated in a youth detention facility. Four participants elected to participate in a group that used manualized RCT group sessions. Results indicated that three of the four participants reported notable changes in at least one domain of relational health as measured by the relational health indices. Lenz et al. (2012) concluded that "RCT may be effective for promoting relational empowerment and engagement with others" (p. 17) with this specific population.

Due to the paucity of research in use of RCT with both adults and children, more research is needed. Based on the few studies that have been published, it appears that RCT is a viable constructivist approach for use with children. Quantitative and qualitative research studies would be appropriate to determine not only the statistical outcomes but also how young people are affected by this particular counseling approach. Qualitative research may also be more conducive to use with younger children with limited reading abilities. Guided Exercise 9.6 is a way to explore how you can create research that informs the counseling profession on the efficacy of using constructivist counseling approaches with children.

Guided Exercise 9.6

Outcome Research

The need for more outcome research on counseling techniques has been a key issue in the counseling profession in the last decade. The connection between documenting techniques that work and the effectiveness of the counseling relationship has not been made, and professional counselors may feel ill-equipped to conduct research. Think about a constructivist counseling approach or method to use with children that appeals to you. What do you want to know about the use of that approach/method (i.e., outcomes)? Are there specific ages or developmental levels of clients to consider? What issues would be best served with the approach/method? How would you want to measure the outcomes in order to inform you about the client as well as you own practice?

Although constructivist counseling approaches are the newest on the counseling scene, they offer counselors the ability to consider diversity and the influence of culture and social systems on clients from the beginning of the counseling relationship. From being humble and respectful in an intentional way, constructivist counselors honor clients as the experts in their lives. The power of language and relationships encourages clients to share their realities with counselors, which provides counselors with insight into how they can work with clients on resolving problematic situations, finding solutions, and connecting with others. These approaches acknowledge that all that is known is not what is perceived.

COUNSELING KEYSTONES

- Meaning can be found in verbal and nonverbal communication and language that children use.
- Communication and language are socially and culturally based.
- Constructivist counseling approaches take a nonpathologizing stance to children's issues and view resiliency and adaptation as coping techniques.
- Constructivist counselors believe that all clients want to change, have the capacity to change, and will do their best to change.
- Clients create narratives that reflect social constructions relevant to their lives. These narratives or stories may change multiple times throughout a person's life.
- By telling their stories, children may learn how relationships can be beneficial in coping with issues and developing strategies that prevent them from occurring in the future.

ADDITIONAL RESOURCES

In Print

Berg, I. K., & Steiner, T. (2003). *Children's solution work*. New York, NY: W. W. Norton & Company.

Kelly, M. S., Kim, J. S., & Franklin, C. (2008). *Solution focused brief therapy: A 360 degree view of research and practice*. Oxford, UK: Oxford University Press.

White, M. (2007). *Maps of narrative practice*. New York, NY: W. W. Norton & Company.

Winslade, J. M., & Monk, G. D. (2006). *Narrative counseling in schools: Powerful and brief* (2nd ed.). Thousand Oaks, CA: Corwin.

On Video

Jordan, J. V. (2009). *Relational-cultural therapy* [DVD]. Washington, DC: American Psychological Association.

Madigan, S. (2009). *Narrative therapy with children* [DVD]. Available at http://www.psychotherapy.net/video/madigan-narrative-therapy-children

Murphy, J. J. (2009). *Solution-focused child therapy*. Available at http://www.psychotherapy.net/video/solution-focused-child-therapy

REFERENCES

American Counseling Association. (2014). *Code of ethics*. Retrieved from http://www.counseling.org/docs/ethics/2014-aca-code-of-ethics.pdf?sfvrsn=4

Berg, I. K., & de Shazer, S. (1993). Making numbers talk. In Friedman, S. (Ed.), *The new language of change: Constructive collaboration in psychotherapy*, (pp. 5–24). New York, NY: Guilford Press.

Berger, P. L., & Luckmann, T. (1966). *The social construction of reality: A treatise in the sociology of knowledge*. London, UK: Penguin Books.

Bertolino, B., & O'Hanlon, B. (2002). *Collaborative, competency-based counseling and therapy*. Needham Heights, MA: Allyn & Bacon.

Bruner, J. (1990). *Acts of meaning*. Cambridge, MA: Harvard University Press.

Cannon, K. B., Hammer, T. R., Reicherzer, S., & Gilliam, B. J. (2012). Relational-cultural theory: A framework for relational competencies and movement in group work with female adolescents. *Journal of Creativity in Mental Health, 7*, 2–16.

Cashin, A., Browne, G., Bradbury, J., & Mulder, A. (2013). The effectiveness of narrative therapy with young people with autism. *Journal of Child and Adolescent Psychiatric Nursing, 26*, 32–41. doi: 10.1111/jcap.12020

Corey, G. (2013). *Theory and practice of counseling and psychotherapy* (9th ed.). Belmont, CA: Brooks/Cole, Cengage Learning.

Cottone, R. R. (2012). *Paradigms of counseling and psychotherapy*. Cottleville, MO: Author.

De Jong, P., & Berg, I. K. (2008). *Interviewing for solutions* (3rd ed.). Pacific Grove, CA: Brooks/Cole.

De Shazer, S. (1988). *Clues: Investigating solutions in brief therapy*. New York, NY: Norton.

De Shazer, S., & Berg, I. (1988). Doing therapy: A post-structural revision. *Journal of Marital and Family Therapy, 18*, 71–81.

Epston, D., & White, M. (1995). Termination as a rite of passage: Questioning strategies for a therapy of inclusion. In R. A. Neimeyer & M. J. Mahoney (Eds.), *Constructivism in psychotherapy* (pp. 339–354). Washington, DC: American Psychological Association.

Freedman, J., & Combs, G. (1996). *Narrative therapy: The social construction of preferred realities*. New York, NY: Norton.

Frey, L. L. (2013). Relational-cultural therapy: Theory, research, and application to counseling competencies. *Professional Psychology: Research and Practice, 44*, 177–185.

Gardner, R. A. (1993). Mutual storytelling. In C. E. Schaefer & D. M. Cangelosi (Eds.), *Play therapy techniques* (pp. 199–209). Northvale, NJ: Jason Aronson.

George, C. M. (2008). Solution-focused therapy: Strength-based counseling for children with social phobia. *Journal of Humanistic Counseling, Education and Development, 47*, 144–156.

Gergen, K. J. (1985). The social constructionist movement in modern psychology. *American Psychologist, 40*, 266–275.

Gergen, K. J. (1992). Social construction and moral action. In D. N. Robinson (Ed.), *Social discourse and moral judgment* (pp. 9–27). San Diego, CA: Academic Press.

Gergen, K. J. (2001). *Social construction in context*. Thousand Oaks, CA: Sage.

Gil, E. (1991). *The healing power of play: Working with abused children*. New York, NY: Guilford Press.

Gingerich, W. J., & Eisengart, S. (2000). Solution-focused brief therapy: A review of the outcome research. *Family Process, 39*(4), 477–498.

Granvold, D. (1996). Constructivist psychotherapy. *Family in Society: The Journal of Contemporary Human Services, 77*, 345–359.

Hannen, E., & Woods, K. (2012). Narrative therapy with an adolescent who self-cuts: A case example. *Educational Psychology in Practice, 28*, 187–214.

Jordan, J. (1991). Empathy, mutuality, and therapeutic change: Clinical implications of a relational model. In J. V. Jordan, A. G. Kaplan, J. B. Miller, I. P. Stiver, & J. L. Surrey (Eds.), *Women's growth in connection: Writings from the Stone Center* (pp. 283–289). New York, NY: Guilford Press.

Jordan, J. V. (2008). Recent developments in relational-cultural theory. *Women & Therapy, 31*, 1–4.

Jordan, J. V. (2009). *Relational-cultural therapy*. Washington, DC: American Psychological Association.

Kalodner, C. R. (2011). Cognitive-behavioral theories. In D. Capuzzi & D. R. Gross (Eds.), *Counseling and psychotherapy: Theories and interventions* (5th ed., pp. 193–213). Alexandria, VA: American Counseling Association.

Kelly, G. A. (1955). *The psychology of personal constructs*. New York, NY: Norton.

Kelly, G. A. (1963). *A theory of personality*. New York, NY: Norton.

Kim, J. S., & Franklin, C. (2009). Solution-focused brief therapy in schools: A review of the outcome literature. *Children and Youth Services Review, 31*, 464–470.

Lenz, A. S., Speciale, M., & Aguilar, J. V. (2012). Relational-cultural theory intervention with incarcerated adolescents: A single-case effectiveness design. *Counseling Outcome Research and Evaluation, 3*, 17–29.

Lyotard, J. (1992). *The postmodern explained: Correspondence 1982–1985*. Minneapolis, MN: University of Minnesota Press.

Maturana, H. R. (1978). Biology of language: The epistemology of reality. In G.A. Miller & E. Lenneberg (Eds.), *Psychology and biology of language and thought*, (pp. 27–63). New York, NY: Academic Press.

Miller, J. B., & Stiver, I. P. (1997). *The healing connection: How women form relationships in therapy and in life*. Boston, MA: Beacon Press.

Monk, G. (1997). How narrative therapy works. In G. Monk, J. Winslade, K. Crocket, & D. Epston (Eds.), *Narrative therapy in practice: The archaeology of hope* (pp. 3–31). San Francisco, CA: Jossey-Bass.

Murphy, J. (2008). *Solution-focused counseling in schools* (2nd ed.). Alexandria, VA: American Counseling Association.

Neukrug, E. S. (2011). *Counseling theory and practice*. Belmont, CA: Brooks/ Cole, Cengage Learning.

Oakley, A., Addison, S., & Piran, N. (2004, June). *Brief psychotherapy centre for women: Results of a comprehensive two-year outcome study of a brief feminist relational-cultural model*. Poster session at the JBMTI Research Forum, Wellesley, MA.

Ramey, H. L., Tarulli, D., Frijters, J. C., & Fisher, L. (2009). A sequential analysis of externalizing in narrative therapy with children. *Contemporary Family Therapy, 31*, 262–279. doi: 10.1007/s10691-009-9095-5

Russo, M., Vernam, J., & Wolbert, A. (2006). Sandplay and storytelling: Social constructivism and cognitive development in child counseling. *The Arts in Psychotherapy, 33*, 229–237.

Sassen, G., Spencer, R., & Curtin, P. C. (2005). Art from the heart: A relational-cultural approach to using art therapy in a group for urban middle school girls. *Journal of Creativity in Mental Health, 1*, 67–80.

Tantillo, M., & Sanftner, J. (2003). The relationship between perceived mutuality and bulimic symptoms, depression, and therapeutic change in group. *Eating Behavior, 3*(4), 349–364.

Taylor, E. R., Clement, M., & Ledet, G. (2013). Postmodern alternative approaches in genogram use with children and adolescents. *Journal of Creativity in Mental Health, 8*, 278–292.

Tucker, C., Smith-Adcock, S., & Trepal, H. C. (2010). Relational-cultural theory for middle school counselors. *Professional School Counseling, 14*, 310–316.

Vicario, M., Tucker, C., Smith-Adcock, S., & Hudgins-Mitchell, C. (2013). Relational-cultural play therapy: Reestablishing healthy connections with children exposed to trauma in relationships. *International Journal of Play Therapy, 22*, 103–117.

White, M. (1995). *Re-authoring lives: Interviews and essays.* Adelaide, South Australia: Dulwich Centre.

Wolter, J. A., DiLollo, A., & Apel, K. (2006). A narrative therapy approach to counseling: A model for working with adolescents and adults with language-literacy deficits. *Language, Speech, and Hearing Services in Schools, 37*, 168–177.

Section III

Chapter 10

Counseling With Very Young Children (0–4) and Their Families

C<small>ATHERINE</small> T<small>UCKER</small>

It is easier to build strong children than to repair broken men.

—Frederick Douglas

INTRODUCTION

The first several years of a person's life are fast-paced and busy for both the child and the people who take care of him or her. Over half of the development of the brain's gray matter, or cortex, occurs after birth (Schore, 1994). As a result, babies and young children experience explosive growth across all developmental domains. Meanwhile, even the most eager and capable caregivers can become exhausted by growing babies' demands for nurturance, stimulation, and safety. Therefore, most of the problems presented in clinical settings involving children from ages 0 to 4 are related either to nontypical development in one or more domains (physical, cognitive, or psychosocial) or to problems of parenting (Zeanah & Zeanah, 2009). Parenting babies and young children takes a tremendous amount of energy under ideal circumstances, and when there are barriers such as poverty, a parent's own mental or physical illness, or relational distress, the task of raising healthy children can feel overwhelming.

It is imperative that counselors who work with very young children view them within the context of the family, regardless of the nature of the presenting problem. Joining with the child's primary caregivers to craft a meaningful and achievable treatment plan is crucial to the success of any intervention with children of this age/ stage. For this reason, many of the interventions we discuss later in this chapter are aimed at increasing the family's ability to problem solve with, communicate to, and nurture each other. Effective intervention with families who are just beginning to raise children can give them tools to prevent the need for intervention in later years. Interventions that do not include the whole family may be effective in one setting, or for a period of time, but are not as likely to yield long-lasting systemic results (Lieberman & van Horn, 2009). One illustration of systemic intervention may be found in Case Illustration 10.1.

Case Illustration 10.1

Jacob presented in the clinic as a smiling, well-groomed, and active 4-year-old. He was accompanied by his aunt, who had gained custody of him a month prior to the first meeting with the counselor. Jacob's aunt, Maria, told the counselor that she met Jacob for the first time when she traveled to another state to pick him up and bring him home with her at the request of child services. Jacob's mother, Maria's sister, lost custody of him when she went to prison on charges of possession of a large quantity of methamphetamine.

When Maria met Jacob and his social worker at the airport, he happily took her hand and got on the airplane with her and never looked back. Once Jacob settled in at Maria's home, she noticed that he had recurring nightmares, avoided a wide array of objects and situations, such as dark corners, the cellar, bathroom stalls in public places, and any object related to fire (cigarette lighters, ashtrays, fireplaces, etc.). Jacob's preschool teacher reported that although he appeared to be very bright, he was very aggressive with the other children and was having trouble making friends.

In order to get a more complete picture of Jacob's current symptoms, the counselor asked Maria and the preschool teacher to complete BASC2 forms (Reynolds & Kamphaus, 2008). Maria and Jacob also participated in the Marschak interaction method (MIM) assessment (Booth & Jernberg, 2010). After reviewing the results of the BASC2, the MIM, and reviewing the medical and school records Maria supplied, the counselor diagnosed Jacob with reactive attachment disorder, disinhibited type, and posttraumatic stress disorder. She also created a treatment plan that included reducing Jacob's fear-based symptoms, such as nightmares, irritability, and aggression with peers and increasing his secure attachment to Maria. The counselor also gave Maria materials to use at home with Jacob to introduce stranger safety.

During the MIM session, it was noted that Maria did a great job on nurturing tasks but struggled with creating and maintaining structure. Therefore, the first series of Theraplay sessions the counselor conducted emphasized structure and engagement, with nurturing activities at the beginning and end of the session (see chart for session description). Weekly sessions were held with both Jacob and

Maria working with the therapist on activities. After 18 weekly sessions of theraplay in the counselor's office, along with specifically prescribed at-home nurturing activities at bedtime, and assistance with discipline methods, Maria noted that Jacob's nightmares had decreased from two or three a week to about one every 2 weeks. She also reported less aggressive and irritable behaviors at preschool. The counselor repeated the BASC-2 and the MIM, both of which showed marked improvements in all previous symptoms. Jacob's counseling was discontinued after two more sessions, the final one being a joyful session of his favorite Theraplay activities. (Note: All activities are taken from the Theraplay book. Authors encourage counselors to seek training prior to using this approach for purposes of fidelity [Booth & Jernberg, 2010].)

Title of Activity	Dimension	Description/Materials Needed
Twinkle song	Engagement	Sing "twinkle twinkle little star," modified to child's specific description, for example, Twinkle twinkle little star, how I wonder who you are, With soft brown skin and Round red cheeks, Big brown eyes from which you peek, Twinkle twinkle, little star, Jacob is who you are!
Bean bag drop	Structure	Place a bean bag or small toy on your head. If the child will tolerate it, place one on his or her head as well. Tell the child to wait until you say a certain word, or blink, or make a facial expression, then you'll both drop the bean bags into your laps at the same time. (Words or expressions should be funny "watermelon" or "elephants" for words and silly faces for expressions work well.) Don't immediately give the signal, but don't exceed the child's ability to wait, either. A list of two to three words is usually about right. Play three to six rounds, changing the signal, as the child tolerates the activity.
Juice	Nurture	Ask caregiver to bring in a juice box to use, or bring one yourself. Caregiver gives juice to child, using the straw on the box, as parents do with young children.
Simon says	Structure	Use the common children's game—the adult is "Simon," child learns to wait for turns and listen for directions. Play a few rounds, according to the child's tolerance.
Newspaper punch	Engagement/structure	Hold up a section of the newspaper, ask child to punch through it, tell him or her how strong he or she is. Add structure by using "code word" to cue punching.
Bubble tennis	Structure	Use bubble wand to blow a few bubbles. Let child pop a few by clapping them. Then tell her you will catch one bubble on your wand and gently blow it to her. Ask her to return it, see how many back and forth rounds you can share with one bubble.

(Continued)

(Continued)		
Lotion	Nurture	Use any nonallergenic lotion. Ask caregiver to rub a small amount of lotion onto child's hand while humming a short song. If the child cannot tolerate this, he or she may rub in the lotion. Do not allow child to apply lotion to adults; this activity nurtures the child.
Good-bye song	Nurture/ structure	Use any children's song, preferably the same each week

In fact, because of their young age and specific needs, some states are now requiring mental health workers to earn specialized credentials to work with young children. If you are considering specializing in working with very young children and their families, be sure to check the requirements for credentialing in your state (Korfmacher, 2014).

After reading this chapter, you will be able to

- describe the typical cognitive, psychosocial, and physical developmental patterns of children from birth to 4 years old;
- explain what sorts of mental health problems children in this age group most often present; and
- describe several possible types of interventions available for children from 0 to 4 and their families when mental health issues are present.

THE BRAIN AND COGNITIVE DEVELOPMENT

During the first years of human life, an astonishing amount of activity occurs in the brain. Infants are born with most of the basic structures of the adult brain intact, however, the wiring, or connection of brain cells to each other, continues at a fast pace for at least the first 2 years of life, as does the development of the gray matter (Sheridan & Nelson, 2009). While the old myth that the brain cannot generate new cells after birth has been refuted, it does appear to be true that only some parts of the brain can generate entirely new neurons during postnatal development (Sheridan & Nelson, 2009). Connections between existing brain cells do appear to continue to form long after birth, quite possibly into adulthood (Schore, 2012).

Soon after birth, the parts of the brain that intercept and interpret sensory information (vision, hearing, taste, etc.) grow dramatically. Growth and connections in the brain appear to be dependent on the quality of experiences the infant has and especially the quality of care he or she receives (Schore, 2012). This is particularly true of the nonverbal right hemisphere of the brain, which develops most rapidly in the first 2 years or so of life. The right brain, which controls such functions as emotion, arousal, and affect regulation, is dominant for the first 3 years of human life. Once the left brain, which generally controls cognition, language, decision making, and other executive functions, comes fully online around age 3, there is a dramatic growth in the child's vocabulary and ability to reason (Schore, 2012). Knowing this is crucial to our understanding of the importance of early caregiving experiences and the negative impact of poor quality care on later childhood behaviors and emotions.

Brain development and what can go wrong when young children experience adversity is covered in detail in Chapter 3. However, all counselors should be aware that caregivers of infants are in the position of being able to set the stage for later mental wellness by being affectionate, calm, and consistently soothing when interacting with infants. Attachments are formed by right brain to right brain contact, which is generally accomplished by holding a long eye to eye gaze (Schore, 2012; Tronick & Beeghly, 2011). The act of gazing lovingly into the eyes of an infant is a very powerful one; to do it often is to put the child on a path to secure attachment and healthy brain development. Lack of early right brain to right brain stimulation appears to lead to a myriad of later problems, including problems of regulation (e.g., attention deficit hyperactivity disorder [ADHD], oppositional defiant disorder [ODD], anger outbursts), problems in relationships (insecure attachment style), and greater vulnerability to other mental illnesses (PTSD, in particular) (Cozolino, 2010).

During the first 2 to 3 years of life, while the nonverbal right brain is dominant, growth is explosive in areas related to sensation, experience, and affect. At around 2 ½ to 3 years, the child's vocabulary increases dramatically, along with his or her ability to comprehend complex sentences (Sheridan & Nelson, 2009). However, parenting children of this age generally means keeping commands very short (one idea at a time) and being very consistent with rules.

In Piaget's terms, toddlers make the transition from sensorimotor to preoperational thinking at around age 2 (Piaget & Inhelder, 1973). During the sensorimotor stage (birth–2), babies take in sensory information and act on it with a minimal amount of additional processing. They also develop object permanence (which is why 1- to 2-year-old children sometimes get upset during games of hiding or peek-a-boo, they think the person hiding might not be there anymore) and often pass through a stage of separation anxiety around 9 to 12 months (Berk, 2006). Anxiety when separated from parents is normal during this stage, as the baby has just figured out that he or she is a separate being from mom or dad, and that not all caregivers are the same person. Usually, this anxiety fades over a few months, but, in some cases, it can remain a problem intermittently until later childhood.

Around the age of 2, children move into Piaget's stage of preoperational thought (Piaget & Inhelder, 1973). Children remain in this stage until around the age of 7 or 8. Preoperational thinking is the stage where magical thinking and imaginative play are most notable (Piaget & Inhelder, 1973). Children in this stage enjoy pretending that the old tree in the yard is a spaceship or that their toy elephant can speak to them. They also enjoy asking "why" and "how" questions, even though their capacity for understanding abstract thought is still quite limited (Berk, 2006). They are also extremely self-focused. To a preoperational child, he or she is the center of the universe; everything and everyone else revolves around himself or herself (Piaget & Inhelder, 1973). Children in this stage often blame themselves for all sorts of events that are not under their control. For example, it is very common for small children to believe their parents are divorcing because they've been naughty, or that Uncle Al died because they stepped on a crack in the sidewalk. Consequently, it is very important that counselors working with very young children understand that simply stating "it's not your fault" may not be adequate to shift a child's beliefs about the cause of upsetting events. The child may need to play, draw, or act out the event over and over until the belief shifts, and the child can say confidently that he or she did not cause the stressful event.

During this period, children have great difficulty understanding the point of view of other people (Piaget & Inhelder, 1973). Learning to share, take turns, and handle small conflicts are major social developmental tasks around the age most children begin school (Berk, 2006). Young children do understand the concept of fairness and are generally able to follow rules if they are simple and are consistently enforced.

PSYCHOSOCIAL DEVELOPMENT

As with the rapid development in other developmental domains, children make tremendous strides in psychosocial realms between birth and age 4. Erikson's stage model of psychosocial development (1963) holds that children pass through two stages of development before the age of about 3 or 4. The first stage of Erikson's theory is called trust versus mistrust. During this stage, the basic conflict infants must address and overcome involves having their basic needs (which includes the need for comfort and nurturing) met in order to successfully move on to the other stages. Children cared for by adequate caregivers will develop a basic sense of trust in the world, whereas children who are neglected or mistreated may develop a basic sense that they cannot trust people to keep them safe or meet other basic needs

(Erikson, 1963). Obviously, there is a great deal of congruence between this early stage in Erikson's theory and the various theories of attachment. Bowlby, Erikson, and other theorists also agree that if this first, foundational, conflict between trust and mistrust is not resolved, there may be lifelong implications for the individual in forming and maintaining healthy connections to other people.

When the trust versus mistrust conflict is successfully resolved, children progress onto the second stage of Erikson's model, autonomy versus shame and doubt (Erikson, 1963). This stage encompasses the toddler period, beginning around 12 months of age and ending usually around age 3. During this phase, children struggle to gain a measure of independence from caregivers; they learn to walk, feed themselves, use the toilet, and talk in entire sentences (Berk, 2006). If children are criticized rather than encouraged in their efforts to be independent, they may develop a sense of doubt about their abilities and may be reluctant to try new things (Erickson, 1963). However, the issue of independence appears to be culturally constructed and variable between European, African, Latin, Asian, and other cultures. While White American and Western European people generally support the idea of individualism and self-reliance, most other cultures of the world value cooperation and interdependence (Vernon & Clemente, 2005). Therefore, when working with toddlers, counselors should be sensitive to cultural beliefs around the value of being independent versus being able to work well with others.

Children between the ages of 0 and 4 often have trouble learning to share and cooperate with peers and siblings. According to Selman's theory of social perspective taking (Selman, 1980), this is explained as the egocentric perspective taking stage, which often extends into kindergarten. During this stage, Selman (1980) states that children begin to know that they are independent from their parents, but believe that everyone has the same ideas and emotions that they do. They do not have the ability yet to discern different points of view. This is why toddlers do not comprehend why grabbing a toy from a peer makes the peer angry; they must develop the capacity to empathize with others. Parents and caregivers of toddlers usually spend a good deal of time teaching children that it hurts when you hit someone, or that it hurts their friend's feelings when the child grabs away their ice cream. Usually by about age 4 or 5, the requisite neural pathways exist to allow empathetic thought to begin to develop, and children are able to understand that other people may have ideas and feelings different from their own (Selman, 1980; Cozolino, 2013).

ISSUES AND CONCERNS

When very young children are referred for mental health care, most often the cause for the referral is either (1) the parents need help structuring the child's environment or giving adequate nurturing to the child or (2) the child has some sort of physical or neurological disability that includes behavioral symptoms (Troutman & Moran, 2011). In the section following, we address an assortment of problems of parenting and problems related to disabilities. We have chosen to include some of the most common problems in both areas; however, this should not be considered an exhaustive inventory of all possible issues faced by families with very young children. In the first guided exercise, you will watch some examples of young children playing together to illustrate these principles.

Guided Exercise 10.1

If possible, gather into groups of three or four students. Each student should identify a major developmental theorist to track for this exercise (Piaget, Erikson, etc.). Using YouTube or a similar video sharing service, search for "child development observations ages 2–4." There are hundreds of videos posted by students of child development from all over the world. Choose two or three short videos to watch, preferably with children from a variety of ethnic, racial, geographic, and gender groups in preschool or play group settings. After viewing the videos, describe the behaviors you observed from the perspective of the developmental theorist you chose at the start of the activity. Then answer the following questions in the group:

1. Were all children at equally advanced stages in all areas, or were they at different levels cognitively, socially, ethically, and so on?

2. Did you observe any overall differences between boys and girls or between groups in different settings?

3. Did you observe any cooperative activities among the children? Did their abilities to share and take turns vary by age, gender, or other factors?

4. Did any of your videos show children who might have behavioral problems (it's impossible to diagnose anything from one short video clip; this is simply a thought exercise)? If so, what recommendations might you, as a consultant, make to the teacher to help the child?

Parenting Typically Developing Babies and Toddlers

Bringing an infant into your home for the first time can be an overwhelming experience. Whether the child is a newborn biological child, a foster child in your care, or is placed in your care as a family placement, finding a rhythm to care for this new life while attempting to continue to adequately address other life roles (worker, spouse, parent of other children, etc.) may take a few days or several months, depending on the health and temperament of the baby, the resources of the adults in the family, and the types and severity of stressors present in the environment.

The immediate needs of infants are simple but incessant: food, shelter, clean diapers, and security. Meeting the needs of an infant all day every day can be physically and emotionally draining, especially if the infant's sleep patterns are erratic. Exhaustion and frustration make the parent's job all that much more difficult, particularly around emotional bonding and secure attachment. While even a very tired and very grouchy adult can usually manage to feed a baby a bottle or change a diaper, offering soothing and protective emotional responses may be beyond the capabilities of new parents at times.

Luckily for us all, babies are relatively resilient; an occasional instance of mom and dad being short tempered is unlikely to cause lifelong emotional scarring (Greenspan & Wieder, 2006). As the baby and his or her caregivers spend time together, particularly time looking into one another's eyes, they develop a pattern of coregulation of affect that is the cornerstone of secure attachment (Schore, 1994). In effect, what Bowlby, Winnicott, Ainsworth, and other theorists have called attachment may in fact be a neurological/emotional regulation process (Schore, 2012; Tronick & Beeghly, 2011). The infant essentially synchronizes his or her state of arousal or calm to match that of the parent figure, which leads to the infant gradually learning how to self-soothe and regulate his or her own emotional states (Schore, 1994). This eye-to-eye, right brain to right brain contact during the first year or so of life is also a critically important cue to growing neural connection in the infant's brain, stimulating rapid growth and increases in connections between brain cells (Cozolino, 2010). (This is discussed at length in Chapter 3.) Regulation, or lack thereof, is thought to be directly related to mental well-being later in life in a number of crucial ways. Although it is possible to repair damage done by lack of coregulation, it is a very difficult and demanding process, making the first few months of life a critical window for the development of good mental health across the lifespan (Schore, 2012).

If the caregivers of the infant manage to be "good enough" at this coregulation of affect and its automatic stimulation of brain growth, the infant will generally develop what Bowlby and others have labeled a secure attachment style (Winnicott, 1973). Securely attached babies and toddlers feel safe exploring the world around them because if they need help, they know their caregiver will be there to provide care and nurturing (Bowlby, 1969). However, if the caregivers are not able to muster a "good enough" response of consistent nurturing and care, coregulation of affect will not go smoothly, and the child may develop an insecure style of attachment (Bowlby, 1969). Depending on which theorist you consult, insecure attachment styles may be referred to with a variety of titles. In this text, we will use Mary Ainsworth's classifications developed as a result of her work with the strange situation experiment (Zeanah & Smyke, 2009). To learn more about this fascinating series of experiments, see Guided Exercise 10.2.

Guided Exercise 10.2

Strange Situation: Many universities and some public libraries now subscribe to the digital service "Films on Demand." If yours does (ask your library staff), find the short film, "Mary Ainsworth: Attachment and the Growth of Love" (2005). If you do not have access to Films on Demand, you can look up other video titles on public access sharing sites like YouTube and supplement that viewing with an article or two by Dr. Ainsworth or her colleagues. After watching some samples of the strange situation, answer the following questions:

1. How have early intimate relationships influenced your current life?

2. Do you think your early relationships have any bearing on your decision to become a counselor?

3. How does this information impact your thinking about working with families who have young children?

4. What else do you want to learn about Ainsworth's work and legacy now that you have seen this basic information?

In addition to creating a warm emotional bond with the baby, parents or caregivers must also create enough structure to help the growing child feel safe. As the baby becomes a toddler, and then a little girl or boy, caregivers begin to add rules to both keep the child safe (Don't touch the stove!) and to help him or her learn to live within the family (Don't hit your brother!). Although it can be difficult to stick to the rules after a long day at work, it is crucial for caregivers to create enough structure in the home to allow the child to explore and play but balance those needs with the safety and well-being of everyone in the home.

Caregivers usually begin to craft household rules for behavior around the time the first child begins to walk. Early rules normally involve safety (don't go outside, don't go down the stairs, etc.). As the baby becomes more independent and learns to do more things, rules must expand to protect the child in this expanded world (don't stick your finger in the outlet, don't run out into the street). At this point, rules must encompass teaching the child to live in harmony with the rest of the members of the household (don't tease the cat, don't bite your sister). Although rules generally develop organically from experience, enforcing them can be another matter. Structure that is inconsistently enforced is confusing to young children and tends to make them even more likely to protest (NO!) than when rules are stable and consistently enforced. In our clinical experience, inconsistent rule enforcement is probably the most common cause of behavior problems in young children. Caregivers who are too tired or distracted to require children to behave within a stable structure of expectations often end up causing themselves more work when children become defiant and resistant to repeated requests to do or not do something.

Autism and Related Disorders

Perhaps the most confounding and puzzling developmental problems of early childhood may be autism and related disorders. Inherent problems in conducting accurate clinical assessments with very young children (Carr & Lord, 2009), along with the diverse array of symptoms and the differences in responses to the same treatment with different autistic children, can leave clinicians feeling a bit overwhelmed and bewildered. Fortunately, emerging medical technology and advances in our understanding of the functions of the human brain are beginning to untangle some of autism's mysteries (Carr & Lord, 2009).

Although commonly referred to simply as "autism" or "autistic spectrum disorders," the cluster of problems typically thought of in this group may be best described by the term *neurological disorders of relating and communicating* (NDRC) (Greenspan, 1992; Greenspan & Wieder, 2006). This cluster of problems encompasses a broad array of neurological and developmental diagnoses but holds in common great difficulty for the child in relating to and communicating with the world and the people in it. Using the term *NRDC*, and its associated subtypes, to describe these conditions could be important both because it allows clinicians to assess the individual child's level of need along the lines of symptomology, and because it helps make a more clear definition of problems for researchers interested in determining what sorts of problems respond to what sorts of interventions (Greenspan & Wieder, 2006).

One current hypothesis to explain what is commonly called autistic spectrum disorders is that at some early point in an infant's development, he or she encounters a problem pairing sensory input with their affective reaction. As the child continues to develop, this problem extends to the pairing of sensory input, the meanings of social gestures, and symbolic language (Greenspan & Wieder, 2006). There is a huge variation between autistic children in terms of ability to communicate and function in the social world; however, it is likely that all of them share this same core disruption. It is very likely that this inability to attach meaning to affect generated by sensory input may also lead to attachment problems, which may then exacerbate behavioral problems later on (Schore, 1994, 2012).

As the infant moves into toddlerhood, parents begin to expect more gestural and later verbal communication to occur. When children affected by NDRC do not progress in their ability to communicate as expected, parents often feel very frustrated and isolated. Emerging research suggests that appropriate early diagnosis not only of overall NDRC, but also the subtypes involved, may allow for more targeted interventions aimed directly at the skill deficits the child is experiencing (Greenspan & Wieder, 2006).

The most promising interventions to date seem to be interdisciplinary, implemented across settings (home, daycare/school, and clinic visits) and aimed at specific skill deficits (Carr & Lord, 2009). Once a very thorough assessment is completed, detailed and specific treatment goals may be determined by the family and treatment team. Interventions may include brief, frequent explicit teaching strategies, attachment-based family play, and sensory exposures, among others (Carr & Lord, 2009). These interventions may be delivered by a wide range of professionals along with the parents.

Due to the complexity of symptoms and our as yet still incomplete medical understanding of NDRC, it is of the upmost importance for counselors to be aware of referral resources available to the families they serve. Often, children with NDRC require a team of professionals to assist them. This team may involve a pediatric neurologist, pediatrician, occupational therapist, physical therapist, speech/language therapist, special education teacher, developmental psychologist, social workers, and school and mental health counselors, among others. The role of the school or mental health counselor is often to help parents sort through what can seem a bewildering array of helpful professionals and ensure that everyone communicates clearly about the child's needs. Counselors may also intervene with parents and siblings of children with NDRC to assist them in learning coping strategies for stress and the adjustment in expectations that can accompany a diagnosis of any developmental disorder. Counselors who seek specialized education about NDRC may also be involved directly in the assessment, diagnosis, and treatment of these disorders. To learn more about one fascinating woman's lifelong journey with autism, have a look at the video in Guided Exercise 10.3.

Guided Exercise 10.3

Watch Temple Grandin's 2010 TED talk titled "The World Needs All Kinds of Brains." TED talks are available on the TED webpage and on YouTube at no charge. After watching the video, consider Dr. Grandin's points about autism as a difference but not a disability. How did her talk influence how you think about children with autism?

Problems Related to Prenatal Exposure to Alcohol

Although exact numbers are not available, most scientists who gather data on birth defects caused by prenatal exposure to alcohol generally seem to agree that between 0.1% and 1% of the United States population is significantly affected by fetal alcohol exposure (CDC, 2015; Wattendorf & Meunke, 2005). Alcohol consumption during pregnancy has long been, and still is, the leading preventable cause of intellectual disabilities, with about 40,000 children born in the United States annually with serious alcohol related problems (May & Gossage, 2001). Because of the large impact alcohol has on our culture as compared to other recreational drugs, we concentrate here only on birth defects caused by alcohol. Information on birth defects caused by street drugs and other hazards can be found here:

- The National Center on Birth Defects and Developmental Disabilities, a division of the federal Centers for Disease Control and Prevention: http://www.cdc.gov/ncbddd/birthdefects
- March of Dimes, a national advocacy organization dedicated to the prevention of birth defects: http://www.marchofdimes.org

Disabilities related to maternal alcohol consumption are all grouped under the large umbrella term *fetal alcohol spectrum disorders*, a nonclinical term used to describe an array of disabilities known to be caused by prenatal exposure to alcohol. Currently, there are three broad categories proposed by the Centers for Disease Control and Prevention (CDC; http://www.cdc.gov/ncbddd/fasd/diagnosis.html) to refine identification of how severe any one person's alcohol related problems are. The three proposed categories are fetal alcohol syndrome (FAS), alcohol-related neurodevelopmental disorder (ARND), and alcohol related birth defects (ARBD). The category of ARND is designed to reflect problems in the central nervous system due to prenatal alcohol exposure without the facial affects seen in FAS, while ARBD is centered around deformities in the organs and skeletal systems of the body (SAMHSA, 2006).

Fetal alcohol syndrome (FAS) is the only category so far to have definite diagnostic guidelines for clinical use. In order to be diagnosed with FAS, a patient must have problems in all three of the areas below. The current guidelines given on the CDC website include the following:

1. Abnormal facial features—commonly, these may include missing ridge between the nose and upper lip (smooth philtrum), a very thin and flat upper lip, and a shorter than usual distance between the inner and outer corners of the eyes.

2. Growth problems (below 10% on the standard pediatric charts).

3. Central nervous system problems—Problems with learning, memory, motor skills, social skills, and sensory information processing may exist. There may be structural differences in the brain as well, which are often visible on an MRI or CAT scan. Children with FAS often, but not always, have lower than average IQ scores and may exhibit problems with impulse control and hyperactivity.

Although FAS is a common cause of learning and other problems, it is very often not diagnosed or recognized. If a child with FAS lives with his or her birth mother, it can be difficult to illicit accurate information about the mother's drinking during pregnancy, due to the overwhelming shame and guilt many mothers feel after delivering a baby with problems. Not all children have the more obvious physical expressions of the syndrome, which can lead clinicians to diagnose ADHD, ODD, borderline intellectual functioning, or other problems instead of correctly diagnosing FAS (CDC, 2015).

Once at daycare or preschool, children with fetal alcohol spectrum disorders (FASD) may present as being very difficult to manage. They may appear to understand an idea or know a song one day, only to appear to forget it on the next day. They may be more easily frustrated than other children, may have trouble telling the difference between patting a friend on the back and hitting the friend, and may exhibit an array of other learning and social problems (CDC, 2015). Unfortunately, there is no cure for FASD. Programs aimed at educating the public on the dangers of drinking during pregnancy are likely the best hope for eliminating FASD. However, there are some promising interventions for children and adults struggling with various disorders related to FASD (SAMHSA, 2014).

Depending on which of the child's body systems are impacted and how severely, the child may require services from an array of health care providers, including occupational therapy, physical therapy, speech and language therapy, medical monitoring and intervention, specialized educational services, and mental health therapy. It is ideal for all of the professionals involved with one child to work together to coordinate services and prevent overlap. Often, the counselor working with the child is most concerned with issues related to social skills and impulse control. The exact approach a counselor should use depends largely on the level of cognitive functioning the child has and must be tailored to fit the needs of the individual child (SAMHSA, 2014). If you suspect a child you are working with may have FASD, you can find much more information about how to find a pediatrician who can help, and how to find appropriate interventions at any of the resources listed at the end of this chapter.

Special Issues With Foster and Adoptive Children

Trauma

The impact of trauma, especially early relational trauma, is covered in great detail in Chapter 3. In this chapter, additional information is provided to the reader about the symptoms and treatment of common problems in very young children who have experienced trauma.

Reactive Attachment Disorder

Reactive attachment disorder (RAD) is a severe form of attachment disturbance caused by abuse, neglect, or other early childhood trauma (APA, 2013). On the continuum of attachment styles, which begins with secure attachment and progresses to disorganized attachment, RAD is found on the most severe end of the insecure styles and is strongly correlated with persistent and extreme abuse and/ or neglect by caregivers. While securely attached children learn they can depend on caregivers to keep them safe from harm and comfort them when distressed, insecurely attached children learn that their caregivers are not dependable, not safe, and/or not able to comfort them (Main & Cassidy, 1988).

The first type of insecure attachment is termed *avoidant attachment*. Avoidant children typically exhibit little distress when separated from a caregiver and are not particularly impressed when the caregiver returns. Ambivalent children (sometimes called *resistant*) respond to being separated from the caregiver by becoming very upset and are difficult to soothe when reunited. The final category, added by Mary Main and her colleagues, is disorganized attachment (Main & Cassidy, 1988). Disorganized attachment is generally considered to be the most serious form of insecure attachment with the strongest correlation to the later development of psychopathology (Zeanah & Smyke, 2009).

All of the insecure attachment styles can be created by inconsistent, neglectful, or abusive caregiving during the first several months of life. In many cases, parents tend to replicate the attachment styles of their own parents or caregivers (Busch & Lieberman, 2007). The most severe insecure attachment, the disorganized style, is often seen in children who have experienced extreme hardships, such as being raised in orphanages with inadequate care or in severely neglectful or abusive homes (Slade, 2007; Zeanah & Smyke, 2009). In addition, parents with disorganized attachment styles may appear frightening, inconsistent, uncaring, or confusing to their own infants (Slade, 2007). In some children with disorganized attachment styles, RAD may arise. RAD is thought to be a rare disorder, with less than 1% of the nonclinical population exhibiting symptoms (Breidenstine, Bailey, Zeanah, & Larrieu, 2011). However, among children living in foster care or in orphanages, the rate of RAD may be as high as 25% to 35% (Zeanah & Smyke, 2009).

There are two subtypes of RAD, inhibited and disinhibited (APA, 2013). Children who display flat affect, lack of typical comfort-seeking behaviors, little social engagement, irritable mood, and withdraw when stressed are categorized as having the inhibited version of RAD (Breidenstine et al., 2011). On the other hand, children with disinhibited RAD are overly social in superficial ways and will happily walk off with any adult who approaches them. These children are indiscriminate about who they will go to for comfort under stress, are rarely shy around new people, and do not appear to prefer comfort from a caregiver over a stranger (Zeanah & Smyke, 2009). In both types of RAD, children may improve when placed with a warm, consistent caregiver (Breidenstine et al., 2011). However, the pace and extent of improvement in symptoms is dependent on factors such as age of the child when he or she finds a safe home; frequency, intensity, and duration of abuse or neglect; and presence of aggravating factors such as autism, low intelligence, and so on.

There are very little data about the long-term impact of RAD on a person's lifetime mental health, although the general impact of childhood abuse and neglect is well established across multiple domains (Dube et al., 2003). However, there is some indication that while the inhibited type of RAD often improves if children are placed in nurturing homes and receive appropriate therapies, the disinhibited type frequently persists into adolescence even after appropriate placements are made (Zeanah & Smyke, 2009). There is emerging research suggesting a connection between a childhood diagnosis of RAD and adult psychopathology, but more longitudinal research is needed to clarify the typical course of development and the role of treatment (Morgan, Brugha, Fryers, & Stewart-Brown, 2012).

PTSD in the Very Young Child

Children who experience overwhelming, frightening events may develop PTSD, much as similarly exposed people of other age groups sometimes do. This possibility has only recently been formally acknowledged in the broader medical/psychiatric community, as evidenced by the preschool subtype's debut in the DSM5 (APA, 2013), decades following the adult diagnosis appearance in the DSM-III. One possible reason for so many professionals' previous denial of PTSD in children might be that the symptoms commonly seen in this age group vary greatly from those often seen in adults.

According to the National Institutes of Mental Health (n.d.), there are three primary groups of symptoms of PTSD: (1) reexperiencing the traumatic event, (2) numbing of affect and responsiveness, with possible developmental delays, and (3) increased arousal and hypervigilence. In this age group, reexperiencing may be observed in repetitive play scenes that depict aspects of the event, sleep disturbances, and/or avoidance of reminders (places, people, animals, smells, anything that triggers sensory memories of the event). Children who have PTSD may also exhibit symptoms related to increased arousal that are frequently mistaken for symptoms of ADHD or ODD (Busch & Lieberman, 2007). Those symptoms may include increased irritability or clinging behavior, lack of attention to tasks, temper tantrums, separation anxiety, aggression toward peers or caregivers, loss of recent developmental gains (often related to toileting), and/or age inappropriate sexualized behaviors. It is critical that clinicians correctly diagnose very young children who have PTSD, since many treatments for ADHD and ODD, including stimulant medications and punitive behavioral regimens, are at odds with appropriate treatment for PSTD (Schore, 2012). According to Follan et al. (2011), it is possible for clinicians to differentiate between these problems in a typical interview setting with caregivers if the interview is appropriately focused on eight core RAD symptoms. The eight core areas include problems with showing affection, seeking comfort, reliance on adults for help, cooperation, exploratory behavior, controlling behavior, reunion responses, and response to strangers (American Academy of Child and Adolescent Psychiatry, 2005).

Many of these symptoms, including intense fears, lack of affect regulation, difficulties with soothing, and tantrums, are also evident in some types of attachment problems. There has long been a great deal of speculation that PTSD and disorganized attachment may, in fact, be related constructs, but more research is needed to confirm or deny this hypothesis (Busch & Lieberman, 2007). Possibly because of an as-yet undocumented common thread between PTSD and attachment problems, it appears that many of the same treatments are effective with both problems (Lieberman & van Horn, 2009). To learn more about the possible prevalence of PTSD in young children, please see Guided Exercise 10.4.

Guided Exercise 10.4

The U.S. Department of Veterans Affairs has a National Center for PTSD research. *PTSD in Children and Adolescents Fact Sheet* (by Hamblen & Barnett) at http://www.ptsd.va.gov/professional/treatment/children/ptsd_in_children_and_adolescents_overview_for_professionals.asp has updated information on PTSD incidence, risk factors, effects on children, and treatment. Consider a setting of your choice. Will you be a school counselor, a mental health counselor, or a family counselor? How likely are you to encounter children with PTSD or some form of traumatic experiences? How will you use these resources to guide your work with children and adolescents?

SUGGESTIONS FOR DEVELOPMENTALLY APPROPRIATE INTERVENTION WITH CHILDREN AGES 0 TO 4

Effective interventions with children aged 0 to 4 involve creating a positive, nurturing, and reasonably structured environment in which the child can develop. Children at this age have very little power or control in their own lives, so involving caregivers in the home and, when possible, in day care or preschool, is necessary to achieve the most positive outcomes. Although many types of psychotherapy for families with young children exist, the authors have chosen to highlight Theraplay in this text. Theraplay was originally designed for use in the Chicago Head Start program in the late 1960s by Ann Jernberg and Phyllis Booth. Using the principles of healthy attachment and child development, Booth and Jernberg fostered a modality for helping very young children that is developmentally appropriate, simple in its implementation, and enjoyable for the child. Theraplay has growing evidence for effectiveness and is well on the way to being qualified as an "evidence-based practice" in various states and/or programs. Readers who wish to implement theraplay with clients should seek further training after reading this chapter prior to attempting the techniques.

As with several interventions used with young children, Theraplay is designed to create a warm, nurturing relationship between caregivers and children. The means of doing so are, however, very different. Theraplay sessions are designed by the therapist to be highly active, engaging, fun, and structured (Booth & Jernberg, 2010). Session activities are chosen ahead of time by the therapist and are introduced to the child and caregiver(s) in a planned sequence based on each family's individual needs.

Often, theraplay therapists design therapy based on information gleaned from the MIM assessment. The MIM poses a variety of tasks for the caregiver-child dyad to complete and provides guidance to clinicians observing the interactions on what actions might be clinically significant. Accurate assessment via the MIM can yield excellent insights into the strengths and weaknesses of caregiver-child relationships, which can then be used to form the basis for treatment planning. The MIM is described by Booth & Jernberg (2010) and is explained in most introductory theraplay training seminars.

Once assessments are complete, the therapist decides which of the four Theraplay dimensions to emphasize during sessions. The four dimensions are nurture, structure, engagement, and challenge. All four dimensions are thought to be crucial in healthy caregiver-child relationships, with some relationships needing to add more of one or the other of the dimensions and possibly reducing others. For example, in my own clinical work, I find that adoptive parents or grandparents who are raising grandchildren often excel at nurturing but need help finding ways to add structure to the child's environment. The children may also reject attempts at structuring their behaviors, making such activities frustrating. It frequently appears that grandparents or adoptive parents who are aware of a child's traumatic past try to "make up" for the child's poor treatment earlier in life by allowing quite a bit of freedom in the home. However, they often find that this can lead to the child feeling unsafe, since the child is not yet prepared to encounter large amounts of freedom, which in turn results in the child becoming bossy, irritable, defiant, and/or aggressive. When the caregivers add more structure to the child's life, perhaps in the form of consistent bed and meal times, more rules about how to interact with others, and consistent, reasonable consequences for mistakes, the child's behavior often improves. Caregivers are taught to increase structure at first within the sessions, using structuring activities and then to transfer those skills to their parenting at home. This process may be used with any of the dimensions. To learn more about using Theraplay, visit http://www.theraplay.org.

Other interventions for use with children age 0 to 4 include the following:

1. Attachment and biobehavioral catch-up (ABC): Designed to help caregivers of children who have experienced trauma develop secure attachments and reduce symptoms of PTSD: http://www.infantcaregiverproject.com/#!

2. Circle of Security: An attachment-based, dyadic therapy to help caregivers and children become securely attached: http://circleofsecurity.net

3. Parent-Child Interaction Therapy: Developed for use with children who have externalizing behavior problems (ODD, CD, ADHD); helps parents find more effective ways to communicate without sarcasm or shaming the child: http://pcit.phhp.ufl.edu

COUNSELING KEYSTONES

- Very young children can have mental health problems. The identification and treatment of these problems requires special care and skill on the part of the counselor. Children are not just short adults!
- Very young children are often best helped within the context of the whole family system. Working with the child alone may help some, but large-scale change almost always requires the whole system to be engaged.
- Counselors working with children in this age group should be very well versed in child development theories and should know how to apply the theories to what they see children do in sessions.
- Using developmentally appropriate interventions is crucial to helping young children. Talk-based counseling will not work with a toddler. Counselors who work with this population need to learn nonverbal interventions using play, movement, and expressive arts techniques and methods.
- Community resources are often important to know about with any client group but are especially important when working with families who might have a child with special needs. Counselors need to be up to date on what resources are available and how parents can access them.

ADDITIONAL RESOURCES

In Print

Arnett, J., & Maynard, A. (2012). *Child development: A cultural approach.* New York, NY: Pearson.

Grandin, T. (2010). *Thinking in pictures: My life with autism.* New York, NY: Vintage.

Grinker, R. (2008). *Unstrange minds. Rethinking the world of autism.* New York, NY: Basic Books.

Schaefer, C., & de Geronimo, T. (2000). *Ages and stages: Parent's guide to normal child development.* New York, NY: Wiley.

Solomon, M., & Siegel, D. (2003). *Healing trauma: Attachment, mind, body, and brain.* New York, NY: Norton.

Dorris, M. (1992). *The Broken Cord.* New York, NY: Harper Perennial.

Zeanah, C. H. (Ed.). (2009). *The handbook of infant mental health.* (3rd ed.). New York, NY: Guilford.

Online

Autism Speaks: http://www.autismspeaks.org/what-autism

Centers for Disease Control and Prevention Adverse Childhood Experiences study: http://www.cdc.gov/ace

Center for the Developing Child at Harvard University: http://www.developingchild.harvard.edu

Child Trauma: http://childtrauma.org

National Alliance on Mental Illness Autism page: http://www.nami.org/Content/NavigationMenu/Inform_Yourself/About_Mental_Illness/By_Illness/Autism_Spectrum_Disorders.htm

National Association for the Education of Young Children: http://www.naeyc.org

National Institutes of Mental Health: http://nimh.nih.gov/health/topics/autism-spectrum-disorders-asd/index.shtml

The Centers for Disease Control and Prevention: http://www.cdc.gov/ncbddd/fasd/index.html

The Fetal Alcohol Spectrum Disorders Center for Excellence: http://fasdcenter.samhsa.gov/index.aspx

The National Child Traumatic Stress Network: http://www.nctsn.org

The National Organization on Fetal Alcohol Syndrome: http://www.nofas.org

Zero to Three: www.zerotothree.org

REFERENCES

American Academy of Child and Adolescent Psychiatry. (2005). Practice parameter for the assessment and treatment of children and adolescents with reactive attachment disorder of infancy and early childhood. *Journal of the American Academy of Child and Adolescent Psychiatry. 44*(11), 1205–1219. doi:10.1097/01.chi.0000177056.41655.ce

American Psychiatric Association (APA). (2013). *Diagnostic and statistical manual*, (5th ed.). Washington, DC: Author.

Berk, L. (2006). *Child development* (7th ed.).New York, NY: Pearson.

Booth, P., & Jernberg, A. (2010). *Theraplay: Helping parents and children build better relationships through attachment-based play* (3rd ed.). San Francisco, CA: Jossey-Bass.

Bowlby, J. (1969). *Attachment and loss. Volume 1: Attachment.* New York, NY: Basic Books.

Breidenstine, A. S., Bailey, L. O., Zeanah, C. H., & Larrieu, J. A. (2011). Attachment and trauma in early childhood: A Review. *Journal of Child & Adolescent Trauma, 4*(4), 274–290. doi:10.1080/19361521.2011.609155

Busch, A. L., & Lieberman, A. L. (2007). Attachment and trauma: An integrated approach to treating young children exposed to family violence. In D. Oppenheim & D. Goldsmith (Eds.). *Attachment theory in clinical work with children: Bridging the gap between theory and practice* (pp. 139–171). New York, NY: Guilford.

Carr, T., & Lord, C. (2009). Autism spectrum disorders. In C. H. Zeanah & A. Smyke (Eds.), *The handbook of infant mental health* (3rd ed., pp. 301–317). New York, NY: Guilford.

Centers for Disease Control and Prevention (CDC). (last updated 2015). Fetal alcohol spectrum disorders (FASDs); Data and statistics. Retrieved from http://www.cdc.gov/ncbddd/fasd/data.html

Cozolino, L. (2010). *The neuroscience of psychotherapy* (2nd ed.). New York, NY: Norton.

Cozolino, L. (2013). *The social neuroscience of education: Optimizing attachment and learning in the classroom.* New York, NY: Norton.

Dube, S. R., Feletti, V. J., Dong, M., Giles, W. H., & Anda, R. F. (2003). The impact of adverse childhood experiences on health problems: Evidence from four birth cohorts dating back to 1900. *Preventative Medicine, 37*(3), 268–77.

Erikson, E. H. (1963). *Childhood and society.* New York, NY: Norton.

Follan, M., Anderson, S., Huline-Dickens, S., Lidstone, E., Young, D., Brown, G., & Minnis, H. (2011). Discrimination between attention deficit hyperactivity disorder and reactive attachment disorder in school aged children. *Research in Developmental Disabilities, 32*(2), 520–526. doi:10.1016/j.ridd.2010.12.031

Greenspan, S. (1992). *Infancy and early childhood: The practice of clinical assessment and intervention with emotional and developmental challenges.* Madison, CT: International Universities Press.

Greenspan, S., & Wieder, S. (2006). *Infant and early childhood mental health: A comprehensive developmental approach to assessment and intervention.* Arlington, VA: APA.

Korfmacher, J. (2014). Infant, toddler, and early childhood mental health competencies: A comparison of systems. Retrieved from http://www.zerotothree.org/public-policy/pdf/infant-mental-health-report.pdf

Lieberman, & van Horn. (2009). Child-parent psychotherapy. In *The handbook of infant mental health* (3rd ed., pp. 439–449). New York, NY: Guilford.

Main, M., & Cassidy, J. (1988). Categories of response the reunion with the parent at age 6: Predictable from infant attachment classifications and stable over a one month period. *Developmental Psychology 24(3)*, 415–426.

May, P. A., & Gossage, J. P. (2001). Estimating the prevalence of fetal alcohol syndrome: A summary. *Alcohol Research & Health 25*(3), 159–167. Retrieved from http://pubs.niaaa.nih.gov/publications/FASDFactsheet/FASD.pdf

Morgan, Z., Brugha, T., Fryers, T., & Stewart-Brown, S. (2012). The effects of parent-child relationships on later-life mental health status in two national birth cohorts. *Social Psychiatry and Psychiatric Epidemiology* (47), 1707–1715. doi: 10.1007/s00127-012-0481-1

National Institutes of Mental Health (n.d.). *What is post-traumatic stress disorder, or PTSD?* Publication # 08-6388. Washington, DC: Department of Health and Human Services. Retrieved from http://www.nimh.nih.gov/health/publications/post-traumatic-stress-disorder-ptsd/index.shtml

Piaget, J., & Inhelder, B. (1973). *Memory and intelligence.* London, UK: Routledge and Kegan Paul.

Reynolds, C., & Kamphaus, R. (2008). *Behavioral assessment scales for children,* (2nd ed.). San Antonio, TX: Pearson Assessments.

Schore, A. (1994). *Affect regulation and the origin of the self: The neurobiology of emotional development.* New York, NY: Earlbaum & Associates.

Schore, A. (2012). *The science of the art of psychotherapy.* New York, NY: Norton.

Selman, R. (1980). *The growth of interpersonal understanding: Developmental and clinical analyses.* New York, NY: Academic Press.

Sheridan, M., & Nelson, C. (2009). The neurobiology of fetal and infant development. In *The handbook of infant mental health* (3rd ed., pp. 40–58). New York, NY: Guilford.

Slade, A. (2007). Disorganized mother, disorganized child. In D. Oppenheim & D. Goldsmith (Eds.), *Attachment theory in clinical work with children: Bridging the gap between theory and practice* (pp. 1226–250). New York, NY: Guilford.

Substance and Mental Health Services Administration (SAMHSA). (2006). *Fetal alcohol syndrome by the numbers.* Retrieved from http://fasdcenter.samhsa.gov/documents/WYNK_Numbers.pdf

Substance Abuse and Mental Health Services Administration (SAMHSA). (2014). *Addressing fetal alcohol spectrum disorders (FASD). Treatment improvement protocol (TIP) Series 58.* HHS Publication No. (SMA) 13-4803. Rockville, MD: Substance Abuse and Mental Health Services Administration.

Tronick, E., & Beeghly, M. (2011). Meaning making and infant mental health. *American Psychologist*, 107–119.

Troutman, B., & Moran, T. (2011). Definition of early childhood mental health. In B. Troutman, T. Moran, K. Pelzel, G. Luze, & S. Lindgren, *Developing a blueprint for training Iowa providers in early childhood mental health.* Retrieved from http://www.dhs.state.ia.us/docs/BlueprintPaperFINAL_11-04-2011.pdf

Vernon, A., & Clemente, R. (2005). *Assessment and intervention with children and adolescents: Developmental and multicultural approaches* (2nd ed.). Alexandria, VA : ACA Press.

Wattendorf, D. J., & Muenke, M. (2005). Fetal alcohol spectrum disorders. *American Family Physician, 72*(2). 279–282, 285.

Winnicott, D. W., (1973). *The child, the family, and the outside world.* London, UK: Middlesex.

Zeanah, C. H., & Smyke, A. (2009). Attachment disorders. In *The handbook of infant mental health* (3rd ed., pp. 421–435). New York, NY: Guilford.

Zeanah, C. H., & Zeanah, P. D. (2009). The scope of infant mental health. In *The handbook of infant mental health* (3rd ed., pp. 1–21). New York, NY: Guilford.

Chapter 11

Counseling With Young Children (5–8) and Their Families

CATHERINE TUCKER

> *Listen to the MUSTN'Ts, child,*
> *Listen to the DON'Ts*
> *Listen to the SHOULDN'Ts*
> *The IMPOSSIBLES, the WON'Ts*
> *Listen to the NEVER HAVEs*
> *Then listen close to me—*
> *Anything can happen, child,*
> *ANYTHING can be.*

—Shel Silverstein (1974)

INTRODUCTION

Once children reach the age of 5, they are usually able to communicate their needs verbally, toilet independently, dress themselves with minimal assistance, play cooperatively with peers for brief periods, follow simple sequences of two or three commands, and are often emerging readers. For a 5-year-old, new abilities and tools with which to explore the world are beginning to come under consistent control; their balance, large and small motor coordination, and verbal abilities are burgeoning during this time (Berk, 2006). Along with these new skills, 5-year-olds often acquire an important new environment, the school. Between the ages of 5 and 8, children in the United States spend an average of a third of their waking hours in formal school settings (OECD, 2013).

In order to succeed in this new setting, children must master the complex social skills of following directions, working cooperatively with others, and handling minor and major frustrations without acting inappropriately. At the same time, the new student must master the very complex cognitive tasks of learning to read, write, and work with numbers. For many children, these social and cognitive challenges are presented by schooling before the child is optimally ready to encounter them developmentally (Berk, 2006). This demand-readiness mismatch, along with organic problems such as serious developmental delays; attention deficit hyperactivity disorder (ADHD); and relational problems such as neglect, abuse, inconsistent caretaking, and poverty can contribute to a child's lack of progress at school. One in eight children between the ages of 8 and 15 were referred to mental health professionals in the United States in 2009, a large percentage of them due to problems at school (SAMHSA, 2012). The estimated prevalence of mental health issues in children has not changed significantly since it was first studied in 1968, but the percentage of children in need of services who receive them has doubled from 10% to 20%, a number still in critical need of improvement (Nuffield, 1968). Children remain an underserved population in spite of over 40 years of documentation of the need for more services (Prout & Brown, 2007). Although only about 20% of children referred to services received them (U.S. Public Health Service, 2000), the greatest number of children who did see a mental health professional saw a school counselor, school psychologist, or school social worker (SAMHSA, 2012). For this reason, much of the focus of this chapter is on the interaction between the child, the family, and the school environment. One of the most helpful strategies school counselors can employ in working collaboratively is the family-school problem-solving meeting, which is outlined in Guided Exercise 11.1.

Guided Exercise 11.1

Problem-solving meetings are often extremely effective in helping students, reducing conflict between teachers and parents or teachers and students, and can save school counselors and administrators a great deal of time when implemented correctly. In order to conduct an effective, nonadversarial problem-solving meeting, follow these steps precisely:

1. Prepare the student: Involve the student in the meeting, and prepare him or her for participation. This step is often left out or not done well and can torpedo the entire effort. The student should almost always be an integral member of the problem-solving team, even if he or she

(Continued)

(Continuod)

is very young, developmental delayed, or facing serious consequences. Involving the student makes your chances for success much greater, keeps the student from imagining worst-case scenarios, and helps you create much more effective intervention strategies. It is imperative that you adequately prepare the student for full participation in the meeting. When I was a primary school counselor, I could usually prepare a student for these meetings in about 20 to 30 minutes. You need to tell the student the purpose of the meeting, who is coming, when and where the meeting will be held, what you expect him or her to do or say, and perhaps most importantly, that you are there to be on his or her side. This doesn't mean you think the student's behavior was ok but that you are there to help create a fair and effective plan for making things better. If you don't know the student well, or have ever suspected domestic violence in the home, now is the time to assess for safety. It is not recommended that you attempt a problem-solving meeting with highly chaotic, violent, or mentally ill parents or caregivers. In those cases, you might meet with the student and teacher only and call the parent to relay any pertinent information, being cautious about what you share. As always, suspicions of child abuse must be reported to the appropriate state agency.

2. Introductions and agenda setting: When everyone has gathered, begin the meeting by introducing everyone and explaining each person's role. Do not assume parents know everyone or understand what a "behavior interventionist" or "dean" or "assistant principal" does or why you invited those people. Keep meetings as small as possible to avoid overwhelming the family. Seat the child between yourself and one of the parents. Explain in one or two sentences what the purpose of the meeting is; for example, "Today we are together to talk about JoAnn's math grades. We will decide on how to help her pass math this year." Talk *to*, not *about*, the student. Explain the steps in the meeting, and if you are using a problem-solving meeting form (which I recommend), show it to everyone at this point and describe who will receive copies after the meeting. I normally make copies for each school staff member, the student, and each household represented.

3. Present your/the school's concerns and inquire about family and student concerns: Limit this to one or two primary concerns. Use your counseling skills to avoid blaming and finger pointing. Avoid allowing teachers or parents to rant about the student. Avoid using professional jargon.

4. Check for consensus about the shared concern: This is the most difficult part of conducting a successful meeting. Do not allow the school staff or parents to run all over the other party. Make sure everyone has an equal say in the process. Identify what will have the most impact for shifting the relationship in the group. This is done by selecting a theme that (1) allows people to be seen in a different light, which will lead to positive change and (2) provides the group with hope rather than adversarial relationships.

5. Develop possible solutions: Each group member should share one or two possible solutions. No solutions are rejected at this point. You can ask for clarification of responses. If the group gets stuck, ask about times the problem was absent, what was different then?

6. Action planning and follow-up: The child should always have an action to do in the plan. The focus of the plan should be on school-related issues. The plan should in some way include parent, teacher, and student. The plan should be appropriate to skill level and roles and positions of participants. The plan should be written on the record form. A copy of the plan should be given to all participants and should specify who will do the tasks, what the tasks will be, by when the tasks will be completed, what the standard of quality for doing the tasks is, and how the plan will be evaluated.

After reading this chapter, you will be able to

- describe the developmental changes that occur in children between the ages of about 5 and 8 cognitively, physically, and psychosocially;
- describe some of the most common problems children in this age group present with in counseling settings;
- explain best practices for working effectively with schools, families, and systems of care to help children;
- tell colleagues about current challenges facing children in this age group who have counseling-related needs; and
- locate reliable information about common childhood problems online or in texts.

THE BRAIN AND COGNITIVE DEVELOPMENT

Although development is slightly less dramatic in middle childhood than in the baby and infant years, there is a marked expansion of capacity and ability during this period. The corpus collosum, the band of tissue that joins the two sides of the brain, thickens during this time, making tasks that require both hemispheres to work together to be more fluid (Rathus, 2008). Skills that require fine motor control, such as writing and playing a musical instrument improve dramatically around the ages of 5 to 8 (Berk, 2006). Gross motor skills, which help with tasks done by larger muscle groups, also improve during this time. As a result, children become steadier on their feet; more competent in sports; and more fluid in using pencils, crayons, computer keys, and other small objects (Berk, 2006). These skills allow school-aged children to become much more independent from adults in self-care tasks and much more able to make their own choices about play and cognitive work.

Play

Children between the ages of 5 and 10 or so engage in pretend play with increasingly more elaborate plots and characters until the onset of the early adolescent period, when pretend play gives way to more structured game play (Frost, Wortham, & Reifel, 2001). Early in middle childhood, children begin to involve friends in their imaginary play schemes with more regularity. Skills and preferences begin to emerge during this time and are reflected in a child's choices of what to play and with whom (Cobb, 2001). Whether they prefer physical games, play with small toys, doll play, household play, or dramatic play, imaginative play during this phase of development is crucial for the healthy development of cognitive and social problem-solving skills. When schools take away free-play time or recess to help boost test scores, they are actively sabotaging the likelihood that students will perform better, as imaginary play is one of the cornerstones of strong cognitive skill development (Frost et al., 2001). To counteract the loss of recess time, parents may need to actively encourage more imaginative play during after-school times. Screen-based games are a new frontier in play and child development. To learn more about this, see Guided Exercise 11.2.

Guided Exercise 11.2

To learn more about the impact of video games on child development, please visit the Vanderbilt University Developmental Psychology blog entry from April 24, 2014: https://my.vanderbilt.edu/developmentalpsychologyblog/2014/04/effect-of-video-games-on-child-development

In this blog, the authors discuss the history of video games in the United States and current trends. After reading the blog, what advice would you give to parents of children in elementary school about video games? Do you think video games occupy the same category of play as toys children can physically manipulate directly? Why, or why not?

Gaining Control

The prefrontal cortex, which governs self-control, planning, and working memory, develops significantly during this time span (Martin & Fabes, 2008). This part of the brain continues to develop until adulthood, making it the last to develop completely (Martin & Fabes, 2008). While the prefrontal cortex continues to develop, children's abilities to remember sequences of commands, control their own behavior, and plan actions also continues to improve until adulthood.

Cognitive Changes

Cognitively, children move from Piaget's preoperational to concrete operational stage around age 7 (Salkind, 2004). Three key advancements concrete operational thinkers make are reversibility, sociocentrism, and decentration (Rathus, 2008). Reversability means that a child can think about categorizing an object in both ascending and descending order. For example, a concrete thinker can say that John is his cousin and then link John in ascending order to his immediate family and then to his extended family. He can also say John is a member of the Smith family and then descend in category size until he identifies John as Joe and Chris Smith's son.

This new skill only applies to concrete problems, however. Abstract thinking does not fully develop until adolescence.

Sociocentrism replaces egocentrism around the age of 7 or 8, meaning that children now see themselves as meaningfully connected to social groups, not as solely independent beings. This switch is vital to the child's ability to get along with peers at school, to form friendships, and to be able to work cooperatively on tasks (Rathus, 2008). They also become aware of how their performance compares to that of peers and siblings (Frost et al., 2001). Children who reach this stage later than others may have difficulty learning to share, take turns, and work for a common group goal. Concrete thinkers are not yet able to imagine accurately what other people are thinking or feeling but do often have rudimentary abilities to determine what they would do or feel in a given situation. Perspective taking is a skill that develops during the formal operations stage.

Finally, decentrism means that children can begin to think about multiple aspects of a problem at once rather than focusing only on the most obvious part of the problem (Piaget & Inhelder, 1973). This ability allows concrete thinkers to perform more complex math and science problems, while not quite yet being able to understand abstract concepts required for advanced algebra or higher math. Concrete thinkers use decentrism to break down problems into parts so that they can each be solved independently, then added back together to solve the whole problem. A good example of this is the steps required in solving math problems using complex fractions; each fraction must first be converted into the same format, then the larger math problem can be solved.

PSYCHOSOCIAL DEVELOPMENT

As children move from the preschool-age stage of initiative versus guilt into the stage of industry versus inferiority, they must learn to perform tasks relatively independently, learn what behaviors please adults and peers, and learn to read social cues (Erikson, 1963). Children who struggled with demonstrating personal power during the initiative versus guilt phase may enter middle childhood appearing shy and withdrawn and may need coaching from adults in order to display their abilities. Meanwhile, children who were allowed too much power and control as preschoolers may now struggle to work in groups and to complete tasks assigned by adults (Erikson, 1963).

Along with the emerging desire to prove their competence at various tasks, children begin to develop an internal locus of control around this time (Cobb, 2001). This means that they are less likely to blame other people or circumstances for mistakes than are younger children, which can lead to feelings of inferiority if taken too far but can also lead to a healthy sense of mastery when tasks are completed successfully.

Friendships begin to emerge in the early elementary years, becoming more meaningful than the typical short-term play alliances of preschool. First friendships can help children learn to see themselves as unique by comparing their personal preferences, histories, and abilities within a group of peers. Friendships are important sources of validation and self-worth for children. As they learn the skills required to be a good friend, there are often ups and downs caused by arguments and misunderstandings that can be very distressing to children, whose lack of experience with relationships does not provide enough context to understand how to repair disconnections. Often, children in elementary school develop very close "best friendships," which can be intense crucibles for forging intimate bonds with people outside of the family (Vernon & Clemente, 2005). Best friendships can be particularly intense for girls, and disruptions in these relationships can be especially distressing for them (Vernon & Clemente, 2005). Help from adults is critical to helping children learn to effectively manage early friendships. See Case Illustration 11.1.

Case Illustration 11.1

Daniel is a 5-year-old kindergartener attending a rural public school. His mother is Caucasian, and his father immigrated from Guatemala as a child. Daniel lives with his married parents and three older sisters. He was referred to the school counselor by his teacher due to frequent problems "being a good friend" to other children in the class.

When the school counselor observed Daniel in class, he was sitting with the other children on the carpet listening to the teacher read a story. He seemed engaged, looked interested in the story, and called out correct answers to her questions. When the children moved into a less structured center time, however, Daniel seemed to have some difficulties. He was assigned to the "puzzle corner" with two other children, a boy named John and a girl named Maria. Daniel seemed to become quickly frustrated when Maria pulled out the first puzzle on the stack and said they should all solve it together. She and John began fitting the pieces into the frame, and Daniel stood back and watched, pouting and muttering "no fair" to himself. When John and Maria seemed to be taking a while to solve the puzzle, he said, "Hey, slow pokes, you're not doing it right!" and tried to grab pieces from them. At this point, the teacher's assistant came over and told Daniel to "calm down and share." After that, Daniel stood back and resumed pouting without trying to rejoin the activity.

In a problem-solving meeting with Daniel, his parents, and his teachers, the problem was identified as Daniel having problems with waiting his turn, stating his needs to friends and siblings, and getting angry quickly. His parents stated that these problems happen frequently at home as well as at school, and the most successful intervention is for one of them to go over to Daniel and the other children involved in the conflict and talk out what happened and what the best thing was to do next. However, his parents said that they are often too busy with other tasks to do this as consistently as they'd like.

The school counselor knows that Daniel's teachers are also very busy in a full-day kindergarten classroom and can't always talk out every conflict between children. They said Daniel seems to be very bright, is on track with his work, and doesn't seem to get into trouble in other ways. At the end of the meeting, the school counselor drew up the following intervention plan for Daniel:

1. The school counselor will meet with Daniel individually once a week for a month for about half an hour each time to talk about ways to solve his friendship problems. She will use age-appropriate books to offer ideas, then use puppets to help Daniel role-play solutions.

2. Each week for a month, the school counselor will visit Daniel's class for 15 minutes during center time to coach him on using his new skills.

3. Daniel's teachers will pay attention to his new skill use during the times of the day when he typically has problems. They will make a special effort to praise him when they see him using his new skills.

4. If the teachers notice new or worsening problems, or don't notice any change in a month, they will report this to the school counselor.

5. The school counselor will send home a note each week briefly telling Daniel's parents about his new skill for the week. They will read the note with Daniel and ask him to show them what he learned. When they notice him using his new skills at home, they will praise him. If he has the old problems at home, they will remind him about his new options for doing something different.

6. The teachers, parents, and school counselor set a time to meet again in a month to review their progress.

For further learning about family and school relationships, please see Chapter 11 of Ellen Amatea's (2012) book, listed in the references section of this chapter.

Children also practice their emerging psychosocial development and skills in formal groups such as Boy and Girl Scouts, sports teams, 4-H, and religious groups. These groups help children learn skills of cooperation, team work, and leadership. Group membership can also be helpful in teaching children to cope with frustration when working in a group (Cobb, 2001).

ISSUES AND CONCERNS

School-aged children who present for counseling most often are referred either for school-related behavioral or emotional problems or due to problems occurring within the family, such as divorce, remarriage, or a death in the family. These problems are sometimes associated with an underlying organic problem such as autism, developmental delay, or ADHD but are often due to relational (including abuse and neglect) or structural problems within the family or classroom (Kestly, 2014).

Parenting

The elementary school years are often characterized as the eye of the storm, situated between the chaotic early years and the frequently stormy adolescent years.

However, parenting elementary school–aged children is not without challenges. The transitions into formal schooling and into more emotionally involved friendships can be stressful for children and parents as they learn to navigate new settings and social groups.

Most parents of elementary-age children face issues related to decisions about how much independence a child should have, how much time they should spend on leisure activities, what chores they should do, and how to go about punishing misbehavior. There are no one-size-fits-all answers to any of these questions. What is best for one child in one family may differ significantly from what is best for another child from another cultural background, geographic area, ability level, or age. In general, however, parents find greater success when rules are perceived to be fair by the children and are enforced consistently. Inconsistent application of rules and consequences can be very confusing to concrete thinkers and is a leading reason for visits to the counselor's office.

Parenting issues may be more complicated if parents divorce, remarry, or change partners. Because children at this stage are usually concrete thinkers who have trouble seeing other people's perspectives, parents who are planning a change in the composition of the home should explain in a calm, matter-of-fact way how and when the change will occur and how the change might impact the child's daily life. Children should be assured that the divorce, remarriage, or other change is not their fault and that the adults in their life will still love and care for them. Ensuring that rules are as similar as possible in shared custody situations also reduces stress and confusion for the child and adults. Books that parents and children can read together, like Marge Heegaard's excellent *When Mom and Dad Separate* (1996), can help parents explain the changes in the home without too many or too few details.

ADHD

According to the Substance Abuse and Mental Health Services Administration (SAMHSA), 11%, or approximately 6.4 million children between the ages of 4 and 17 in the United States have been diagnosed with attention deficit hyperactivity disorder (ADHD) (SAMHSA, 2013), in spite of a statement of expected prevalence of 5% in the DSM-5 (APA, 2013), meaning that over more than 3 million children and adolescents have been diagnosed than would be expected. Rates of diagnosis have increased by about 5% a year every year since 2003 (CDC, 2015). The rate of diagnosis varies by gender and geographic location. Almost twice as many boys as girls are diagnosed with ADHD, and more children in the south than in the north or west are diagnosed (from a low of 5.6% of children in Nevada to a high of 18.7% in Kentucky). Children from lower income homes are also diagnosed more frequently than children from middle and upper income families (Akinbami, Liu, Pastor, & Reuben, 2011).

What is not yet known is whether these differences in levels of diagnosis reflect actual differences in how many children have ADHD in various states and income groups or whether access to health care, level of physician training, or bias accounts for some or most of the differences. Until more investigations are completed, it is wise for counselors to advise very thorough assessments of all children in their care before a diagnosis of ADHD is made. A detailed medical and developmental history that includes questions about various forms of trauma, direct observation of the child in multiples settings, and rating forms completed by multiple caregivers should be standard aspects of an evaluation prior to any mental health diagnosis of a child (American Academy of Pediatrics, 2011). This is especially crucial for disorders like ADHD where powerful drugs are often used as part of treatment. The psychostimulants used in the treatment of ADHD can also be used as drugs of abuse and must be monitored carefully (National Institute on Drug Abuse, 2014).

Although the DMS-5 estimates that up to 1 in 20 people in the United States may have ADHD, there is a strong likelihood that many of the 6 million children and adolescents who have been told they have ADHD have been misdiagnosed. Many of the common symptoms of ADHD, like difficulty concentrating, trouble completing tasks, and daydreaming, can also be symptoms of other disorders. Anxiety disorders, posttraumatic stress disorder, pediatric bipolar disorder, and childhood depression can all produce similar symptoms to ADHD. However, each of these disorders responds to different treatments. Giving a child with PTSD psychostimulant medication, for example, is likely to exacerbate symptoms of heightened arousal and paranoia (Cozolino, 2010).

Once a child is diagnosed with ADHD, a multifaceted treatment plan is most likely to be effective in helping the child control the symptoms of the disorder. The American Academy of Pediatrics (2011) states that stimulant medication may be one part of treatment, but counseling, classroom accommodations, and careful structuring of at-home time is usually also needed to achieve the best results. School counselors should work closely with teachers, parents, and medical professionals to ensure that medication side effects are managed and that any needed accommodations are implemented (not every child with ADHD will need any additional help academically). School or mental health counselors can also help children with ADHD by providing a warm, accepting environment for the child to express his or her frustrations, practice any needed social skills, develop organizational practices, and discuss problems with academics or social settings. Recent research has shown that child centered play therapy, a developmentally appropriate approach to use with children ages 5 to 8, is effective in helping children with ADHD (Schottelkorb & Ray, 2009). This approach is discussed in detail later in this chapter.

ODD

Oppositional defiant disorder (ODD) is the most commonly diagnosed mental health disorder among children, with between 2% and 14% of the general child population being affected (Fahim, Fiori, Evans, & Pérusse, 2012). ODD is characterized by irritable or angry mood, argumentative and defiant behavior, and/or vindictive, spiteful behaviors. These symptoms may be present in only one setting in milder cases or across all settings in more severe cases (APA, 2013). Boys are diagnosed with ODD far more often than girls, and it is often diagnosed along with ADHD (APA, 2013).

Parenting or teaching children with ODD can be very challenging. Children with ODD are often prone to public temper tantrums, poor relationships with peers and siblings, and frequent disciplinary problems in school (Drugli, Larsson, Fossum, & Mørch, 2010). Children who have more problems with irritability than with defiance and vindictiveness seem to be at higher than average risk for mood disorders in adulthood, while children with higher incidents of defiance and vindictiveness are more likely to go on to develop conduct disorder, antisocial or borderline personality disorder than other children (Burke, 2012).

The causes of ODD are still largely unknown. However, a recent study by Fahim et al. (2012) using advanced scanning technology to view the brains of children with and without ODD showed significant anatomical brain differences between the two groups. In children with ODD, parts of the frontal cortex concerned with mood regulation and impulse control were smaller than average, while parts of the frontal cortex associated with aggressive and antisocial behaviors were larger than average. These findings suggest that children with ODD have anatomical brain changes but do not answer whether these changes are a cause or a result of ODD. Another study using parent-child observations and DNA testing (Willoughby, Mills-Koonce, Propper, & Waschbusch 2013) along with family histories determined that children with genetic markers for ODD along with harsh and negative intrusive parenting styles made the later development of the disorder far more likely than either factor alone. This finding supports interventions that reduce harsh and negative parenting styles, especially when a family history of mental illness is present. It is possible that harsh, negative, and intrusive teaching styles are also harmful to children who have or are likely to develop ODD or other conduct related problems; research is needed to confirm this hypothesis. However, assisting teachers in using more positive, encouraging, and assertive (rather than aggressive or passive) methods of interaction with students is highly unlikely to harm them and may be of benefit.

Another neurobiological study found that one reason ODD is so difficult to treat is that children with ODD seem to have less responsiveness to rewards and punishments than other children (Matthys, Vanderschuren, Schutter, & Lochman, 2012). Matthys et al. (2012) go on to say that because of neurocognitive differences between children with ODD, treatment needs to be tailored to the individual child and family rather than following a manual for all children with ODD. Children who do not seem to have much response to rewards for good behavior or punishments for negative behavior may need more time with empathy training before behavior management tools are introduced.

Other studies that used interviews with parents of children with ODD about family history have found a relationship between ODD and having a parent with antisocial personality disorder, depression, or anxiety (Burke, 2012). It appears likely that there are some hereditary factors in the development of ODD and certainly differences in neurobiology. However, effective treatment of children with the disorder still proves difficult. The most effective interventions studied to date heavily involve parents (Matthys et al., 2012) and were able to vary the rewards, interventions, and consequences of behaviors as the child progressed. Most evidence-based interventions for ODD involve multiple modes of treatment, such as parent training, teacher training, along with cognitive restructuring or psychoeducational activities with the child (Matthys et al., 2012). Depending on the individual child's sensitivity to rewards and consequences, and how able he or she is to learn new social cues and behaviors, some parts of the intervention may need to be altered.

Play therapy, especially play therapy that involves parents, seems to have a positive impact on the disorder (Bratton, Ray, Rhine, & Jones, 2005). Play therapy is developmentally appropriate for children in the age group of 5 to 8, can be implemented in school and clinical settings, and creates a less-stressful way for children and parents to interact than they may commonly experience. Stress-reducing and de-escalating help for teachers, such as the CONNECT program outlined by Helker, Shottelkorb, & Ray (2007) and school-based approaches discussed in the volume *Counselor as Consultant* (Scott, Royal, & Kissinger, 2015) in this series is also strongly recommended.

Specific Learning Disabilities

For about 1 in 10 to 15 students, beginning school involves the discovery of cognitive disabilities (USDE, 2015). The process of recognizing, diagnosing, and creating a plan of action for a formal disability can be extremely stressful for the child and the family. According to the United States Department of Education (2015), the total number of children identified as having a disability that interferes with the educational process has increased from 8.3% in 1976 to 13%, or roughly 6.4 million, in 2011. The largest increase during that time span was in the area of specific learning disability, an area that includes problems in processing information in reading, math, or another specific academic area (USDE, 2015). Only one other of the 14 federal categories of educational disability increased during that same time period; autistic children represented 0.4% of the total public school enrollment in 1976 and 0.8% in 2011. (The preschool category was added in 1986 and therefore has had a 100% gain in enrollment since that time. However, the increase in enrollment does not necessarily reflect a change in identification standards or prevalence of the problem.) Federal law governs much of special education policy, but states and school districts do vary in some ways. To learn more about special education law, see Guided Exercise 11.3 (see also Chapter 2).

Guided Exercise 11.3

The United States Department of Education's National Center for Education Statistics houses a large body of data and research about special education. Browse their website at http://nces.ed.gov for data and reports on children with disabilities. The federal government sets the 14 categories and requires all 50 states to provide services to children who qualify for them. However, each state may provide more services, but not fewer, than the federal law requires (USDE, 2015). After reading through some of the documents available at the nces.ed.gov website, visit http://idea.ed.gov to view federal laws and policies related to educational services for children with disabilities. What new provisions were added to the Individuals with Disabilities Education Act (IDEA) in 2005? Next, visit your state's department of education website. What are you able to learn about how your state handles special education? What information do you think is missing? How else might you locate it?

Although the exact requirements to qualify for help for a specific learning disability vary by state, the general premise is that the child has an average or above level of overall intelligence and ability, does not have another reason to do poorly in one subject (such as an acute illness, behavioral problems, frequent moves, homelessness, etc.) but performs lower in one academic area than others. The most common form of specific learning disability is related to problems with learning to read (USDE, 2015).

Counselors working with parents who are learning that their child has a disability often need to assist the parents with the process of grieving. Parents often have ideas about what their child might be or do as an adult; some disabilities may preclude these ideas from occurring. While not all parents feel a significant sense of loss when a child is found to have a learning disability, counselors should be able to identify and assist those who do. Many resources are available to counselors working with parents in this situation online and in libraries. Counselors should, of course, review the materials before suggesting them to parents to ensure that they are appropriate to the situation at hand.

SUGGESTIONS FOR DEVELOPMENTALLY APPROPRIATE INTERVENTION WITH CHILDREN AGES 5 TO 8

Most well-established theories of counseling have existing adaptations for working with children. A quick search of your university library or bookstore should turn up resources offering guidance on using most of the standard approaches. A key element of adapting any general, adult-based theoretical approach to the developmental needs of children involves adding in some element of play. Talk therapy and other highly abstract forms of counseling are often not developmentally appropriate for work with children before the age of about 15 or 16, when they make the transition into the abstract cognitive developmental stage (Piaget & Inhelder, 1973). Even for people who are able to think abstractly, using play as a part of counseling can be very powerful, particularly if the person has a history of trauma (the exact science behind this can be explored in detail in Theresa Kestly's (2014) wonderful book *The Interpersonal Neurobiology of Play: Brain-building Interventions for Emotional Well-Being.*

Some of these brain-building approaches are discussed in other chapters of this text. For this chapter on counseling children from ages five to eight, we have chosen to discuss two approaches in some detail. In particular, we chose two approaches that have models of teacher consultation, since children facing mental health challenges at this age are in school and counselors, including those in community agencies or private practices, often need to work alongside teachers and parents to help solve problems. The two approaches we chose are (1) child-centered play therapy (CCPT) and person-centered consultation and (2) solution-focused brief therapy (SFBT) and its corollary for consultation. In our opinion, SFBT is best used when problems are acute and less complex. More complicated or severe problems, especially related to trauma, should not be treated with SFBT alone. Complex trauma in particular needs a more in-depth and multisensory approach (van der Kolk, 2014). SFBT is excellent for use with acute, short-term, and largely external problems, especially when short-term solutions need to be found and implemented in the classroom. Case Illustration 11.2 at the end of this chapter illustrates the parent-teacher problem-solving meeting, which is a form of SFBT consultation.

CCPT in Schools and Clinical Settings

Child-centered play therapy was first described in a book by Dr. Virginia Axline in 1947. Axline was a colleague of Carl Rogers, who developed person-centered counseling (Landreth, 1991). In her approach to working with children, Axline (1947/1969) outlined eight core principles:

1. The therapist must develop a warm, friendly relationship with the child, in which good rapport is established as soon as possible.

2. The therapist accepts the child exactly as he or she is.

3. The therapist establishes a feeling of permissiveness in the relationship so that the child feels free to express his or her feelings completely.

4. The therapist is alert to recognize the feelings the child is expressing and reflects those feelings back to him or her in such a way that he or she gains insight into his or her behavior.

5. The therapist maintains a deep respect for the child's ability to solve his or her own problems if given the opportunity to do so. The ability to make choices and institute changes is the child's.

6. The therapist does not attempt to direct the child's actions or conversations in any way. The child leads the way; the therapist follows.

7. The therapist does not attempt to hurry therapy along. It is a gradual process and is recognized as such by the therapist.

8. The therapist establishes only those limitations necessary to anchor the therapy to the world of reality and to make the child aware of his or her responsibility in the relationship.

Almost 50 years later, Axline's eight principles remain the core of CCPT. CCPT implements a few simple but powerful techniques to achieve the conditions described by Axline. Van Fleet and Sywulak (2010) provide a list of four basic skills for use in CCPT and title them structuring, empathic responding, imaginative play, and limit setting. *Structuring* refers to the basic parameters for the session and the process set out by the counselor at the start of therapy. This often entails the length of the sessions, whether or not the parent or guardian is allowed to be in the playroom, whether or not bathroom breaks are allowed, and the like. Most CCPT therapists begin the first session by introducing the child to the playroom by saying something like "This is a special room. In here, you can say anything you like, and you can do most anything you like. I'll let you know if there are things not to do." CCPT therapists do not begin by reeling off a list of the "don'ts" for the playroom. This would inhibit the free-flowing, caring atmosphere they are trying to create.

The next skill, *empathic responding,* is also sometimes referred to as "tracking" in the play therapy literature. Guidelines for how often and in exactly what ways the therapist should use this skill vary, but the essence of empathic responding is to start out at the beginning of the relationship by remarking frequently (I tell my students to do this about once every 30 to 60 seconds or so) on what the child is doing, without attaching any judgment or praise. For example, you might say, "You're using the blue car to chase the red car." At this point, the therapist does not make any remarks about the child's affect or possible meanings of the play. Later in the therapy process, the therapist will remark on the child's affect (That dinosaur is making you really mad!) or the possible meanings of the play (That dog puppet talks just like your dad.). In fact, many CCPT therapists decline to make any remarks about meanings of play throughout the process. In my own practice, I decide whether or not to use these sorts of statements based on how accepting the child seems to be of my remarks about affect. If the remarks about meaning are not well received, I do not make any more such statements. However, I have often found them to be very helpful in moving the child out of a "stuck" pattern where the same problem is introduced repeatedly without a good resolution.

The third basic skill is closely related to the second. In *imaginative play,* the child may engage the therapist in the play or may play alone with the therapist as witness. Again, there are some CCPT therapists who do not believe in engaging in the play, while others do. As a beginning therapist, I advise you to try both and decide which style works best with your own personality and approach. If you do not engage in the play scenarios the child creates, you continue to make empathic responses frequently to the play while continuing to create the atmosphere to allow and contain the play. If you do chose to join the play (which you only do if invited by the child), you must ensure that the child continues to direct the play. Many therapists employ a stage whisper technique to do this, frequently asking the child in a whisper tone of voice, "What does the lion do now?" rather than deciding independently what happens next within the play.

The fourth skill, *limit setting,* is the one I most often see beginning students struggle to use appropriately. In CCPT, we want to create a permissive atmosphere where scary and unpleasant memories and ideas can be expressed and contained. Therefore, too many rules are not helpful to the process. Limits should generally only be set to keep the child and therapist safe. Landreth's (1991, p. 223) ACT model of limit setting is useful in many settings:

A = Acknowledge the child's feelings, wishes, and wants.

C = Communicate the limit.

T = Target alternatives.

For example, if the child throws a hard plastic toy at you, you might respond by stating, "I see that you think it's fun to throw that car at me. Throwing things at people isn't ok in here. You can roll it to me, but you can't throw it at me. If you throw it again, I will put that toy in the cabinet for the rest of the hour." Usually, setting the limit once or twice is enough to let the child know what the boundaries of his or her freedom are in the playroom, and that will end the problem. Sometimes, however, children will push beyond those limit-setting statements. If that occurs, the therapist then has to decide whether to end the session early or not. This is the choice of last resort, used only when the play has become unsafe for child or therapist or both. If the session must be ended, it is best to attempt some calming exercises with the child before returning him or her to the parent or classroom. If unsafe behaviors are presented more than once in the playroom, CCPT may not be the best approach. Some children with autism or complex trauma have great difficulty managing their emotions in a permissive environment and may do better, at least initially, with a more structured approach such as Theraplay (see Chapter 10).

Though these skills may seem simple, they can be extremely powerful when implemented faithfully and are very difficult to master. Being faithful to Axline's vision of using play therapy to allow a child to explore his or her own inner world, express himself or herself through play and the use of toys, and to build a warm, caring relationship in which both child and therapist feel able to authentically be themselves, is still a very challenging direction to take for many counselors. Over the years I have taught graduate students to use CCPT, I have seen many students initially dismiss CCPT as too simplistic and complain they feel they are not "doing anything." What I typically find when I watch these students counseling with young clients is that they are not consistently using all eight of Axline's principles. In order for CCPT to be effective, the counselor has to establish a warm, permissive atmosphere that is free of the *pressure to perform* that so many of us spend our lives inhabiting. Counselors who wish to use CCPT have to first truly believe that children can solve their own problems, and that children are capable of leading the flow of counseling.

Person-Centered Consultation in Schools and Clinical Settings

When working with parents and teachers using the CCPT approach, staying with the basic humanistic principles of person-centered counseling allows for a consistent presentation of the person of the counselor. Teaching elementary school is a very challenging profession and is made far more complex when one or more students in a classroom exhibit defiant, disrespectful, or generally noncompliant behaviors. School or mental health counselors who are consulting with teachers can help them discharge some of the stress they feel and find workable solutions to the management of difficult students by using person-centered consultation. In the person-centered teacher consultation approach (Ray, 2007; Schottelkorb & Ray, 2009), parallel to person-centered therapy, the counselor is congruent, manifests unconditional positive regard, and communicates empathy to the other person.

Much like CCPT, person-centered consultation requires that the counselor be fully emotionally and cognitively present and engaged with the other people and the helping process. This sounds deceptively simple but can be rather difficult to apply in practice. Counselors who wish to use this approach require a great deal of practice and a general sense of calm in order to be effective.

In person-centered consultation, the consultant focuses on the basic person-centered skills of reflecting content, reflecting feelings, confrontation, and enlarging the meaning of narratives (Ray, 2007). In this type of consultation, the focus is not always on one identified problem but is sometimes more about the person presenting the problem. Rogers stated that the goal of counseling is to help people become more congruent between their idealized selves and their current reality (Rogers, 1980). Person-centered consultation has the same basic goal but instead of having a single client, the consultant may be working within a large system, such as a school or business organization. However, the goal of reaching greater congruence remains appropriate. What is the teacher's ideal view of himself or herself as a teacher? What is the teacher's current view of himself or herself as a teacher? How might the counselor and teacher work toward bringing those two images into closer alignment? These are all excellent beginning points for teacher consultation and may be translated to parent or other consultations as well.

SFBC Techniques

In contrast to CCPT, SFBC is a very directive, short-term, focused approach (Sklare, 2014). When I was working as a school counselor with children in this age range, I found SFBC to be extremely helpful in working with children who presented with acute problems (e.g., a child stops doing her homework after the birth of a sibling) and in doing consultation with parents and teachers who were facing difficulties or who were difficult to work with. Research supports the use of SFBC in school settings where time is a limited resource and with children who have single-event problems. Other counseling approaches that more deeply explore the cause and history of current problems and focus on strong therapeutic bonds are more appropriate for children presenting with traumatic or abusive histories (Flamez & Watson, 2014).

Sklare (2014, pp. 13–16) offers six rules for the effective use of SFBC:

1. Focusing on success leads to solutions. This means that rather than trying to trace the origins of the problem, the counselor guides the child to talk about what life will be like without the problem. This is often accomplished via use of the miracle question. The miracle question is "If you woke up tomorrow and a miracle had happened overnight while you were asleep, and the problem disappeared, what would your life be like?" It is important to ask the

child to give concrete and realistic details in answer to this question. Young children often like to add in fantasies such as "I'd live in a huge house on the moon" or "My mean sister would be gone and I'd be living with a nice princess and a pony instead." While these fanciful additions are creative and interesting, they are not terribly helpful in constructing realistic solutions. It is often helpful to have the child draw or make a written list of exactly how life would be after "the miracle."

2. Every problem has identifiable exceptions. When attempting to generate solutions to the problem, the counselor needs to find out about times and situations when the problem does not exist. This can be accomplished by simply asking, "Tell me about some times you didn't (fill in problem)." Again, it is important to help a younger child come up with concrete examples and stay away from fantasy stories. Sometimes you may need input from teachers or parents to generate a good list.

3. Small changes have a ripple effect. Even if the problem is large and impacts many aspects of a child's life, a small change in one area can help to create changes in other areas. For example, if the child is failing the second grade, you might start by helping him or her raise his or her grade in reading by doing homework every night. If he or she begins to get in the habit of doing homework right after school every day, his or her math grade may improve as well.

4. Be efficient with your interventions. In SFBC, no time in session is spent on history gathering or examining root causes. Although these practices are crucial in treating trauma, for acute problems, this total focus on the present allows the counselor to be very economical in locating and trying out possible solutions.

5. Focus on the present and future, and while you might relate the past to the present, do not dwell on it.

6. Focus on actions rather than insights. Both Rules 4 and 5 ask the counselor to home in on what is happening in the child's life right now, today, and craft solutions for that problem. Counselors using SFBC use language to help uncover strengths and solutions (Flamez & Watson, 2014). For example, instead of asking *if* the problem goes away what will life be like, the counselor would ask *when* the problem goes away what life will be like. Presuming that change is possible, that solutions exist to all problems, and that people are capable of change are key beliefs for counselors using this approach (Sklare, 2014). This use of positive language is also very helpful in averting blaming talk and reducing hostility in meetings, as seen in our example of a parent-teacher problem-solving meeting in Case Illustration 11.2.

Case Illustration 11.2

Nora is an 8-year-old Caucasian third grader at a public elementary school in a small city. The school social worker referred Nora to the school counseling intern for additional support due to her challenging home circumstances and family structure. This student currently lives in a community home with two other displaced families. Nora and her older brother are under the guardianship of their paternal grandmother who is also the house mother within the community home. Nora is close to her grandmother and speaks fondly of her. While this home is located within one block of Nora's school, she continues to have poor attendance. Nora's classroom teacher notes that she is bright, pleasant, and kind to all peers. Her teacher additionally adds that "Nora's mind seems to wander in class." Despite her very transient history, eight school transfers within a 3-year period, Nora has managed to remain an A/B student.

Nora's mother was recently released from being incarcerated and lives with her mother. Through a family drawing, the school counseling intern was able to informally assess Nora's family dynamics and gain a better understanding of her family structure. During her mother's incarceration, Nora's younger brother, age 3, was sent to live with his father, and her younger sister, age 2, was placed in foster care. Nora worries about the safety of her younger sister and becomes somber when speaking of this sibling whose whereabouts are unknown to Nora. Her parents are separated, and her father lives with his grandmother in a town nearby. While Nora occasionally sees both parents, her mood is usually solemn after a weekend visit at her mother's home. Nora feels as if she vies with her older brother for their mother's attention. Nora often notes that her mother is planning on getting all of her children back under one roof after she receives her "tax money," but is leery of her "mother's empty promises."

Since she was referred to the intern near the end of the school year, there was time for only nine sessions. Therefore, helping Nora acquire some coping skills she could use on her own was the focus of the sessions. Capitalizing on Nora's intelligence and creativity, the intern used the following techniques to help Nora with some additional coping skills:

1. The school counseling intern supplied Nora with a journal for her to write her thankful entries in. Nora enjoys sharing these details and typically lists her grandmother, the community home where she lives, and her best friend. She can write stories, make lists, or draw pictures to record the positive attributes in her life. When she feels stressed, she can review these entries.

2. The intern helped Nora identify her strengths. She can easily identify her positive qualities and the encouraging people in her life. Nora has noted that she wants to be a doctor so that she can "take care of her family members." She speaks often of becoming a foster parent and supplying these children with a good and safe home.

3. The intern encouraged Nora to make a habit of going to bed at a reasonable time and improving her attendance. While grandmother has been a more stable force in Nora's life, her good intentions have often enabled Nora to dictate the day's agenda, and attendance is not always a priority. Nora enjoys school and is academically successful, but her teacher is concerned about her disconnections during class and poor attendance. The counselor will talk with grandmother about setting a consistent bedtime and encourage her to get Nora on the bus every morning. The counselor will also use a point system to support Nora's improvement in attendance.

Note: Special thanks to Sarah Pesavento for providing this Case Illustration.

COUNSELING KEYSTONES

- Counselors who work with children in this age group need to be very familiar with the finer points of typical child development across physical, cognitive, psychosocial, and intrapersonal domains. If you do not know what *typical* is for a child of any given age, you cannot possibly determine whether or not there is a more serious problem.
- Counselors need to use extreme caution when making any diagnosis of a child. Many of the children you will see in your office will be presented as "having major problems" when what they really have is teachers and/or parents who need to use a different set of skills in working with them. This is not to say that some children are not difficult to be around but that many behavioral problems in children tend to be related to their living and learning environments.
- In order to be successful in helping children, counselors must become very good at effective consultation with parents and teachers. Blaming and finger pointing are not helpful to anyone. Learn to defuse and de-escalate tense, angry meetings.
- Keep an updated log of community resources, including both a child psychiatrist and a pediatric neurologist, for instances when your child clients or students need more intervention than you can provide.
- New scientific findings about the brain are being made almost daily. A lot of these discoveries directly impact counseling practices, so be sure to check various scientific news sources to stay current.
- Elementary school counselors are often the only mental health professionals in the school building. When this is the case, it is absolutely critical to engage in ongoing professional supervision. Supervision keeps your skills sharp, helps you think more clearly about challenging students, and brings additional credibility and professionalism to your role.

ADDITIONAL RESOURCES

In Print

Axline, V. (1964). *Dibs in search of self.* New York, NY: Random House.

Cozolino, L. (2013). *The social neuroscience of education: Optimizing attachment and learning in the classroom.* New York, NY: Norton.

Heegaard, M. (1996). *Drawing out feelings series* (four workbooks and facilitator guide). Chapmanville, WV: Woodland Press. Available via used book sources.

Vernon, A., & Clemente, R. (2005). *Assessment and intervention with children and adolescents: Developmental and multicultural approaches* (2nd ed.). Alexandria, VA: ACA Press.

Online

Center for School Mental Health at the University of Maryland: http://csmh .umaryland.edu/index.html

Children's Defense Fund: http://www.childrensdefense.org

General child development information for parents: http://childdevelopmentinfo.com

General statistics and information about child and adolescent physical and mental health in the United States: http://www.childstats.gov/index.asp

National Child Traumatic Stress Network: http://www.nctsn.org

Science Daily online: http://www.sciencedaily.com/news/mind_brain

REFERENCES

Akinbami, L. J., Liu, X., Pastor, P. N., & Reuben, C. A. (2011). Attention deficit hyperactivity disorder among children aged 5–17 years in the United States, 1998–2009. *NCHS data brief, no 70*. Hyattsville, MD: National Center for Health Statistics. 2011.

Amatea, E. (Ed.). (2012). *Building culturally responsive family-school relationships,* 2nd ed. New York, NY: Pearson Higher Education.

American Academy of Pediatrics. (2011). *Implementing the key action statements: An algorithm and explanation for process of care for the evaluation, diagnosis, treatment, and monitoring of ADHD in children and adolescents.* Retrieved from http://pediatrics.aappublications.org/content/suppl/2011/10/11/ peds.2011-2654.DC1/zpe611117822p.pdf

American Psychiatric Association (APA). (2013). *Diagnostic and statistical manual of mental disorders*, (5th ed.): *DSM-5.* Washington, DC: American Psychiatric Association.

Axline, V. (1947/1969). *Play therapy.* Boston, MA: Houghton-Mifflin.

Berk, L. (2006). *Child development* (7th ed.). New York, NY: Pearson.

Bratton, S. C., Ray, D., Rhine, T., & Jones, L. (2005). The efficacy of play therapy with children: A meta-analytic review of treatment outcomes. *Professional Psychology: Research and Practice, 36*(4), 376–390. doi:10.1037/0735-7028.36.4.376

Burke, J. D. (2012). An affective dimension within oppositional defiant disorder symptoms among boys: Personality and psychopathology outcomes into early adulthood. *Journal of Child Psychology & Psychiatry, 53*(11), 1176–1183. doi:10.1111/j.1469-7610.2012.02598.x

Centers for Disease Control and Prevention (CDC). (last updated 2015). *Data and statistics report on ADHD.* Retrieved from http://www.cdc.gov/ncbddd/adhd/data.html#

Cobb, N. (2001). *The child: Infants, children, and adolescents.* Mountain View, CA: Mayfield.

Cozolino, L. (2010). *The neuroscience of psychotherapy* (2nd ed.). New York, NY: Norton.

Drugli, M., Larsson, B., Fossum, S., & Mørch, W. (2010). Five- to six-year outcome and its prediction for children with ODD/CD treated with parent training. *Journal of Child Psychology & Psychiatry, 51*(5), 559–566. doi:10.1111/j.1469-7610.2009.02178.x

Erikson, E. H. (1963). *Childhood and society.* New York, NY: Norton.

Fahim, C., Fiori, M., Evans, A. C., & Pérusse, D. (2012). The relationship between social defiance, vindictiveness, anger, and brain morphology in eight-year-old boys and girls. *Social Development, 21*(3), 592–609. doi:10.1111/j.1467-9507.2011.00644.x

Flamez, B., &Watson, J. (2014). *Solution focused therapy.* In R. Parsons & N. Zhang (Eds.), *Counseling theories* (pp. 311–342). Thousand Oaks, CA: Sage.

Frost, J., Wortham, S., & Reifel, S. (2001). *Play and child development.* Upper Saddle River, NJ: Merrill.

Heegaard, M. (1996). *When mom and dad separate: Children can learn to cope with grief from divorce.* Minneapolis, MN: Woodland Press.

Helker, W., Shottelkorb, A., & Ray, D. (2007). Helping students and teachers CONNECT: An intervention model for school counselors. *Journal of Professional Counseling: Practice, Theory, & Research,* 35(2), 31–45.

Kestly, T. (2014). *The interpersonal neurobiology of play: Brain-building interventions for emotional well-being.* New York, NY: Norton.

Landreth, G. (1991). *Play therapy: The art of the relationship.* Levittown, PA: Accelerated Development.

Martin, C., & Fabes, R. (2008). *Discovering child development.* New York, NY: Cengage.

Matthys, W., Vanderschuren, L., Schutter, D., & Lochman, J. (2012). Impaired neurocognitive functions affect social learning processes in oppositional defiant disorder and conduct disorder: Implications for interventions. *Clinical Child & Family Psychology Review, 15*(3), 234–246. doi:10.1007/s10567-012-0118-7

National Institute on Drug Abuse. (2014, January). *Drug facts; Stimulant ADHD medications: Methylphenidate and amphetamines.* Retrieved from http://www.drugabuse.gov/publications/drugfacts/stimulant-adhd-medications -methylphenidate-amphetamines

Nuffield, E. J. (1968). Child psychiatry limited: A conservative viewpoint. *Journal of the American Academy of Child Psychiatry, 7,* 210–212.

OECD. (2013). *Education at a glance 2013: OECD indicators.* OECD iLibrary. Retrieved from http://dx.doi.org/10.1787/eag-2013-en

Piaget, J., & Inhelder, B. (1973). *Memory and intelligence.* London, UK: Routledge and Kegan Paul.

Prout, D. H., & Brown, D. (2007). *Counseling and psychotherapy with children and adolescents: Theory and practice for school and clinical settings* (4th ed.). New York, NY: Wiley

Rathus, S. A. (2008). *Children and adolescence: Voyages in development.* Belmont, CA: Thomson Wadsworth.

Ray, D. C. (2007). Two counseling interventions to reduce teacher-child relationship stress. *Professional School Counseling, 10*(4), 428–440.

Rogers, C. (1980). *A way of being. Boston,* MA: Houghton Mifflin.

Salkind, N. J. (2004). *An introduction to theories of human development.* Thousand Oaks, CA: Sage.

Schottelkorb, A. A., & Ray, D. C. (2009). ADHD symptom reduction in elementary students: A single-case effectiveness design. *Professional School Counseling, 13,* 11–22.

Scott, D., Royal, C., & Kissinger, D. (2015). *Counselor as consultant.* Thousand Oaks, CA: Sage.

Silverstein, S. (1974).*Where the sidewalk ends.* New York, NY: Harper & Row.

Sklare, G. (2014). *Brief counseling that works: A solution-focused therapy approach for school counselors and other mental health professionals.* New York, NY: Corwin.

Substance Abuse and Mental Health Services Administration (SAMHSA). (2012). *Mental health, United States, 2010.* HHS Publication number (SMA) 12-4681. Rockville, MD: SAMHSA.

Substance Abuse and Mental Health Services Administration (SAMHSA). (2013). *Mental and substance use disorders, U.S., 2013.* Retrieved from http://www .samhsa.gov/disorders

United States Department of Education (USDE, National Center for Education Statistics. (2015). *Digest of education statistics, 2013 (NCES 2015-011),* Retrieved http://nces.ed.gov/fastfacts/display.asp?id=64

U.S. Public Health Service. (2000). *Report of the surgeon general's conference on children's mental health: A national action agenda.* Washington, DC: Department of Health and Human Services.

van der Kolk, B. (2014). *The body keeps the score.* New York, NY: Penguin.

Van Fleet, R., & Sywulak, A. (2010). *Child centered play therapy*. New York, NY: Guilford.

Vernon, A., & Clemente, R. (2005). *Assessment and intervention with children and adolescents: Developmental and multicultural approaches* (2nd ed.). Alexandria, VA: ACA Press.

Willoughby, M. T., Mills-Koonce, R., Propper, C. B., & Waschbusch, D. A. (2013). Observed parenting behaviors interact with a polymorphism of the brain-derived neurotrophic factor gene to predict the emergence of oppositional defiant and callous–unemotional behaviors at age 3 years. *Development & Psychopathology, 25*(4pt1), 903–917. doi:10.1017/S0954579413000266

Chapter 12

Counseling With Older Children (9–11)

JACQUELINE SWANK AND CLARENCE ANTHONY

Through others we become ourselves.

—Lev S. Vygotsky

INTRODUCTION

Older children, ages 9 through 11 years, typically attend upper elementary grades and the beginning year of middle school in most school systems in the United States (fourth through sixth grade). This developmental stage is sometimes described as a "grace period between the dependence of early childhood and the stresses of early adolescence" (Finnan, 2008, p. 2). However, this transitional stage is also marked by a variety of crucial changes in key developmental areas essential to successfully navigating the transition to adolescence.

After reading this chapter, you will be able to

- discuss the cognitive, psychosocial, and physical development considerations for older children;
- explain challenges experienced by children in this development stage; and
- describe developmentally appropriate counseling interventions to use with older children.

THE BRAIN AND COGNITIVE DEVELOPMENT

During older childhood, children develop more sophisticated modes of processing and understanding information. This developmental process includes a child's mental capacity to categorize, plan, reason, problem solve, create, and fantasize (Berk, 2003). Within this section, we summarize the work of two prominent theorists (Jean Piaget and Lev Vygotsky). Additionally, we include information about brain development.

Brain Development

During older childhood, the frontal lobe and cerebral cortex are further developing, which allows children to have an increased capacity for several cognitive functions (Finnan, 2008). The gray matter, neurons in the cerebral cortex, has peak volumes in the frontal and parietal areas generally by the age of 12 (Zembar & Balter Blume, 2009). Additionally, researchers have found that children have significant synaptic pruning during this stage, which involves unstimulated neurons losing their connective fibers. This pruning leads to the development of a more differentiated brain that facilitates enhanced capacity for learning (Zembar & Balter Blume, 2009). Therefore, older children are able to complete tasks in a more fluid manner compared with their performance at a younger age. This includes improvements in areas such as memory, reasoning, planning, and categorizing, which are consistent with the theoretical premises proposed by Piaget.

Cognitive Development

According to Piaget's (1964) cognitive development model, children between the ages of 9 and 11 are in the later part of the concrete operations stage. During this stage, children master operations/skills that are used to solve problems and make predictions about what may happen in concrete situations which they have experienced or observed during childhood. However, they are not able to perform these operations beyond the context of concrete situations, and abstract thinking has not yet developed. For example, children can tell you that if they are not at the bus stop on time then they will miss the bus, without actually having this demonstrated to them in the moment. However, they do not fully understand more abstract concepts, such as freedom and liberty, until the formal operations stage. The operations that children begin developing during Piaget's (1964) concrete operations stage include conservation, decentration, reversibility, hierarchical classification, seriation, and spatial reasoning. (An explanation of these operations is provided in Table 12.1.)

The concrete operational stage is also marked by a decline in egocentric thought. Older children gradually develop an awareness of the perspectives of others and

Table 12.1 Piaget's Concrete Operational Stage Concepts

Concepts	Definition	Example
Conservation	Amount of something remains constant even if the appearance changes (relates to numbers, mass and length, and area)	Related to conservation of area, which is typically the last to develop around age 9, children understand that blocks spread out on a table take up as much space as when they are grouped together on the table.
Decentration	Ability to focus on multiple characteristics or attributes of an object or situation, involves development of short-term memory, basis for multitasking	A child can look at a story and see words that make up the sentences in addition to individual letters.
Reversibility	The ability to think in a series of steps and then reverse those steps to return to the starting point	A balanced scale becomes unbalanced when weight is added to one side and can be rebalanced by removing the weight.
Hierarchical classification	Sort things into general and more specific groups	A child can divide animals into groups (e.g., mammals vs. nonmammals, types of mammals).
Seriation	Put things in order according to magnitude	Child arranges blocks from smallest to largest.
Spatial reasoning	Understand and draw conclusions about direction and distance	Child develops a map of their neighborhood with landmarks and approximate distances between places.

integrate these viewpoints to interpret the world. The ability to consider the perspectives of others assists children in working effectively with others. Enhanced cognitive skills correlate with the development of social skills and the ability to relate to, and work cooperatively on tasks, with others.

While Piaget (1964) wrote that language development depends on earlier skills related to categorization, Vygotsky (1978) believed that thought and language developed in parallel, but fundamentally different, trajectories during early childhood. Then, in late childhood, Vygotsky (1978) believed that children are on their way to establishing fairly stable internal narratives that help them make meaning of the world and the people around them. Not all children develop the same skills at the same time or in the same order (Vygotsky, 1978). A child's culture is a significant contributing factor in cognitive and intellectual development (Smith, Dockrell, & Tomlinson, 1997). Interactions between society and the individual are crucial to the cognitive development process, including interactions with peers and adults. Children create meaning by participating with other people in their culture. How, when, and in what order children develop cognitive skills is dependent on the values placed on these skills by the adults around them.

Psychosocial

During older childhood, children encounter psychosocial tasks that help them recognize who they are as individuals and who they are as members of groups and society. This section presents an overview of Erikson's (1963) psychosocial stages and Kohlberg's (1969) moral stages of development. Furthermore, this section includes information about language development, development of self, socialization, career development, and cultural considerations.

Erikson's Psychosocial Stages

According to Erikson's (1963) theory of development, older children are in the industry versus inferiority stage. During this stage, children focus on mastering knowledge and developing skills. Children who struggle with developing key areas of knowledge and skills and balancing their multiple areas of involvement may develop a sense of inferiority and feel incompetent. For example, children who receive encouragement in their efforts to perform well academically or athletically develop self-confidence in their abilities to achieve goals and success. In contrast, children who have their efforts discouraged, restricted, or not acknowledged by adults begin to doubt their abilities and struggle with reaching their potential.

Moral Development—Moral Reasoning

In working with children, it is crucial to consider their present stage of moral development because this is related to the decision-making process. During upper elementary school, children typically enter the second level of moral reasoning (conventional morality) of Kohlberg's (1969) cognitive development model of moral development (Finnan, 2008). This level contains the third and fourth stages of moral development. Older children are generally within stage 3: mutual interpersonal expectations, relationships, and interpersonal conformity. Within this stage, decision making is characterized by the desire to be a "good person" and to please others, and thus to be accepted by peers and influential adults. Therefore, children may be reluctant to discuss negative behaviors because they don't want adults to perceive them negatively. Moral reasoning is also guided by following consistent rules established by adults and developing their own rules that are viewed as fair. In doing so, they also hold others accountable to these rules, including adults. Furthermore, children often want to engage in caring behaviors and are aware that negative behaviors are wrong and could negatively affect others (Finnan, 2008).

Moral Development—Forgiveness

Enright, Santos, and Al-Mabuk (1989) proposed a model of forgiveness that was comparable to Kohlberg's (1969) model of moral reasoning. The researchers found that fourth graders' behaviors were usually within the second stage of forgiveness development (restitutional or compensational forgiveness), expecting replacement for something that was broken or an apology that acknowledged wrongdoing. This corresponds to Kohlberg's second stage (individualism, instrumental purposes, and exchange), which is one stage lower in regard to the development of moral reasoning than what Finnan (2008) described as being typical for children in upper elementary school. Children in Kohlberg's third stage of development, as described in the moral reasoning section, would be in the expectional forgiveness stage. Within this stage, children show forgiveness because it is expected of them or they feel pressured to forgive someone. Enright and colleagues (1989) reported that the third stage was common for tenth graders who were significantly influenced by their peers.

Language and Communication

Older children are able to verbally communicate more effectively with peers and adults, with the increase in a child's vocabulary from roughly 10,000 to approximately 40,000 words (Berk, 2003) by this developmental period. Humor and riddles contribute to language development through the expansion of brain processes and the development of an understanding of semantics and a larger vocabulary (Finnan, 2008). Furthermore, humor provides an opportunity for children to relate to others in ways that they have not previously done. In further discussing language development, Finnan (2008) emphasized that there is a reciprocal relationship between the ability to communicate and the development process, with communication being both a contributor and a product of the developmental process. Children at this stage of life often enjoy "gross out" and bathroom humor, which although often not appreciated by adults, helps them forge friendships based on a common sense of humor.

Development of Self

Older children view themselves as more independent from their parents and adults in their lives than do younger children; however, they continue to seek affirmation from adults as they struggle with finding a balance between autonomy and relatedness (Finnan, 2008). Additionally, older children continue to view themselves as related to their competencies (e.g., "I am smart."); however, the advances in their cognitive abilities allow them to also begin to incorporate the perspectives of others (peers and adults) into their understanding of themselves, which was absent at younger ages (Harter, 2006). Children's ability to make social comparisons between themselves and others is influenced by the environments in which they are socialized, including the school, home, and wider cultural context. Children are also exposed to adults in these environments comparing children to each other (Harter, 2006).

Older children develop the ability to integrate both positive and negative viewpoints and emotions simultaneously. This demonstrates growth in the area of emotional development, as children at earlier developmental stages deny having opposing emotions at the same time (Harter, 2006). Older children also experience more complex emotions (e.g., guilt, pride) and are able to relate emotions to actual situations (Vernon, 2009).

As children grow, they also develop the increased ability to consider the perspectives of others. Older children have the ability to recognize that others may have different views and feelings about a situation than they do. According to Selman's (1976) developmental model of perspective taking, children are still likely within the self-reflective role taking stage at the beginning of older childhood; however, they will likely transition to the mutual role taking stage around the age of 10. Within the self-reflective stage, children recognize that others have different viewpoints and feelings. However, as children transition into the mutual role-taking stage, they develop the ability to take the perspective of a spectator. Thus, social perspective-taking skills related to higher expectations and standards that others have for them including societal standards, the development of social comparison skills used to evaluate oneself, and the ability to differentiate the real from the ideal self may contribute significantly to a child's view of oneself (Harter, 2006). Therefore, it is crucial to provide support as older children struggle with constructing a balanced perspective of themselves and developing a healthy self-concept.

The self-concept of older children is influenced by their own perceptions of their abilities and competencies, comparing their ideal selves to their real selves. Additionally, older children are influenced by the perspectives of others, including adults and, increasingly, peers (Harter, 2006). While some children develop a balanced perspective of themselves, others may need assistance in developing a healthy self-concept. Counselors may use individual or group interventions that help children identify positive qualities about themselves, including abilities and areas of competency, and challenge negative thoughts about oneself. Group counseling provides children with an opportunity to recognize that everyone has areas that they struggle with, in addition to having strengths.

Family

The family is the first source of socialization for a child, and it remains a crucial influence in promoting a child's sense of belonging during older childhood, despite the desire children have to be more independent and spend increasing amounts of time with their peers outside of the home (Finnan, 2008; Harter, 2006). In addition to parents providing nurturing and support, upper elementary school children may also provide this within the family by recognizing the emotions of others and responding in ways to help relieve stress within the family (Finnan, 2008). Parenting style is a key factor in fostering a sense of belonging and accomplishment among older children. The three major styles of parenting are authoritarian, permissive, and authoritative. Permissive parents are reluctant to set and enforce rules and instead require children to regulate themselves. Authoritarian parents are rigid and demanding in setting and enforcing rules. Finally, authoritative parents set and reinforce rules while also being nurturing and supportive and strive to balance freedom and responsibility (Santrock, 2011). Parents who use an authoritative parenting style, instead of an authoritarian or permissive style, promote positive child development through fostering strong relationships with children and offering older children a greater role in the decision-making process (Finnan, 2008; Santrock, 2011). Older children generally receive less physical punishment and are encouraged to take greater responsibility for their actions and to develop self-regulation skills (Santrock, 2011). Thus, parents help children gradually develop greater autonomy while maintaining a strong level of support that is essential as children spend more time with their peers and other adults (e.g., teachers, coaches) outside of the home.

Peer Socialization and Friendship

In regard to socialization, overall peer interactions increase to 30% in this stage compared to 10% for toddlers. Additionally, interactions become less supervised and peer groups increase in size (Rubin, Bukowski, & Parker, 2006). The settings in which children interact with their peers also expand and become more diverse as children advance through childhood (Finnan, 2008; Rubin et al., 2006). Involvement outside of school may include involvement with religious group activities (e.g., youth group) and community organizations (e.g., boy/girl scouts, sports leagues). Furthermore, activities become more structured and coordinated, involve the increase of games and sports, and encompass both positive and negative behaviors (Rubin et al., 2006).

Older childhood is characterized by the emergence of fewer groupings focused on inclusion of everyone to differentiated groupings through the formation of cliques. With the formation of these differentiated groups, an emphasis is placed on power, status, and attention. A popularity hierarchy also becomes apparent during this stage (Finnan, 2008; Rubin et al., 2006). Additionally, the nature of friendship continues to evolve during childhood developmental stages. Young children conceptualize friendship in the here and now and relate friendship to the activity of engagement. This shifts to perceiving friendship as lasting beyond a single activity to encompassing a more long-term relationship as children enter school. Then, as children enter the upper grades of elementary school they begin to view shared values as important and loyalty is viewed as an essential component of friendship. Friendship serves also as a protective factor for children, and the dissolution of friendship during late childhood can have a significant effect on children (Rubin et al., 2006). Therefore, children may need opportunities to process their experiences with their peer groups as they journey through the upper elementary school years and transition to middle school.

Vocational Development

Donald Super researched vocational development across the lifespan, grouping older children within the growth stage of career development, which included children ages 4 to 13 (Super, Savickas, & Super, 1996). According to Super and colleagues (1996), children develop work habits and attitudes, begin thinking about career interest for the future, and learn to value achievement and success during the elementary school years. Thus, older children need an opportunity to learn about different types of careers and what is required to enter them; practice responsibility and positive work habits through assignment of appropriate chores and tasks; and understand positive work ethics exhibited by role models.

Importantly, counselors need to be wary of children in this developmental stage closing off career options prematurely. Gottfredson's stages of circumscription focus on children excluding occupational choices based on inadequate information about careers. Older children are typically in the orientation to social valuation stage, which is characterized by considering the status of careers (Gottfredson, 2002). Children in this stage typically exclude occupations that have low prestige. Additionally, they often reject jobs that are perceived to be too difficult or present a high risk of failure. Furthermore, older children from a higher socioeconomic status may experience greater pressure to pursue career choices with a higher level of prestige to avoid being considered a failure by their social group (Gottfredson, 2002).

Palladino Schultheiss, Palma, and Manzi (2005) explored career development among 49 fourth and fifth graders. The children's responses revealed eight of the nine dimensions of childhood career development proposed by Super (1990). The eight dimensions present were (a) exploration, (b) information, (c) key figures, (d) interests, (e) locus of control, (f) time perspective, (g) self-concept, and (h) planfulness. In exploring the responses further, some child participants showed an awareness of the importance of an income, helping others through work, and having a home for the family, with influential adults being crucial in their understanding of the concept of work. Thus, career education and interventions for children in this stage of development are foundational to later decision making.

Cultural Considerations

With the increase in peer interactions, children in this stage become more focused on being accepted by others and "fitting in" (Finnan, 2008). They have greater awareness of how they are similar and different from others and are drawn toward peers who are similar to them. In making this shift, children develop a greater awareness of their ethnic/racial identify and the existence of racism (Finnan, 2008). In examining interethnic and interracial friendships among kindergarteners compared to fourth and fifth graders, Pica-Smith (2011) found that younger children had more positive perceptions of interracial friendships, with older children becoming more selective in forming and maintaining friendships. Older children also recognize socioeconomic differences as they become more interested in their possessions and the clothes they wear and acknowledge that these differences influence their values and group interactions (Finnan, 2008). Recognition of these ethnic/racial and socioeconomic differences may lead to negative interactions with peers. Negative interaction styles change during this stage as children engage in more verbal and relational aggression (e.g., gossip, insults), instead of physical aggression. Bullying and victimization and support for negative, aggressive behaviors also become more apparent in older childhood (Rubin et al., 2006).

Differences are also evident in the socialization patterns of girls and boys during this stage. Girls are interested in more feminine activities and may also begin to express interest in boys (e.g., having a crush on a famous male actor). In contrast, boys remain interested in socializing primarily with other boys through sports and physical activities. Girls may view boys as immature, while boys are confused by the changes they see in the girls who were once their playmates (Finnan, 2008). In examining the interactions of third through fifth graders ($N = 56$ triads), Lansford and Parker (1999) found that girls sought emotional connections, as expressed through sharing more personal information, while boys demonstrated more aggressive behaviors.

Motor Skill Development

During older childhood, continued changes in physical development (e.g., growth in limbs, changing center of gravity) are related to enhanced gross motor skills. Children expand upon the skills developed in early childhood (e.g., running, jumping) through the development of greater agility, flexibility, and balance (Zembar & Balter Blume, 2009). These improved abilities translate to involvement in more complicated physical activities including skateboarding and organized sports (e.g., basketball, baseball, football). Zembar & Balter Blume (2009) also described the development of perceptual-motor skills. Specifically, a child's ability to process complex sensory information contributes to improved gross motor skills (e.g., using eye, ears, and hands to make a basket in basketball). Furthermore, children demonstrate improved fine motor skills during older childhood (i.e., coordination and precision; Zembar & Balter Blume, 2009). Examples of improved fine motor skills include playing an instrument and improved handwriting.

Physical

In the latter part of older childhood, children begin to experience a growth spurt that is characterized by rapid growth of arms, legs, hands, and feet. This growth spurt may lead to awkwardness and clumsiness as children strive to adjust to their disproportional bodies (Zembar & Balter Blume, 2009). Additionally, girls may surpass boys in average height and weight, which typically continues until boys enter puberty (Zembar & Balter Blume, 2009).

Herdt and McClintock (2000) described two pubertal processes (adrenal and gonadal) that occur during the older childhood period. They reported that adrenal puberty occurs between the ages of 6 and 10, becoming stable during older childhood at the age of 10. As the adrenal pubertal process becomes stable, children become more aware of gender roles, develop sexual awareness, and experience feelings of attraction for their peers. McClintock & Herdt (1996) proposed that the emergence of sexual attraction prior to adolescence might be partially associated with an increased cognitive capacity to understand the social environment and adult sexual interactions. Children observe adult behavior and begin to imitate these behaviors with their peers (McClintock & Herdt, 1996). In contrast, gonadal puberty (secondary sex traits) begins at the end of the older childhood phase of development and throughout adolescence, beginning around age 11 for girls and age 12 for boys (Herdt & McClintock, 2000). Researchers have also acknowledged that children are entering puberty at an earlier age due to genetic and environmental factors that influence how youth interact with each other and with adults (Zembar & Balter Blume, 2009).

Body image and appearance becomes increasingly important for older children, with relevance to both females and males (Phares, Steinberg & Thompson, 2004). Children begin to have greater awareness of their weight and overall physical appearance. Additionally, they become more attuned to messages communicated by others about the importance of appearance (Finnan, 2008). Older children may need help in understanding and processing changes in their physical development and how this relates to their views about themselves. Guided Exercise 12.1 provides an example.

Guided Exercise 12.1

Observe older children interacting with each other. You may choose to observe children on a playground, in the school cafeteria, or so on. Alternatively, you can view a YouTube video. What do you notice about the cognitive, psychosocial, and physical development of the children? Do some children appear to be more advanced in specific areas of development than others? Are any issues apparent that you think need to be addressed? If so, what are they, and what recommendations do you have for addressing them?

ISSUES AND CONCERNS

Older children experience various issues and concerns that counselors need to have awareness of in working with this age group. We present three major issues experienced by older children: (a) obesity, (b) bullying, and (c) transition to middle school. The discussion of these areas includes the scope of the issue and implications for counselors.

Obesity

The National Center for Health Statistics (2012) reported that according to the findings from the 2009–2010 National Health and Nutrition Examination Survey (NHANES), 18% of all children ages 6 to 11 are obese. More specifically, obesity was higher among boys in the 6 to 11 age group (20.1%) compared with girls (15.7%). Additionally, obesity among boys was higher in this age group, when compared with the other two age groupings (2 to 5 years, 12 to 19 years). Although obesity is not generally considered to be a mental health–related issue, concerns about body image, teasing, and emerging eating disorders are all obesity-related concerns often seen by counselors. Therefore, school counselors may consider adding wellness and healthy eating themes to the developmental school counseling curriculum and encourage school administrators to lengthen recess and other activity periods throughout the school day.

Bullying

Bullying is repeated aggressive behavior with an imbalance of power and strength between at least two parties (Nansel et al., 2001; Olweus, 1993). Additionally, bullying may involve physical, social, and psychological (e.g., rumor spreading, social exclusion, and friendship manipulation) dimensions (Jimerson, Swearer, & Espelage, 2010). In examining the long-term effects of bullying among children ages 9 to 16 who were both victims and perpetrators, Wolke, Copeland, Angold, and Costello (2013) found elevated rates of adult and child psychiatric disorders. Additionally, the researchers found that childhood bully victims that were ages 9 and 11 were more likely to have higher rates of negative health, financial, and social outcomes when compared to children who were not bullied (Wolke et al., 2013). Furthermore, with the development of information and communication technologies, a new form of bullying, cyberbullying, has emerged during the last decade (Cassidy, Faucher, & Jackson, 2013). Although older children might be skilled in navigating games and using social media within the online world, Cassidy and colleagues (2013) acknowledged that youth struggle with addressing situations in the online world, as they do in real life face-to-face interactions. Thus, the cyber world and face-to-face interactions both present situations where children may experience bullying. In Guided Exercise 12.2, we explore bullying and cyberbullying in more depth.

Guided Exercise 12.2

In small groups, discuss the issue of bullying, including a review of the bullying policy for the local school district. Who is responsible for addressing bullying? What recommendations do you have for addressing bullying? An extension of this exercise may include interviewing a school or community counselor about bullying, discussing the prevalence of the issue and interventions used with older children to address bullying.

Promoting a strong school connection may enhance children's academic behavior, performance, and health (Durlak, Weissberg, Dymnicki, Taylor, & Schellinger, 2011). Parent involvement through reinforcing lessons taught at school about bullying may also be beneficial (Twemlow & Sacco, 2013). Twemlow and Sacco

(2013) outlined several concepts that involve bullying in schools such as altruism, being aware of school climate, and the notion that student development occurs when children feel valued and safe. Although any student can be a victim of bullying, children who identify as LGBTQ are more frequently at risk and their safety may be of particular concern to counselors. Resources for LBGTQ youth can be found at the following websites: Stop Bullying. Gov (http://www.stopbullying .gov/at-risk/groups/lgbt, The Trevor Project: http://www.thetrevorproject.org, and It Gets Better project: http://www.itgetsbetter.org.

A caring school environment helps children thrive. In contrast, a high frequency of bullying behaviors contributes to a fearful environment where students feel unhappy and unwelcome (Sanders & Phye, 2004). Therefore, it is crucial for professionals to implement strategies to help prevent and address bullying to promote a positive, safe learning environment. Interventions to address bullying may involve teaching and promoting empathy and active listening skills (Smith, Cousins, & Stewart, 2005). It is also beneficial to empower students by developing peer-led programs (Salmivalli, 2001).

Developing a peer mediation program can be time extensive, involving recruiting, selecting, and training mediators and then ongoing monitoring of the program. However, this may help students take ownership for addressing bullying in their school. Counselors may also implement systemic interventions that would run concurrently to the peer mediation program. This may involve implementing an antibullying code and facilitating activities and discussions that focus on antibullying (Olweus, 1993; Olweus et al., 2009). Furthermore, counselors may seek involvement from parents to enhance the learning environment and form a cohesive bond between the school and the home environment. In Case Illustration 12.1, we describe a school counseling intervention focused on addressing bullying and promoting diversity.

Case Illustration 12.1

Various bullying incidents had been occurring at Sanders Elementary School. Specifically, one student had been the target of acts of physical and verbal aggression from other students within the classroom for the past few days. The student, an African-American male named Darius, had complained about insults relating to skin color, his name, hair texture, and the way that he spoke in class. Then, an insult from another student led to a physical altercation within the classroom. Darius's parents reported that he had expressed feeling sad and angry and that he no longer wanted to attend school.

The school counselor decided to survey all students, school personnel, and parents about their knowledge, beliefs, and attitudes about bullying and diversity, and their perspectives about bullying incidents occurring in the school. The school counselor then developed a task force of teachers, administrators, and parents to share the data with and to develop policies and procedures to address bullying and promote diversity within the school. Simultaneously, the counselor began working with teachers and other

(Continued)

(Continued)

school personnel to implement a program focused on valuing diversity and addressing bullying across all fourth and fifth grade classrooms, with a plan to gradually involve more grades to provide a school-wide program. The counselor conducted classroom guidance lessons focused on respecting and valuing differences and bullying prevention and intervention. Specifically, the counselor focused on diversity and differences in culture (race specifically), addressing the emotional effects of bullying, and teaching students strategies for intervening when they saw another student being bullied. In helping students explore various aspects of diversity, the counselor worked with students to acknowledge and appreciate differences and similarities among them. The counselor also helped them process their thoughts and feeling about the bullying incidents that had occurred in the school. The counselor also met individually with Darius to provide further support. Additionally, the counselor worked with the teachers to implement classroom meetings following the Olweus program (Olweus et al., 2009), with the goal of promoting the classroom as a safe, caring learning environment. Furthermore, the counselor developed a schoolwide peer mediation program, selecting fourth and fifth grade students as peer mediators.

Transition to Middle School

At about age 11, children experience a major transition that can present a variety of issues and concerns. This transition normally entails the completion of fifth grade (leaving elementary school) and beginning sixth grade (entering middle school) for students in the United States. The transition to middle school involves many significant changes including attending school in a typically larger building, larger class sizes, and constant transition to different classrooms with different teachers throughout the day (Barber & Olsen, 2004). Additionally, children transition from being the oldest in elementary school to the youngest in middle school so there may be concerns about being bullied, experiencing a shift in the level of homework, being able to do the work, concerns about older pupils, and new expectations and the rules of secondary school (Rice, 2011). Middle school students may also be expected to take more personal responsibility and to have higher levels of motivation due to the increased difficulty in the academic curriculum and higher grading standards (Rudolph, Lambert, Clark, & Kurlakowsky, 2001). Young people also experience changes in peer groups and friendships during this transition (Kingery, Erdley, & Marshall, 2011; Xie, Dawes, Wurster & Shi, 2013), which includes more brief periods of social interaction, such as transitions between classes instead of recess. Furthermore, peer support may shift from supporting academic behaviors to supporting aggressive and rule-breaking behaviors (Xie et al., 2013). School belongingness is said to help ease problems with this transition and promote mental health in middle school (Vaz et al., 2014). Close peer relationships, teachers, and school climate do seem to make an important difference.

Akos and Galassi (2004) explored students' ($n = 173$), parents' ($n = 83$), and teachers' ($n = 12$) perspectives about the transition from elementary to middle school and identified concerns in three primary areas (academic, procedural, social). In regard to transition concerns, students and parents identified getting lost and the amount of homework as concerns. Parents and teachers were both concerned about students making friends, while students and teachers were both concerned about students navigating the school. All three groups viewed the opportunity to make friends and choose classes as positive aspects of middle school. In contrast, students identified homework, teachers, and classes as challenges, and parents reported responsibilities and peers as the greatest challenges for their children. In considering successful adjustment to middle school, teachers identified maturity, cooperation, and motivation as key factors. Participants also discussed strategies for promoting a successful transition period, which included discussions about middle school during elementary school and implementing various activities during the transition phase (e.g., orientation, team building, opportunities to ask questions, programming on fostering positive peer relationships).

Barber and Olsen (2004) assessed changes among youth transitioning to middle and high school in Utah. There were 933 families involved in the study that examined students' transition from Grades 5 to 8. In comparing students' fifth and sixth grade reports, students reported positive changes, including higher self-esteem, lower levels of depression and loneliness, increased support from teachers, and more time spent on homework in sixth grade. However, negative changes were reported in the following areas: (a) decline in grades, (b) increased need for organization at school, and (c) decreased quality in father-child relationships. Kingery and colleagues (2011) also examined the transition period from elementary school to middle school ($N = 365$) focusing on the influence of peer relationships and found that social interactions were related to academic success. Peers served as a strong support system in helping address the academic challenges of transitioning to middle school. Thus, students with limited peer support in the upper elementary school grades may experience greater difficulty in transitioning to middle school.

Elementary school counselors can facilitate large group guidance lessons and small groups focused on skills that help promote success in transitioning to middle school. Skill building in the areas of problem solving, social skills, and coping strategies may help facilitate academic success in middle school (Kingery & Erdley, 2007; Kingery et al., 2011). Additionally, as discussed previously, Akos and Galassi (2004) recommended facilitating discussions with elementary school children about middle school. They also recommended implementing a variety of activities to promote a successful transition including orientation, team building, and programming on fostering positive peer relationships.

Community and school counselors can help children prepare for the transition to middle school by facilitating discussions about middle school. This may involve role-plays to address "what if" scenarios. School counselors may also involve current middle schools students to provide a student's perspective in discussions to address fears and dispel myths about middle school. Counselors can identify students' fears and beliefs about middle school by asking students to write a fear or belief about middle school on a piece of paper anonymously and putting it into a container. The counselor can take out the slips of paper and discuss the comments or have the students take turns reading the comments. This intervention offers the counselor an opportunity to identify, validate, and discuss the thoughts and feelings of the students, while facilitating a safe environment for students to share by having students write their comments anonymously. Middle school tours can also be arranged that give elementary school students an opportunity to become familiar with the middle school and to meet with middle school teachers and students. Furthermore, school counselors may establish a mentoring program to help students adjust to middle school. It might be difficult to establish a mentor for every student; therefore, this intervention could be used with students who are identified as having a particularly difficult time with adjusting to middle school. Thus, community and school counselors can implement a variety of group and individual counseling interventions to assist youth with making a successful transition to middle school. Case Illustration 12.2 focuses on a counselor's work with an older child in a community setting who is struggling with preparing for the transition to middle school.

Case Illustration 12.2

Sadie is an 11-year-old female in fifth grade. She excelled academically throughout elementary school and had reportedly always enjoyed attending school. Sadie also appeared to have a strong peer group and stated that she had known her best friend since they started elementary school together. Sadie's mother reported that following a discussion at school about transitioning to middle school, Sadie "changed." Her mother stated that Sadie often became tearful in the morning before school, and her grades began to decline. Sadie's mother also reported that Sadie was often sad and would not talk about what was wrong. Furthermore, she stated that Sadie had always been a happy, well-adjusted child, and due to her extreme change in demeanor and behavior, she decided to seek counseling for Sadie.

Sadie was initially reluctant to meet with the counselor and was very quiet during the first session. After meeting with Sadie and her mom together, the counselor met with Sadie alone and offered her the opportunity to play a game while they talked. Sadie shared that she liked to play Uno, and she gradually began to talk with the counselor as they played the game. Sadie agreed to come again the following week and asked if they could play Uno again. The counselor continued to focus on building rapport with Sadie as they played and talked during the sessions. As counseling continued, Sadie shared that she was sad about finishing fifth grade because her best friend would not be attending the same middle school. She stated that she was told that the classes were bigger in middle school and that the schoolwork was more difficult. She expressed feeling anxious and scared and doubting her ability to be successful in middle school. The counselor worked with Sadie to help her explore her self-concept and fears about middle school and develop strategies to cope with change and anxiety through creative writing and art. Sadie drew pictures and created collages of herself and her fears and described them in her writings. Sadie was then able to talk about how she felt about herself and her fears through a discussion about her writings and art. Sadie shared with the counselor that she thought writing and drawing helped her express her feelings and feel less anxious because she didn't feel pressured to just talk about them. Additionally, the counselor role-played with Sadie middle school scenarios that she depicted through her writing and art and had her practice coping strategies. Sadie also practiced talking with her mom about her anxiety through letter writing and art. Furthermore, with the mother's consent, the counselor contacted the sixth grade school counselor at the middle school where Sadie would be attending and arranged a time for Sadie to meet her, talk about extracurricular activities available at the school, and to take a tour of the school.

SUGGESTIONS FOR DEVELOPMENTALLY APPROPRIATE INTERVENTIONS WITH CHILDREN AGES 9 TO 11

Counselors may integrate a variety of counseling inventions within their work with older children. However, in order to practice ethically, it is important for counselors to have training in using the specific interventions. Additionally, counselors should experience the techniques and explore their thoughts and feelings about using the interventions before using them in their work with clients. We discuss five categories of interventions: (a) social skills and cognitive behavioral, (b) expressive arts, (c) bibliotherapy, (d) game play, and (e) nature-based interventions.

Social Skills and Social–Emotional Learning

Because children in this age group experience dramatic changes, their interpersonal and social skills, social skills building, and cognitive coping skills are commonly goals targeted by counselors in schools and clinical settings (Kingery & Erdley, 2007; Kingery et al., 2011). Social skills curricula, such as *Second Step: Student Success Through Prevention for Middle School* (Espelage, Low, Polanin & Brown, 2013), are widely available for this age group and tend to address basic social skills (e.g., empathy, problem-solving skills, risk assessment, decision making, and goal setting) as well as increased emphasis on understanding relationships and aggression and conflict resolution. Broader aims of social skills programs include reducing peer conflict and school safety and increasing positive school climate, which, as discussed, are critical to this age group. Though these interventions are commonly used as schoolwide (universal) programs, they can also be modified for use in individual, small group, and family counseling/consultation. Other evidence-based social skills program that are available for use with older children include *A Curriculum for Children's Effective Peer and Teacher Skills* (ACCEPTS) (Walker et al., 1988); *Social Skills Intervention Guide* (K-12) (Gresham & Elliot, 2008); *Promoting Alternative Thinking Strategies* (PATHS) (Kusche & Greenberg, 1997); and *Student Success Through Prevention for Middle School* (Lemberger, Selig, Bowers, & Rogers, 2015). More resources are available at the Collaborative for Academic, Social, and Emotional Learning (CASEL) at http://www.casel.org and the Institute of Educational Sciences (IES) What Works Clearinghouse at http://ies.ed.gov/ncee/wwc/interventionreport .aspx?sid=578.

Expressive Arts

Though older children are capable of verbalizing their thoughts and feelings, counselors may want to consider using alternatives to "talk therapy" because children this age may still have difficulty expressing the range of thoughts and emotions they experience. A few examples that are applicable to counseling older children include using art to address behavioral issues and promote communication (Saunders & Saunders, 2000), drama to promote adjustment and well-being (McArdle et al., 2002), music to promote social competence (Gooding, 2011), and dance/movement to promote a positive body image (Muller-Pinget, Carrard, Ybarra, & Golay, 2012). Researchers have also found play therapy, which may encompass a variety of expressive arts, to be effective in addressing various emotional and behavior concerns, for older children (Bratton & Ray, 2000).

Counselors can adapt a variety of expressive arts techniques with older children. For example, counselors may have children create collages involving words and pictures to describe themselves. Counselors can creatively use this activity by having children make a personalized license plate or design the packaging for a cereal box to describe their strengths. This provides children with an opportunity to be creative and express themselves in a way that may be new and different. Additionally, the use of drama in counseling may involve acting out fictional scenes from books or movies or real life scenarios and then processing the experiences during sessions. Counselors may also integrate music in counseling with older children by having them create a music collage of their favorite songs that they can play and discuss with the counselor during session. Furthermore, counselors may combine music with dance/movement techniques to provide an opportunity for clients to engage in self-expression. Therefore, counselors may integrate a variety of expressive arts techniques into their work with clients to build rapport and address a variety of concerns.

Bibliotherapy

Bibliotherapy is a particularly helpful therapeutic intervention to use with older children because literature can be matched to their developmental issues and concerns.

Through the use of bibliotherapy, counselors can help children discuss a topic that is difficult to talk about, develop a greater understanding of themselves, acknowledge that they are not alone in what they are experiencing, and learn about strategies to address the issues that they are experiencing (Stamps, 2003). Bibliotherapy can be used in various ways within counseling to address a variety of counseling issues (e.g., grief and loss, trauma, divorce, self-esteem, anger, social skills). For example, the counselor might use books to approach a topic and then give children an opportunity to write their own endings to the stories or act out the stories. This provides children with an opportunity to relate stories to their own lives by obtaining ownership of the stories. In using bibliotherapy in practice, counselors should discuss with children how this approach differs from schoolwork, since children often associate books with school. Furthermore, it is crucial for counselors to read and review books before integrating them into their work with children (Pehrsson, Allen, Folger, McMillen, & Lowe, 2007).

Game Play

Games are enjoyable for older children, and counselors may use them in addressing a variety of counseling issues (Swank, 2008). Specifically, counselors may use game play in helping children develop social skills and engage in problem solving (Serok & Blum, 1979). Games are useful because children often interact with each other through the use of games. Game may include active physical games, board or card games, or video games. Counselors may use games that are specifically designed for counseling, modify existing games, or create their own games to use with children. Creating new games or modifying existing games allows counselors to tailor games to address specific issues (Swank, 2008; Swank & Swank, 2013). For example, Swank (2008) described modifying charades and Pictionary in working with groups of children regarding a variety of issues by creating playing cards that focus on specific aspects of the issue. As with any intervention, it is important to consider what is appealing to the child and to choose games that address the therapeutic goals. For steps on how to modify existing games or develop new games to use for therapeutic purposes, see Swank (2008).

Nature-Based Intervention

Counselors may also consider the use of interventions that involve a nontraditional counseling space. The natural environment provides a unique, therapeutic counseling setting (Swank & Shin, 2015). Researchers have found that the integration of nature-based interventions may improve child well-being, as well as reduce behavioral problems (Swank, Shin, Cheung, Cabrita, & Rivers, 2015) and promote empathy (Feral, 1998). Thus, counselors may integrate various interventions in the natural outdoor environment. For more information about the integration of nature-based play see Swank and Shin (2015). For additional information about using therapeutic gardening to address personal, social, career, and academic development, see Swank and Swank (2013).

Guided Exercise 12.3

In small groups, brainstorm how you would use one of the five intervention areas to address self-esteem with older children within a setting of your choice (e.g., agency, private practice, school) using an individual or group format. Identify the counseling goals, describe one specific intervention that you would use from one of the five areas (e.g., a specific book you would use in bibliotherapy, a game you would modify or develop), and explain how you would measure the effectiveness of the intervention.

COUNSELING KEYSTONES

- During older childhood, children pursue greater independence while still seeking support from adults.
- While older children spend an increasing amount of time with peers, the family remains influential during this developmental stage.
- Self-esteem is a crucial issue for older children as they become more focused on how they are viewed by others, and they begin to experience physical changes.
- In working with older children, counselors need an understanding of child development theories, challenges commonly experienced within this developmental stage (e.g., bullying, transitioning to middle school), and developmentally appropriate interventions.

ADDITIONAL RESOURCES

In Print

Daunic, A. P., Smith, S. W., Robinson, T. R., Landry, K. L., & Miller, M. D. (2000). School-wide conflict resolution and peer mediation programs: Experiences in three middle schools. *Intervention in Schools & Clinic 36*(2), 94–101.

Taylor, J. V., & Trice-Black, S. (2007). *Girls in real life situations, grades 6–12: Group counseling activities for enhancing social and emotional development* (Book and CD). Champaign, IL: Research Press.

Online

Bullying.gov: http://www.stopbullying.gov

Bullying in U.S. Schools: 2013 Status Report: http://www.violenceprevention works.org/public/index.page

"Don't Laugh at Me" video on YouTube: https://www.youtube.com/watch?v =NaDn3hBERw8

Edutopia: Transition resources for parents, teachers, and administrators: http:// www.edutopia.org/blog/transition-resources-teachers-matt-davis

Favorite therapeutic activities for children, adolescents, and families: Practitioners share their most effective interventions: http://www.lianalowenstein. com/e-booklet.pdf

Operation Respect: Don't Laugh at Me: http://www.operationrespect.org/ curricula

The Best Children's Books: http://www.best-childrens-books.com/bibliotherapy .html

The Carnegies Library of Pittsburg: http://www.carnegielibrary.org/research/ parentseducators/parents/bibliotherapy

The Collaborative for Academic, Social, and Emotional Learning (CASEL): http:// www.casel.org

The NED Show (Career Day Video Lessons): http://www.youtube.com/playlist ?list=PLkwL1rGISbRlAtmdyqUzMcWRmhWYXhYKI

U.S. Department of Education and Institute of Educational Sciences. What Works Clearinghouse. Social Skills: http://ies.ed.gov/ncee/wwc/pdf/ intervention_reports/wwc_socialskills_020513.pdf

REFERENCES

Akos, P., & Galassi, J. P. (2004). Middle and high school transitions as viewed by students, parents, and teachers. *Professional School Counseling, 7,* 212–221.

Barber, B. K., & Olsen, J. A. (2004). Assessing the transitions to middle and high school. *Journal of Adolescent Research, 19(1),* 3–30. doi:10.1177/0743558403 258113

Berk, L. E. (2003). *Child development* (6th ed.). Boston, MA: Pearson Education.

Bratton, S., & Ray, D. (2000). What the research shows about play therapy. *International Journal of Play Therapy, 9,* 47–88. doi:10.1037/h0089440

Cassidy, W., Faucher, C., & Jackson, M. (2013). Cyberbullying among youth: A comprehensive review of current international research and its implications and application to policy and practice. *School Psychology International, 34,* 575–612. doi:10.1177/0143034313479697

Durlak, J., Weissberg, R. P., Dymnicki, A. B., Taylor, R. D., & Schellinger, K. B. (2011). The impact of enhancing student's social and emotional learning: A meta-analysis of school-based interventions. *Child Development, 82,* 405–432. doi:10.1111/j.1467-8624.2010.01564.x

Enright, R. D., Santos, M. J. D., & Al-Mabuk, R. (1989). *Helping clients forgive: An empirical guide for resolving anger and restoring hope.* Washington, DC: American Psychological Association.

Erikson, E. H. (1963). *Childhood and society.* New York, NY: Norton.

Espelage, D. L., Low, S., Polanin, J. R., & Brown, E. C. (2013). The impact of a middle school program to reduce aggression, victimization, and sexual violence. *The Journal of Adolescent Health, 53(2),* 180–186.

Feral, C. H. (1998). The connectedness model and optimal development: Is eco-psychology the answer to emotional well-being? *The Humanistic Psychologist, 26,* 243–274. doi:10.1080/08873267.1998.9976975

Finnan, C. (2008). *Upper elementary years: Ensuring success in grades 3–6.* Thousand Oaks, CA: Corwin.

Gooding, L. F. (2011). The effect of a music therapy social skills training program on improving social competence in children and adolescents with social skills deficits. *Journal of Music Therapy, 48,* 440–462. doi:10.1093/jmt/48.4.440

Gottfredson, L. S. (2002). Gottfredson's theory of circumscription, compromise, and self-creation. In D. Brown & Associates (Eds.), *Career choice and development* (4th ed., pp. 85–148). San Francisco, CA: Jossey-Bass.

Gresham, F. M., & Elliott, S. N. (2008). *Social skills intervention guide.* Minneapolis, MN: Pearson.

Harter, S. (2006). The self. In W. Damon & R. M. Lerner (Eds.), *Handbook of child psychology* (pp. 505–570). Hoboken, NJ: John Wiley & Sons.

Herdt, G., & McClintock, M. (2000). The magical age of 10. *Archives of Sexual Behavior, 29,* 587–606. doi:10.1023/A:1002006521067

Jimerson, S. R., Swearer, S. M., & Espelage, D. L. (2010). International scholarship advances sciences and practice in addressing bullying in schools. In S. R. Jimerson, S. M. Swearer, & D. L. Espelage, (Ed.), *Handbook of bullying in schools* (pp. 1–6). New York, NY: Routlege.

Kingery, J. N., & Erdley, C. A. (2007). Peer experiences as predictors of adjustment across the middle school transition. *Education and Treatment of Children, 30,* 73–88. doi:10.1353/etc.2007.0007

Kingery, J. N., Erdley, C. A., & Marshall, K. C. (2011). Peer acceptance and friendship as predictors of early adolescents' adjustment across the middle school transition. *Merrill-Palmer Quarterly, 57,* 215–243. doi:10.1353/mpq.2011.0012

Kohlberg, L. (1969). Stage and sequence: The cognitive-developmental approach to socialization. In D. A. Goslin (Ed.), *Handbook of socialization theory and research* (pp. 347–480). Chicago, IL: Rand McNally.

Kusche, C. A., & Greenberg, M. T. (1997). *PATHS: Promoting alternative thinking strategies.* South Deerfield, MA: Channing-Bete.

Lansford, J. E., & Parker, J. G. (1999). Children's interactions in triads: Behavioral profiles and effects of gender and patterns of friendships among members. *Developmental Psychology, 35,* 80–93. doi:10.1037/0012-1649.35.1.80

Lemberger, M., Selig, J., Bowers, H., & Rogers, J. (2015). Effects of the student success skills program on the executive functioning skills, feelings of connectedness, and academic achievement in in a predominantly Hispanic, low-income middle school district. *Journal of Counseling and Development, 93,* 25–36.

McArdle, P., Moseley, D., Quibell, T., Johnson, R., Allen, A., Hammal, D., & LeCouteur, A. (2002). School-based indicated prevention: A randomised trial of group therapy. *Journal of Child Psychology and Psychiatry, 43,* 705–712. doi:10.1111/1469-7610.00091

McClintock, M. K., & Herdt, G. (1996). Rethinking puberty: The development of sexual attraction. *Current Directions in Psychological Science, 5,* 178–183. doi:10.1111/1467-8721.ep11512422

Muller-Pinget, S., Carrard, I., Ybarra, J., & Golay, A. (2012). Dance therapy improves self-body image among obese patients. *Patient Education and Counseling, 89,* 525–528. doi:10.1016/j.pec.2012.07.008

Nansel, T. R., Overpeck, M., Pilla, R. S., Ruan, W. J., Simons-Morton, B., & Scheidt, P. (2001). Bullying behaviors among U.S. youth: Prevalence and association with psychosocial adjustment. *Journal of the American Medical Association*, 285, 2094–2100. doi:10.1001/jama.285.16.2094

National Center for Health Statistics. (2012). *NCHS data on obesity.* Retrieved from http://www.cdc.gov/nchs/data/factsheets/factsheet_obesity.htm

Olweus, D. (1993). *Bullying at school: What we know and what we can do.* Cambridge, MA: Blackwell.

Olweus, D., Limber, S. P., Snyder, M., Mullin, N., Riese, J., & Flerx Crocker, V. (2009). *Class meetings that matter: K-12.* Center City, MN: Hazelden.

Palladino Schultheiss, D. E., Palma, T. V., & Manzi, A. J. (2005). Career development in middle childhood: A qualitative inquiry. *Career Development Quarterly, 53,* 246–262. doi:10.1002/j.2161-0045.2005.tb00994.x

Pehrsson, D. E., Allen, V. B., Folger, W. A., McMillen, P. S., & Lowe, I. (2007). Bibliotherapy with preadolescents experiencing divorce. *The Family Journal, 15,* 409–414. doi:10.1177/1066480707305352

Phares, V., Steinberg, A. R., & Thompson, J. K. (2004). Gender differences in peer and parental influences: Body image disturbance, self-worth, and psychological functioning in preadolescent children. *Journal of Youth and Adolescence, 33*, 421–429. doi:10.1023/B:JOYO.0000037634.18749.20

Piaget, J. (1964). Part 1: Cognitive development and learning in children: Piaget development and learning. *Journal of Research in Science Teaching*, 2, 176–186. doi:10.1002/tea.3660020306

Pica-Smith, C. (2011). Children's perceptions of interethnic and interracial friend-ships in a multiethnic school context. *Journal of Research in Childhood Education, 25*, 119–132. doi:10.1080/02568543.2011.555495

Rice, F. (2011). Assessing pupil concerns about transition to secondary school. *British Journal of Educational Psychology, 81*, 244–263.

Rubin, K. H., Bukowski, W. M., & Parker, J. G. (2006). Peer interactions, relation-ships, and groups. In W. Damon & R. M. Lerner (Eds.), *Handbook of child psychology* (pp. 571–645). Hoboken, NJ: John Wiley & Sons.

Rudolph, K. D., Lambert, S. F., Clark, A. G., & Kurlakowsky, K. D. (2001). Nego-tiating the transition to middle school: The role of self-regulatory processes. *Child Development, 72*, 929–946. doi:10.1111/1467-8624.00325

Salmivalli, C. (2001). Peer-led intervention campaign against bullying: Who considered it useful, who benefited? *Educational Research, 43*, 263–278. doi:10.1080/00131880110081035

Sanders, C., & Phye, G. D. (2004). *Bullying: Implications for the classroom.* San Diego, CA: Elsevier.

Santrock, J. W. (2011). *Child development* (13th ed.). New York, NY: McGraw-Hill

Saunders, E. J., & Saunders, J. A. (2000). Evaluating the effectiveness of art therapy thorough a quantitative, outcome-focused study. *The Arts in Psychotherapy, 27*, 99–106. doi:10.1016/S0197-4556(99)00041-6

Selman, R. L. (1976). Social-cognitive understanding: A guide to educational and clinical practice. In T. Lickona (Ed.), *Moral development and behavior: Theory, research, and social issues* (pp. 299–316). New York, NY: Holt, Rinehart, and Winston.

Serok, S., & Blum, A. (1979). Games: A treatment vehicle for delinquent youths. *Crime & Delinquency, 25*, 358–363. doi:10.1177/001112877902500306

Smith, J. D., Cousins, J. B., & Stewart, R. (2005). Antibullying interventions in schools: Ingredients for effective programs. *Canadian Journal of Education, 28*, 739–762.

Smith, L. S., Dockrell, J., & Tomlinson, P. (1997). *Piaget, Vygotsky, and beyond: Future issues for developmental psychology and education.* New York, NY: Routledge.

Stamps, L. S. (2003). Bibliotherapy: How books can help students cope with concerns and conflicts. *Delta Kappa Gamma Bulletin, 70*(1), 25–29.

Super, D. E. (1990). A life-span, life space approach to career development. In D. Brown, L. Brooks, & Associates (Eds.), *Career choice and development* (2nd ed., pp. 197–261). San Francisco, CA: Jossey-Bass.

Super, D. E., Savickas, M. L., & Super, C. M. (1996). The life-span, life-space approach to careers. In D. Brown & L. Brooks (Eds.), *Career choice and development* (3rd ed., pp. 121–178). San Francisco, CA: Jossey-Bass.

Swank, J. M. (2008). The use of games: A therapeutic tool with children and families. *International Journal of Play Therapy, 17*(2), 154–167. doi:10.1037/1555-6824.17.2.154.

Swank, J. M., & Shin, S. (2015). Nature-based child-centered play therapy: An innovative counseling approach. *International Journal of Play Therapy, 24(3),* 151–161.

Swank, J. M., Shin, S. M., Cheung, C., Cabrita, C., & Rivers, B. (2015). Initial investigation of nature-based child-centered play therapy: A single-case design. *Journal of Counseling and Development, 93(4),* 440–450.

Swank, J. M., & Swank, D. E. (2013). Student growth within the school garden: Addressing personal/social, academic, and career development. *Journal of School Counseling, 11*(21), 1–31. Retrieved from http://jsc.montana.edu/articles/v11n21.pdf

Twemlow, S. W., & Sacco, F. C. (2013). Bullying is everywhere: Ten universal truths about bullying as a social process in schools and communities. *Psychoanalytic inquiry, 33,* 73–89. doi:10.1080/07351690.2013.759484

Vaz, S., Falkmer, M., Parsons, R., Passmore A. E., Parkin, T,, & Falkmer, T. (2014). School belongingness and mental health functioning across the primary-secondary transition in a mainstream sample: Multi-group cross-lagged analyses. *PLoS ONE 9*(6), 1–10.

Vernon, A. (2009). *Counseling children and adolescents* (4th ed.). Denver, CO: Love.

Vygotsky, L. S. (1978). *Mind and society.* Cambridge, MA: Harvard University Press.

Walker, H., McConnell, S., Holmese, K., Todis, B., Walker, J., & Golden, N. (1988). *The Walker social skills curriculum: A curriculum for children's effective peer and teacher skills* (ACCEPTS). Austin, TX: Pro-ed

Wolke, D., Copeland, W. E., Angold, A., & Costello, E. J. (2013). Impact of bullying in childhood on adult health, wealth, crime, and social outcomes. *Psychological Science*, 24, 1959–1970. doi:10.1177/0956797613481608

Xie, H., Dawes, M., Wurster, T. J., & Shi, B. (2013). Aggression, academic behaviors, and popularity perceptions among boys of color during the transition to middle school. *American Journal of Orthopsychiatry, 83,* 265–277. doi:10.1111/ajop.12039

Zembar, M. J., & Balter Blum, L. (2009). *Middle childhood development: A contextual approach.* Upper Saddle River, NJ: Pearson Education.

Chapter 13

Counseling With Young Adolescents (12–14)

Andrea L. Dixon, Robert E. Rice, and Amanda Rumsey

The changes during adolescence are not something to just get through; they are qualities we actually need to hold on to in order to live a full and meaningful life in adulthood.

—Daniel J. Siegel, *Brainstorm: The Teenage Brain From the Inside Out*

INTRODUCTION

The unique period of the lifespan occurring between the ages of 12 to 14 is best known as early adolescence. Much like the older childhood years (9–11), this is considered a time of life in which youth undergo rapid physical, cognitive, and social transformations. However, at this stage, these developmental patterns intensify. In fact, throughout the past 30 years, and most likely long before, early adolescence has entailed periods of extreme upheaval, and even stress, for young adolescents and for others involved in their lives as they navigate the physical, cognitive, emotional, academic, and personal/social transitions during middle school and into early high school. The stereotypical images of younger adolescents being "trapped" in changing, awkward bodies and confused by the effects of their "raging hormones" has been pervasive among counselors, pediatricians, parents, and educators for decades (Arnett, 1999; Buchanan & Hughes, 2009; Hollenstein & Lougheed, 2013). Thus, the difficulties associated with transitioning from childhood to early adolescence have historically received a great deal of attention in research, leading to numerous specialized approaches for communicating and working with young adolescents.

Because educators and researchers recognize early adolescence as a period of development that is unique and distinct from late childhood and later adolescence, this developmental stage brings about unique challenges that highlight the need for counseling specific to working with young adolescents.

After reading this chapter, you will be able to

- describe varying developmental considerations during young adolescence,
- outline specific concerns and issues that emerge during this time of life,
- understand a variety of counseling approaches and interventions to use with young adolescents, and
- illustrate practical, developmentally suitable approaches to counseling with young adolescents in schools and clinical settings.

DEVELOPMENTAL CONSIDERATIONS

Because individuals are not yet adults and no longer children, early adolescence is a time of extreme growth and development in various areas. It is also a time of confusion, excitement, and discovery (Forbes & Dahl, 2010). In this section we provide an overview of the physical, cognitive, psychosocial, and identity developmental growth during early adolescence.

Physical and Brain Development

Physical growth during this time varies greatly among and between genders and is greatly influenced by the onset of puberty. Typically girls will begin onset of puberty between ages 9 and 11 and boys between ages 10 and 13, however, puberty seems most pronounced during the middle schools years, around ages 12 through 14. The onset of puberty triggers the release of three endocrine events: (1) adrenarche (usually starting around ages 8 and 9), (2) gonadarche (around ages 11 and 12), and (3) the activation of the hypothalamic-pituitary-gonadal axis, resulting in ovulation or maturity of viable sperm (Blakemore, Burnett, & Dahl, 2010). The first of these, adrenarche, sets the stage for the later stages of puberty by increasing the output of the adrenal glands, often causing acne outbreaks and body hair growth. The gonadarche process activates the ovaries and testes that produce the gonadal steroids estrogen and testosterone. These events are accompanied by the development of secondary sex characteristics, such as enlargement of breasts in girls and testicles in boys and the appearance of body hair in both. These changes in appearance (or lack of changes in some) and surge of hormones are a source of mystery, confusion, and concern for these early adolescents (Forbes & Dahl, 2010).

Generally, girls' physical growth in height, muscle, and fine motor coordination appears earlier than boys, but these developments are outpaced by boys later in adolescence. However, it is not unusual to see both early and late maturation in groups of children Grades 6 through 8 (Forbes & Dahl, 2010). At the extremes, early or late maturation can be a source of stress because the child appears different from the average. The growth is often not graduated but comes in spurts, which can interfere with motor control. It is typical for these early adolescents to bump into objects, trip, and have difficulty controlling other gross and fine motor activates until they have practiced the acts in their environment (Blakemore et al., 2010; Konrad, Firk, & Uhlhaas, 2013). Another aspect contributing to growth spurts is food intake. For many adolescents, the need for food and the images presented to them of desirable bodies are often in conflict. This can lead to eating disorders, obesity, or health related problem such as diabetes (Mäkinen, Puukko-Viertomies, Lindberg, Siimes, & Aalberg, 2012). The process of gaining control over their bodies, motor control, and eating habits can be very disturbing and frustrating for some, particularly in environments where they are exposed to youths at differing early adolescent stages (Buchanan & Hughes, 2009; Konrad et al., 2013).

Physical growth can influence brain development in a number of ways, and one of these may be due to the onset of puberty. Blakemore et al. (2010) posit that puberty may have a role in both white and gray matter brain development. During puberty, an increase in gray matter occurs sending the brain though a sort of blooming period (growth of neuron connections). The brain then begins to thin out unneeded neurons to increase efficiency and speed. As the individual experiences the environment, connections are made in the brain. The brain retains wanted connections and prunes unused or unwanted connections. This allows the desired connections to strengthen (Kadosh, Linden, & Lau, 2013).

At the same time, myelination (the growth of fatty tissue around the neuron cells) is taking place (Blakemore et al., 2010; Konrad et al., 2013). It is thought that puberty and nutrition speed the growth of myelin. This fatty tissue acts as insulation, which aids in conduction of electrical impulses that speed up the signals throughout the brain. Myelination and selective pruning crystalizes certain behaviors, which helps to shape the individual's conduct as he or she reacts to the environment. These two processes of synaptic pruning and myelination occur throughout adolescence and into adulthood but are most active during early and mid adolescence (Konrad et al., 2013). Understanding the importance of how behaviors develop can be useful to parents, teachers, and counselors as they help guide students through the challenges of these early adolescent years. Encouraging positive behaviors may help young people crystalize those behaviors (Kadosh et al., 2013).

Two prominent areas of the brain significant to early adolescence are the cerebellum and the prefrontal cortex. The cerebellum coordinates some motor functions as well as social and other higher order thinking processes (Burnett,

Bird, Moll, Frith, & Blakemore, 2008; Konrad et al., 2013). Growth in this area of the brain increases during adolescence and continues until completed in adulthood. As the adolescent interacts with the environment, control over body movement, socialization, and higher order thinking take place.

Equally significant to the adolescent is the growth of the prefrontal cortex. This is one of the last areas of the brain to develop and begins primarily to develop during and throughout adolescence, ages 12 to 25 (Konrad et al., 2013). Remember that the cortex is often called the executive functioning part of the brain because it controls impulses and decision making. While the area of the brain that controls information processing, the amygdala, is almost fully developed, the prefrontal cortex is still immature. As the cerebellum continues to connect and interpret the world, the amygdala sends reactions to those encounters. Without a fully functioning prefrontal cortex, the adolescent is prone to react to these messages without control, foresight, and logical or long-range reason. The result is that adolescents often select risky behaviors not simply out of impulse (though they often are impulse) but because the long-range results are not believed possible (Burnett et al., 2008; Konrad et al., 2013).

Cognitive Development

Jean Piaget's (1954) approach to cognitive development states that around age 12 children began to move from concrete operational thought to formal operational thought. Adolescents are moving from the application of logic to concrete problems to the application of more abstract thought to problems. One of the primary differences is in moving more from a focus on the here and now to seeing future possibilities. Adolescents begin to hypothesize their own theories and test them out to form concrete answers. As their experiences and testing continues, their thinking becomes more complex. Concrete logic gives way to propositional thought, and the adolescent increasingly uses abstract thought and logic even without concrete examples. Of course, this way of thinking creates a lot of questions. This natural evolution of cognitive processing can be frustrating for both the adolescent and adult by creating arguments and questioning of rules and authority (Piaget, 1954).

As discussed in Chapter 12, Lev Vygotsky proposed a more fluid model of developmental than did Piaget. He was one of those who believed that social interaction and experiences were the drivers of cognition. Vygotsky (1978) viewed children's functional developments as happening on two levels; first, in the interaction or communication with others and second, in the inward processing of the interaction. Every development leading to higher functioning can be traced to social relationships between individuals. This is best described in his concept of the zone of proximal development and scaffolding. The idea is to take what is known or doable and what is not known or doable and determine what can be done with some help (scaffolding). This is significant in middle school when concepts taught are moving from concrete operations to more abstract operations, when behaviors for academic and social success are being challenged, and as identity development is primary.

Psychosocial and Identity Development

Eric Erikson (1968) understood that the influence of physical and brain development can be seen in the early adolescent's psychosocial and identity development. Erickson's theory of social development also followed a stage approach but did not require mastery at each stage. He posited that humans go through eight stages from birth to late adulthood, and development is brought about by a combination of biological and social influences. The period between ages 6 to 12 is called industry versus inferiority and is represented by an individual trying to accomplish goals and develop capabilities. As individuals experience success or failure at accomplishing tasks and answers to the logic they use in concrete and formal operational stages, they develop a sense of both competence and mastery if they are successful or, if less successful, a feeling of lack of skill or ineptitude. This can have a positive or negative effect as the child moves into adolescence, which is characterized by a search for identity versus identity confusion. This stage is paramount throughout adolescence and into early adulthood. The middle school years (Grades 6 to 8), ages 11 to 14, are particularly challenging as the individual both transitions between the Piagetian stages of concrete and formal operational thought and determines his or her role in Erickson's stages of industry versus inferiority and identity versus identity confusion, (Erikson, 1968).

The level of cognitive understanding, maturity of the amygdala, and the immaturity of the prefrontal cortex converge when these early adolescents interact with each other and older people. Belief in one's ability is often tied to how the individual is perceived by his or her peers or by significant others. The adolescent brains react to a greater extent to emotional stimuli and often see neutral stimuli as threating. Some of this may be due to the changes brought on by puberty in hormone levels. There is a decrease in serotonin levels and an increase in dopamine levels. Regardless of the cause, adolescents experience more events as stressful than either preadolescents or adults and are more susceptible to depression (Burnett et al., 2008; Konrad et al., 2013). This is in large part due to how others react to young adolescents' efforts to perform, contribute, feel attraction to others, and belong.

As an individual experiences success or failure with a task or idea, the formation of a concept of self-abilities begins to form. The development of a healthy self-concept or clear view of one's abilities is critical to how adolescents see their total self-worth (self-esteem). In middle school, identity is often tied to the student's capabilities. Determining what the student is good at becomes one of the goals in middle school. Self-concept and self-esteem also appear to be tied to body image. Both girls and boys are vulnerable to concerns about their weight. Girls tend to be more affected and try to reach the ideal body image put forward by the media and society or are underweight for their age. They feel dissatisfaction at normal weight for their age and the most dissatisfaction when overweight. Boys suffer if they are out of the norm but are most concerned when they are overweight (Mäkinen et al., 2012; Pollack, 1998).

While keeping up with the newest clothes, music, and other fads is important to many adolescents, being from a family with lower socioeconomic status should not affect the development of a healthy self-image if there are strong family supports and values in place; even when faced with limited financial resources the adolescent with strong social support is open and engaging and emotionally stable (Pollack, 1998). Perhaps a greater risk for boys of all socioeconomic statuses is believing in the myths of manhood (i.e., societal stereotypes for men and boys). These include the pressures to always be tough, fearless, never disrespected, virile, strong, and confident, and they are difficult challenges for the early adolescent male struggling with the many changes in the mind and body (Pollack, 1998). Complicating events for both girls and boys is the increase of estrogen and testosterone brought on by puberty. Adolescents may now experience feelings of desire and romance toward others who were friends during elementary school. This becomes a source of confusion as girls may seek attention and closeness, and boys may have more sexual feelings and want less attachment. Developing healthy relationships with both genders while living in a society with media-driven images (often not positive) is a very real challenge as these early adolescents try to develop their identities (Forbes & Dahl, 2010; Veselska et al., 2010).

Research shows that mass media can greatly influence adolescents' perceptions and behavior in relationships (Brown, Halpern, & L'Engle, 2005; Gentile, 2014; Kaiser Family Foundation, 2001). Goldberg, Smith-Adcock, & Dixon (2011) recommended using popular films and other popular media with adolescents to help them critically examine these messages. In Guided Exercise 13.1, we illustrate an activity that will help you and the adolescents you work with to examine changing selves and relationships.

Guided Exercise 13.1

Popular Media Activity

Helping young people to critically examine the media's potentially harmful influence is important. In Goldberg et al. (2011), a list of movies is provided to illustrate both healthy friendships, for example, *The Sisterhood of the Traveling Pants* (Chase, Di Novi, Kosove, Johnson, & Kwapis, 2005), and unhealthy friendships, for example, *Mean Girls* (Michaels & Waters, 2004). Create your own list of films that depict healthy identity formation and relationships and those that do not. Some categories of lists of films and other popular media you might create include (but are not limited to) parent-child relationships, friendships, early dating relationships, sibling relationships, or relationship to self (self-understanding and identity development). Some mass media sources might include TV, films, books, magazines, YouTube videos, and so on.

Compounding this is the task of succeeding academically in school. Girls and many minority boys struggle with the concept of academic success and failure (Matusov, DePalma, & Smith, 2010). To be too smart is often not an asset for many girls or African-American and Hispanic boys but rather can be a source of ridicule or outcast. So many find themselves in a dilemma of not reaching their potential for fear of being cast as something other than their stereotype (Matusov et al., 2010).

James Marcia's (1967) expansion of Erikson's model casts the adolescent as experiencing four categories of identity development: (1) foreclosure, (2) identity diffusion, (3) moratorium, and (4) identity achievement. Adolescents experiencing identity foreclosure make a commitment based on how others perceive their success. They believe they must behave or act a certain way because that is what others see as their strength. Adolescents in this category are often happy and self-confident. They tend to seek social approval and yet are controlling and seek leadership. The second of Marcia's categories is identity diffusion. This is when the adolescent has no idea who he or she is or what he or she will do. There is no real commitment in this stage, but it is very prevalent in early adolescence when the child is faced with so many possibilities and cannot decide what works best for him or her. This adolescent may be withdrawn and find it difficult to have close relationships (Marcia, 1967). Adolescents in the moratorium status choose to explore many different areas and not make a commitment. They appear to be carefree, open to new experiences, and seek intimacy with others. They also may experience anxiety and psychological conflict. Within the final stage of identity achievement, adolescents make active decisions, and the stage ultimately occurs when success in an area is made. These students tend to have tried many things and settled on what makes them feel the most successful. According to Marcia, students in this identity status are psychologically adjusted, academically motivated, and have high self-esteem (Marcia, 1967).

It is important to note that racial and ethnic minority adolescents in today's diverse schools have additional challenges. They must decide whether to merge their ethic culture with the majority culture, assimilate into the majority culture, or maintain bicultural identities. Identity formation occurs over time and requires teachers, administrators, parents, and counselors to be sensitive to the explorations adolescents may have about their culture and how that culture interacts in the world (Matusov et al., 2010). Overall, within the boundaries of social norms and school and family boundaries, young adolescents are faced with numerous issues and concerns that affect their daily self-worth, interpersonal connections, and maturation. In Case Illustration 13.1, we describe these developmental changes for a middle school student.

Case Illustration 13.1 School Counseling Case Example

Morgan is a 13-year-old seventh-grade Black male, who is tall for his age at about 5′ 11″. Morgan is the only child of two middle-age working African-American professionals. His mother is in business, and his father works in the media center of a local university. The family lives in a predominantly Black, middle class neighborhood. As a family, they travel, go to local cultural events, museums, and openly talk with one another. While Morgan feels comfortable talking to both his mother and father, he does not talk about his social issues.

Morgan has been in a gifted honors program since the third grade with the same group of 100 students. He is now in a middle school of over 800 students in Grades 7 and 8. While the middle school has a large African-American population, his honors program is mostly made up of Caucasian and Asian students; however, his elective classes are not restricted to honors students. Morgan has friends in school of both genders and many races but tends to have more male friends than girls. While he has tried to mix with all the students, most of his friends are from his years in the honors program. Morgan does not like to associate with the "in" crowd and has a group of peers that he hangs out with who he calls "loners" and a group of "Internet friends" that he really likes. He enjoys playing games on the Internet with these friends because when you lose no one really knows you. Though he is tall, he feels awkward physically and does not like sports.

As the school year progressed, Morgan began to grow increasingly depressed, isolated, and angry, even avoiding his "loner" friends. He went on academic probation for the first time and recently was suspended for fighting. When he met with is counselor, he said he was being called "White" and "gay" by both Black and White students. He said girls no longer want to talk to him, even one who he has been friends with since third grade (she happens to be White). In tears, he explained that he does not fit in with the White or Black kids, and he hates it.

The counselor believed that Morgan was suffering from identity diffusion brought on by peer relationship and self-concept concerns. Morgan's struggles were complicated by his early adolescent struggles with physical and cognitive development issues and have ultimately affected his academic performance. The counselor suggested Morgan attend a small psychoeducational group of other male students with relationship and identity concerns. He also met with Morgan in two individual sessions using rational emotional behavior therapy (REBT; with homework). The counselor connected Morgan with a school club, and weekly check-ins were instituted to monitor grades and social process. With Morgan's concurrence, the counselor contacted his parents and developed a plan to help him manage his time on the Internet. The counselor also suggested the parents should encourage exposure to successful Black college students.

ISSUES AND CONCERNS FACING YOUNG ADOLESCENTS

As children mature into young adolescents, they continue to experience rapid growth and development, which likely brings about an enormity of confusion and concerns. Wolfe, Jaffe, and Crooks (2006) identify parallels between young adolescents and young children in the areas of problem behaviors and emotional regulation. Young adolescents differ from young children with regard to what is expected from them by their environment and biology (Wolfe et al., 2006). From a developmental perspective, a young child is expected to build relationships with his or her caregivers, and an adolescent is expected to develop independence and begin detaching from his or her caregivers (Erikson, 1968). Many adolescents are able to make that transition without major issues or concerns, however, that detachment process along with rapid physical and emotional changes can be difficult and present many vulnerabilities.

Identity Issues

As mentioned above, as youth pull away from their parents and move toward their peer groups, they begin to explore aspects of their identity and how they fit in with others. Younger adolescents tend to have a growing awareness of social comparisons and judgments of social attributes, with increased self-consciousness and a greater concern with being "popular" (Ryan & Shim, 2008). This can present challenges as most young adolescents do not have a strong sense of identity and are experimenting with different roles to figure out who they are and how they fit in with peers. As Pledge (2004) proposes, this insecurity can make some young people very vulnerable to potential abuse in relationships.

Gender identity has been defined as the "extent to which a person experiences oneself to be like others of one's gender" and develops in accordance with physical characteristics (Steensma, Kreukels, deVries, & Cohen-Kettenis, 2014, p. 289). For young adolescents, this can present many challenges, as they are all developing at different levels, and there is a focus on social comparisons and judgments. Insecurities are easily triggered, and teasing may be experienced by those who have developed early, for those who are late bloomers, and for those who are experiencing incongruence between assigned gender and experienced gender. For adolescents that do identify as a sexual minority, there are issues with establishing an integrated sexual identity and navigating the coming-out process (Wolfe et al., 2006).

Interpersonal Relationships

All of the insecurities that arise as young adolescents navigate the course of social, physical, and emotional growth can lead to many interpersonal challenges. Complaints about parents and dilemmas with friends are common troubles with young adolescents. Often, conflict in parent-child relationships evolves as young adolescents exert independence. As they find their peer group increasingly important, there can be newfound issues and concerns with developing and maintaining friendships. There is often an emergence of dating relationships; although, between the ages of 12 and 14 they tend to be brief and somewhat superficial in nature.

Acquiring a sense of belonging in school and a belief that one is liked, respected, and valued as a unique individual is important for young adolescents (Osterman,

2000). Relational aggression such as teasing, spreading rumors, and social isolation, as well as other more outward signs of physical aggression and violence are all behaviors that seem to increase between the ages of 12 and 14 and can challenge those desired feelings of belonging and social support. First coined by Crick and Grotpeter (1995), *relational aggression* can be defined as impending threats of withdrawal from, and dissolution of, relationships among individuals. Relational aggression among young adolescents occurs when both covert and direct tactics, including acts of hostility exhibited through rumor spreading, eye rolling, rejection and alienation, and exclusion and isolation, are used to impose bullying tactics and social harm that damage relationships or social standing (Ostrov, Hart, Kamper, & Godleski, 2011; Weber & Kurpius, 2011). In addition, bullying has been defined as a behavior that leaves a child "exposed, repeatedly and over time, to negative actions on the part of one or more other students" (Olweus, 1993, p. 9). Powell and Ladd (2010) identify both direct and indirect types of relational aggression and bullying as well as cyberbullying, all of which can have drastic effects on the students who bully, their victims, and the families involved. Behaviors that indicate a child or adolescent may be a victim of relational aggression include but are not limited to loss of interest in school, school avoidance or school phobia, withdrawal from family interactions, psychosomatic symptoms, more emotional than usual, loss of appetite, trouble sleeping, and bruising or torn clothing (Powell & Ladd, 2010). A discussion of bullying remediation and prevention may be found in Chapter 12.

Grief and Loss

Although the loss of loved ones may occur at any time in a person's life, losses that occur during the turbulent middle school years may seem to be particularly difficult to the person experiencing the loss. Feelings of grief may be triggered by the death of a family member, friend, or pet or by other forms of loss and change, such as moving to a new place, changing schools, divorcing parents, or an older sibling leaving home. The pain of loss during the early adolescent years may be particularly acute when the young person has not developed an adequate array of coping skills yet or when the loss is sudden or traumatic.

School counselors can help to lessen the impact of grief and loss by presenting curricular lessons aimed at developing strong coping skills before a loss occurs. There are a wide variety of such programs available for purchase. The American School Counselor Association (ASCA) maintains a resource page on the members only section of its website that lists many commercial curricula and individual lesson plans. This site also has resources to assist school counselors in the creation of effective crisis plans, which all schools should have and regularly update. A comprehensive crisis plan that is easy to locate and follow in the event of a schoolwide or community-wide tragedy can make the school staff members' response much more streamlined and thoughtful. It is often very difficult to make decisions regarding how, when, and where to intervene after a tragedy has occurred. Planning ahead can save valuable time and anguish in the days following a tragic event. Community agencies should have similar plans for responding to large-scale crisis events. Links to webinars and websites are available through ASCA, *Helping Kids During Crisis*, at http://www.schoolcounselor.org/school -counselors-members/professional-development/2015-webinar-series/learn-more/ helping-kids-during-crisis.

After a loss has occurred, counselors in any setting can seek resource material from the National Child Traumatic Stress Network's website (http://nctsn.org). An extensive collection of resources are maintained on the site and are free to access. NCTSN includes a specific section on dealing with schoolwide tragedies, such as the death of a teacher or student, or the aftermath of a school shooting. This website may be shared with parents or students as appropriate. Resources for dealing with grief and loss across the lifespan can also be accessed at the Dougy Center: The National Center for Grieving Children & Families at http://www.dougy.org/ grief-resources/kids-and-funerals. This website has easy to access information that can be used in school and clinical settings.

Internalizing Problems

Heightened sensitivity, mood swings, the propensity to act out, and inhibition of behavior are identified as affective states and behaviors that are characteristic of adolescents (Brown & Prout, 1989). For some adolescents, depressive symptoms, anxiety, and other mood disorders extend beyond the typical adolescent experience with emotional variability. Internalizing disorders, in which "the tendency is to turn symptoms onto themselves as opposed to acting out against others" (Pledge, 2004, p. 137) are present; however, with younger adolescents, there is more of a tendency to display outward signs of distress. With regard to depression, adolescents often display more anger and irritability, along with uncommunicativeness and hypersensitivity to criticism. "Although rebelliousness toward parents and a tendency to 'shut them out' is normal in adolescence, those behaviors become more extreme and more constant in depressed youth" (Pledge, 2004, p. 139).

Externalizing Problems

Externalizing problems can be defined as issues or concerns that occur when symptoms are displayed in an outward manner or acted out against self or others. Those actions include aggression and violence toward self and others. Today's adolescents are exposed to an unprecedented amount of violence through digital technology and the mass media, including television, movies, music videos, the internet, and video games (Finkelhor, Turner, Ormrod, Hamby, & Kracke, 2009; Wolfe et al., 2006). Not all exposure will lead to problems with aggression and violence, but there is a desensitization effect that may occur with continued exposure to violence.

In addition to acting out behaviors, young adolescents are at a peak risk period for the following types of victimization: assault with a weapon, sexual harassment, kidnapping, witnessing a family assault, and witnessing intimate partner (interparental) violence (Finkelhor et al., 2009). Another concern for this age group is the onset of issues with self-harm. In a 2013 study exploring self-harm among young adolescents, Stallard, Spears, Montgomery, Phillips, and Sayal (2013) found that girls between the age of 13 and 14 had increased odds for developing self-harming thoughts and behaviors. Among the young adolescents studied, 1 in 5 reported thoughts and 1 in 10 reported at least one act of self-harm over a 6-month period. Therefore, given the ever-increasing numbers of social and personal issues and concerns facing young adolescents, counselors in schools and mental health agencies must be prepared with developmentally appropriate counseling interventions in order to aid this group of individuals in their coping and growth and development throughout middle school and into their high school years.

SUGGESTIONS FOR DEVELOPMENTALLY APPROPRIATE INTERVENTIONS WITH CHILDREN AGES 12 TO 14

Due to the unique plasticity and developmental challenges of individuals in early adolescence, a variety of counseling approaches and interventions should be used. Contemporary counselors should employ interventions that are effective and designed to help young adolescents acquire the knowledge, attitudes, and skills for functioning more effectively in the school community, at home, and in society. Examples of some of these interventions include individual counseling, small group counseling approaches, classroom guidance curriculum activities, consultations with teachers and parents, and possible peer-based interventions.

Individual Counseling

Individual counseling with young adolescents can take on many unique approaches that may include play counseling, counseling with art and music, bibliotherapy, as well as talk therapy. These supportive approaches take place in both schools and mental health agencies, dependent upon where the young adolescent is seeking help and should focus upon academic or social and emotional needs. Individual sessions can be important and should be used as more intimate and concentrated interventions are required. It is likely that supportive, individual therapeutic interventions can assist young adolescents in learning healthy ways of relating to others (Klem, Owens, Ross, Edwards, & Cobia, 2009), which can take many forms when working with individuals in the in-between stages of childhood and young adulthood.

Young adolescents can benefit greatly from creative counseling approaches such as play counseling, art and music interventions, bibliotherapy, and journaling (ASCA, 2012). When used along with talk therapy, these approaches can help young adolescents explore issues and concerns and label feelings and thoughts that are difficult for them to articulate with words or expressions. Allowing them to play and explore in an unstructured and safe environment allows young adolescents the permission to express themselves openly and to work through specific concerns via toys and art forms. Puppets, clay, drawings, and other creative forms of toys and art expression are suggested in allowing less articulate and younger adolescents freely share their hopes, thoughts, fears, desires, and needs. An age-appropriate example might involve a young adolescent being asked to draw how he or she is feeling in the present regarding a specific class he or she may be having academic trouble in and then draw how he or she would like to feel in that specific class or subject. A counselor can then discuss the drawings with the adolescent in order to provide guidance for helping the student make the changes needed to move toward the feelings and outcome he or she wants.

Music is often another important component in young adolescents' lives; therefore, asking them to bring in popular songs that explain how they are feeling or that represent themselves in specific manners also allows for creative expression without placing verbal expectations on young individuals who may not be able to put words to their thoughts and feelings.

Counselors use readings or books in the form of a bibliotherapy process to help young adolescents in individual counseling. Many useful books exist that are appropriate for this age group (e.g., *Dr. Bird's Advice for Sad Poets* by Evan Roskos, *Playing Tyler* by T. L. Costa, and *Being Bullied* by Kate Petty and Charlotte Firmin. Please see additional books that can be used with young adolescents in the Additional Resources list.) that cover the wide range of issues and concerns facing young adolescents and that can be used to help them to relate to characters in the readings that may be facing similar concerns. Finally, using written expression can be useful for young adolescents in individual counseling, which can take place through assigned journaling or free writing. This can be something that adolescents can be invited, but never forced, to share in counseling sessions with counselors. Again, this type of intervention, as well as the other creative approaches listed above, can lead to developed rapport between clients and counselors, and thus, deeper and more meaningful talk therapy.

As with any age group across the lifespan, there are many young adolescents who may feel comfortable opening up verbally in individual sessions as well as an equal amount who may not. This is to be expected and should not deter counselors attempting this approach with young adolescents. However, it is critical that these clients thoroughly understand the limits of confidentiality and are allowed to take their time in building rapport and trust with counselors. Because they are at a critical point in their development where they want to think for themselves and question authority, it may also be critical that adolescents at this age provide their assent to counseling. In Chapter 2, we discussed confidentiality and assent to counseling treatment. In Guided Exercise 13.2, consider confidentiality issues and practice asking teen clients to assent to counseling.

Guided Exercise 13.2

Adolescent Confidentiality and Assent to Counseling

Review the section on confidentiality in Chapter 2. In particular, consider the importance of allowing children to assent to counseling interventions. For this particular group of young people, ages 12 to 14, what are their prevailing concerns? Choose a partner and role-play how to ask early adolescents to participate in a counseling intervention of your choice. In developmentally appropriate language, describe confidentiality, the purpose of the counseling interventions, and his or her responsibility to make decisions and act on his or her own behalf as he or she participates (or does not participate) in counseling.

Combining creative approaches described above with talk therapy can allow young adolescents to begin the process of self-reflection and potential behavior and thought modification as needed. These individual approaches can be effective in encouraging adolescents to build their personal self-esteem and social skills that will aid them throughout their lives with parents, teachers, peers, and others. In Case Illustration 13.2, we describe how counseling interventions are applied in a clinical setting with a young adolescent.

Case Illustration 13.2 Mental Health Counseling Case Study

Jaden is a biracial 12-year-old, seventh grader who lives with his mother and two younger siblings. His parents went through a tumultuous divorce when he was 10, and his father moved several states away. He now has limited contact with his father. He was brought to counseling by his mother because of concerns regarding recent changes she is seeing in his behavior. They used to get along well, and he

(Continued)

(Continued)

has been a good big brother to his younger siblings. He has always enjoyed playing basketball and planned to try out for the middle school team when he got to seventh grade. He has always made As and Bs in school but is increasingly disorganized and seems to lose things often.

Lately Jaden's mother has seen these changes in him, and he is not open or willing to talk to her. She states that he no longer wants to try out for the school team, and even more concerning, he has had trouble controlling his anger toward her. He does not associate with his old friends and has made a few friends that don't seem to be a good influence. She is concerned that he may start doing drugs or drinking. She reports that he picks on his siblings and has been progressively more defiant at home. He refuses to do his homework and wants to sleep all the time. When she wakes him up or asks him to do anything around the house, he gets very angry. She is concerned about him because he will not talk about what is going on, and things seem to be escalating.

Jaden appears willing and open to talk to the counselor. He reports that his mother does not understand him and treats him like a baby. She nags him to do everything and does not trust him. He also states that she does not give him any privacy at home and expects him to be the man of the house but treats him like a child. He wishes he could go and live with his father who moved to another state 2 years ago. Whenever he gets the opportunity talk to his father, his father tells Jaden that he can come live with him soon.

When asked about school, Jaden reports that he does not really fit in with a group anymore. He thinks he is too skinny, too short, and he does not like the color of his skin. He reports that he used to be friends with the "popular" kids, but now they tease him and call him "gay." He also reports that he has given up in some classes because the teachers don't like him. He hates going to school and would rather stay home and sleep. He wishes his mother would trust him more and leave him alone.

Jaden is displaying outward signs of distress that are impacting him at home and in school. His apparent withdrawal from friends and activities he previously enjoyed, along with his increasing anger, are symptoms that may indicate issues with depression. The counselor believes that the childhood experience of parental conflict and loss of relationship with his father has contributed to Jaden's current presentation of symptoms. The counselor chooses to explore issues related to Jaden's relationships with his parents and his identity development. Understanding that identity and self-esteem are both delicate at this age, the counselor maintains a strength-based approach to interventions. A family mapping activity is used to collaboratively explore the patterns and dynamics within the family relationships. Cognitive behavioral strategies are used to assist Jaden in identifying and changing maladaptive ideas that are contributing to emotional distress. Along with individual counseling to support Jaden, the counselor recommends family counseling to support the relationship between Jaden and his mother.

Small Group Counseling

Small group counseling is a proven-effective intervention for young adolescents for many of the same reasons it is effective with adults, in addition to other reasons that are specific to young adolescents' levels of cognitive, emotional, behavior, and social development (Akos, Hamm, Mack, & Dunaway, 2007). Groups enable young adolescents to form unique bonds with their peers in a structured and safe environment and help them to understand that their concerns are not unique to them, and that there is nothing "wrong with them." And, as is also the case with small groups with adults, small groups with young adolescents in schools and mental health agencies enable counselors to reach more young people more quickly and at lower costs to families relative to individual counseling.

Overall, small groups that address specific needs in the areas of personal/social and academic goals are appropriate because young adolescents need to belong and interact with each other. Some of the topical areas that are most useful for individuals in this part of the lifespan include exploration of values, self-concept, social skill development, and identity; planning and time management, organization, study skills, and learning styles; understanding and handling conflict with peers and adults; and coping with stress and anger. There are many additional small group topics that can be useful for young adolescents as they face specific life situations such as parental divorce, family financial concerns, grief and loss, and so on.

In general, the Association for Specialists in Group Work recommends that small groups with young adolescents should be semistructured, if not completely structured; should include creative, hands-on activities that facilitate group cohesion and member engagement; and should be time-limited, leader-centered, and usually focused on specific issues and behavioral goals (ASGW, 2007a; ASGW, 2007b; Erford, 2011; Greenberg, 2003). Many of the creative approaches that can be used in individual counseling sessions can also be implemented in small group sessions, including art, music, journaling, and talk therapy. In addition, small group work allows for dyad and triad work within the larger group, allowing for opportunities for members to get to know one another and discuss their commonalities in stages. Finally, small group counseling can allow for affirmations that aid in adolescents understanding that they are not alone in their concerns and experiences and offer new knowledge and skills to help them to excel academically, personally, and socially. Small groups are highly indicated, both in school and clinical settings, to help structure change for early adolescents.

In Guided Exercise 13.3, explore ideas for small groups for varied issues faced by children aged 11 to 14.

Guided Exercise 13.3

Group Counseling With Young Adolescents

Structured groups are carefully planned and time limited. Group sessions are organized around a focused topic and usually follow a set of lessons or activities. Structured groups are scheduled for a specified number of sessions, focus on a single topic, and follow a preestablished agenda. Structured groups are also closed groups, meaning that group members are selected based on similar goals or life experiences, and once the group is established, no new members are invited.

(Continued)

(Continued)

Small counseling groups for children aged 11 to 14 can be structured around many topics: academic support and study skills, social skills, divorce/changing families, grief/loss, or coping with stress and anger (Brigman & Earley Goodman, 2008). Brainstorm with other students in your class about how you would structure a group counseling curriculum for any one of these topics, or one of your choosing, in a setting of your choice. Answer the following questions:

1. What is the purpose of your group?
2. Who would attend? How would you select members?
3. How much time do you need? How long and how often would the group sessions be held?
4. What particular concerns would you have for managing the group dynamics?
5. What are activities you would include?

Classroom Guidance Curriculum Activities

Classroom guidance curriculum activities, which are delivered in schools regularly by school counselors, should aid in the development of academic and personal skills during early adolescence (ASCA, 2012). This allows for smoother transitions at both ends of middle school. Classroom guidance curriculum that first introduces social personal, then moves to academic (college and career readiness skills), and finally career exploration may be more developmentally sound. These classroom interventions are offered to large groups of students and mimic classroom lessons delivered by teachers daily. They can be developed around academic, personal/social, or college and career readiness concerns. School counselors are trained to design, deliver, and evaluate these in-classroom interventions that can be helpful for young adolescents in learning new knowledge and coping skills that can aid them in handling their daily concerns with school, parents, teachers, and peers. Within these lessons, school counselors often employ an educational component as well as experiential activities that help students apply what they have learned in a variety of potential situations that are similar to their daily lives outside of the classroom. Most importantly, school counselors are able to serve a larger group of students and work closely in consultation with parents and teachers.

Consultation With Teachers and Parents

All counselors who work with young adolescents, and other individuals under the age of 18, work in concert with other adults in the adolescents' lives. Consultations with teachers and parents can actually serve as preinterventions and are needed to make sure counselors' interventions used with young adolescents are reinforced in the classroom or at home. This is a critical component for learning about the young adolescents we work with and allows counselors to plan interventions that work with the plasticity these young people experience. In addition, young adolescents can be included in the consultation meetings as appropriate so that they feel a part of the planning of the work they will be doing in counseling, individual or small group.

Peer-Based Interventions

Young adolescents are drawn especially to their peers during this time in their lives and experience an innate need to belong and matter to their friends and other peers (Dixon & Tucker, 2008). Thus, it is likely that the use of peer-based interventions may be additional unique interventions for working with young adolescents. This can be particularly helpful in middle schools when eighth graders may be able to help or guide students in sixth or seventh grades in resolving conflicts, bullying situations that may arise, and other adolescence-related concerns. These peer helpers are trained and supervised by school counselors who offer them the skills and knowledge needed to work with younger students. Students selected for the peer helpers/leaders/mentoring program can be nominated by teachers, administrators, or other students and should be trained in a systemic way, including basic development in communication and conflict resolution skills (ASCA, 2015). In addition, there is evidence that peer tutoring can provide both academic and social/personal support for middle school students (Bowman-Perrott et al., 2013). Peer tutoring primarily focuses on academic issues, but the act of tutoring by another student can provide the tutored student with modeling, self-efficacy, and internal motivation. This is yet another example where young adolescents can be useful in providing facilitative support and modeling that can help school counselors reach more students and can lead to new relationships for all of the adolescents involved.

Many of the counseling approaches and interventions suggested here for use with young adolescents are in response to this unique period of the lifespan. With counselors' appropriate accommodation of the interventions used, counselors can help young adolescents acquire the knowledge, attitudes, and skills for functioning more effectively in their schools, homes, families, and in society.

COUNSELING KEYSTONES

- Young adolescence remains a period of the lifespan filled with developmental struggles and identity individuation for individuals moving through it.

- Developmentally, young adolescents are caught in between elementary and high school, and their experiences are unique and distinct from late childhood and later adolescence.
- Fortunately, counselors working with young adolescents can serve as additional support as individuals navigate their academic, personal, and social goals, ultimately aiding in young adolescents successfully bridging their transitions into later adolescence in meaningful manners and with appropriate guidance and direction.

ADDITIONAL RESOURCES

In Print

Siegle, D. (2013). *Brainstorm: The power and purpose of the teenage brain.* New York, NY: Penguin Putnam.

Additional Bibliotherapy Resources

Davis, D. (2010). *Something is wrong at my house: A book about parents' fighting.* Seattle, WA: Parenting Press.

De la Peña, M. (2009). *We were here.* New York, NY: Delacorte Press.

Juby, S. (2004). *Miss Smithers.* New York, NY: HarperCollins.

Myracle, L. (2009). *Luv ya bunches.* New York, NY: Amulet Books.

Rue, N. (2010). *Motorcycles, sushi and one strange book.* New York, NY: Harper Collins.

Watts, G. (2009). *Hear my roar: A story of family violence.* New York, NY: Annick Press.

Online

American Counseling Association (ACA) Grief reactions over the lifespan: https://www.counseling.org/docs/trauma-disaster/fact-sheet-12---grief-reactions-over-the-life-span.pdf?sfvrsn=2

ASCA, Helping kids during crisis: http://www.schoolcounselor.org/school-counselors-members/professional-development/2015-webinar-series/learn-more/helping-kids-during-crisis

Dr. Dan Siegel's video clips at http://www.drdansiegel.com/resources/video_clips/

Frontline: Inside the teenage brain: http://www.pbs.org/wgbh/pages/frontline/shows/teenbrain

The Dougy Center National Center for Grieving Children & Families' developmental grief responses: http://www.dougy.org/grief-resources/developmental-grief-responses/

REFERENCES

Akos, P., Hamm, J. V., Mack, S., & Dunaway, M. (2007). Utilizing the developmental influence of peers in middle school groups. *Journal for Specialists in Group Work, 32*(1), 51. doi:10.1080/01933920600977648

American School Counselor Association (ASCA). (2012). *ASCA national model for school counseling programs* (3rd ed.). Alexandra, VA: Author.

American School Counselor Association (ASCA). (2015). The school counselor and peer helping programs. Retrieved from https://www.schoolcounselor.org/asca/media/asca/PositionStatements/PS_PeerHelping.pdf

Arnett, J. J. (1999). Adolescent storm and stress, reconsidered. *American Psychologist, 54*(5), 317–326. doi:10.1037/0003-066X.54.5.317

Association for Specialists in Group Work (ASGW). (2007a). Special issue on group work in the school: Innovative thinking and practice to support school improvement initiatives. *The Journal for Specialists in Group Work, 32*(1).

Association for Specialists in Group Work (ASGW). (2007b). Special issue on group work in the school: More innovative thinking and practice to support school improvement initiatives. *The Journal for Specialists in Group Work, 32*(2).

Blakemore, S., Burnett, S., & Dahl, R. E. (2010). The role of puberty in the developing adolescent brain. *Human Brain Mapping 31*, 926–933.

Bowman-Perrott, L., Davis, H., Vannest, K., Williams, L., Greenwood, C., & Parker, P. (2013). Academic benefits of peer tutoring: A meta-analytic review of single-case research. *School Psychology Review, 42(1)*, 39–55.

Brigman, G., & Earley Goodman, B. (2008). *Group counseling for school counselors: A practical guide.* Portland, ME: J. Weston Walch

Brown, D. T., & Prout, H. T. (Eds.). (1989). *Counseling and psychotherapy with children and adolescents: Theory and practice for school and clinic settings* (2nd ed.). Brandon, VT: Clinical Psychology.

Brown, J. D., Halpern, C. T., & L'Engle, K. L. (2005). Mass media as a sexual super peer for early maturing girls. *The Journal of Adolescent Health, 36*(5), 420–427. doi: 10.1016/j.jadohealth.2004.06.003

Buchanan, C. M., & Hughes, J. L. (2009). Construction of social reality during early adolescence: Can expecting storm and stress increase real or perceived storm and stress? *Journal of Research on Adolescence, 19*(2), 261–285.

Burnett, S., Bird, G., Moll, J., Frith, C., & Blakemore, S. (2008). Development during adolescence of the neural processing of social emotion. *Journal of Cognitive Neuroscience 21*(9), 1736–1750.

Chase, D. M., Di Novi, D., Kosove, A., & Johnson, B. (Producers), & Kwapis, K. (Director). (2005). *The sisterhood of the traveling pants* [Motion picture]. Los Angeles, CA: Alcon Entertainment.

Costa, T. L. (2013). *Playing Tyler*. Nottingham, UK: Strange Chemistry Books.

Crick, N. R., & Grotpeter, J. K. (1995). Relational aggression, gender, and social-psychological adjustment. *Child Development, 66*(3), 710–722. doi:10.1111/1467-8624.ep9506152720

Dixon, A. L., & Tucker, C. (2008). Every student matters here: Enhancing strengths-based school counseling through the application of mattering. *Professional School Counseling, 12,* 123–126.

Erford, B. T. (Ed.). (2011). *Group work: Process and applications.* Upper Saddle River, NJ: Pearson.

Erikson, E. H. (1968). *Identity, youth, and crisis.* New York, NY: W. W. Norton.

Finkelhor, D., Turner, H. A., Ormrod, R. K., Hamby, S. L., & Kracke, K. (2009, April). Children's exposure to violence: A comprehensive national survey. *Juvenile Justice Bulletin* (pp. 1–11). Washington, DC: U.S. Department of Justice. doi: 10.1016/0278-2391(95)90744-0

Forbes, E. E., & Dahl, R. E. (2010). Pubertal development and behavior: Hormonal activation of social and motivational tendencies. *Brain and cognition. 72*(1), 66–72.

Gentile, D. A. (2014). *Media violence and children: A complete guide for parents and professionals* (2nd ed.). Westport, CT: Greenwood.

Goldberg, R. M., Smith-Adcock, S., & Dixon, A. L. (2011). The influence of the mass media on relational aggression among females: A feminist counseling perspective. *Journal of Aggression, Maltreatment, & Trauma, 20,* 376–394. doi: 10.1080/10926771.2011.678995

Greenberg, K. R. (2003). *Group counseling in K-12 schools: A handbook for school counselors.* Boston, MA: Allyn and Bacon.

Hollenstein, T., & Lougheed, J. P. (2013). Beyond storm and stress: Typicality, transactions, timing, and temperament to account for adolescent change. *American Psychologist, 68*(6), 444–454. doi:10.1037/a0033586

Kadosh, K., Linden, D. J., & Lau, J. F. (2013). Plasticity during childhood and adolescence: Innovative approaches to investigating neurocognitive development. *Developmental Science, 16*(4), 574–583.

Kaiser Family Foundation. (2001). *Teens and sex: The role of popular TV.* Menlo Park, CA: Author.

Klem, J., Owens, A., Ross, A., Edwards, L., & Cobia, D. C. (2009). Dating violence: Counseling adolescent females from an existential perspective. *Journal of Humanistic Counseling, Education, and Development, 48(1),* 48–64.

Konrad, K., Firk, C., & Uhlhaas, P. J. (2013). Brain development during adolescence. *Deutsches Aerzteblatt International, 110*(25), 425–431.

Mäkinen, M., Puukko-Viertomies, L., Lindberg, N., Siimes, M.A., & Aalberg, V. (2012). Body dissatisfaction and body mass in girls and boys transitioning from early to mid-adolescence: Additional role of self-esteem and eating habits. *BMC Psychiatry, 12,* 35.

Marcia, J. E. (1967). Ego identity status: Relationship to change in self-esteem, general "maladjustment," and authoritarianism. *Journal of Personality, 35*(1), 118.

Matusov, E., DePalma, R., & Smith, M. (2010). The creation and maintenance of a "learning loving minority" in conventional high schools: A research-based response to John Ogbu. *Oxford Review of Education, 36*(4), 463–480.

Michaels, L. (Producer), & Waters, M. (Director). (2004). *Mean girls* [Motion picture]. Hollywood, CA: Paramount Pictures.

Olweus, D. (1993). *Bullying at school: What we know and what we can do.* Oxford, UK; Cambridge, US: Blackwell.

Osterman, K. F. (2000). Students' need for belonging in the school community. *Review of Educational Research,* (3), 323.

Ostrov, J. M., Hart, E. J., Kamper, K. E., & Godleski, S. E. (2011). Relational aggression in women during emerging adulthood: A social process model. *Behavioral Sciences and the Law, 29(5),* 695–710.

Petty, K., & Firmin, C. (1992). *Being bullied.* London, UK: Bracken Books.

Piaget, J. (1954). *The construction of reality in the child* (Margaret Cook, Trans.). New York, NY: Basic Books.

Pledge, D. S. (2004). *Counseling adolescents and children: Developing your clinical style.* Australia; Belmont, CA : Thomson/Wadsworth.

Pollack, W. S. (1998). *Real boys: Rescuing our sons from the myths of boyhood.* New York, NY: Random House.

Powell, M., & Ladd, L. (2010). Bullying: a review of the literature and implications for family therapists. *American Journal of Family Therapy, 38*(3), 189–206. doi:10.1080/01926180902961662

Roskos, E. (2013). *Dr. Bird's advice for sad poets.* Boston, MA: Houghton Mifflin Harcourt.

Ryan, A. M., & Shim, S. (2008). An exploration of young adolescents' social achievement goals and social adjustment in middle school. *Journal of Educational Psychology, 100*(3), 672–687. doi:10.1037/0022-0663.100.3.672

Stallard, P., Spears, M., Montgomery, A. A., Phillips, R., & Sayal, K. (2013). Self-harm in young adolescents (12-16 years): Onset and short-term continuation in a community sample. *BMC Psychiatry, 13*(1), 1–25. doi:10.1186/1471-244X-13-328

Steensma, T., Kreukels, B., de Vries, A., & Cohen-Kettenis, P. (2014). Gender identity development in adolescence. *Hormones and Behavior, 64*(2), 288–297. doi: 10.1016/j.yhbeh.2013.02.020

Veselska, Z., Geckova, A. M., Gajdosova, B., Orosova, O., Van Dijk, J. P., & Reijneveld, S.A. (2010). Socio-economic differences in self-esteem of adolescents influenced by personality, mental health and social support. *European Journal of Public Health 20*(6), 647–652.

Vygotsky, L. S. (1978). In M. Cole, V. John-Steiner, S. Scribner, & E. Souberman (Ed.), *Mind in society: The development of higher psychological processes*. Cambridge, MA: Harvard University Press.

Weber, D., & Kurpius, S. R. (2011). The importance of self-beliefs on relational aggression of college students. *Journal of Interpersonal Violence, 26*(13), 2735–2743.

Wolfe, D. A., Jaffe, P. G., & Crooks, C. V. (2006). *Adolescent risk behaviors: Why teens experiment and strategies to keep them safe*. New Haven, CT: Yale University Press.

Chapter 14

Counseling With Older Adolescents (15–19)

Derrick Paladino and Leigh DeLorenzi

The hardest thing about adolescence is that everything seems too big.
There's no way to get context or perspective. Pain and joy without limits.
No one can live like that forever, so experience finally comes to our rescue.
We come to know what we can endure, and also that nothing endures.

—Sara Paretsky, *Bleeding Kansas*

INTRODUCTION

Late adolescence is a time in human development when a young person is transitioning from dependency to autonomy. As with previous generations, the primary task of growing into adulthood is to develop a sense of identity and social connectedness. This can also be a confusing and stressful time for older adolescents who have spent most of their lives relying on caregivers for instruction and assistance when making choices, with cultural practices, parenting styles, and peer relationships heavily influencing this transition. People in late adolescence benefit from strong support and understanding as they begin to make key decisions in the areas of relationships, education, careers, and lifestyle practices that could having a lasting impact on their lives for years to come.

This chapter gives an overview of the older adolescent through a developmental, cultural, and clinical lens.

Specifically, at the end of this chapter, you will be able to

- understand the unique characteristics and strengths of the older adolescent,
- understand the neurological changes that occur during late adolescence,
- understand various identity development assumptions and experiences as applied to the older adolescent,
- enhance your knowledge regarding specific issues connected to the millennial and postmillennial generations, and
- build clinical knowledge and skills for counseling the older adolescent.

A TIME OF RAPID GROWTH AND CHANGE

While individuals in late adolescence may appear to be adults on the outside, their brains are still developing in important areas related to decision making, impulse control, and reasoning (U.S. Health and Human Services, 2001), leaving caregivers feeling frustrated, worried, and helpless when confronted with high-risk behaviors and suboptimal decision making. Sneaking out after hours, speeding while driving, mood swings, fighting in school, poor attention in class, talking back to authority figures, engaging in unprotected sex, and experimenting with drugs or alcohol are only a few examples of high-risk behavior that are often identified as reasons for counseling referrals. Findings from the National Youth Risk Behavior Survey (YRBS) show that 70% of adolescent deaths result from motor vehicle crashes, bodily injuries, homicide, or suicide (Eaton et al., 2012), highlighting the need for counselors to better engage and support adolescents and their caregivers through these transitional years. Moreover, because symptoms for many mental disorders first appear in adolescence (U.S. Health and Human Services, 2001), it is important for counselors to understand the role of brain development on a client's presenting concerns.

Behaviors historically blamed on raging hormones are often better explained in the context of genes, childhood experiences, environment, and brain development. Late adolescence is a time when the brain is undergoing a massive reorganization of neuronal connections. The area of the brain that governs decision making, impulse control, and reasoning (i.e., the prefrontal cortex) is the last part of the brain to fully mature. According to researchers, brain immaturity, coupled with lower levels of dopamine, causes adolescents to feel understimulated by activities that used to thrill them in childhood (Giedd, 2011). The early maturation of subcortical brain areas and delayed maturation of the prefrontal control areas result in a period of neural imbalance (Konrad, Firk, & Uhlhaas, 2013). As a result, adolescents may seek greater behavioral risks in order to experience their previous childhood levels of excitement (Powell, 2006). Furthermore, the transition from puberty into adulthood involves the production of gonadotropin releasing hormone (GnRH) neurons, leading to increases in gonadal steroid hormones. These processes work together to remodel and activate neural circuits in the adolescent brain, creating increases in sexual interest and behaviors (Sisk & Foster, 2004).

In addition to changes in the brain, adolescents are influenced by home environments and social structure in a manner that forces them to question, "Who am I?" and "Am I allowed to be who I want to be?" Older adolescents may find themselves in a tug-of-war between developing their identities and forces of autonomy. The social environment of late adolescents stretches their sense of identity, while the home and familial environment may simultaneously constrict it. Furthermore, older adolescents experience intense personal exploration within the areas of sexual, moral, social, cultural, spiritual, gender, and religious identities.

Guided Exercise 14.1

Introduction: The following illustrates the case of Jeff. Jeff is an 18-year-old White sophomore studying at a community college in his hometown. In addition, he lives with his parents who are paying his tuition and living expenses (e.g., car, car insurance, lives and eats at home for free). We encounter Jeff partway through his first session.

Dr. Rood: Jeff, from what I'm hearing it sounds like you are experiencing confusion around what your parents have raised you to believe and what you have been encountering since your time at college.

Jeff: They are VERY strict when it comes to our faith, and I guess my doubt started a couple of years ago. The friends I've met at school come from religious backgrounds that are different from mine, and they're awesome people. I can't sit in front of them and believe that they're all going to hell, as my mom would say. They are good people.

Dr. Rood: It sounds like your friends are making your question your faith, the faith you grew up with.

Jeff: I guess. I mean, I would never tell them that. Who knows how they would react.

Dr. Rood: Jeff, what do you think your parents would say if they knew you were struggling with these thoughts?

Jeff: Probably, "You're cut off!" So there's no way they're hearing this from me. I can't afford college and a car. You have to understand, the level of connectedness my entire family has to our church, it . . . it would just destroy them.

Dr. Rood: I'm hearing a few things here, Jeff. On the one hand, your experiences as of late and the wonderful friends you've made have brought out a "wondering" if your faith is the correct one for you. On the other hand, I can tell that you care about your parents and worry about how they would take this news. Needing their support, financially, throws in wrench in this for you as well.

(Continued)

(Continued)

Reflection and Discussion: Reflect on how Jeff's environments are affecting him. What are the specific environments of significance to him? What are the realities of these environments? What is his struggle between them? Placing yourself in Jeff's shoes, what are your feelings, thoughts, and beliefs regarding your current situation? Finally, placing yourself in Dr. Rood's shoes, what are your overall thoughts on how to work with Jeff? What might be some counseling goals, and how will you assist Jeff in this exploration?

Two major social transitions occur between early adolescence (ages 12–14) and late adolescence (ages 15–18) (Tanti, Stukas, Halloran, & Foddy, 2011). Early adolescents experience a major transition from primary school to secondary school, and older adolescents experience another transition from secondary school to college or work. As older adolescents transition to college or work, they experience fluctuations in autonomy. Autonomy can be experienced in many ways, as the postsecondary transition is different for every person. For example, an individual entering the workforce without his or her family's financial support may experience greater autonomy. Autonomy can also be experienced as a construct of confusion for the individual who is attending college away from home but is fully financially supported by his or her guardians. In both of these cases, the individual is struggling with what Erikson (1993) discusses as issues of identity exploration and creation and role confusion. This time of transition (i.e., when one moves toward becoming an independent adult) can be greatly affected by, but not limited to, variables such as financial means, parental expectations, educational limitations, and motivation. In addition, even after an individual chooses a direction (e.g., work, school, both, or neither), the above factors can have a great effect on success and longevity. For example, if one is accepted into a 4-year college with a full academic scholarship, he or she may still run into variables such as university alienation (Burbach, 1972; Burbach & Thompson, 1971) and cultural congruity (Gloria & Robinson Kurpious, 1996) that can impact his or her experience and success.

Tanti et al. (2011) found that peer groups influence the transition from dependency to autonomous adult functioning, stating that older adolescents experience, "some relative change in their social identity in response to the significant change in social context they experience" (p. 557). Practitioners working with adolescents should avoid making overgeneralizations about the adolescent experience because of the complex interplay between age, individual maturity, and differing peer group influences. Furthermore, important cognitive, behavioral, and affective differences among older adolescents make it crucial to view later adolescence as its own unique stage. The next few sections discuss the concepts of psychosocial and cultural identity development in late adolescence.

MODELS OF ADOLESCENT IDENTITY DEVELOPMENT

Stages of Psychosocial Development

Pioneering developmental theorists agreed that younger adolescents react differently from older adolescents to the emergence of autonomy (Erikson, 1959; Marcia, 1966; Chickering, 1969). More often than younger adolescents, older adolescents face heightened pressure to make key decisions in the areas of (a) what they stand for, (b) where they find importance, (c) who they choose to partner with in platonic and romantic relationships, and (d) what will become their life's work and mission (Schwartz, Zamboanga, Meca, & Ritchie, 2012). Erik Erikson (1959, 1968, 1993) highlighted a similar decision-making process in his model explaining psychosocial stages and transitions that occur across the life span. Erikson described eight periods when psychological and biological changes occur and are influenced by sociocultural demands that span from caregivers to peers. In particular, the stage of identity versus role confusion sheds light on adolescent identity and challenges.

According to Erikson (1993), identity versus role confusion spans the ages of approximately 12 to 19 and is a psychosocial stage during which adolescents begin their exploration into and development of identity. Erikson suggests that adolescents begin to explore and discover (a) their identities within the context of their social lives (e.g., "with whom do I best fit in?") and (b) their identities within the context of their abilities and goals. As adolescents begin to explore these possibilities, they gain a sense of who they are within their core sense of self. He further explains this ideology, "The sense of ego identity, then, is the accrued confidence that one's ability to maintain inner sameness and continuity (one's ego and psychological sense) is matched by the sameness and continuity of one's meaning for others" (Erikson, 1993, p. 94). Should the adolescent fail to develop this clear sense of identity and purpose, he or she falls into identity diffusion, causing him or her to overidentify or even lose his or her identity due to the failure to commit. However, individuals do not become stuck in a particular stage; rather, they carry these traits with them into the next stage of psychosocial development until it is rectified. In the older adolescent, this crisis becomes magnified because he or she has less time to acclimate to a more autonomous life, which may include college, work, and/or a separation from caregivers.

Guided Exercise 14.2

With Whom Do I Best Fit In?

Direction: Erikson suggests that adolescents experience the psychosocial stage, "identity versus role confusion"—a time when they begin their identity exploration. In order to make a more empathic connection to your older adolescent client, this exercise will allow you to reconnect with yourself during that time. Reflect on your time between ages 15 to 19 (i.e., high school through early college). Think about your experiences, what you accomplished, what you tried, barriers you overcame, what you were curious about, and any additional events or milestones that occurred during this time. Most importantly, think about who you were with during these experiences.

With Whom Do I Best Fit In?				
Social groups I identified with and/or was a part of	Why I became a part of these groups	Impact of these groups then	Impact of these groups now	How this experience can be transferred to client empathy

Identity Status Theory

James Marcia (1966) was another influential theorist in the area of identity formation and ego development. Marcia focused his work on the older adolescent by viewing Erikson's theoretical notions on identity formation through an empirical lens. Marcia (1980) suggested that an individual's identity formation is created through an intertwining experience of two key variables: (a) exploration (i.e., crisis versus no crisis) and (b) commitment (i.e., commitment versus no commitment). The exploration variable "involves the questioning of values and goals defined by parents [or caregivers] and weighing various identity alternatives and their potential repercussions" (Evans, Forney, Guido, Patton, & Renn, 2010, p. 52). For example, the parents of a 17-year-old Myles pressure him to choose their college alma mater as his next educational step. This pressure, according to Marcia, may (or may not) place Myles in crisis, ushering in a period of internal exploration that could include questioning, immediately accepting, or rejecting his parents' wishes. As Myles moves toward a decision (or nondecision) he next enters into the commitment variable. Evans et al. (2010) state, "Individuals that have solidified their commitments have made conscious decisions about which they are confident . . . not only do they confirm their goals, they also take action toward realizing them" (p. 52). In the example above, Myles might commit to attend his parents' college alma mater, or he may choose to attend another school. There is also the possibility that Myles will forgo college and choose to go straight into the workforce. The variables of exploration (crisis versus no crisis) and commitment (commitment versus no commitment) are what Marcia (1966) used to identify four distinct categories of identity status in adolescents: foreclosure, moratorium, identity diffusion, and identity achievement.

Foreclosure. Marcia defined foreclosure as an adolescent avoiding any crisis and settling on a commitment. Individuals in the foreclosure status experience a lack of a crisis period, "yet have firm, often parentally determined commitments" (Marcia, 1967, p. 119). Most individuals in this status accept their parental suggestions, plans, and values without question and become the individual that others have intended them to become (Evans et al., 2010; Marcia, 1966, 2002), thus firming their ideology and not requiring any exploration. It is the "endorsement of authoritarian values" (Marcia, 1966, p. 557) that leads our older adolescent, Myles, to choose his parents alma mater without question or thought. He is firm in his commitment, though he may not have personal awareness surrounding it.

Moratorium. On the other hand, an adolescent in the midst of crisis (exploration) leading to no commitment falls within the moratorium status. The crisis period leaves the adolescent with rather vague commitments as he or she is in an active struggle searching for answers (Marcia, 1966). Moratorium comes with an active questioning of parental wishes and values. These are still seen as significant to the adolescent, but he or she is working diligently to examine alternatives and negotiate a compromise between his or her parents, society, and personal capabilities (Marcia, 1966, 2002). In this identity status, Myles would be actively grappling with his decision to apply to or forgo attending his parents' college alma mater. Since this is an ongoing exploration,

Myles may find himself traveling, getting a job, or perhaps doing nothing while he makes up his mind. In many cases, the moratorium stage gives way to identity achievement because the exploration eventually comes to an end after alternatives are fully explored (Marcia, 2002).

Identity diffusion. When an adolescent experiences neither crisis nor commitment, he or she is said to be in the state of identity diffusion. These individuals either "refuse to or are unable to firmly commit" (Evans et al., 2010, p. 54). Because the adolescent has not entered into a crisis, the lack of commitment is filled with aimless wandering with little to no concern about the outcome (Marcia, 1966, 2002). This individual is "either uninterested in ideological matters or takes a smorgasbord approach in which one outlook seems as good to him as another" (Marcia, 1966, p. 552). This indecisive attitude allows the adolescent to go with the flow and take the path of least resistance. If Myles was in this identify status, he would not recognize his parents' wishes and values as a crisis. Moreover, he would likely lack the appearance of identity achievement that can be found in the foreclosure identity status (Marcia, 1967). These individuals lack an identity as well as a secure sense of self (Marcia, 2002), so there is a high probability that Myles would go along with whatever his parents wished but then change, without concern, when something new came along.

Identity achievement. Lastly, when adolescents experience a crisis and make a commitment to ideology, they are said to be in the identity achievement status (Marcia, 1967). This identity status is distinguished by a strong ego identity within the individual. The adolescent has the ability to tolerate a stressful experience for a longer period of time due to his or her strong ego identity and aspirational drive (Marcia, 1966). In this identity status, Myles would be able to explore his parents' wishes and his own from a place of comfortable crisis. He may require information, but an individual in this status infrequently requires guidance (Marcia, 2002). Discerning between all alternatives, Myles would have the ability to make a commitment regarding his parents' hopes of him attending their alma mater that reflected his own goals, values, and beliefs.

Developmental Vectors

As older adolescents move forward in their identity development, they often encounter the issue of competence. Chickering (1978) is well known for his college student development model, and while not every older adolescent will transition to higher learning, the essence of his model can still be applied. Chickering posited that students encounter the following seven vectors: (a) achieving competence, (b) managing emotions, (c) becoming autonomous, (d) establishing identity, (e) freeing interpersonal relationships, (f) clarifying purposes, and (g) developing integrity. Because this theory is examined closely in the next chapter, only the first vector will be briefly introduced here. Achieving competence is a task that all older adolescents will encounter regardless of whether they enter into the work force or attend college. Chickering (1978) believed that competence is identified as the confidence in one's ability to cope with what he or she is faced with as well as the ability to achieve success. The vector of achieving competence is made up of three main components: (a) intellectual competence, (b) physical and manual skills, and (c) interpersonal competence. These components have tasks including knowledge and skills, critical thinking and reasoning, comprehension, attention to wellness, manual activities, communication and social skills, and leadership ability (Chickering and Reisser, 1993). As competence increases, the older adolescent is poised to achieve in other vectors or areas of his or her life.

Identity development models (Erikson, 1959; Marcia, 1966; Chickering, 1969) serve as an important conceptual foundation for practitioners working with any older adolescent. Counselors should understand that identity development models are sometimes normed on a single population. Developmental issues such as autonomy and competence can vary considerably based on the intersection of identities. An adolescent's racial, cultural, ethnic, gender, and sexual identity may differ from the models' normed population, thus clinicians should be mindful not to use direct comparisons between their clients and the identity development models.

TOWARD A GLOBAL UNDERSTANDING OF ADOLESCENT IDENTITY DEVELOPMENT

It is important to note that many historical identity development models fail to adequately address the role of culture and ecological influences; constructs that significantly impact many parts of identity development. To better illustrate this idea, let's reexamine the case of Myles through the lens of Marcia's (1966) theory of identity status. If Myles belongs to a culture where it is expected that he follow his parents' values and authoritarian rearing, then foreclosure would be the expected identity status. If Myles were to go against his expected cultural values and practices, the discussion on the theoretical variables of crisis and exploration becomes much more complex.

Examining the influence of culture and ecology within identity development is best accomplished through exploring different racial and cultural populations. One population of note that is significantly connected to varied identity development experiences is the multiracial population. Other name iterations of this group are biracial, mixed-race, mixed-heritage, and multiple heritage. The 2000 Census recorded 6.8 million multiracial individuals (2.4% of the population), rising to slightly over 9 million (2.9% of the population) in 2010. Moreover, about 92% of people who self-identified as multiracial reported exactly two races. With the population rising, more research and clinical knowledge is needed in this area. In addition, a 20% increase of interracial marriages since the 2000 Census yields a proportional increase of multiple heritage decedents from this population (U.S. Census Bureau, 2010). What makes this population significant for clinical consideration with older adolescents is the incredible amount of variance in developmental experiences that come along with diverse racial and cultural backgrounds. Even if an older adolescent does not identify as multiracial, an ecological framework speaks directly to the influences and contexts in which he or she lives. Counseling with any older adolescent through the lens of a multiracial older adolescent allows the counselor to view the client through multiple contexts and ultimately pulls away bias and stereotype in counseling to allow the client to be the expert on how his or her environment, family, and cultural background is influencing his or her development or presenting issue. The section that follows further describes this population in relationship to their identity development journey.

Though research has been increasing, much remains to be learned about this growing population—especially as it relates to the adolescent experience of multiracial individuals. It was not until the 2000 Census that individuals were given the option to self-identify as belonging to more than one race. Prior to this, the only other identifiers were mulatto (1890–1920), quadroon, and octoroon (1890)—labels that were created to ensure that mixed individuals with African ancestry would not fall into the White category (Henriksen & Paladino, 2009). This can be traced back to the "one-drop rule" (or the rule of hypodescent) in which individuals who had "one drop" of Black blood were forced to identify themselves as Black or another minority ethnicity (Davis, 1991; Wehrly, Kenney, & Kenney, 1999). In addition, it was not until 1967 in the landmark civil rights case of *Loving vs. Virginia* (1967) that the antimiscegenation statute (a law criminalizing interracial marriage) was deemed unconstitutional. Needless to say, this history caused a lot of mistrust and identity confusion amongst the multiracial population.

Multiracial adolescents may come from parents who are multiracial themselves or who each hold a different monoracial identity. Either way, multiracial adolescents experience their world through their own unique lenses, and their navigation of society begins at a very young age. One's culture, identity, and developmental level intertwine, shaping how he or she interacts with and perceives the world. Harris and Sim (2002) conducted a study that explored youth living with multiple racial identities within varied contexts. In their study, they discovered that 8.6% of youth reported being multiracial at home or in school, and only 1.6% identified themselves as multiracial in both contexts. Though this study solely focused on race, it is important to note the impact one's ecological world can have on disclosure and comfort with identity. Parents, guardians, extended family, peers, and teachers all may create certain biases in their worlds, and due to this, multiple heritage youth must carefully examine which environments are safe regarding any identity exposure. All of these constructs make up a significant component of the older adolescent's world and are variables that affect decisions they make through their identity development process.

Identity Development in a Multiracial World

Identity development models (IDMs) describe some of the experiences multiracial individuals encounter and their decision process in self-identifying. This can be a complex process for the individual and was described as early as 1937 by Everett Stonequist in *The Marginal Man*. Stonequist (1937) described the multiracial individual or "marginal man," as someone who is condemned to live in two societies that differ. His depiction illustrates a suffering individual who struggles to navigate between two antagonistic worlds and differs in culture from his or her biological parents. Though this piece was written many years ago, it still connects to the potential struggle that some multiracial individuals experience. There has been an evolution of IDMs in examining both the struggle and strength of this population. Carlos Poston (1990) created a linear IDM that focuses on the biracial individual or a person that identifies as only two races. Since then, theorists such as Root (1999, 2002) and Henriksen and Paladino (2009) have viewed multiracial and multiple heritage development from a more ecological and fluid position.

Ecological Model of Racial Identity Development

Furthering this idea of ecological world, culture, and identity development, Maria Root (1994) introduced six major themes that impact the experience of multiple heritage individuals: uniqueness, acceptance and belonging, physical appearance, sexuality, self-esteem, and identity. These themes not only affect the way these individuals interact with the world, but they can have a large impact on identity development. Older adolescents encounter these variables as they develop, but as we examine the influence of culture, we see how complex adolescent identity development can be. The first theme, *uniqueness*, consists of feelings that one is different and is constantly misunderstood. The multiple heritage individual may feel like no one else can relate to his or her experience living with multiple identities. This experience has the potential to influence the individual's behaviors to align with the majority population. The *acceptance and belonging* theme is a concept related to feeling accepted and connected to environment, peers, family, and the dominant society. When there is low connectivity to the above domains, there is a high potential for the emergence of feeling isolated and alienated. The multiple heritage individual struggles to find fit. The *physical appearance* theme generates beliefs that one does not look like the dominant or minority population. These individuals believe they need to continually explain their personal background and race. In addition, individuals may believe that they cannot fully belong to any specific racial or cultural group. The fourth theme, *sexuality*, is commonly associated with women. It rests on the myth that mixed heritage women are more desirable than their single heritage or monoracial peers, and it can affect how they relate to peers and enter relationships. The *self-esteem* theme interacts with all themes. "Much of a person's self-esteem comes from feeling special, valued, connected and accepted" (Root, 1994, p. 471). Therefore, if there are negative personal experiences in the aforementioned themes, it is likely that self-esteem will be affected. Finally, the last theme is *identity*. This theme relates to feeling connected with and a part of one's multiracial heritage or the larger synthesized multiple heritage identity.

Root's (1999, 2002) ecological model of racial identity development speaks to the influence of the multiracial individual's ecological world on identity development. Root adds the contexts gender, class, sexual orientation, and regional and generational history of race and ethnic relations to basic identity development. These are looked at through lenses of family functioning and socialization, racial and ethnic identity, traits and aptitudes, community attitudes and racial socialization, and phenotype and are further broken down by additional variables.

Multiple Heritage Identity Development Model

Henriksen and Paladino's (2009) multiple heritage identity development model (MHID), which is based on Henriksen's (2000) study, offers a nonlinear model through which to view multiple heritage identity. For the purposes of this model, a multiple heritage individual is described as one who is exploring different heritages and combinations of identities such as ethnicity, gender, sexual orientation, national origin, religion/spirituality, indigenous heritage, and language. With the fluidity of this model, the MHID can be applied to individuals of any age. In addition, periods can be experienced concurrently and recycled as additional experiences are encountered. The MHID contains six periods: neutrality, acceptance, awareness, experimentation, transition, and recognition (Henriksen & Paladino, 2009). When applied to older adolescents, the MHID illuminates the ever-changing influences of this age group and allows for a deeper and more multifaceted understanding of their experiences from a counseling standpoint. The ecological model of racial identity development (Root, 1999, 2002) and the MHID (Henriksen & Paladino, 2009) also assist when selecting clinical interventions and approaches for the older adolescent.

Case Illustration 14.1

Amanda

Amanda is a 16-year-old junior at Stevenson High School in Michigan. Her father, Jerry, is Caucasian, and her mother, Juanita (who is from the Philippines), identifies as Filipino. She lives in a small town where her mother is one of the few minorities, and her high school has roughly 500 students attending it with the majority being White. Amanda attends counseling at her high school because she is experiencing pressure from her parents to select a college that specializes in engineering. Her parents are both successful electrical engineers and believe that "this is the correct path" for her life. Amanda feels conflicted about this, as her actual passions are acting, improv, and music-aspirations that are constantly dismissed by her parents. "I'm struggling to find a way to just tell them that engineering isn't for me. I mean, I'm very good at those subjects, it's that I just don't care enough about them." Amanda wants to be able to attend a school for the performing arts.

In the first session Amanda becomes quiet and begins to cry. She discloses that her mother and father exercise an authoritarian parenting style. "Whatever they say, goes!" Additionally, Amanda reports difficulty fitting in with some of her peers due to the way she looks. "Most of the kids at my school have the same kind of look. And here I am . . . the outsider. It's exhausting having to continually explain that my parents come from two different places, so sometimes I just lie and tell people I'm White." She says she wishes she looked more like her Caucasian father—a sentiment that has caused additional strain with her Filipino mom, Juanita. She admits that she has never talks to her parents about race and only knows about her mother's background through stories told by that side of the family. "I have so much going on that I just don't feel ready for the world."

ISSUES AND CONCERNS: LATE ADOLESCENCE IN THE POSTMILLENNIAL GENERATION

Mental Health Research

The millennial and postmillennial generations, also known as *Generation Y, the Selfie Generation*, or the *Digital Natives* (Caumont, 2014), face a unique set of challenges in adolescence when compared to previous generations. Twenge (2011) concluded in his analysis of historical patterns of adolescent mental health that the current incidence of youth mental health disorders is "unacceptably high" (p. 469), with consistent evidence demonstrating a sharp rise in anxiety, depression, and other mental health issues. While more serious problems, such as suicide and depression, have decreased in some studies, feeling overwhelmed and psychosomatic complaints have continued to increase. The rise of antidepressant use and talk therapy may account for the stabilization of some of these numbers (Twenge, 2011).

Recent research highlights the importance of identifying mental health issues, such as depression and anxiety, in late adolescence because they can predict the onset of related mental health disorders in adulthood (Wolitzky-Taylor et al., 2014).

Yet mental health issues, such as depression, in late adolescence are missed by practitioners more frequently than in adults (Leaf et al., 1996), possibly because of a barrage of other related symptoms that appear to be the primary presenting problem, such as mood reactivity, eating disorders, academic problems, substance abuse, or unexplained physical symptoms (Thapar, Colishaw, Pine, & Thapar, 2012). Moreover, depression in adolescents is a major risk factor for suicide, which is ranked by varying sources as either the second or third leading cause of death in this age group (Windfuhr et al., 2008).

The effects of stressful life events and associated emotions have a measurable impact on the adolescent brain. For example, daily life stress and negative emotions, specifically sadness and loneliness, in late adolescence are related to major depressive disorder, hypothalamic-pituitary-adrenal (HPA) axis functioning, and fluctuating cortisol levels (Doane et al., 2013). Researchers also found a link between stressful childhood environments and the development of anxiety in late adolescence. Factors such as certain parenting styles, peer victimization from bullying, parent history of depression and anxiety, and chronic feelings of frustration and loss of control in childhood were identified as risk indicators of anxiety in late adolescence (van Oort, Greaves-Lord, Ormel, Verhulst, & Huizink, 2011).

Studies reveal a stigma exists among adolescents seeking out mental health services, especially for males (Chandra & Minkovitz, 2006). An adolescent's dependency on caregivers can present challenges in the therapeutic environment, especially if the source of the adolescent's distress is the inability to escape from a chaotic environment in his or her home. During late adolescence, mixed messages about autonomy with caregivers both encouraging them to make decisions for themselves, while simultaneously monitoring (and vetoing) those decisions can lead to increased confusion and conflict. Some adolescents are powerless to exercise autonomous decision making in their own lives if they are required to garner parental compliance for job, educational, and relationship choices. Furthermore, given that most adolescents are financially dependent on caregivers, their entrance into counseling oftentimes requires parental involvement. The inherent dependence of adolescent clients on their caregivers brings forth important considerations for the clinical relationship. These issues are further discussed later in the chapter.

Adolescent Relationships in a Virtual World

Because an adolescent's social world is of paramount importance in late adolescence (Larson & Hartl, 2013), it is crucial for clinicians to understand how the modern adolescent connects to his or her peer group. Today's adolescents spend hours every day nurturing social relationships within a technological landscape. In our technology-driven society, communication and interactional patterns between adolescents have changed more in the last 10 years than in the preceding 500 years (Giedd,

2011). With the invention of technological gadgets, cellular smart phones, and tablets, today's adolescents are plugged into and immersed in technology as a primary form of communication with the world around them. These patterns of communication and engagement are markedly different than previous generations, as individuals born in the mid to late 1990s have never known a world without computers.

Labeled the *digital natives*, these adolescents are averaging 11.5 hours of media time a day—a figure that is increasing steadily (Giedd, 2011). Polls show that more than 50% of adolescents visit a social media site more than once a day, with 22% of adolescents logging on to their favorite social media site more than 10 times a day (Common Sense Media, 2009). Due to the fast pace of social media innovation, this list will likely change quickly. With over 75% of adolescents owning cell phones, the emotional and social development of today's adolescents is influenced by technology (O'Keeffe, Clarke-Pearson, & Council on Communications and Media, 2011).

Guided Exercise 14.3

Tortured by Technology

Directions: Read the following case example, and make a list of all the ways technology might be influencing the client's life.

Lydia is a 16-year-old Caucasian adolescent who was referred to you for counseling by her mother. During the first session, you observe that Lydia seems somber. She rarely makes eye contact with you and fidgets with her hands while you explain the counseling process to her. After a period of silence, you hear a buzzing sound coming from her chair. She perks up, quickly grabs her cell phone, and spends a moment reading through a stream of incoming texts. Each buzz sound indicates she has received a new text, and the constant stream of buzzing does not stop for 30 to 45 seconds. Her eyes get narrow, she frowns, and then slams the phone down on her lap. You check in with her about it.

Counselor: That's a cool phone. Is that one of those new models that just came out last week?

Lydia: Yea. My mom got it for me for my birthday last week.

Counselor: How do you like it so far?

Lydia: (Sighs) Well . . . it should be exciting, but it's sort of making my life miserable.

Counselor: Miserable?

Lydia: Yea. I can't go 5 minutes without my phone exploding with texts. Ever since . . . *(her eyes look down and she begins to cry)*

Counselor: Ever since what, Lydia?

Lydia: *(Wiping her tears with her hand)* I guess that's why I'm here. I should never have joined that dating website.

(Continued)

(Continued)

Counselor: You're regretting a decision you made to join a dating website. Tell me more.

Lydia: It's called cupidarrow.com. Haven't you seen the commercials?

Counselor: I think I remember those commercials. But do they have a dating section for adolescents? I thought it was an adult dating website. Then again, I'm not up to date on the latest technology.

Lydia: I made myself a profile and lied about my age. It doesn't cost any money, so my mom didn't know about it. At school . . . boys don't really know I'm alive. But when I joined cupidarrow.com, guys seemed to love me. They asked me questions and complimented me. For once, it felt like I wasn't invisible. And it was easier for me to talk to a guy without having to be in the same room with him. There were no awkward moments. I could just take my time and write emails, maybe even flirt if the guy was cute. I've never had confidence like that with the boys at school, so I thought it was a good thing. Until . . .

Counselor: Until . . .

Lydia: His name is Asher. He's 17 and goes to the high school in the next town over. I was excited to talk to a guy my own age. He is pretty much drop dead gorgeous, and I really started to like him. I gave him my phone number, and we started texting almost every day. My mom was always complaining that I never looked up from my phone all day, but that's how moms are. He friended me on Facebook, Instagram, and Vine. He even started following my photography blog. He knew I loved photography and would always leave the nicest comments about my photos.

Counselor: It sounds like you were excited to meet someone you connect with.

Lydia: I was! When he texted asking to be my boyfriend, I was so excited to finally change my relationship status to "in a relationship" on Facebook. After that happened, everyone started paying attention to me. I would show the girls at school his profile pictures, and they were all so excited for me. Even though I'd never met him before, I was becoming more popular for having this hot new boyfriend. *(Her eyes fill with tears again)*

Counselor: I can see you are feeling really sad as you talk about this.

Lydia: I'm so embarrassed! He turned out to be a huge jerk! *(She sobs)* He asked me to send him a naked picture of myself, and I did. He would pressure me via text to send him pictures every day. I was nervous at first, but after I would send them, he would say the nicest things to me. Even that he loved me.

Counselor: I see.

Lydia: It was all a lie. Asher texted the photos I sent him to his friends, and they posted them online! Now everyone at his high school and my high school have seen them. The police found out that I was 16, and now I'm in trouble with my school and my parents. My friends aren't talking to me. They ignore me at school and post awful things online about me, saying I'm a slut. And all these texts you're hearing? *(she holds up the phone)* These are just random numbers from kids at school—they all say the same thing. "You're a slut" or "You're a whore." I never want to show my face again. I wish we could just move!

While research shows the human brain adapts well to changing environments (Giedd, 2011), daily interactions among adolescents via technology are shaping cultural practices. Studies also show that steep increases in screen time are ushering in a new set of challenges for adolescents, including decreased face-to-face contact, increased sedentary lifestyles, cyberbulling, changing social skills, increased isolation, loneliness, and higher rates of depression and anxiety (Selfhout, Branje, Delsing, Bogt, & Meeu, 2009). Furthermore, because of the adolescent's inherent limited capacity for self-regulation and vulnerability to peer pressure, online social interactions can be risky (O'Keeffe et al., 2011). Other research shows that cyberbullying (Patchin & Hinduja, 2006), privacy issues, sexting, Internet addiction, and sleep deprivation are some of the issues that can develop for adolescents (Christakis & Moreno, 2009). Although there is little research on how adolescents' wide use of electronic communication may affect family communication, it appears to be reinforcing peer communication at the expense of communication with parents (Subrahmanyam & Greenfield, 2008). Despite these risks, technology undoubtedly offers adolescents a virtual space to shape interpersonal connections and identity development—two important tasks of adolescence (Subrahmanyam & Greenfield, 2008).

In previous generations, an adolescent's capacity for emotional connectedness was a function of daily, in-person interaction. It remains unclear if intimacy is restricted by society's increasing reliance on gadgets, as this field of research has been inconclusive. According to Pew Internet Research (Lenhart, 2009), modern adolescents text more frequently than they talk face-to-face. Moreover, while the invention of video chatting has provided the illusion of face-to-face contact, it also plays a role in maintaining distance between users. Since the invention of the telephone, gone are the days when someone had to look another person in the eyes to have a conversation, discuss their day, vent frustrations, argue with one another, or even ask someone to prom. Consequently, cultural practices for dating and relationships have changed drastically in the last 15 years (Clark, 1998; Wilson & Peterson, 2002).

Millions of young people are initiating relationships through dating websites, social media, texting, e-mail, and video chatting. In some instances, people begin dating via the Internet long before they ever meet in person. Research is showing that this technological innovation may leave people feeling more isolated than connected (Fischer, 2009). Because technology is a growing platform to both initiate and end romantic relationships, today's adolescent may be blindsided with a breakup via text message or social media relationship status change. While in many ways it is too soon to tell how these social practices may influence adolescent mental health, these are important considerations for counselors working with adolescents in a technologically advanced world.

Relational Violence in Late Adolescence

Unfortunately, today's adolescents are no less vulnerable to the dangers of relational violence and trauma exposure than were previous generations. Almost a quarter of all adolescents experience "extreme stressors" as described by the *Diagnostic Statistical Manual for Mental Disorders*, (5th ed.) (*DSM-V*; American Psychiatric Association, 2013; Costello, Erkanii, Fairbank, & Angold, 2005). Research establishes that many adolescents experience or witness multiple forms of relational violence in their childhood and adolescence. In fact, the phenomena of family violence, dating violence, and community violence are interconnected. Saunders (2003) reveals that most adolescent victims of violence are victims of more than one type of violence. Adolescents who report a single exposure to violence are in the minority, with most child victims of abuse being exposed to several types of violence on multiple occasions. Out of previous studies that reached the same conclusion (Finkelhor & Dzuiba-Leatherman, 1994; Green, 1998; Kilpatrick & Saunders, 1999), a series of National Survey of Adolescents (NSA) studies stands out from the rest (Acierno et al., 2000; Crouch, Hanson, Saunders, Kilpatrick, & Resnick, 2000). In a telephone survey on the abuse and violence exposure of randomly sampled adolescents ($N = 4.032$) from 12 to 17 years old, researchers found that nearly 50% of the sample reported experiencing at least one out of four types of violence. Of these children, 40% (20% of the total sample) reported experiencing at least two types of violence. Moreover, of those children who either witnessed community violence or survived physical or sexual abuse by a parent, 50% admitted exposure to domestic violence. Additionally, of those children reporting caregiver domestic violence, between 40% and 80% stated they were victims of one of the other types of violence also.

The Centers for Disease Control and Prevention reports that intimate partner violence (IPV) often begins at a young age, with 9% of high school students reporting exposure to dating violence (Eaton et al., 2012). The report also shows that 22.4% of females and 15% of males who first experienced IPV in adolescence also experience rape, physical violence, or stalking by an intimate partner in their adult lives. Research on relational violence over the last 20 years has consistently shown a link between violence in adolescence and a continued pattern of abuse well into adulthood. Factors that exacerbate these risks include poverty, deprived neighborhoods, stress, dysfunctional family patterns, parental discord, and violence between parents, among others (Tolan, Gorman-Smith, & Henry, 2006).

Much of the mental health research community agrees that prevention is the best way to combat relational violence. Recent IPV prevention efforts, such as the Start Strong: Building Healthy Adolescent Relationships initiative, are showing promise (Spivak et al., 2014). Using the social-ecological model of public health, this violence prevention effort educates youths, caregivers, and school personnel and includes creative social marketing and social media efforts focused on youths and parents.

Trauma in Adolescence

Finkelhor (2009) argues that children and adolescents are the most criminally victimized population in American society. According to the U.S. Department of Justice National Crime Victimization Survey (NCVS) derived from detailed interviews with over 100,000 citizens annually between the years of 1993 and 2003, researchers found that the rate for aggravated assault, rape, and overall violence against youths 12 to 17 years old more than doubled the rate for the general population. Furthermore, nearly half (47.2%) of all active duty members of the military are under the age of 25 (Department of Defense, 2012). A wealth of research outlines the potential impact of trauma on children and adolescents, including depression, anxiety, decreased self-esteem, anger, guilt and shame, disturbances in sleeping and eating, aggressive behaviors, dissociation, suicidal behaviors, substance abuse and dependence, impaired social functioning, personality disorders, intimate relationship problems, posttraumatic stress disorder, and a number of health risks including diabetes, cancer, heart disease, and gastrointestinal disorders (Kendall-Tackett, 2009).

Given these startling statistics, counselors need to be prepared to work effectively with adolescent survivors of trauma. Research demonstrates that traumatized youth receiving treatment often experience measureable benefits on personal, interpersonal, and societal levels (Briere, 1992; Cohen & Mannarino, 2008; Ducharme, Atkinson, & Poulto, 2000; Finkelhor, 1998; Harvey & Taylor, 2010; Saywitz, Mannarino, Berliner, & Cohen, 2000). As a primary goal, clinicians focus on ensuring the adolescent's safety and reducing or diminishing the effects of the traumatization on the adolescent (Foa, Keane, Friedman, & Cohen, 2009; Glaser, 1991). In empirically supported therapies for traumatized youth such as trauma-focused cognitive behavioral therapy, over 80% of traumatized children show improvement within 12 to 16 sessions occurring once a week for 60 to 90 minutes (Cohen, Mannarino, Berliner, & Deblinger, 2000; Deblinger, Lippmann, & Steer, 1996).

SUGGESTIONS FOR DEVELOPMENTALLY APPROPRIATE COUNSELING INTERVENTIONS WITH ADOLESCENTS AGES 15 TO 19

Several variables should be considered when working with older adolescents in a clinical setting. For example, a clinician's approach depends on whether the adolescent client is attending sessions voluntarily or whether his or her entrance into counseling is mandated by a parent, court, or some other outside system. Counseling that occurs in school has a different set of parameters when compared to counseling that occurs in a community agency. Moreover, an adolescent's social, emotional, and cognitive developmental stage often dictates the set of interventions used in counseling. For example, while younger children and early adolescents respond better to nondirective approaches centered in play, older adolescents tend to engage better to insight-oriented talk therapy fused with expressive arts activities (Sori & Heckler, 2003).

Moreover, counselors should exercise thoughtful triage decision making during the screening process with adolescent clients. If an adolescent is receiving trauma therapy for abuse and either his or her nonoffending parent(s) is not supportive, abuse is ongoing in the home with no safety plan, or domestic violence is occurring in the home, the counselor should (a) consult the child abuse hotline and make a report if he or she suspects the child is in danger and (b) refer the caregivers for more specialized couples, individual, or family services until the parenting issues are resolved (Tavkar & Hansen, 2011; SAMHSA, 2014).

Moreover, an important part of trauma counseling involves training the adolescent to engage in healthier coping behaviors. Many survivors of abuse adopt maladaptive coping skills (e.g., avoidance, shutting down, numbing, substance abuse, eating disorders, or self-injury) to deal with the overwhelming negative thoughts, feelings, and sensations they experience when triggered. Counselors should inform caregivers about treatment goals, including lessons on assertiveness training, healthy boundary-setting, and healthy emotional expression to ensure parents understand, support, and nurture the child's learning at home (Cohen et al., 2000).

Some parents may perceive increased emotional expression as disrespect or disobedience and may choose to punish the child for practicing the very skills he or she is learning in counseling. For example, a counselor may encourage an adolescent to practice assertive statements such as "When you yell at me, it hurts my feelings." While these practices benefit passive adolescents who are learning to better protect themselves from future abuse, some parents may view these statements as defiance and punish their child as a result. Therefore, in addition to assessing symptomology, therapists should carefully consider an adolescent's level of readiness, caregiver support, physical and emotional safety, and ability to attend sessions regularly prior to engaging in counseling.

As a minor, the older adolescent client below the age of 18 still requires parental permission for counseling. Yet, even though counseling outcomes improve with parent involvement, it can have a significant influence on client disclosure. Helitzer, Sussman, Hernandez, & Kong (2011) state "a balance must be found between maintaining adolescent confidentiality and involving parents in preventing poor adolescent outcomes resulting from risky behaviors" (p. 404). While orienting an adolescent client to the process of counseling, the clinician should begin a discussion with the client and caretaker regarding hopes for counseling and parameters of confidentiality. The goal is to create an environment where the adolescent client can experience freedom to discuss topics without worrying that the counselor will break confidentiality and share information with the parents without the adolescent's consent (except in instances where the clinician is mandated to break confidentiality). Sommers-Flanagan and Bequette (2013) suggest that the main challenges in the initial stage of working with this population are finding balance between the clinician's assessment, building a relationship, caretaker/parent management, and case formulation.

Building rapport, fostering trust, and nurturing the relationship are, above all else, the most important factors in laying the foundation for successful work with adolescents. Findings suggest that alliance is significantly associated with positive counseling outcomes such as decreased symptoms, improved family relationships, increased self-esteem, and a higher perception of social support (Hawely & Garland, 2008). Rogers (1957) suggested three elements that assist in creating this intentional environment and alliance: (a) empathy, (b) congruence (or genuineness), and (c) unconditional positive regard. With *empathy*, the clinician possesses an understanding of the client's internal frame of reference and endeavors. This client-centered framework is best described in Rogers's own words: "To be of assistance to you, I will put aside myself—the self of ordinary interaction—and enter into your world of perception as completely as I am able. I will become, in a sense, another self for you" (Rogers, 1951/2003, p. 35). *Congruence* describes a clinician who is "freely and deeply himself," (Rogers, 1957, p. 97) and is someone who is a genuine, integrated person as he or she sits with the client. Lastly, *unconditional positive regard* describes a clinician who possesses warm acceptance of the client. This is especially useful when working with adolescents displaying high-risk behaviors. If counselors can foster these conditions, they will have a greater connection with their adolescent clients.

Case Illustration 14.2

Jazmine

Jazmine is a 17-year-old female entering her senior year at Hamilton High School in Florida. She arrives for counseling well dressed, polite, and reports enjoying school. "School is my escape," she says during the first session. She reports having aspirations of joining the military or becoming a doctor one day—but the counselor notices she has little information about how to attain those goals. During the intake session with her father, Jazmine presents as somber, quiet, and fearful. Born in Jamaica and living as a legal resident, Jazmine and her father, Harold, immigrated to the United States 2 years ago without her

(Continued)

(Continued)

mother. They both work at the same grocery story to pay the bills while she finishes high school. Her father presents with a mixture of ambivalence and sarcasm toward his daughter's desire for counseling.

Jazmine's father agreed to show up to the first appointment "to sign paperwork" but only at the urging of his sister—Jazmine's aunt and the matriarch of the family living in the United States. Last week, Jazmine disclosed to a police officer at school that she was molested by an older man in their neighborhood. "If you ask me, she knew what she was doing," her father says to the counselor while filling out forms. After orienting Jazmine and Harold to the process of counseling and discussing confidentiality, the counselor invites Harold to sit in the waiting room to get better acquainted with Jazmine. She sits silently and won't make eye contact with the counselor. Finally, she admits, "I can't tell you anything. My father blames me for what happened and told me that I will get grounded if I tell you about our family's personal business." Although Jazmine says she genuinely wants to speak freely to the therapist, she states she is used to "having to survive life alone without anyone else's help."

Multiracial literature offers additional suggestions for working with children and adolescents in creating an alliance. Herring (1995) suggests that it is important to create an environment where a client can experience safety and feels the freedom to self-ventilate. The client's presenting issue may be vocalized for the first time in the counseling session so it must be treated with utmost respect, and the client's perception should be honored. Counselors should be prepared to observe a variance in the openness of the client's issue in connection to family and peer knowledge of it. Counselors should also examine their own attitudes and biases toward older adolescents. It is important for counselors to self-reflect, as any bias held will disrupt the therapeutic relationship and potential progress. In addition, this self-examination should encompass clinical knowledge, competence, and areas for growth concerning working with adolescents and the presenting issue.

Counselor training should include information on adolescent identity development as well as facilitation skills with this population. Specific issues, such as trauma, eating disorders, substance abuse, or self-harming behaviors, may require additional training. While there are web-based resources available to counselors, it is important to ensure that the website and content are valid. The California Evidence-Based Clearinghouse for Child Welfare (CEBC; http://www.cebc4cw.org) is a prime example of a helpful resource for clinicians. The CEBC offers research on which evidence-based practices work best with a particular issue. In addition, counselors can be equipped with assessment and screening tools. You can download free counseling toolkits at samhsa.gov. Websites like SAMHSA's and the CEBC provide excellent resources; however, counselors should ensure that they are competent to use them.

Adolescents are developing within an ecological world swirling with pressures and curiosities on all aspects of life and relationships. For this reason, counselors would benefit from using genograms and ecomaps in session. Geno-grams (McGoldrick, Gerson, & Petry, 2008) are visual tools constructed collabora-tively between client and therapist that map out pertinent patterns within a client's family history and relationships, and they can assist in revealing current influences on the adolescent's presenting issues. The ecomap (Logan, Freeman, & McRoy, 1987) provides an understanding of current ecological and contextual influences. The ecomap is similar to the genogram in that it depicts family influence, but it also extends to external networks and environments that provide support or discourage-ment. Both interventions allow the counselor to gain a large amount of background on the client relatively quickly. In addition, the client will also gain more awareness regarding his or her identity through these personal explorations.

Psychoeducation allows clients to use media and literature in self-exploration. Bibliotherapy, journaling, storytelling, movies depicting adolescent issues, and websites can help adolescents learn more about their social, cognitive, and emo-tional world. Through psychoeducation, clients will be validated and empowered to examine themselves in a new way, while also planning for the future as they transition into adulthood. Psychoeducation may also bring out particular interests (e.g., art and music) of the client that can be used to further exploration.

For older adolescents entering postsecondary education, college counseling cen-ters offer a great resource to assist them in areas such as adjustment issues (e.g., transition to college, becoming independent, being away from home), relationships (e.g., peer, family, significant other, communication issues), academic difficul-ties (e.g., study skills, time management), and additional significant issues (e.g., disordered eating, depression, anxiety, suicidal ideation, substance use, sexual victimization, ADHD). In all, the college counseling center offers many services such as individual counseling, group counseling, crisis intervention, medication and diagnosis, and consultation and outreach (Sharkin, 2012). Fortunately for students, many college counseling centers have their cost built into tuition to cre-ate a free resource to assist older adolescents while on their road to academic and developmental success. College counselors are typically versed in college student development theories such as Chickering's seven vectors, Kolb's theory of experi-ential learning, Perry's cognitive theory of student development, and Schlossberg's transition theory (Evans et al., 2010) and specific clinical issues connected to the postsecondary experience and associated developmental levels (Grayson & Meilman, 2006).

Lastly, counselors must not forget to view their adolescent client through a cultural lens. This lens assists the counselor to shape interventions to each client's specific needs. Understanding and applying multiracial themes and identity devel-opment models can offer a comprehensive way to holistically view a client while revealing the influences of caregivers, peers, community, and societal messages.

COUNSELING KEYSTONES

- Older adolescents are in the stage of development where they are navigating from dependency toward autonomy. This can be a particularly stressful transition.
- The digital age has been a strong part of the millennial and postmillennial generations and has greatly impacted the ways in which older adolescents communicate.
- Adolescent behaviors can be better explained in the context of genes, childhood experiences, environment, and brain development.
- Personal and life exploration is a key feature of the older adolescent.
- Within the transition toward autonomy, the older adolescent may experience life constraints that may come in the form of financial concerns or family beliefs.
- The older adolescent's ecological world is vast and can shape identity development.
- Creating an intentional environment of trust is important for connecting with the older adolescent.

ADDITIONAL RESOURCES

In Print

Hansen, S. A. (2013). *The executive functioning workbook for adolescents: Help for unprepared, late, and scattered adolescents.* Oakland, CA: New Harbinger.

Naar-King, S., & Suarez, M. (2011). *Motivational interviewing with adolescents and young adults.* New York, NY: Guilford Press.

Online

Center for Disease Control and Prevention STRYVE: http://vetoviolence.cdc.gov/apps/stryve

Drug Strategies: http://www.drugstrategies.org

The California Evidence-Based Clearinghouse for Child Welfare (CEBC): http://www.cebc4cw.org

Trauma-Focused Cognitive Behavioral Therapy website: http://tfcbt.musc.edu

REFERENCES

Acierno, R., Kilpatrick, D. G., Resnick, H. S., Saunders, B. E., de Arellano, M., & Best, C. L. (2000). Assault, PTSD, family substance use, and depression as risk factors for cigarette use in youth: Findings from the National Survey of Adolescents. *Journal of Traumatic Stress*, 13, 381–396.

American Psychiatric Association. (2013). *The diagnostic and statistical manual of mental disorders: DSM 5*. Washington, DC: Author.

Briere, J. N. (1992). *Child abuse trauma: Theory and treatment of the lasting effects*. Newbury Park, CA: Sage.

Burbach, H. J. (1972). The development of a contextual measure of alienation. *Pacific Sociological Review, 15*, 225–234.

Burbach, H. J., & Thompson, M. A. (1971). Alienation among college freshmen: A comparison of Puerto Rican, Black, and White students. Journal of College Student Personnel, 12(4), 248–252.

Caumont, A. (2014, March 12). What would you name today's youngest generations of Americans? *Pew Research Center*. Retrieved from http://www .pewresearch.org/fact-tank/2014/03/12/what-would-you-name-todays-youngest -generation-of-americans

Chandra, A., & Minkovitz, C. S. (2006). Stigma starts early: Gender differences in adolescent willingness to use mental health services. *Journal of Adolescent Health*, 38(754), 1–8.

Chickering, A. W. (1969). *Education and identity*. San Francisco, CA: Jossey-Bass

Chickering, A. W. (1978). *Education and identity*. San Francisco, CA: Jossey Bass.

Chickering, A. W., & Reisser, L. (1993). *Education and identity* (2nd ed.). San Francisco, CA: Jossey Bass.

Christakis, D. A., & Moreno, M. A. (2009). Trapped in the net: Will internet addiction become a 21st century epidemic? *Archives of Pediatrics & Adolescent Medicine, 163*(10), 959–960.

Clark, L. S. (1998). Dating on the net: adolescents and the rise of "pure" relationships. In S. G. Jones *Cybersociety 2.0: Revisiting computer-mediated communication and community* (pp. 159–83). Thousand Oaks, CA: Sage.

Cohen, J. A., & Mannarino, A. P. (2008). Psychotherapeutic options for traumatized children. *Current Opinions in Pediatrics*, 22(5), 605–609.

Cohen, J. A., Mannarino, A. P., Berliner, L., & Deblinger, E. (2000). Trauma-focused cognitive behavioral therapy for children and adolescents an empirical update. *Journal of Interpersonal Violence*, 15(11), 1202–1223.

Common Sense Media. (2009). Is technology networking changing childhood? A national poll. San Francisco, CA: Common Sense Media. Retrieved from http://www.commonsensemedia.org/sites/default/files/CSM_adolescent_ social_media_080609_FINAL.pdf

Costello, J. E., Erkanii, A., Fairbank, A., & Angold, A. (2005). The prevalence of potentially traumatic events in childhood and adolescence. *Journal of Traumatic Stress, 15*(2), 99–112.

Crouch, J. L., Hanson, R. F., Saunders, B. E., Kilpatrick, D. G., & Resnick, H. S. (2000). Income, race/ethnicity, and exposure to violence in youth: Results from the National Survey of Adolescents. *Journal of Community Psychology, 28,* 625–641.

Davis, F. J. (1991). *Who is Black? One nation's definition.* University Park: Pennsylvania State University Press.

Deblinger, E., Lippmann, J., & Steer, R. (1996). Sexually abused children suffering posttraumatic stress symptoms: Initial treatment outcome findings. *Child Maltreatment, 1*(4), 310–321.

Department of Defense, Office of the Deputy Assistant Secretary of Defense. (2012). *2012 demographics profile of the military community.* Retrieved from http://www.militaryonesource.mil/12038/MOS/Reports/2012_Demographics _Report.pdf

Doane, L. D., Mineka, S., Zinbarg, R. E., Craske, M., Griffith, J., & Adam, E. K. (2013). Are flatter diurnal cortisol rhythms associated with major depression and anxiety disorders in late adolescence? The role of life stress and daily negative emotion. *Development and Psychopathology, 25,* 629–642.

Ducharme, J. M., Atkinson, L., & Poulton, L. (2000). Success-based noncoercive treatment of oppositional behavior in children from violent homes. *Journal of the American Academy of Child & Adolescent Psychiatry, 39*(8), 995–1004.

Eaton, D. K., Kann, L., Kinchen, S., Shanklin, S., Flint, K. H., Hawkins, J., . . . Wechsler, H. (2012). Youth risk behavior surveillance-United States, 2011. *Morbidity and mortality weekly report. Surveillance summaries, 61*(4), 1–162.

Erikson, E. H. (1959). *Identity and the life cycle.* New York, NY: Norton.

Erikson, E. H. (1968). *Identity: Youth and crisis.* New York, NY: Norton.

Erikson, E. H. (1993). *Childhood and society.* New York, NY: Norton.

Evans, N. J., Forney, D. S., Guido, F. M., Patton, L. D., & Renn, K. A. (2010). *Student development in college: Theory, research, and practice* (2nd ed.). San Francisco, CA: Jossey-Bass.

Finkelhor, D. (1998). *Child sexual abuse: New theory and research.* New York, NY: Collier Macmillan.

Finkelhor, D. (2009). The prevention of childhood sexual abuse. *Future Child, 19*(2), 169–194.

Finkelhor, D., & Dziuba-Leatherman, J. (1994). Children as victims of violence: A national survey. *Pediatrics, 94*(4), 413–420.

Fischer, C. S. (2009). The 2004 GSS finding of shrunken social networks: An artifact? *American Sociological Review, 74*(4), 657–669.

Foa, E. B., Keane, T. M., Friedman, M. J., & Cohen, J. A. (Eds.). (2009). *Effective treatments for PTSD: Practice guidelines from the International Society for Traumatic Stress studies.* New York, NY: Guilford Press.

Giedd, J. (2011). Development of the young brain. *National Institute of Mental Health*. Retrieved from http://www.nimh.nih.gov/news/media/2011/giedd.shtml

Glaser, D. (1991). Treatment issues in child sexual abuse. *British Journal of Psychiatry, 159*, 769–782.

Gloria, A. M., & Robinson Kurpious, S. E. (1996). The validation of the cultural congruity scale and the university environment scale with Chicano/a students. *Hispanic Journal of Behavioral Sciences, 18*, 533–549.

Grayson, P. A., & Meilman, P. W. (2006). *College mental health practice.* New York, NY: Routledge

Green, A. H. (1998). Factors contributing to the generational transmission of child maltreatment: Clinical perspectives. *Journal of the American Academy of Child & Adolescent Psychiatry, 37*(12), 1334–1336.

Harris, D. R., & Sim, J. J. (2002). Who is multiracial? Assessing the complexity of lived race. *American Sociological Review, 67*, 614–627.

Harvey, S. T., & Taylor, J. E. (2010). A meta-analysis of the effects of psychotherapy with sexually abused children and adolescents. *Clinical Psychology Review, 30*(5), 517–535.

Hawley, K. M., & Garland, A. F. (2008). Working alliance in adolescent outpatient therapy: Youth, parent and therapist reports and associations with therapy outcomes. *Child & Youth Care Forum, 37*(2), 59–74.

Helitzer, D. L., Sussman, A. L., Hernandez, B. U., & Kong, A. S. (2011). The "ins" and "outs" of provider-parent communication: Perspectives from adolescent primary care providers on challenges to forging alliances to reduce adolescent risk. *Journal of Adolescent Health 48*(4), 404–409.

Henriksen, R. C. (2000). Black/White biracial identity development: A grounded theory study (Doctoral Dissertation, Texas A&M University–Commerce, 2000). *Dissertation Abstracts International, 61/07*, 2605.

Henriksen, R. C., & Paladino, D. A. (Eds.). (2009). *Counseling individuals, couples, and families with multiple heritages.* Alexandria, VA: American Counseling Association.

Herring, R. D. (1995), Developing biracial ethnic identity: A review of the increasing dilemma. *Journal of Multicultural Counseling & Development, 23*, 29–38.

Kendall-Tackett, K. A. (2009). Psychological trauma and physical health: A psychoneuroimmunology approach to etiology of negative health effects and possible interventions. *Psychological Trauma, 1*, 35–48.

Kilpatrick, D. G., & Saunders, B. E. (1999). *Prevalence and consequences of child victimization: Results from the National Survey of Adolescents: Final report* (NIJ Grant No. 93-IJCX-0023). Charleston, SC: Author.

Konrad, K., Firk, C., & Uhlhaas, P. J. (2013). Brain development during adolescence: Neuroscientific insights into this developmental period. *Deutsches Ärzteblatt International, 110*(25), 425.

Larson, B., & Hartl, A. C. (2013). Understanding loneliness during adolescence: Developmental changes that increase the risk of perceived social isolation. *Journal of Adolescence, 36*, 1261–1268.

Leaf, P. J., Alegria, M., Cohen, P., Goodman, S. H., Horwitz, S. M., Hoven, . . . Regier, D. A. (1996). Mental health service use in the community and schools: Results from the four-community MECA study. *Journal of the American Academy of Child & Adolescent Psychiatry, 35*(7), 889–897.

Lenhart, A. (2009). Teens and mobile phones over the past five years. Washington DC: Pew Research Center. Retrieved from http://www.pewinternet .org/files/old-media/Files/Reports/2009/PIP%20Teens%20and%20 Mobile%20Phones%20Data%20Memo.pdf

Logan, S. L., Freeman, E. M., & McRoy, R. G. (1987). Racial identity problems of bi-racial clients: Implications for social work practice. *Journal of Intergroup Relations, 15*(2), 11–24.

Loving v. Virginia, 388 U.S. 1 (1967).

Marcia, J. E. (1966). Development and validation of ego identity status. *Journal of Personality and Social Psychology, 3*, 551–558.

Marcia, J. E. (1967). Ego identity status: Relationship to change in self esteem, "general maladjustment," and authoritarianism. *Journal of Personality, 35*(1), 118–133.

Marcia, J. E. (1980). Identity in adolescence. In J. Adelson (Ed.), *Handbook of adolescent psychology* (pp. 159–187). Hoboken, NJ: Wiley.

Marcia, J. E. (2002). Adolescence, identity, and the Bernardone family. *Identity: An international journal of theory and research, 2*(3), 199–209.

McGoldrick, M., Gerson, R., & Petry, S. S. (2008). *Genograms: Assessment and intervention*. WW Norton & Company.

O'Keeffe, G. W., Clarke-Pearson, K., & Council on Communications and Media. (2011). The impact of social medial on children, adolescents, and families. *Pediatrics, 127*, 800–804.

Paretsky, S. (2008). *Bleeding Kansas*. New York: Putnam Adult.

Patchin, J. W., & Hinduja, S. (2006). Bullies move beyond the schoolyard: A preliminary look at cyberbullying. *Youth Violence and Juvenile Justice, 4*(2),148–169.

Poston, W. S. C. (1990). The biracial identity development model: A needed addition. *Journal of Counseling and Development, 69*, 152–255.

Powell, K. (2006). Neurodevelopment: How does the adolescent age brain work? *Nature, 442*, 865–867.

Rogers, C. R. (1951/2003). *Client-centred therapy*. London, UK: Constable & Robinson.

Rogers, C. R. (1957). The necessary and sufficient conditions of therapeutic personality change. *Journal of Consulting Psychology, 21*(2), 95–103.

Root, M. P. P. (1994). Mixed-race women. In L. Comez-Diaz & B. Green (Eds.), *Women of color: Integrating ethnic and gender identities in psychotherapy* (pp. 455–478). New York, NY: Guilford.

Root, M. P. P. (1999). The biracial baby boom: Understanding ecological constructions of racial identity in the 21st century. In. R. H. Sheets, R. Hernandez, & E. R. Hollins (Eds.), *Racial and ethnic identity in school practices: Aspects of human development* (pp. 67–89). Mahwah, NJ: Erlbaum.

Root, M. M. P. (2002). Methodological issues in multiracial research. In G. C. Nagayama, S. Okazaki, (Eds.), *Asian American psychology: The science of lives in context* (pp. 171–193). Washington, DC: American Psychological Association.

Saunders. (2003). Understanding children exposed to violence: Toward an integration of overalapping fields. *Journal of Interpersonal Violence, 18,* 356–36.

Saywitz, K. J., Mannarino, A. P., Berliner, L., & Cohen, J. A. (2000). Treatment for sexually abused children and adolescents. *American Psychologist, 55,* 1040–1049.

Schwartz, S. J., Zamboanga, B. L., Meca, A., & Ritchie, R. A. (2012). Identity around the world: An Overview. In S. J. Schwartz (Ed.), *Identity around the world. New Directions for Child and Adolescent Development, 138,* 1–18.

Selfhout, M. W., Branje, S. T., Delsing, M., Bogt, T. M., & Meeu, W. J. (2009). Different types of Internet use, depression, and social anxiety: The role of perceived friendship quality. *Journal of Adolescence, 32*(4), 819–833.

Sharkin, B. S. (2012). *Being a college counselor on today's campus: Roles, contributions, and special challenges.* New York, NY: Routledge.

Sisk, C. L., & Foster, D. L. (2004). The neural basis of puberty and adolescence. *Nature Neuroscience, 7*(10), 1040–1047.

Sommers-Flanagan, J., & Bequette, T. (2013). The initial psychotherapy interview with adolescent clients. *Journal of Contemporary Psychotherapy, 43,* 13–22.

Sori, C., & Heckler, L. (2003). *The therapist's notebook for children and adolescents: Homework, handouts, and activities for use in psychotherapy.* New York, NY: The Hayworth Clinical Practice Press.

Spivak, H. R., Jenkins, E. L., VanAudenhove, K., Lee, D., Kelly, M., & Iskander, J. (2014). CDC grand rounds: A public health approach to prevention of intimate partner violence. *MMWR. Morbidity and Mortality Weekly Report, 63*(2), 38–41.

Stonequist, E. V. (1937). *The marginal man: A study in personality and culture conflict.* New York, NY: Russell & Russell.

Subrahmanyam, K., & Greenfield, P. (2008). Online communication and adolescent relationships. *The Future of Children, 18*(1), 119–146.

Substance Abuse and Mental Health Services Administration (SAMHSA). (2014). *SAMHSA's Concept of Trauma and Guidance for a Trauma-Informed Approach.* HHS Publication No. (SMA) 14-4884. Rockville, MD: Author. Retrieved from http://store.samhsa.gov/shin/content/SMA14-4884/SMA14-4884.pdf

Tanti, C., Stukas, A. A., Halloran, M. J., & Foddy, M. (2011). Social identity change: Shifts in social identity during adolescence. *Journal of Adolescence, 34*(3), 555–567.

Tavkar, P., & Hansen, D. J. (2011). Interventions for families victimized by child sexual abuse: Clinical issues and approaches for child advocacy center-based services. *Aggression and Violent Behavior, 16*(3), 188–199.

Thapar, A., Colishaw, S. Pine, D. S., & Thapar, A. K. (2012). Depression in adolescence. *The Lancet, 379,* 1056–1067.

Tolan, P., Gorman-Smith, D., & Henry, D. (2006). Family violence. *Annual Review of Psychology, 57,* 557–583.

Twenge, J. M. (2011). Generational differences in mental health: Are children and adolescents suffering more, or less? *American Journal of Orthopsychiatry, 81*(4), 469–472.

U.S. Census Bureau. (2010). The two or more races population: 2010. Retrieved from http://www.census.gov/prod/cen2010/briefs/c2010br-13.pdf

U.S. Department of Health and Human Services. (2001). Adolescent age brain: A work in progress. National Institute of Mental Health, Publication No. 11-4929. Retrieved from http://www.nimh.nih.gov/health/publications/the-adolescent-brain-still-under-construction/adolescent-brain.pdf

van Oort, F. V. A., Greaves-Lord, K., Ormel, J., Verhulst, F. C., & Huizink, A. C. (2011). Risk indicators of anxiety throughout adolescence: The TRAILS study. *Depression and Anxiety, 28*(6), 485–494.

Wehrly, B., Kenney, K. R., & Kenney, M. E. (1999). *Counseling multiracial families.* Thousand Oaks, CA: Sage.

Wilson, S. M., & Peterson, L. C. (2002). The anthropology of online communities. *Annual Review of Anthropology, 31,* 449–467.

Windfuhr, K., While, D., Hunt, I., Turnbull, P., Lowe, R., Burns, J., . . . National Confidential Inquiry into Suicide and Homicide by Young People with Mental Illness. (2008). Suicide in juveniles and adolescents in the United Kingdom. *Journal of Child Psychology and Psychiatry, 49*(11), 1157–1167.

Wolitzky-Taylor, K. B., Dour, H., Zinbarg, R., Mineka, S., Vrshek-Schallhorn, S., Epstein, A., . . . Craske, M.G. (2014). Experiencing core symptoms of anxiety and unipolar mood disorders in late adolescence predicts disorder onset in early adulthood. *Depression & Anxiety, 31,* 207–213.

Chapter 15

Counseling Emerging Adults (18–21): A Time of Uncertainty and Hope

Laura Choate

What used to occur during the teenage years is now happening far later.
Twenty-five is becoming the new fifteen. And it's not just delaying our kids'
maturity, it's changing who they become.

—Allen & Allen, (2009, p. 25)

INTRODUCTION

The late teens and early 20s form a particularly important developmental period, as these years lay the foundation for continued growth throughout the lifespan. The life choices an individual makes during this time can be highly influential on the rest of his or her life (Zarrett & Eccles, 2006). In recent years, scholars have shown great interest in examining this developmental window, realizing that the writings of dominant theorists such as G. Stanley Hall (1904) and Erik Erikson (1968) may no longer capture the experiences of young people in this age group. Historically this period included a time of separation from family and settling into stable adult roles. There was a rather clear-cut pathway to adulthood, with most people marrying and entering a full-time career by age 20. By the beginning of the 21st century, this was certainly no longer the case, as it is now normative for individuals to spend several years exploring possibilities and keeping as many doors open as possible in the areas of intimate relationships and work, often delaying what has traditionally been thought of as "adulthood" until the late 20s or early 30s.

Arnett (2000, 2004, 2007) was the first to identify the age period between the late teens and mid-20s as a distinct developmental period known as *emerging adulthood*. Several cultural changes have enabled this in-between period to surface in recent decades. For example, the age of first marriage has risen sharply and is now 28.6 for men and 26.6 for women (U.S. Census Bureau, 2013). Further, there is an increasing need for a higher education degree in order to secure a well-paying job, which has resulted in a record number of high school graduates enrolling in college (68.2%; National Center for Education Statistics, 2011) and delaying entry into full-time work. Most emerging adults claim that they want to wait until they have finished their education and to secure a full-time, stable job before they consider marriage or parenthood, viewing these as choices to be avoided rather than milestones to be achieved (Settersten & Ray, 2010). Overall, while this can be a time to experiment with different roles and beliefs, learning who one is and who one wants to be, at the same time, the emerging adult years can also be a period of instability, uncertainty, and transition.

Because there are no longer specific milestones in America to indicate healthy or on-time development within this age group (Arnett, 2007; Garrett & Eccles, 2009), counselors who work with emerging adults need assistance in understanding this developmental period and how to best work with clients in their late teens and early 20s who may feel unsettled or confused by the choices offered to them during this time.

To this end, after reading this chapter, you will be able to

- describe the broad features of emerging adulthood,
- explore the physical and cognitive changes that are still occurring during the emerging adulthood period,
- discuss identity development as the central and most salient developmental task for the emerging adult period, and
- describe developmental challenges and associated counseling interventions.

EMERGING ADULTHOOD

Arnett (2004) identified five primary features of emerging adulthood, which are explained in the paragraphs that follow:

a. *It is an age of identity exploration regarding self, relationships, and work.* In his writings from over 40 years ago, Erikson (1968) recognized the need for a psychological moratorium—a time when adult responsibilities are delayed so that young people can experiment and find their niche in society through a period of free role exploration (Arnett, 2000). This is now considered an important aspect of the emerging adult years, as individuals have the freedom to try out different possibilities for life while gradually transitioning toward a clearly defined identity.

b. *It is an age of instability and anxiety.* As is explored later in the chapter, emerging adults can become confused and overwhelmed at all of the choices available to them. Many report that they like the feeling of being unsettled but nevertheless experience anxiety about the unknown future. Still others experience frustration and resentment when their choices are foreclosed due to lack of financial resources or unexpected life circumstances (e.g., birth of a child, death of a parent).

c. *It is an age of being self-focused.* During this period, individuals don't generally have to take others into account when making decisions. They are primarily concerned about themselves and their own needs.

d. *It is an age where one feels caught between adolescence and adulthood.* Generally, emerging adults reply "yes and no" when asked whether they feel they are an adult (Arnett, 2004). Emerging adults define adulthood primarily through qualities of character rather than by specific milestones like college graduation, marriage, or parenthood. Instead, when asked about how they describe adulthood, the most common responses are (a) accepting responsibility for yourself, (b) making independent decisions, and (c) becoming financially independent. Overall, it seems that emerging adults see adulthood as a time when one finally becomes a self-sufficient person, whether or not this includes traditionally defined adult roles (Arnett, 2007).

e. *It is an age of possibilities.* Most emerging adults report that they enjoy this period of semiautonomy and freedom from role obligations and are often pleased with their increasing self-sufficiency. They are often excited by their perceived unlimited future potential. They may see the future as brimming with possibilities and believe that they have the flexibility to transform their lives into the ideal that they dream for themselves.

Arnett (2007) notes that these five features are not universal but are more common during emerging adulthood than in any other developmental period. He also notes that this is the most heterogeneous period of life, and that the described opportunities and freedoms are not available to all emerging adults. It is clear that individuals who have greater financial resources and family support will be more likely to experience extended periods of role exploration and freedom from adult responsibilities. Those emerging adults who must work and meet challenging life demands often struggle during these years, as they are forced to enter the adult world without adequate preparation and support (Settersten & Ray, 2010). In Guided Exercise 15.1, reflect on your current perceptions about the developmental period knows as the emerging adult.

Guided Exercise 15.1

Self-Exploration Exercise: Emerging Adulthood

(a) After reviewing the five features of emerging adulthood, which ones stand out for you as the most significant for understanding this developmental period?

(b) Most emerging adults define adulthood in the following manner: (a) accepting responsibility for yourself, (b) making independent decisions, and (c) becoming financially independent. They seem to base their definition around self-sufficiency and not on a particular life event or milestone. Take a moment to consider how you define adulthood. How does your view shape your perception of your emerging adult clients? How might your views influence your beliefs about what a client should or should not be doing by a particular age or stage of development?

PHYSICAL AND COGNITIVE DEVELOPMENT

Compared to earlier stages of development, there are not as many physical changes occurring to the body, but an emerging adult is still likely adjusting to the massive physical changes to body size and shape that occurred in earlier adolescence. Physically, young women are generally fully developed by this stage, while young men continue to gain weight, height, muscle mass, and body hair into their 20s (American Academy of Child and Adolescent Psychiatry, 2011). Emerging adults are also still undergoing changes to their brain structure and function. It was previously assumed that brain development was complete during the adolescent period, with the transition from concrete to abstract thinking becoming solidified during this time. As noted by Piaget, during early adolescence, most youth are still operating at concrete operations stage (Piaget, 1972), meaning that they think concretely, are unable to use abstract thinking, make decisions based primarily on their feelings, and are often unable to determine the most practical solution to a problem. With the onset of formal operational reasoning in middle adolescence, adolescents become capable of thinking through a problem with logic and a sense of *multifinality* (e.g., ability to imagine various options, perspectives, plans, or outcomes for the same situation). As these skills are developed in older adolescence, youth have the ability to think qualitatively differently about the world: with the skills of logical, abstract thinking and empathy, they have the capacity to manage their own learning and problem solving, process information more efficiently, reflect on their inner experiences and life circumstances, plan for educational and occupational goals, moderate risk-taking behaviors and delay gratification, display empathy for others and understand their perspectives, become more skilled at conflict resolution, and develop an appreciation for the larger cultural context in which they live (American Academy of Child and Adolescent Psychiatry, 2011; Simpson, 2001).

However, recent brain research reveals that the prefrontal cortex of the brain is not fully reorganized and developed until an individual reaches his or her mid to late 20s. This is the area that controls the executive functions of the brain (i.e., functions that control self-regulation, self-initiation, and flexibility in problem solving and that organize and direct cognitive activity, emotional regulation, and behaviors) so that even in emerging adulthood, individuals do not yet have the capability to fully regulate and control their impulses or to engage in purposeful, logical, goal-oriented behavior (Pharo, Sim, Graham, Gross, & Hayne, 2011). In other words, while the executive functions of the brain are still solidifying and can be effective at times, they are not yet used in a consistent manner, making an emerging adult's behavior unpredictable and hard for adults to understand at times. Parents might question why emerging adults have so many challenges in moving toward consistent, logical, goal-oriented, decision making that is based on a core sense of beliefs and values. They may remain perplexed at how their emerging adult son or daughter may sometimes make mature decisions, while at other times display an inability to plan, carry out these plans, take others' perspectives into consideration, or to regulate his or her emotions (Allen & Allen 2009; Steinberg, 2014).

In addition, older adults often do not understand the extreme risk-taking behavior that occurs and often peaks during these years. Because of variations in the development of executive functions in the brain, research indicates that emerging adults who have lower levels of executive function development are also more likely to engage in risk-taking behavior (Pharo et al., 2011). Similarly to adolescents, emerging adults continue to evaluate the costs and benefits of risky behaviors differently from adults. Compared with adults, emerging adults prioritize the rewards of risky behaviors more highly than any potential negative consequences. They clearly understand the risks involved but value the pros and cons differently; for them, benefits such as peer acceptance or short-term gratification far outweigh the negative consequences in a situation (Mahalik et al., 2013). Because they rate the benefits so highly, even when they do consider the risks involved, they engage in the behavior regardless of known risks (Institute of Medicine and National Research Council, 2011). This is why it is important for counselors to understand the inconsistent behavior of emerging adults and how supplying education about the risks of certain situations is not necessarily effective in reducing high-risk behavior.

IDENTITY DEVELOPMENT

The development of a positive identity is one of the most important psychosocial tasks of both the adolescent and emerging adult years. According to Erikson (1968), *adolescence* is a time to discover who you are in order to establish a workable self-definition; however, Arnett (2004) argues that this process primarily takes place during the emerging adult years. Ideally, essential aspects of identity are formed, including the ability to function independently as well as in connection to others. Identity formation also involves the integration of the various facets of identity that have emerged in terms of gender, physical appearance, sexuality, ethnicity, personality, vocational direction, personal values, and other key aspects of the self (Simpson, 2001). Emerging adults may look at themselves and "see a complex collage of bits and pieces which do not quite fit together; they have to create some coherence in that collage" (Knefelkamp, Widick, & Parker, 1978, p. 6).

CHICKERING'S VECTORS OF IDENTITY DEVELOPMENT

Arthur Chickering (1969; Chickering & Reisser, 1993) proposed a model of identity development that operates within the Eriksonian framework and is helpful for understanding emerging adulthood. Chickering's model of seven vectors describes the process through which a person becomes more comfortable with himself or herself and others and develops a personal value system that guides his or her behavior. While all seven vectors are interrelated and influence one another, individuals will not progress at the same pace in all seven areas simultaneously, seldom progress in a linear fashion, and do not necessarily progress at the same rates as others of the same age. A discussion of the vectors is included in the paragraphs that follow. Remember that Chickering's vector one, *competence*, also was discussed in Chapter 14. The seven vectors are presented in greater detail below.

Vector One: Developing Competence

Competence refers to the belief in one's general intellectual, physical, and interpersonal competence (Chickering, 1969). As competence develops, an individual comes to terms with his or her physical appearance (strength, fitness, self-discipline), ability to form relationships with peers, and ability to achieve in the area of academics. It also involves an overall confidence that one can handle life demands, including stressors such as adjusting to leaving home for the first time, transitioning to college, or managing the demands of a part- or full-time job. For example, Amanda, a 19-year-old college student, took on part-time employment for 10 hours per week during her first semester of college, even though she was hesitant to do so because she was already enrolled in 18 hours of college courses. However, at the end of her first year, she was pleased with her increasing ability to manage her time well and to maintain a solid GPA.

Vector Two: Managing Emotions

This developmental task refers to the ability to become aware of, understand, and manage one's emotions rather than being controlled by them; to have the ability to regulate emotions; and to tolerate strong emotions. As stated previously, due to the uneven growth in the prefrontal cortex, emerging adults experience a correspondingly uneven progression in learning to appropriately channel feelings, find a cathartic release for feelings, to delay gratification, and to tolerate some anxiety without becoming overwhelmed. This capacity in particular can be improved through counseling (see Suggestions for Counseling Interventions section). Jacob, a 20-year-old who had a 3.0 GPA in college and was a student leader at his school, began having strong emotional outbursts and periods of depression following a breakup with his girlfriend. Everyone who knew him was surprised by his ability to remain so calm and emotionally stable in other situations but to not be able to manage his feelings related to this breakup.

Vector Three: Interdependence

The purpose of this developmental task is to learn to function independently as well as to recognize the need to connect with and work well with others in achieving one's goals. This involves both emotional and instrumental independence: Emotional independence refers to the ability to act and make decisions without the need for constant reassurance or approval from others. Instrumental independence, in turn, refers to one's ability to set realistic goals, make plans to meet them, and to recognize the need for interdependence with others (Chickering & Reisser, 1993). Olivia was able to move out of her parents' home and start to make some of her own decisions about her career path and her relationships, but she realized that she still needed her parents for their occasional financial contributions and their ability to serve as a sounding board when she needed support in making a decision.

Vector Four: Establishing Identity

Chickering believed that positive identity is dependent on the first three vectors of competence, emotions, and autonomy, which then set the stage for the next three vectors: mature interpersonal relationships, developing purpose, and integrity (Chickering, 1969). So, vector four is the pivotal point in the vectors; the first three tasks are needed for establishing identity, and the last three tasks are dependent upon a clear sense of identity. As stated previously, identity is solidified through creating a coherent collage of all aspects of one's self-concept. Evans, Forney, Guido, Patton, and Renn (2009) delineate these aspects as including but not being limited to personal characteristics (including acceptance of body and appearance); gender; sexuality (including sexual orientation); ethnicity, race, and cultural identity; family, education; social class; and religion. Weaving these aspects together into a stable identity is one of the most challenging but essential aspects of the emerging adulthood period. Guided Exercise 15.2 is an opportunity to reflect on your own identity development.

Guided Exercise 15.2

Consider your own process of identity development. At what point did you start to recognize yourself as a congruent "self" that was distinct from your family and friends? How did you start to define yourself in terms of your appearance, gender, sexuality, ethnicity, race, cultural identity, family, education, social class, and religion? As you reflect on how you were able to establish your own identity, how can you learn to help your emerging adult clients through this process?

Vector Five: Developing Mature Interpersonal Relationships

The tasks in this vector are primarily about developing intimate and lasting relationships in three areas: with peers, with romantic partners, and renegotiating an adult relationship with one's parents and family of origin. According to Chickering (1969), to be able to develop mature relationships, an emerging adult needs a growing tolerance and appreciation of differences in people, acceptance of inevitable flaws in one's self and in others, and a deepening capacity for empathy and mutuality in relationships.

In addition to these features, an individual needs a sense of self, a personal identity, in order to develop intimate relationships with others (Erikson, 1968). Erikson describes intimacy as a willingness to engage in supportive, tender relationships without also losing oneself in the relationship. In other words, identity development is a key precursor for the ability to connect with others in mature, intimate, authentic relationships (Montgomery, 2005). If an emerging adult does not yet know who he or she is, it will be easy to lose a sense of self in an intimate relationship.

During adolescence, friendships and the peer group become increasingly important, are primarily activity based, and generally serve as a primary source of companionship and recreation. As an adolescent matures, friendships transition toward relationships that are still activity based but now are also more selective and based upon mutual levels of self-disclosure. These relationships can serve as a safe place for conversations about who one is and who one hopes to be (Radmacher & Azmitia, 2006). As adolescents enter into the emerging adulthood years, however, the impact of peer relationships on behavior starts to decline. Romantic relationships begin to increase in influence above friends and even parents. In fact, when an emerging adult is involved in a romantic relationship, his or her friends' influence on his or her level of overall happiness is quite weak; the influence of the romantic relationship plays a far greater role in overall happiness and overall adjustment (Demir, 2010; Meuus, Branje, van der Valk, & de Wied, 2007). Research indicates that having a healthy romantic relationship in the emerging adult years is related to greater mental and physical health and is also related to having better intimate relationships in adulthood (Zarret & Eccles, 2006). Being part of a healthy romantic relationship enables a young adult to explore emotional and physical intimacy and to consider the possibility of long-term commitments, cohabitation, and even marriage (Young, Furman, & Laursen, 2011). While emerging adults engage in a series of committed romantic relationships, with each partner the individual can continually refine answers to such questions as, "What kind of person do I want for a lifetime partner?" or "Does the person I am dating have those qualities?"

The final relationship of significance to this developmental period is the family of origin. While an emerging adult separates from the family and becomes increasingly self-sufficient, it is also important to maintain close ties with supportive family members, who can provide not only guidance and advice but also emotional support, and often, financial support. This requires families to renegotiate a relationship that is based on both separateness and closeness. Emerging adults desire that parents continue to provide a secure base; as they explore the world and try out new things, they still want to be able to come back to a home they can count and depend on, even as they move away from parents and into the world of love and work outside the family (Jordan, 2000; Worell, 2006). In fact, emerging adults' emotional closeness with their parents is an important aspect of their overall well-being; close emotional relationships are correlated with psychosocial adjustment, academic functioning, career maturity, and autonomy (Arnett, 2007).

Another issue in emerging adulthood is whether the individual continues to live at home or moves back into the family home. The popular perception is that parents resent the fact that many emerging adults continue to live with them, and that this is a major source of stress in their lives. A recent poll of parents of emerging adults reveals a different picture: "The perception that most parents are grumbling when their 18–29 year-old kids are living with them is utterly false. Parents understand that their kids face an unstable job market, poorly paid first jobs, high rents, and unstable relationships—a vastly different world than they may have faced 30–40 years ago" (Clark University News, 2013). Of the parents in the 2013 poll, 61% said they were mostly positive and only 6% were mostly negative about their emerging adult children living at home or having moved back home. Most parents also said that they felt closer to their children because they live with them: 67% said having emerging adult children living at home causes them to feel closer to their children, 73% report mostly positive relationships, and 86% of parents view their children as a source of enjoyment. While popular media perpetuate a stereotype that parents view emerging adult children with disdain and label them as lazy and selfish, poll data indicate that parents are welcoming their children to live at home and supporting them during this transitional time in their lives (Clark University Poll of Parents of Emerging Adults, 2013). For example, Anna had to move back in with her parents after graduation from college when her first job did not provide enough income for her to live on her own. While she did not like having to live by her parents' rules again, she did appreciate the fact that they continued to support her financially, and she did occasionally enjoy spending time with them doing leisure activities.

Vector Six: Developing Purpose

Developing purpose, the sixth task, involves the integration of priorities in various aspects of the person's life, including vocational, personal, and interpersonal commitments, in order to develop a sense that one's life has a meaningful purpose and direction. To achieve this task, the emerging adult must become more intentional in questioning the impact he or she wants to have on the world. As with other aspects of emerging adulthood, many individuals in their late teens and early 20s are resistant to setting a direction for their lives just yet; they want to explore all available options and keep as many doors open as possible. It is not until later in adulthood that they feel ready to commit to a specific life course. Dillon was 20 and still had not made a decision about whether he wanted to go to college or remain working at the retail store where he had been employed since high school graduation. He knew he wanted more from his life than working at the store, but he resisted going to college because he was not sure of what career path he might want to follow. He felt that he wanted to keep his options open and that committing to a career or major would close off too many possibilities.

Vector Seven: Developing Integrity

The final task, developing integrity, requires an emerging adult to intentionally clarify a personally valid set of beliefs that consistently provides a guide for behavior. Due to the complexity and importance of this vector, the process of integrity development is explored through the frameworks of emerging adult cognitive and moral development.

William Perry (1970) identified stages of cognitive development specific to emerging adults in his studies of college students. These stages describe ways that emerging adults typically approach knowledge acquisition, learning, and ultimately develop their beliefs and values, which also are known as *personal epistemologies* or *epistemic beliefs* (Elby & Hammer, 2001; Muis, 2007; Murphy, Alexander, Greene, & Hennessey, 2012). Perry's scheme of intellectual and ethical development describes nine positions through which intellectual and ethical development unfolds. Because it was developed with college students, his approach is particularly valuable for understanding the ways that college students develop. Many students enter college still viewing the world through a dualistic lens; knowledge is viewed as either right or wrong, and students expect an expert to hand them the right "answer" for every problem. As formal operational thought becomes more developed, however, students move toward recognizing the existence of multiple perspectives in understanding an issue, and these are viewed as relative, equally valid, contingent, and contextual. In keeping with the other features of emerging adulthood, many emerging adults show resistance to choosing any alternative, keeping all options open about what is "truth" or "right" for their lives.

Over time, however, relativism can become overwhelming, and students start to realize that a personal commitment is necessary in order to ease this tension. Students recognize for the first time that their own ideas are valid and become committed to their own personal belief systems and ways of processing information. While placing importance on their own views, they are still able to recognize and appreciate that others have alternative perspectives from their own. In fact, Perry (2007) writes that the goal of college should be to help relativistic students learn how to make intellectual and personal commitments. In order to do this, students must learn to accept responsibility for themselves rather than conforming to standards of others (Brownlee, Boulton-Lewis, & Purdie, 2002). This becomes difficult because students must grapple with the issue of responsibility for their lives, and they may struggle with the question, "If all I have been taught up to now is open to question, then my sense of who is responsible shifts radically from the outside to me" (Perry, 1970, p. 34). It might be easier for students to conform to social and institutional demands rather than take a personal stand about what they think and believe. To be able to break with others' views requires maturity, character, and autonomy, which can only be achieved with experience, critical reflection, and a sense of responsibility (Halonen et al., 2003; Perry, 1970).

Perry's (1970) scheme has been criticized for lack of inclusion of women in the normative sample. In *Women's Ways of Knowing* (Belenky, Clinchy, Goldberger, & Tarule, 1986), the authors present a model to complement Perry's scheme, exploring women's development in terms of how women think about themselves, authority, truth, and life options. Their idea that is particularly relevant for emerging adults is the concept of *self-silencing*—viewing knowledge as outside the self and silencing one's own voice in order to focus on the voices of others. With the right develop mental conditions, however, knowers can move to "constructed knowing" whereby the knower understands himself or herself as an integral part of what is known. At this point, an individual can "value multiple approaches to knowing and insist on bringing the self and personal commitment into the center of the knowing process" (Goldberger, 1996, p. 5). This process is similar to Baxter Magolda's (1992) idea of "self-authorship"—the internal capacity to define one's personal beliefs, identity, and social relationships, and after choosing one's beliefs, having the courage to stand up for them. To make this transition, one must accept responsibility for one's own behaviors, beliefs, and values, rather than an overreliance on the standards of others (Hensley, 2001). An example is provided in Case Illustration 15.1.

Case Illustration 15.1

The Case of Millie

Millie showed up for class on the first day of her freshman year of college, ready to do what she had so successfully done throughout her high school years: Memorize the information from lecture and then just spit it back out on the test. She had grown proficient at passively taking in class material and then repeating it successfully on multiple-choice tests. In college, however, she found that this strategy did not seem to work. She became frustrated because the professors no longer just gave her the information; they presented it but then forced her to come up with her own conclusions and answers. She realized that she would have to piece it together herself. She thought, "If only they would just give me the answer, I would memorize it, and then I would be okay. Why do they make it so hard?" Slowly, she came to realize that others in her classes were going through the same struggles, that they had multiple points of view, and that they all had valid points to share in class. As she listened to them, she began to believe that maybe there are no "truths" to just memorize, and that all views could be equally believable and valid. By the time she reached her senior year, however, she had moved to a place where she was able to formulate her own voice. She had slowly learned to take a personal stand on such issues as her political beliefs and religious views. She learned to move from simply being a recipient of information toward becoming a cocreator of knowledge wherein she realized that she had an important part to play in the learning process.

Lawrence Kohlberg (1976) also examined the developmental shift past relativism toward personal commitment. Kohlberg described the hierarchical, qualitatively distinct stages of reasoning that people use when making decisions about social justice. In adolescence, most individuals are at moral reasoning levels that emphasize conformity to groups. Gradually, they begin questioning beliefs held by their family of origin, realizing that rules are not absolutes but rather agreements formed to help people get along with one another, and that rules can be questioned or changed if they do not fit with a particular situation. While this moral decision-making style works well for them in interpersonal relationships, older adolescents start to realize that they need a framework for understanding the larger issues facing society. During emerging adulthood, therefore, they face the need for what Kohlberg termed a *postconventional principled morality*, which involves a concern with maintaining the social order, so that in decision making one considers not only the other person's feelings but also whether or not good is maintained for society as a whole (Kohlberg, 1976). As he or she matures, an emerging adult increasingly considers fundamental human rights and values in his or her moral values, and there is increasing congruence between his or her values and actual behaviors.

It should be noted that Gilligan (1982) later proposed that Kohlberg's theory of moral reasoning favored the abstract rights orientation of men and therefore did not adequately capture the nature of women's development. Gilligan believed that women possess a voice of care, connection, and responsibility in their moral reasoning, while men tend to use an abstract, impersonal, and rights-oriented mode of reasoning. Gilligan's assertions have been questioned through empirical research (Jaffee & Hyde, 2000), yet they have considerably broadened our understanding of moral development to include an emphasis on caring and responsiveness to the needs of others. It is after going through a period of questioning, evaluating, and ultimately considering both the needs of others as well as the greater good that emerging adults are able to develop more personally meaningful values and worldviews to guide their choices and behavior (Simpson, 2001).

ISSUES AND CONCERNS IN EMERGING ADULTHOOD

There are several challenges that are often salient during the emerging adult period. First, the current context for emerging adulthood does not always provide the conditions needed to help individuals achieve the developmental tasks identified for this stage of life. Erikson's (1968) ideal environment in which identity development occurs is one in which there is (a) time for experimentation with various roles, (b) experience with making choices that might result in some meaningful achievement, (c) freedom from excessive anxiety, and (d) time for reflection and introspection. Historically, attending college provided this opportunity for students—a time to discover a sense of independence, individuation from parents, freedom to make lifestyle choices, to pursue a broad range of life experiences, to reflect on the self, and also to delay many adult responsibilities (Zarrett & Eccles, 2006). While this describes the optimal life for an emerging adult, it is hardly the typical experience for most of today's 18 to 21 year olds. While in the past the typical college setting might have served as a ripe environment for self-discovery, today only a minority of college students are able to have the time and luxury for experimentation and intro-spection without interruptions. Instead, school is just one more role in the busyness of working, parenting, and financial burdens. For today's emerging adults, most higher education is pursued in a nonlinear way, with periods of stopping and restart-ing, and is frequently combined with work responsibilities (Arnett, 2007). Because of its challenges, just over half of students persist to receive their initial degree within 6 years (National Center for Education Statistics, 2013).

Second, even more difficult problems occur for those who move directly from high school into the world of work. While 68.2% of high school graduates go to college at least initially, the remaining students move into work and nonwork set-tings (U.S. Bureau of Labor Statistics, 2013). Students who choose a vocational path rather than college will not likely have the advantage of a period of explora-tion and experimentation. These emerging adults often find themselves on a diffi-cult, lonely path without much support along the way. Without a college education, it is often harder to accomplish the developmental tasks of identity development and to establish long-term financial independence (Settersten & Ray, 2010). For example, older adolescents who dropped out of high school are at particular risk as they enter emerging adulthood, as they have limited options for finding work that will provide financial stability and are more at risk for alcohol and drug abuse, smoking, high-risk sexual activity, criminal activity, and gang related behavior than are other emerging adults (Henry, Knight, & Thornberry, 2011). Lack of family structure and community support also contributes to increasingly difficult prob-lems for youth from vulnerable populations such as children aging out of the foster care system or those returning to society after being part of the criminal justice system (Arnett, 2007).

Case Illustration 15.2

The Case of Dillon

Dillon is a 19-year-old male from a family comprised of a single mother and two sisters. He had aca-demic and behavioral problems in school beginning in the elementary years and ended up dropping out of school at age 16. He began to hang out with an older crowd, where he was exposed to alcohol, smoking, and illegal substances. He soon became a regular user and learned how to deal drugs in order to make money to support himself. After an arrest and serving time in a juvenile detention center, Dillon now sees few options for himself. His girlfriend of 2 years is pregnant. Without a high school diploma, much less a college degree, he is not sure how to pull his life out of poverty and substance use. Even if he wanted to take care of his girlfriend and baby, he isn't sure how he would do so. He is feeling hopeless, and he is only 19 years of age.

A third problem area for emerging adults stems from the very qualities that also make it appealing—while emerging adulthood is a time that often offers freedom from responsibility and the promise of wide-open possibilities, the uncertainty and lack of structure during this period can also translate into anxiety and risks for other mental health problems. Several types of high-risk behaviors peak during the emerging adult years, including unprotected sex, most types of substance use and abuse, and risky driving behaviors such as driving at high speeds or driving while intoxicated (Pharo et al., 2011). As reviewed previously, while novel and sensation-seeking drives are strong, the prefrontal cortex of the brain (which serves to inhibit these drives) is not yet fully formed. This makes it difficult to regulate and appropriately express emotions, which can also lead to impulsive decision making and behavior.

The emerging adult period provides ample opportunities to experiment and pursue risky or intense experiences because individuals often do not yet have the responsibilities of adulthood (e.g., family to support, young children to consider) but no longer operate under the social control or adult monitoring that occurred during the adolescent years. Emerging adulthood is the period in which problems related to alcohol use and abuse are highest, and these problems can set the stage for problems in later adulthood, including difficulty establishing intimate relationships with others, graduating with some type of college credential, or maintaining career and financial responsibilities (Stone, Becker, Huber, & Catalano, 2012). Substance abuse during the emerging adult years also places an individual at higher risk for increased drug use, criminal and antisocial behavior, high risk sexual activity, and deteriorating mental health during the adult years (Stone et al., 2012). However, even while substance use and abuse rises to peak levels in the early 20s, it declines as emerging adults take on adult responsibilities; rates decline sharply after entering into marriage and decline further during entry to parenthood (Arnett, 2007).

In addition to these externalizing problems, the emerging adult years can result in the onset of mental health disorders, including depression and anxiety. Surveys of university and college counseling center directors indicate that students are coming to college with more severe mental health problems, and that anxiety and depression are among top concerns (Reetz, Krylowicz, & Mistler, 2014). When asked about the most predominant presenting concern among college students, 47.4% of directors reported anxiety, followed by depression (39.7%), and relationship problems (33.7%). In sum, it seems that while some individuals benefit from having an extended period to make decisions about career and relationship commitments, other emerging adults seem to flounder in the uncertainty of their futures.

SUGGESTIONS FOR DEVELOPMENTALLY APPROPRIATE COUNSELING INTERVENTIONS FOR EMERGING ADULTS

Due to the unique features and challenges of emerging adulthood, several counseling approaches and interventions are suggested.

Counselors Should Address High-Risk Behaviors Within the Developmental Context of Emerging Adulthood

When counseling emerging adults, it is often difficult to understand why they engage in high-risk behaviors that are harmful to themselves and others. If an emerging adult lacks full capacity to plan for and set goals, to solve problems logically, and to manage impulses, then it makes sense that he or she will act in inconsistent ways during these years, sometimes appearing to engage in adult-like decisions and behaviors, while at other times acting impulsively or recklessly. As part of building a counseling relationship, the counselor should respect the client's worldview, validating the positive role that high-risk behaviors may play in their lives. Using motivational interviewing techniques, instead of only pointing out the risks, counselors can *express empathy*—conveying an understanding of the benefits of behaviors such as substance use or other impulsive behaviors. Heavy drinking, for example, bonds them to their peers and delays worries about the responsibility of adulthood, including academic and career concerns. The goal, then, is to help emerging adults recognize for themselves that the negative consequences of high-risk behaviors do indeed outweigh the perceived benefits (Miller & Rollnick, 2012). Until this is perceived as true for them, emerging adults will not be motivated to change.

Counselors Can Assist Emerging Adult Clients in Building Social Support

In reviewing the developmental tasks of emerging adulthood, it is clear that many of them require social and emotional competence that comes through experiences with forming intimate relationships with peers and romantic partners. This is essential for emerging adults, as the difficult task of clarifying one's sense of self is made possible through interacting with and exploring one's beliefs and values with others with whom one feels supported and safe (Jordan, 2000). Counselors can serve as important sources of support during the transition to adulthood (Young, Marshall et al., 2011). Counselors can assist their clients in building sources of social support with positive peers and help them to evaluate their romantic relationships to determine if they are positive or negative supports in their lives. If the counselor is in a position to work with the entire family system, counselors can encourage parents to provide continued support and guidance while also promoting their child's self-sufficiency. In the absence of beneficial relationships with parents, emerging adults can also form positive relationships with other adult role models (e.g., teachers, pastors, work supervisors; Liang, Spencer, Brogan, & Corral, 2007).

Counselors Can Teach Emotion Regulation Skills

Because the ability to understand feelings, regulate feelings, express them appropriately, and tolerate a certain amount of discomfort is a developmental task of emerging adulthood, counselors can assist clients in learning appropriate skills for emotion regulation. Dialectical behavior therapy (DBT), a therapy approach first developed by Marsha Linehan for clients with borderline personality disorder (Linehan, 1993) teaches emotion regulation as an essential skill set. In drawing upon DBT emotion regulation techniques in an individual or group format, counselors assist emerging adults in learning how to identify, observe, and describe emotions; regulate intense or painful emotions; increase positive emotions; and reduce vulnerability to negative emotions. As they practice emotion regulation, clients recognize that they do have control over how they react to emotional experiences, and that they can be empowered to change their emotional responses. As suggested by Miller, Rathaus, and Linehan (2007), other skills include reducing vulnerability (i.e., decreasing the likelihood of negative emotions by caring for oneself physically), increasing positive emotions (i.e., increasing daily pleasant events), and building mastery (i.e., completing daily activities that contribute to a sense of competence and mastery).

Counselors Can Promote Emerging Adults' Identity Development Through Recognizing Their Strengths and Areas of Competence

An important aspect of identity development is for emerging adults to begin to reflect on themselves, who they are, and who they are becoming. As identified in Chickerings's vector one, they can begin the process of accepting themselves as they are: their physical appearance, including weight and body shape, their academic and vocational strengths, and the character qualities that define who they are. Clients can benefit from a realistic assessment of their abilities and learning to structure their environment to make most of their assets. Counselors can also assist clients in finding resources for providing support to help develop areas that need growth.

Counselors Can Facilitate Emerging Adults' Development Toward a Sense of Purpose and Commitment to Beliefs and Values

Counselors can facilitate the identity development of emerging adult clients as they attempt to understand themselves and to find meaning in their lives. While they may not feel comfortable doing so with peers or even parents, many emerging adults can benefit from the safe holding environment that the counseling relationship provides. In this space, an emerging adult can discuss new ways of knowing themselves, others, and their views about the world. Instead of an overreliance on the views of peers or parents, counselors can help clients explore their personal values and meaning-making systems, perhaps for the first time. Counselors can encourage clients to take steps outside of the safety of the peer group or family as they clarify their beliefs and become authors of their own new stories (Hensley, 2001).

The emerging adult period can be a time of both struggle and excitement for individuals in their late teens to early 20s. Developmentally, emerging adults are caught in an in-between time when they are building self-sufficiency and autonomy while still needing strong adult support and guidance as they weigh their life options. Counselors can help their clients to create a bridge across the chasm between adolescence and adulthood, intentionally determining an identity with meaningful purpose and direction, so that they can transition more successfully to their next stage of life.

Case Illustration 15.3

The Case of Kerrie

Kerrie is a 20-year-old junior enrolled at a local university when she comes to see you for counseling at a local mental health center. She says that she did not want to go to her university's counseling center because she was too embarrassed to have anyone know that she needs counseling. According to Kerrie, her presenting problem is anxiety that manifests through occasional panic attacks, difficulty concentrating when studying, and anxiety when taking tests. She says that the anxiety has been occurring ever since her first year of college, when she thought she was going to major in biology and go to medical school after graduation. Unfortunately, after receiving Cs and Ds in her biology and chemistry classes during her first year, she decided that her lifelong dream of becoming a doctor was no longer a reality. She first changed her major to English, then psychology, then political science. During her sophomore and now junior year of college she is not interested in school and goes out drinking with her friends several nights per week. At least when she is drinking, she says, she doesn't have to think about anything but having fun. She reports that her friends don't know what they are going to do after graduation, so it helps her to spend time around students that also seem to be "wandering aimlessly," but she often feels like she is an impostor when she is with them. Unlike her friends, she likes being able to hang out at college and have fun, but she also believes she is capable of doing more than she is. It really scares her to think about the time when this will end and she will have to "grow up." She also feels as if she has let her family down because they have sacrificed for her to attend college full-time and expected her to go to medical school after college, so she doesn't feel comfortable sharing any of her confusion and fears with her parents. She knows they are highly disappointed in her mediocre grades, and she thinks her parents believe they have wasted their money on her because "I am not on track to make anything out of my life." She says that when she has to slow down and think about her life, like when she is studying alone, she really starts to feel panic about her parent's expectations and her own future. She does not know what she wants to do, where she wants to live, does not have a significant other, and feels like she is "just going in circles." As long as she is partying and having fun, everything seems to be okay, but she is frightened by the constant anxiety that seems to be simmering just under the surface. She doesn't know exactly what she wants from counseling, but she is hoping that you can "just make all of her anxiety go away."

Discussion questions:

1. Where would you start with Kerrie? How do you conceptualize her concerns within a developmental framework?

2. What specific developmental obstacles is Kerrie facing, and how are they contributing to her anxiety?

3. Which of Chickering's identity development vectors seems most relevant to target with Kerrie?

4. What counseling interventions might be helpful for Kerrie?

COUNSELING KEYSTONES

- The ages of 18 through the mid-20s is a distinct developmental period known as emerging adulthood.

- The primary features of emerging adulthood are a period of identity exploration; instability and change; self-focus; a time of feeling caught between adolescence and adulthood; and an age of opportunity.

- The area of the brain that controls the executive functions is not fully mature until the mid-20s, thus affecting emerging adults' ability to think logically and make rational decisions on a consistent basis.

- Perry's stages of cognitive development are helpful for understanding college–age students' knowledge acquisition, learning, and development of their beliefs and values about the world.

- Problems occur in emerging adulthood when young adults don't experience the conditions needed for optimal growth. For example, students who don't go to college find it harder to accomplish the tasks of identity development and long term financial independence.

- The emerging adult years are a period in which several significant mental health problems first occur, the most common of which are depression and anxiety.

- Counseling interventions for emerging adults can include strategies to promote identity development, emotion regulation skills, social support, and a sense of purpose and direction.

ADDITIONAL RESOURCES

Online

Child and adolescent mental health from National Institutes of Mental Health: http://www.nimh.nih.gov/health/topics/child-and-adolescent-mental -health/index.shtml

Youth-Nex Center to Promote Positive Youth Development: http://curry .virginia.edu/research/centers/youth-nex

The teen years explained: A guide to healthy adolescent development: http:// www.jhsph.edu/research/centers-and-institutes/center-for-adolescent -health/_includes/interactive%20guide.pdf

REFERENCES

Allen, J., & Allen, C. (2009). *Escaping the endless adolescence: How we can help our teenagers grow up before they grow old.* New York, NY: Ballantine Books.

American Academy of Child and Adolescent Psychiatry. (2011, December). *Normal adolescent development, part II.* Retrieved from http://www.aacap.org/App_ Themes/AACAP/docs/facts_for_families/58_normal_adolescent_development .pdf

Arnett, J. J. (2000). Emerging adulthood: A theory development from the late teens through the twenties. *American Psychologist, 55*(5), 469–480. doi: 10.1037/0003-066X.55.5.469

Arnett, J. J. (2004). *The emerging adult: The winding road from the late teens through the 20's.* New York, NY: Oxford University Press.

Arnett, J. J. (2007). Emerging adulthood: What is it, and what is it good for? *Child Development Perspectives, 1*(2), 68–73. doi: 10.1111/j.1750-8606.2007.00016.x

Baxter Magolda, M. B. (1992). *Knowing and reasoning in college: Gender related patterns of knowing in students' intellectual development.* San Francisco, CA: Jossey-Bass.

Belenky, M. F., Clinchy, B. M., Goldberger, N. R., & Tarule, J. M. (1986). *Women's ways of knowing: The development of self, voice, and mind.* New York, NY: Basic Books.

Brownlee, J., Boulton-Lewis, G., & Purdie, N. (2002). Core beliefs about knowing and peripheral beliefs about learning: Developing an holistic conceptualisation of epistemological beliefs. *Australian Journal of Educational & Developmental Psychology, 2,* 1–16.

Chickering, A. W. (1969). *Education and identity.* San Francisco, CA: Jossey-Bass.

Chickering, A. W., & Reisser, L. (1993). *Education and identity* (2nd ed.). San Francisco, CA: Jossey-Bass Publishers.

Clark University News. (2013, June 17). What is the key to being an adult? Clark releases new poll findings. Retrieved from http://news.clarku.edu/news/2013/06/17/what-is-the-key-to-being-an-adult-clark-releases-new-poll-findings

Clark University Poll of Parents of Emerging Adults. (2013, May 13). Clark poll: Parents welcome emerging adults back to the nest. Retrieved from http://news.clarku.net/news/2013/05/08/clark-poll-parents-welcome-emerging-adults-back-to-the-nest

Demir, M. (2010). Close relationships and happiness among emerging adults. *Journal of Happiness Studies, 11*(3), 293–313. doi: 10.1007/s10902-009-9141-x

Elby, A., & Hammer, D. (2001). On the substance of a sophisticated epistemology. *Science Education, 85*, 554–567. doi: 10.1002/sce.1023

Erikson, E. H. (1968). *Identity: Youth and crisis*. New York, NY: Norton.

Evans, N. J., Forney, D. S., Guido, F. M., Patton, L. D., & Renn, K. A. (2009). *Student development in college: Theory, research, and practice* (2nd ed.). New York, NY: Jossey Bass.

Garrett, J. L., & Eccles, J. S. (2009). *Transition to adulthood: Linking late-adolescent lifestyles to family and work status in the mid-twenties. Transitions from school to work.* (1st ed., pp. 243–264). Cambridge MA: Cambridge University Press. doi: 10.1017/CBO9780511605369.011

Gilligan, C. (1982). *In a different voice*. Cambridge, MA: Harvard University Press.

Goldberger, N. R. (1996). Looking backward, looking forward. In N. Goldberger, J. Tarule, B. Clinchy, & M. Belenky (Eds.), *Knowledge, difference, and power: Essays inspired by women's ways of knowing* (pp. 1–21). New York, NY: Basic Books.

Hall, G. S. (1904). *Adolescence: Its psychology and its relations to physiology, anthropology, sociology, sex, crime, religion, and education*, 2 vols. New York, NY: Appleton.

Halonen, J. S., Bosack, T., Clay, S., McCarthy, M., Dunn, D. S., Hill IV, G. W., . . . Weaver, K. A. (2003). A rubric for learning, teaching, and assessing scientific inquiry in psychology. *Teaching of Psychology, 30*, 196–208. doi: 10.1207/S15328023TOP3003_01

Henry, K. L., Knight, K. E., & Thornberry, T. P. (2011). School disengagement as predictor of dropout, delinquency, and problem substance use during adolescence and early adulthood. *Journal of Youth and Adolescence, 41*(2), 156–166. doi: 10.1007/s10964-011-9665-3

Hensley, L. H. (2001). College student binge drinking: Implications for a constructivist approach to college counseling. *Journal of College Counseling, 4*, 100–112.

Institute of Medicine and National Research Council, Committee of Science of Adolescence. (2011). *The science of adolescence risk taking* [workshop report]. Washington, DC: National Academic Press.

Jaffee, S., & Hyde, J. (2000). Gender differences in moral orientation: A meta-analysis. *Psychological Bulletin, 126*(5), 703.

Jordan, J. V. (2000). The role of mutual empathy in relational cultural therapy. *In session: Psychotherapy in practice, 55,* 1005–1016.

Knefelkamp, L., Widick, C., & Parker, C. (1978). *New directions for student services: Applying new developmental findings.* San Francisco, CA: Jossey-Bass.

Kohlberg, L. (1976). Moral stages and moralization: The cognitive-developmental approach. In T. Lickona (Ed.), *Moral development and behavior*, (pp. 31–53). New York, NY: Holt, Rinehart, and Winston.

Liang, B., Spencer, R., Brogan, D., & Corral, M. (2007). Mentoring relationships from early adolescence through emerging adulthood: A qualitative analysis. *Journal of Vocational Behavior, 72,* 168–182. doi: 10.1016/j.jvb.2007.11.005

Linehan, M. M. (1993). *Skills training manual for treating borderline personality disorder.* New York, NY: Guilford Press.

Mahalik, J. R., Coley, R. L., Lombardi, C. M., Lynch, A. D., Markowitz, A. J., & Jaffee, S. R., (2013). Changes in health risk behaviors for males and females from early adolescence through early adulthood. *Health Psychology, 32*(6), 685–694. doi: 10.1037/a0031658

Meeus, W. H. J., Branje, S. J. T., van der Valk, I., & De Wied, M. (2007). Relationships with intimate partner, best friend, and parents in adolescence and early adulthood: A study of the saliency of the intimate partnership. *International Journal of Behavioral Development, 31,* 569–580.

Miller, A. L., Rathaus, J. H., & Linehan, M. M. (2007). *Dialectical behavior therapy with suicidal adolescents.* New York, NY: Guilford Press.

Miller, S., & Rollnick, S. (2012). *Motivational Interviewing: Helping people change* (3rd ed.). New York, NY: Guilford Press.

Montgomery, M. J. (2005). Psychosocial intimacy and identity: From early adolescence to emerging adulthood. *Journal of Adolescent Research, 20*(3), 346–374. doi: 10.1177/0743558404273118

Muis, K. R. (2007). The role of epistemic beliefs in self-regulated learning. *Educational Psychologist, 42,* 173–190.

Murphy, P. K., Alexander, P., Greene, J., & Hennessey, M. (2012). Examining epistemic frames in conceptual change research: implications for learning and instruction. *Asia Pacific Education Review, 13,* 475–486. doi: 10.1007/s12564-011-9199-0

National Center for Education Statistics. (2011). Back to school statistics. Retrieved from http://nces.ed.gov/fastfacts/display.asp?id=372

National Center for Education Statistics. (2013), Graduation rates. Retrieved from http://nces.ed.gov/fastfacts/display.asp?id=40

Perry, W. G. (1970). *Forms of intellectual and ethical development in the college years: A scheme.* New York, NY: Holt, Rinehart, and Winston.

Pharo, H., Sim, C., Graham, M., Gross, J., & Hayne, H. (2011). Risky business: Executive function, personality, and reckless behavior during adolescence and emerging adulthood. *Behavioral Neuroscience, 125*(6), 970–978. doi: 10.1037/a0025768

Piaget, J. (1972). Intellectual evolution from adolescence to adulthood. *Human Development, 15,* 1–12.

Radmacher, K., & Azmitia, M. (2006). Are there gendered pathways to intimacy in early adolescents' and emerging adults' friendships? *Journal of Adolescent Research, 21*(4), 415–448. doi: 10.1177/0743558406287402

Reetz, D. R., Krylowicz, B., & Mistler, B. J. (2014), *The association of university and college counseling center directors' annual survey report.* Retrieved from http://www.aucccd.org/assets/documents/2014%20aucccd%20monograph%20-%20public%20pdf.pdf

Settersten, R., & Ray, B. E. (2010). *Not quite adults: Why 20-somethings are choosing a slower path to adulthood, and why it's good for everyone.* New York, NY: Bantam.

Simpson, A. R. (2001). *Raising teens: A synthesis of research and a foundation for action.* Boston, MA: Center for Health Communication, Harvard School of Public Health.

Steinberg, L. (2014). *Age of opportunity: Lessons from the new science of adolescence.* New York, NY: Houghton Mifflin Harcourt.

Stone, A. L., Becker, L. G., Huber, A. M., & Catalano, R. F. (2012). Review of risk and protective factors of substance use and problem use in emerging adulthood. *Addictive Behaviors, 37*(7), 747–775. doi: 10.1016/jaddbeh.2012.02.014

U.S. Bureau of Labor Statistics. (2013, April 17). *College enrollment and work activity of 2014 high school graduates.* Retrieved from http://www.bls.gov/news.release/hsgec.nr0.htm

U.S. Census Bureau. (2013, November 22). Families and living arrangements. Retrieved from http://www.census.gov/hhes/families/data/marital.html

Worell, J. (2006). Pathways to healthy development: Sources of strength and empowerment. In J. Worell & C. D. Goodheart (Eds.), *Handbook of girls' and women's psychological health* (pp. 3–14). New York, NY: Oxford University Press.

Young, B. J., Furman, W., & Laursen, B. (2011). Models of change and continuity in romantic experiences. In F. Fincham, & C. Ming (Eds.), *Romantic relationships in emerging adulthood* (pp. 44–66). New York, NY: Cambridge University Press.

Young, R. A., Marshall, S. K., Foulkes, K., Haber, C., Lee, C. S. M., Penner, C., & Rostram, H. (2011). Counseling for the transition to adulthood as joint, goal-directed action. *Journal of Vocational Behavior, 79,* 325–333. doi: 10.1016/j .jvb.2011.02.005

Zarrett, N., & Eccles, J. (2006). The passage to adulthood: Challenges of late adolescence. *New Directions for Youth Development, 111,* 13–28. doi: 10.1002/ yd.179

Index

ABC (attachment and biobehavioral catch-up) intervention, 265

A-B-C-D-E (Assessment, Benefit, Consequences and Consultation, Duty, Education) worksheet, 50

ABFT (attachment-based family therapy), 213

Abuse/neglect of children, 14–15, 39–40, 125

ACA (Affordable Care Act), 18

ACA (American Counseling Association), 52

Academic skills, 336

Acceptance theme, 353–354

ACCEPTS (A Curriculum for Children's Effective Peer and Teacher Skills) (Walker), 312

ACE (Adverse Childhood Experiences), 6, 70, 83–84, 83 (table)

Activating events, 171

ACT model, 113–114, 285

Act to Establish Public Schools, 9

Addison, S., 237–238

ADHD (attention deficit hyperactivity disorder), 194, 212–213, 262–263, 278–279

Adler, Alfred, 125, 129, 132–133, 136, 173

Adolescents
ages of, 65
attachment-based family therapy for, 213
attitudes toward, 100–101
challenges of working with, 104–105
critical tasks of, 104
culture of, 99
dialectical behavior therapy for, 179–180

uniqueness of, 5–7
See also Older adolescents (15–19); Therapeutic alliances; Young adolescents (12–14)

Adoptive children, 260–262

Adulthood, 375
See also Emerging adults (18–21)

Adverse Childhood Experiences (ACE), 6, 70, 83–84, 83 (table)

Advocacy for children, 36–37, 85–86

Affective-reflective dialogue, 134

Affordable Care Act (ACA), 18

African American child labor, 13

Aggression, 329, 330–331, 360–361

Aguilar, J. V., 238

Ainsworth, Mary, 126, 130, 255–256

Air traffic control system metaphor, 65

Akos, P., 309

Alcohol, prenatal exposure to, 258–260

Alfoadari, K., 179

Al-Mabuk, R., 299

Amatea, Ellen, 191–218

Ambivalent children, 261

American Academy of Pediatrics, 279

American Counseling Association (ACA), 52

American Psychological Association (APA), 52

American School Counselor Association (ASCA), 51, 52, 210, 329–330

Amygdala, 67, 323, 324

Analysis of State Bullying Laws and Policies (Stuart-Cassel, Bell, & Springer), 42

Anger onion intervention, 87

Angold, A., 306

About the Editors

Sondra Smith-Adcock holds a PhD in counseling and counselor education from the University of North Carolina at Greensboro. She has taught at the University of Florida for the past 15 years in both the school counseling and mental health programs. She has authored more than 40 publications on counseling-related topics, with emphasis on counseling children and adolescents. She has counseling experience in schools, agencies, and private practice settings with diverse children of all ages.

Catherine Tucker holds a PhD in counselor education from the University of Florida. She teaches in the counseling area programs at Indiana State University. She holds school counseling licenses in the states of North Carolina and Indiana and is a licensed mental health counselor in Indiana. She is also a registered play therapist supervisor. She has over 10 years of direct clinical counseling experience and has authored multiple journal articles and book chapters on counseling related issues. She is president-elect of the Association for Child and Adolescent Counseling from 2015 to 2017.

About the Contributors

Ellen Amatea is a professor of counselor education in the College of Education at the University of Florida where she teaches graduate courses in school counseling and family counseling, with a focus in counseling children and adolescents and their families. Her research interest focuses on how school, family, and community relationships influence children's and adolescents' academic achievement and emotional development. She is especially interested in the impact of poverty on children's schooling and mental health service delivery.

Clarence Anthony completed his bachelor's degree from the University of Florida in 2010 and his master's from Columbia Teachers College in 2012. He currently is a doctoral candidate in counseling and counselor education at the University of Florida. He is passionate about counseling college student athletes, career counseling, adolescent development, racial identity, and addressing bias in mental health and society.

Laura Choate, EdD, LPC-S is a graduate of the College of William and Mary Counselor Education and Supervision program and has 15 years of experience as a counselor educator at Louisiana State University and 16 years as a licensed professional counselor. She is the author of four books and has over 40 counseling-related publications, most of which have been related to girls' and women's wellness. She served as guest editor for the 2012 special themed issue on eating disorders in the *Journal of Counseling and Development* and is former editor of the *Journal of College Counseling*. She is the past recipient of the American College Counseling Association Research Award, the LSU Phi Kappa Phi Non-tenured Faculty Award for Humanities and Social Sciences, and the 2014 College of Human Sciences and Education Distinguished Research Award.

Leigh DeLorenzi, PhD, is an assistant professor at Stetson University in the graduate counselor education department. In addition to teaching, she volunteers her services at a local child advocacy center for child and adolescent survivors of abuse and trauma. Her research interests include developing standards of conduct in graduate counselor preparation programs, treatment attrition prevention for child sexual abuse victims, concurrent family violence, and triage decision making at child advocacy centers. She has developed trainings and taught courses related to counseling children and adolescents with trauma, family therapy, and the impact of trauma therapies on the developing brain. Dr. DeLorenzi is also the founder of the Stetson University Trauma Therapy Certificate program.

Andrea L. Dixon is an associate professor in the Department of Counseling and Psychological Services at Georgia State University in Atlanta, GA. She received her PhD at the University of North Carolina at Greensboro in Greensboro, NC. Her research and teaching interests are in the areas of multicultural counseling with racial/ethnic diverse individuals, adolescents, mattering and meaning making, school counseling, and school counselor education. She is the author of a number of articles and book chapters on topics regarding the concerns of child and adolescent and racial/ethnic minority concerns. She has coauthored several publications regarding counseling with youth and adolescents.

Ceymone Dyce is a doctoral student fellow studying counseling and counselor education at the University of Florida. A New Jersey native, Dyce graduated from Xavier University of Louisiana with a BS in psychology and from Indiana State University with an MS degree in clinical mental health counseling. Her research interests include integrated community mental health care for marginalized communities and children's mental health.

Donna M. Gibson is an associate professor of counselor education in the Department of Counselor Education at Virginia Commonwealth University. As a counselor educator for 15 years, she has researched and published in the areas of professional identity development, leadership development, advocacy, and constructivist theories related to relational development. She also is a licensed professional counselor and has worked with clients in schools, hospitals, group residential settings, college counseling centers, and private practice.

Carol Hudgins-Mitchell, MEd, LSW, NBCCH, is a certified trauma specialist. She provides training and consultation on the topics of trauma, attachment, child therapy, mindfulness, and self-care for helping professionals. With a background in special education and counseling, she has over 30 years of experience in trauma treatment with a specialty in early childhood, relational, and play therapy and is certified in forensic interviewing as well as a nationally certified clinical hypnotherapist. Her focused trainings help counselors to translate the neurobiology of trauma into practical everyday interventions for children's services, foster care agencies, and parents.

Shajuana Isom-Payne is a counselor education and supervision doctoral student in the Department of Counselor Education and executive director of academic advising at Virginia Commonwealth University. As a counselor, she has worked with clients in high schools and college settings. Her research interest areas are multicultural competencies, professional identity development, life-work balance, international student advocacy, and women's leadership development.

Sandra Logan is a doctoral fellow in the Counseling and Counselor Education program at University of Florida and the lead field supervisor at Lamar University. She earned her master's degree and credential in school counseling at Chapman University in California. Prior to pursuing her doctorate, she worked as an elementary and middle school counselor. Sandra has also been an independent college counselor and private tutor. Her specific research interests include school counseling supervision, leadership development, and professional identity development of counselors.

Derrick Paladino, PhD, LMHC, NCC is an associate professor in the Department of Graduate Studies in Counseling at Rollins College in Winter Park, Florida. His clinical and scholarship interests fall within the areas of multiple heritage/multiracial identity, college counseling, and college student development. He is the coauthor of the book *Counseling Multiple Heritage Individuals, Couples and Families*, published by the American Counseling Association. In addition, Dr. Paladino is a taskforce member and an author of the "Competencies for Counseling the Multiracial Population" adopted and endorsed by the American Counseling Association.

Jenn Pereira is a graduate of the counseling and counselor education program at the University of Florida. She is currently clinical assistant professor at Arizona State University. She is a licensed mental health counselor, registered play therapist supervisor, and clinical traumatologist. Jenn's area of interest has always been children and adolescents, and she has worked with them therapeutically for 14 years in school and clinical settings. She provides workshops in play and sandtray therapy and holds continuing education provider status with the state of Florida and the Association for Play Therapy. Her passion is training others to fully understand, work with, and honor the culture of children and adolescents.

Robert E. Rice is an assistant clinical professor and the school counseling coordinator in the Department of Counseling and Psychological Services at Georgia State University in Atlanta, Georgia. He received his PhD at in counseling education and practice (CACREP) at Georgia State University. He has been a school counselor for 18 years (middle and high schools) and began his work as a counselor educator in 2013. His interests include school counseling, adolescents, peer leadership in k-12 schools, school leadership, multicultural advocacy in schools, college and career readiness, and group work.

Amanda Rumsey, MA is a professional school counselor and a doctoral student in the counselor education and practice program in the Department of Counseling and Psychological Services at Georgia State University, Atlanta, Georgia. She has worked with adolescents in clinical mental health and school settings for over 20 years. Her primary areas of interest revolve around adolescents and include social justice and advocacy, violence and trauma, wellness, and mental health in schools.

Tina Smith-Bonahue is coordinator of graduate programs and associate Professor of special education, school psychology, and early childhood studies at the University of Florida. She received her PhD from the University of North Carolina at Chapel Hill in school psychology, with an emphasis on early intervention. Her research and teaching interests include teacher beliefs related to young children's behavior and diversity and interventions for challenging behaviors and relational aggression.

Jacqueline Swank is an assistant professor of counselor education at the University of Florida. She is a licensed mental health counselor, licensed clinical social worker, and a registered play therapist-supervisor. Her clinical experience includes working with children and adolescents and their families in residential, inpatient, day treatment, and outpatient settings. Her research interests include children and adolescents, play and nature-based interventions, counselor development, and assessment.

Kaitlyn Tiplady received a dual degree in psychology and human development from Virginia Polytechnic Institute and State University. Presently, she is working toward her doctorate in school psychology with a specialization in early childhood development at the University of Florida. She has extensive experience working with Head Start children and teachers and currently teaches in UF's Unified Early Childhood Program.

Mary Vicario is a licensed professional clinical counselor supervisor (LPCC –S) and a certified trauma specialist with over 30 years experience working with children and families. She has experience in school counseling and agency work specializing in trauma survivors. She trains nationally and internationally translating the latest trauma and brain chemistry research into counseling interventions for all ages and ability levels. She is a recipient of the Strong Families Safe Communities Grant and is in the final year of that grant developing and testing neuroscience-based sensorimotor and expressive interventions to coordinate care across life domains for trauma survivors with developmental disabilities.

Dayna Watson is an assistant professor and the clinical placement coordinator for the counselor education program at the University of Alabama at Birmingham. She has experience and training in clinical supervision and mental health counseling, specializing in counseling children, adolescents, and young adults. She has taught coursework in community-school collaboration, counseling theories, counseling skills, and ethics. Her research interests include issues of social class and poverty in mental health counseling, community-school collaboration, and counseling student development.

Elaine Wittman, MAEd, is a licensed professional counselor/supervisor in North Carolina, registered play therapist and supervisor, and an approved APT provider. She has presented workshops on working with children and families in their creative processes at international conferences, state conferences across the United States, and classes at universities and is a frequent presenter in the southeast. Elaine has a private practice, Rainbows End Retreat and Training Center, in Beech Mountain, North Carolina, where she trains clinicians in the use of play therapy including sandtray therapies, provides supervision, facilitates personal process, and offers retreats to caring professionals. She also maintains a counseling practice, Pathways Counseling and Wellness, in Banner Elk, North Carolina.

66090119R00241